SUNSHINE ON PUT

Ben Thompson made his first (and only) appearance as a stand-up comedian in the winter of 1986–7, reading a photocopied Ronnie Corbett monologue to an unreceptive student audience. He has subsequently written for the *Daily Telegraph*, *The Face*, *GQ*, the *Independent*, *Mojo*, *NME*, *New Statesman & Society*, the *Observer*, *Sight & Sound* and the Saturday *Telegraph* Magazine, and (as comedy critic of the *Independent On Sunday*, from 1994–7) politely declined annual invitations to join the Perrier Award judging panel.

Also by Ben Thompson

Seven Years of Plenty
Ways of Hearing

SUNSHINE ON PUTTY

The Golden Age of
British Comedy, from
Vic Reeves to *The Office*

BEN THOMPSON

FOURTH ESTATE · *London and New York*

First published in Great Britain in 2004 by
Fourth Estate
A Division of HarperCollins*Publishers*
77–85 Fulham Palace Road
London W6 8JB
www.4thestate.com

1 3 5 7 9 10 8 6 4 2

A catalogue record for this book is
available from the British Library

ISBN 0-00-713583-1

Typeset by Rowland Phototypesetting Ltd,
Bury St Edmunds, Suffolk
Printed in Great Britain by
Clays Ltd, St Ives plc

'Be content to laugh and try not to know why'
Dugas, *La Psychologie de rire*, 1902

Contents

Contents

Introduction

'Comedy has ceased to be a challenge to the mental processes. It has become a therapy of relaxation, a kind of tranquilising drug'

The great American humorist James Thurber wrote those words in 1961. More than four decades later, they sum up – with uncanny precision – the hollow feeling inspired by watching a self-satisfied university graduate entertaining a roomful of pissed-up twenty-somethings with bad jokes about *Star Trek*.

Complacency, escapism, the inability to take anything seriously . . . These were just a few of the obvious flaws in Britain's cultural DNA which could be (and often were) laid at the door of an ever-burgeoning comedic community in the last years of the twentieth century. For this was a period during which (in the words of another visiting US wit, Rich Hall) 'Everyone who didn't want to lift stuff seemed to become a comedian'; a time when every aspect of the nation's collective experience – politics, sport, art, literature, religion – seemed at some point to be becoming another branch of light entertainment.

Amid the suited-up hubbub of Jongleurs comedy club in Camden on a Friday night in the mid-1990s, the brutal, even bestial, simplicity of the venue's motto – 'Eat, laugh, dance, drink' – perfectly encapsulated the careless hedonism of the epoch. And yet, if the experience of live stand-up could sometimes seem like a short cut to all that was most objectionable in British public life, on the higher – televisual – plane, comedy also provided a kind of lifeline: maintaining vital contact with some of the noblest and most beleaguered aspects of our cultural heritage in an era of encroaching blandness and conformity.

From *Vic Reeves Big Night Out* and *The Day Today* at one end of the period, to *The Royle Family* and *The Office* at the other, the best British TV comedy of 1990–2002 not only offered a home to ideas and ideals of community which could no longer find one elsewhere, it also gave us a clearer picture of what was happening to our nation than any other form of artistic endeavour.[1] This double-headed vision of comedy – as both prophecy of what's to come and memorial to what has been lost – might seem a little on the grandiose side, but it is not a view without historical precedent.

'Successful comedy often anticipates future newsreel coverage'

In Iain Sinclair's book *Lights Out for the Territory*, the film-maker Chris Petit reflects on the way an old Dick Emery sketch – in which an explosive device was hidden in a lunchbox on a bus – seemed to contain an eerie premonition of the IRA bombing campaign which began shortly afterwards.

Dancing a strange backwards jig around Petit's assertion that 'successful comedy often anticipates future newsreel coverage', the newsreel footage in 2001's neurotically self-justificatory Sex Pistols memoir *The Filth and The Fury* is intercut with clips of olde-English comedic legends such as Max Wall and Tommy Cooper. 'If you want to know the root core of something, *go* to the root core,' John Lydon told *Mojo* magazine's Andrew Male in the spring of 2002. 'Comedians . . . Shakespeare . . . *that's* English culture.'

More than twenty years before, the man then known as Johnny Rotten had wanted Monty Python's Graham Chapman to direct the original Sex Pistols film, *The Great Rock 'n' Roll Swindle*. But if Lydon is to be believed (which he isn't always), the group's manager Malcom McLaren was so disgusted by Chapman's party trick involving the pub dog, a pint of cider and a certain inti-

---

[1.] The apparent incongruity between the artistic audacity of a new generation of small-screen pioneers and the ritualized underachievement of a booming live circuit is just one of the many fascinating contradictions with which the annals of this comedic era are littered.

mate part of his anatomy, that he gave the job to Julien Temple instead.[2]

This was one strange cultural linkage which somehow escaped the all-seeing eye of Greil Marcus. Marcus's landmark 1989 volume *Lipstick Traces*[3] sought to clear away the soil from the roots of punk rock by making ingenious connections between obscure sixteenth-century Dutch heretics and members of the Sex Pistols who happened to have similar names. Within the shared cultures of appreciation which have grown up around pop music (or film, or literature, come to that), such extravagant intellectual conceits are, if not exactly ten-a-penny, certainly far from unheard of. Yet British comedy's ever-increasing cultural prominence has so far proved resistant to such ambitious interpretations.

One of the main aims of the book you currently hold in your hands is to stop people wondering why no one has ever attempted something similar in the entertainment field which Jethro and Ken Dodd call home. But before we can begin to see if this lofty goal can be achieved, two important questions must be answered.

1. Was the Reeves/*Office* era really a golden age, and if so, how and why did it come about and what were its exact parameters?

In years to come, the old folk will gather at the seaside. As the coastal waters lap ever closer to the top of the Thames Barrier, the veined and the venerable may be seen pottering up and down the promenade, lost in heated debate about the glory days of their youth.

'Ah yes,' one of them will say, sucking meditatively on an olde-English Alcopop drink, 'the early to mid-1990s: *The Day Today*, Alan Partridge, *Shooting Stars*, Paul Calf, *The Fast Show*, *Father Ted* . . . Never again would we have it so good: the attention to detail, the mordant wit: why did those great days ever have to end?'

A contemptuous expostulation from a nearby bench might

[2.] History does not relate whether Temple ever performed the same trick.
[3.] A book which he ironically dedicated to *Monty Python's Flying Circus*.

upgrade this nostalgic monologue into a vicious row. 'But what of the magical autumn of 2002 – with the third series of *The League of Gentlemen,* and the second of *The Office, I'm Alan Partridge* and *Phoenix Nights . . .* ? Surely this was a vintage the like of which would never be equalled?'

Learned observers of this rose-tinted spectacle might quote Sigmund Freud to the effect that comedy itself is a form of nostalgia, as it attempts to 'recapture the state of childhood in which we did not know the comic, were incapable of wit and did not need humour to make us happy'.[4] Sceptics of a more populist bent will no doubt cite the number of people who used to watch *The Morecambe and Wise Christmas Special* as evidence of a narrowing of both the focus and the range of British comedy in the aftermath of the 1970s heyday of what dewy-eyed nostalgia fiends of an earlier generation like to call 'One Nation TV'.

Both parties will have a point.

And yet the bald facts of the situation are these. First, that the period which authoritative historical evidence set out in the following pages will prove started with *Vic Reeves*[5] *Big Night Out* was one wherein comedy and comedians had an unprecedented impact on this nation's intellectual and emotional life. Secondly, that – without surrendering entirely to the mania for pointless list-making which is the symptom of a culture on the brink of nervous collapse – it would be fair to say that the best ten British TV comedy shows of this era (the other nine being *The Day Today, Father Ted, The Fast Show, Shooting Stars, Brass Eye, I'm Alan Partridge, The Royle Family, The League of Gentlemen* and *The Office* . . . with *Spaced, Black Books,* the funny bits in *Smack the Pony,* the first series of *Big Train* and the great lost Paramount Channel sketch series *Unnatural Acts* pressing hard on their heels, since you asked) not

---

[4.] Freud has no explanation for small boys rolling around helpless with laughter on the living-room carpet in front of *The Goodies* or Spike Milligan's *Q8,* but he couldn't be expected to think of everything.

[5.] I know it looks like there should be an apostrophe here and – as photographic evidence in Bruce Dessau's *Reeves & Mortimer* conclusively proves – in the *Big Night Out*'s early live onstage days, there used to be one, but it somehow got lost in the move to TV.

only stand comparison with, but actually *overshadow* the small-screen landmarks of any previous era.

Far from merely echoing such past glories as *Fawlty Towers* or *That Was The Week That Was*, the finest moments of late twentieth- and very early twenty-first-century UK comedy actually represent a worthy culmination of everything that had happened in the preceding fifty years. Not just in terms of evolving comic traditions – from Hancock to Steptoe to *The Royle Family*; or Spike Milligan to Monty Python to Eddie Izzard – but also with regard to the changing character of the broader culture from which those traditions have emerged.

In the more distant past, it has been possible for astute commentators to discern precise causes of particularly successful periods of comedic endeavour. For example, the golden age of Wilde and Whistler could be ascribed to the healthy state of a late-Victorian Fleet Street which, then still some way short of becoming – in the eloquent estimation of D. B. Wyndham Lewis[6] – 'the sedulous ape of New York tabloidery', none the less 'recognised the existence of a small, cultivated, leisured evening newspaper public and strove to meet its taste'. And the aura of celebrity which enveloped the notoriously sharp and combative wit of Alexander Pope in the early 1820s was the product (in the memorable estimation of Dilys Powell)[7] not only of the cessation of press censorship but also of 'a time when the exercise of critical reason was as much applauded as today the eye of a Bradman or the punch of a Louis'.[8]

Turning to our own mirthful epoch in search of similarly clear-sighted explication, readers of Michael Bracewell's generally estimable *The Nineties: When Surface Was Depth* will have had to be satisfied with a rather downbeat theory of causation. 'The country was still watery-eyed and winded', apparently (and therefore, presumably, in dire need of a good laugh), 'from being punched below the intellect by the recession of the late eighties.'

[6.] D. B. Wyndham Lewis in *English Wits*, ed. Leonard Russell.

[7.] Dilys Powell in ibid.

[8.] Early twenty-first-century readers might wish to substitute here 'the imaginative hairstyles of a Beckham or the fecundity of a Zeta Jones', while reassuring themselves that the extraordinary parallels between the careers of Pope and Steve Coogan will be dealt with at a later stage.

Other, somewhat more specific, economic factors suggest themselves. Without diving too deeply at this early stage into the sewage-encrusted gravel pit of media politics, it would be fair to say that the rise of independent production companies in the mid to late 1980s – set in train by changes in the remit of the BBC and the advent of Channel 4 – was a vital precursor to the explosion of comedic creativity in the next decade. The break-up of the mass TV audience with the dawn of the digital era was another essential precondition.

Where comic performers of earlier times might have had to hold on to an eight-figure following to be considered a viable star of the small screen, it was now possible – by the magic of advertisers' demographics and Friday-night channel-branding entertainment packages – to sustain a major TV career on the basis of an audience of two million.

The expansion of creative extremity and fearlessness thus facilitated would stand a new comedic epoch in good stead. But what were the conditions for membership of this new generation, and how – and against what – would it come to define itself?

The preceding, 'alternative' era had kicked off in headily coincidental and clear-cut style, as the opening of former insurance salesman Paul Rosengard's Soho Comedy Store synchronized helpfully with Margaret Thatcher coming to power. (At the start of William Cook's 1994 book *Ha Bloody Ha: Comedians Talking*, it is even suggested – somewhat controversially – that the former of these two historical events might have been of more lasting historical significance.)

The start of the generation currently under consideration is a slightly more staggered affair – less a clean break and more a jagged edge. Paul Whitehouse is part of it, but Harry Enfield isn't.[9] Ben

---

9. The extent of Harry Enfield's bitterness in this regard is revealed in a late 2002 TV documentary about *Derek and Clive*, where Enfield – adopting a bizarre, almost Damon Albarnesque cockney accent – talks of Peter Cook's tendency to bully the less talented but more successful Dudley Moore (an unappealing trait about which Cook himself is seen to express regret in the course of the same programme) in terms so oddly glowing as to only be explicable in terms of some imagined (not to say dementedly inapt) parallel between the Cook/Moore and Enfield/Whitehouse dynamics.

Elton isn't allowed within sniffing distance, but his erstwhile *Friday Night Live* colleague Jo Brand is (or was, until she started presenting lame late-night advert-clip TV shows). Patrick Marber, whose late-eighties stand-up persona gave no signal of the sophistication of his later work on *The Day Today* and *Knowing Me Knowing You, With Alan Partridge* (let alone his subsequent career as an internationally acclaimed playwright), is definitely included, yet Jennifer Saunders – for all the great leap forward into modernity represented by *Absolutely Fabulous* – for some reason isn't.

Don't ask me why. I don't make the rules.

One thing which is as clear as Ricky Gervais's conscience[10] is that whatever is particular to the post-alternative epoch begins with Vic Reeves and Bob Mortimer (readers keen to find out why it ends with *The Office* are advised to stock up on tinned goods and dry biscuits and sit it out till the conclusion). Throughout their fifteen-year light-entertainment odyssey, this unique pairing have demonstrated an all-the-more-uncanny-for-apparently-being-unconscious propensity for anticipating – in their failures as well as their successes – the future movements of the comedic barometer.

A source of huge delight to their admirers, this laughter-diviners' gift has not gone unnoticed by their enemies either. In his 2000 short-story collection *Barcelona Plates*, erstwhile alternative overlord Alexei Sayle 'created' a comic double act called Nic and Pob. Nic and Pob are a pair of 'apparently genial rubbish-talking Northerners' who live (as Vic Reeves and Bob Mortimer almost did, at the time Sayle was writing) in 'back to back Kentish mansions'.

'Their arrival on the comedy scene', asserts that man who himself rose to public prominence at the turn of the previous decade with that fearsome piece of lyrical dialectic 'Ullo John, Got A New Motor', 'had fortunately coincided with the rise of stupidity.' Never mind poacher-turned-gamekeeper, this is pickpocket-turned-chief-of-police, and the apparent self-awareness of Sayle's qualifying phrase ('the public having tired of being shouted at by fat men

---

[10.] 'I think it was David Baddiel who said that "comedy is your conscience taking a day off",' observed the co-creator of *The Office* in the autumn of 2002. 'I don't agree with that at all. I have to be able to justify everything that I put out morally – I can't just go, "Oh shut up, it was a joke."'

about things that weren't their fault as a form of entertainment') does nothing to dispel the overpowering stench of sour grapes.

Neither does the fact that the ill-intentioned little story which follows is an abysmally sub-Vic-and-Bob farrago of half-assed voodoo ritual and blatant product placement. Still, the notoriously fragrance-conscious Reeves has not been averse to the stink of a spoiled vine in his time (at the height of his mid-nineties pomp, he once imagined himself in later life 'sitting outside the BBC throwing pieces of coal at newcomers'), and they do say that in comedic circles outright frontal assault comes second only to imitation as the sincerest form of flattery.

Reeves and Mortimer have certainly not wanted for the latter tribute in recent years. Watching the *Big Night Out* on an ancient video now is like watching a blueprint for the next thirteen years of British TV in the form of a very strange dream. From *The All-New Harry Hill Show* to *I'm A Celebrity Get Me Out Of Here!*, from the unrepentantly Jackie Milburnesque enunciation of the *Big Brother* narrator Marcus Bentley to more or less every aspect of the onscreen demeanour of ITV's new kings of prime-time Ant and Dec,[11] it's all in there. The miraculous thing is that at the same time as being eerily familiar, the show still manages to seem like a transmission from another planet, picked up randomly from the ether.

2. What in the name of Bob Monkhouse's stolen jokebook does 'Sunshine on Putty' mean?

The title *Sunshine on Putty* originates exactly one hundred years before the first Channel 4 edition of *Vic Reeves Big Night Out* which marks our story's official starting-point. The people we have to thank for it are English lesbian literary icons Katherine Bradley and her niece and lover Edith Cooper. This mercurial pairing wrote eleven plays and thirty volumes of poetry together under the coyly

---

[11.] Which stands in approximately the same relation to Vic and Bob as Pat Boone's cover versions did to the original recordings of Little Richard, but in a good way.

macho pen-name of Michael Field (on the grounds – understand-able in a Victorian England whose perennially unamused matriarch could not bring herself to accept the existence of Sapphic love – that 'we have things to say that people will not hear from a woman's lips').

Perhaps the best known of these hilariously florid and overblown works is an epic poem about their dog, rejoicing in the title *Whym Chow: Flame of Love*. The eponymous canine's real-life role as 'sex symbol, god made flesh and embodiment of the masculine principle' was, their biographer Emma Donoghue later noted,[12] 'a heavy burden of meaning for one small dog to bear . . . Not surprisingly, it went to his head and he became a tyrant.' On one occasion, when Whym Chow's foul temper had prevented them from going to the beach, Bradley and Cooper excused him in verse with the classic couplet 'Bacchic cub, Thou could'st not bear to face the sea'. But, in the immortal words of Ronnie Corbett, I digress.

In the summer of 1890, on meeting the celebrated Irish play-wright and novelist George Moore, Bradley and Cooper noted in their diary that his smile was 'like sunshine on putty'. It is hard to be sure exactly what they meant by this observation, though they probably did not intend it as a compliment. (Moore is one of those tragic whipping boys of destiny – like Sir Geoffrey Howe or Bobby Davro – who seem destined to be remembered chiefly as the butt of other people's insults.)[13]

However, if the phrase 'sunshine on putty' is dramatically uprooted from its original context and applied with a reckless flourish to the recent history of British comedy, its ambivalence becomes entirely felicitous. On the one hand it evokes a pleasurable sensation – a feeling of warmth and light in a clammy and mutable world – on the other, a specific impact: a sense of helping along a process of coalescence that was already ongoing.

Consider for a moment the almost innumerable ways in which daily life in this country is different now from the way it was at the

---

[12.] In *We Are Michael Field*.
[13.] 'Do I know George Moore?' Oscar Wilde once mused brutally when his compatriot's name was mentioned. 'Oh, I know him so well that I have not spoken to him in ten years.'

beginning of the last decade. Who would have predicted in 1990 that within little more than ten years it would be hard to remember what it was like to live under a Tory government (or at least one which called itself that)? Or that the thirsty need no longer dream of pubs that would be open all day, and the hungry could entertain the real possibility of a decent sandwich in almost every town and city in Britain (so long as they had the money to pay the premium for Pret à Manger pine nuts)? Or that Scotland and Wales would have their own parliaments and someone who wasn't a neo-Nazi might fly the flag of St George on the front of their car? Or that on the days when Sara Cox managed to get out of bed for the breakfast show, you could listen to Radio 1 all day from 7 a.m. till 5.45 p.m. and Jo Whiley would be the only DJ you'd hear who didn't come from Manchester or Leeds?[14] Or that a terrestrial TV programme would exist which would keep a twenty-four-hour watch on a group of wannabe daytime travel-show presenters in the hope that a drunken maverick cockney dental nurse might embark upon an ill-advised sexual adventure?

It would be easy (not to mention quite fun) to go on like this all day, but when it comes to the trickier business of establishing the connection between these almost subliminal changes in the fabric of everyday life and the recent history of British comedy, only a famous French philosopher who sounds like he ought to play for Arsenal can help us.

What Henri Bergson has to say about all this

The French philosopher Henri Bergson's 1900 intellectual land-mark *Le Rire* – helpfully translated into English as *Laughter* in 1911 – is most celebrated for its contention that much of what is considered comic can be boiled down to moments where 'the human reduces

---

14. As late as the early eighties, a BBC booklet affirmed that the recommended speech patterns of continuity announcers should be those 'of the person born and brought up in one of the home counties, educated at one of the established southern universities and [a big concession this, accent-wise, if not in terms of gender] not so set in his ways that all linguistic change is regarded as unacceptable'.

itself to the automatic'. In a less frequently quoted passage of the book, Henri makes the seemingly straightforward assertion that 'to understand laughter we must put it back into its natural environment, which is society'.

'Laughter appears to stand in need of an echo,' Bergson notes. 'It can travel within as wide a circle as you please; the circle remains, none the less, a closed one.' To illustrate this notion, he uses the example of travellers sharing a joke in a railway carriage while another passenger sits across the aisle, forbidden by basic etiquette from joining in. 'Had you been one of their company,' Bergson chuckles, 'you would have laughed like them.'

Obviously this was before mobile-phone radiation had fatally eroded our conception of personal space in public places, but when you consider the peculiarly modern spectacle of individuals on buses or trains performing virtual stand-up comedy routines into Nokia handsets for the benefit of faraway friends, while flesh and blood audiences of complete strangers sit around them in stony silence, it actually underlines the truth of Bergson's observation rather than undermining it.

'However spontaneous it seems,' Bergson argues, 'laughter always implies a kind of secret freemasonry.' If you could mark the points at which this freemasonry either breaks down or is particularly strong, you would end up with a kind of dot-to-dot relief map of the national subconscious.

Based – as it is – on how much, in terms of ideas or emotions, a performer is able to share with their audience, comedy can teach us a great deal about who is swimming with society's tide and who is swimming against it. Consider in this regard the following two incidents of live onstage trauma: the first reassuringly trivial, the second rather less so.

Rory Bremner got rid of his original Scottish accent in response to social pressure applied within the English public school system, but soon learned to pick up others in its place. A few years later, after this facility had turned into a career, the BBC's determination to keep him in a light-entertainment strait-jacket pushed him to Channel 4, where he made a startlingly successful transformation (at least in his own mind) from boyish purveyor of sports commentators and weathermen to diamond-hard political satirist.

Away from the safety of the small screen, however, the construction of appropriate showcases for impressionistic virtuosity can still be a perilous business. In the first flush of his reinvention, amid the plaintive cry of the Essex gulls at the elegant Southend Cliffs Pavilion, Bremner's inaptly confident 'Does anybody here listen to Radio 4?' is met with a fairly crushing silence. What price a dazzling impression of crusty, rugby-obsessed, radio sports eminence Cliff Morgan in the cold, hard world of the east-coast riviera?

The second incident involves Scott Capurro – a raffish, catty, minutely boss-eyed, gay comedian from San Francisco, who briefly set down his picnic blanket on the banks of the British comedy mainstream in the early to mid-nineties. The high point of his career was probably an appearance on *Pebble Mill*, where Alan Titchmarsh asked him the immortal question 'So you're a gay comedian, how do you go down in America?'

The fun in a Capurro live show comes from a consensual overstepping of the mark. ('Are you heterosexual?' he taunts straight audience members. 'Really? You were the last one I would have expected.') The edge comes from our – and his – awareness of how easily consensus can turn to conflagration.

At an early live appearance at the Hackney Empire, a gang of rough-looking individuals in the front row begin to get restive about five minutes into Capurro's set. One of them calls him a 'faggot'. Capurro says: 'I want to love you – help me.' The situation simmers and then gets uglier. People at the back of the crowd start to shout at the people in the front, one of whom gets onstage, grabs the microphone and roars in fury and bewilderment, the scar down the side of his face pulsing eerily, 'What is it, are you *all* faggots?'

The rest of the audience shouts 'Leave! Leave! Leave!' – at first tentatively, but then with increasing fervour as the Hackney Empire remembers its former status as the home of alternative cabaret. Eventually, the front row gets up and storms off *en masse*, Capurro's taunts – 'He wants me!', etc – ringing rather half-heartedly in their ears. The violence in the air has hobbled the comedian's instinctive bravado, but though visibly and understandably shaken, he still manages to have the last word: 'Oh, I was wrong, it wasn't the gay thing . . . It was the Vietnam thing.'

At Last, The Theodore Hook in 1812 Show

In the mid-1960s, when John Cleese and a group of his up-and-coming acquaintances (including the brace of comic colossi who would later be known as The Two Ronnies) were looking for a title for their shiny new topical TV revue, they called it *At Last The 1948 Show* in a bid to sum up frustration (previously and more vehemently expressed by their non-Oxbridge-educated role model, Spike Milligan) with the slow-moving institutional nature of the BBC.

Any true appreciation of what is or is not golden about the Reeves/*Office* age will have to avoid overestimating the differences between this and other periods of comedic endeavour. Especially as one of the main creative themes of the period will prove to be reconnection with preceding generations after the supposed ideological breaches of the 1980s.

Consider the brilliant career of nineteenth-century rabble-rouser Theodore Hook, editor of such outspoken publications as *John Bull* and *The Arcadian*. A. J. A. Symons's 1934 biographical essay[15] outlines an armoury of comedic attributes which will not be unfamiliar to comedy *aficionados* of the present day.

Alongside the mid-stream political horse-swapping of the afore-mentioned Mr Rory Bremner ('his power of producing in parody a complete House of Commons debate, imitating one speaker after another . . . taking off Peel, Palmerston or the Duke [of Wellington] without a moment's pause'), the eagle-eyed might discern the poker face of Jack Dee ('his extreme power of keeping a straight face when all his listeners were eclipsed in mirth'), or the institutional subversion of Chris Morris. (Taking up position on an empty cart by the roadside, Hook once posed as an itinerant preacher. Having assembled a suitably rustic audience, the metropolitan mischief-maker 'suddenly altered the tone of his voice, thundered the most appalling curses at the throng and ran for his life'.)

Even the legendary drinking prowess of Johnny Vegas gets a look in. Symons describes Hook 'drinking experimental gin and

---

[15.] In *English Wits*.

maraschino cocktails by the pint with an American *bon vivant*, before dining soberly at Lord Canterbury's where he ascribed his poor appetite to "a biscuit and a glass of sherry rashly taken at luncheon"'.

This is not to say that life was necessarily richer or more satisfying – comedywise – in the early 1800s, but it is probably worth bearing in mind that the late twentieth century was not the first historical moment at which the professional laughter-maker has loomed large in our culture. The medieval scholar Erasmus disparagingly described the mid-thirteenth century as a time when 'Fools [i.e. jesters] were so beloved by great men that many could not bear to eat or drink without them, or to be without their company for a single hour'.

The picture of the wearer of cap and bells painted in R. H. Hill's *Tales of the Jesters* – 'Stealing titbits from the kitchen, falling into fits of violent fury without reason, breaking furniture and crockery, fighting with the pages and worst of all giving himself insufferable airs' – will not be wholly unfamiliar to anyone lucky enough to have spent time with Britain's turn-of-the-millennium comedic élite.

Elements of unexpected continuity are just as rich a source of fascination in the history of comedy (or, indeed, anything else) as unarguable new departures. To achieve a true understanding of the achievements of the Reeves/*Office* epoch, it will be necessary to delve deeply into the historical (as well as the comedic) background of the previous half-century – from the victorious memory of the Second World War to the traumatic loss of the British empire; from the bright new dawn of the swinging sixties to the sour fag-end of Thatcherism. At the same time, the dramatic unfolding events of the 1990s and early 2000s will be recounted – wherever possible[16] – in the present tense, in the hope of capturing the immediacy with which these developments were initially experienced.

If by these means it were somehow possible to root the glorious comic legacy of this illustrious era in timeless verities of national character and cultural heritage, well, that would certainly be a goal worth aiming at. In his lofty 1946 panegyric *The English Sense of Humour*, Harold Nicolson describes that most oft-speculated-upon

---

16. And sometimes where it isn't, really.

of national attributes (whose ethnic remit is, for the purpose of this volume – and in acknowledgement of the partial success of Tony Blair's devolutionary reforms – graciously also extended to the Scots, the Welsh and even the Irish) as 'existing at a level of consciousness between sensation and perception'.

In the hope of getting across how this idea worked, Nicolson came up with a novel illustrative formula. To approximate what he called the 'simultaneous awareness of doubleness and singleness' which it entailed, he invited his readers to enjoy for themselves 'the curious sensation produced when we cross the middle finger over the index and then push the v-shaped aperture up and down the nose'.[17]

[17.] The illusion of 'having two noses and one nose at the same time' may or may not turn out to be the key which unlocks the gate of comedic enlightenment, but if this book can persuade a new generation of readers to savour that experience for themselves, then something of lasting value will certainly have been achieved.

Chronological Timeline

Dawn of time–1990	Pre-history
Summer 1990	First series of *Vic Reeves Big Night Out*
Autumn 1990	Margaret Thatcher resigns
Autumn 1991	First series of Radio 4's *On The Hour*
Winter 1991–2	Saddam Hussein invades Kuwait
Spring 1992	John Major leads the Tories to a fourth successive election victory
Autumn 1992	Black Wednesday. Britain withdraws from the European Community Exchange Rate Mechanism in circumstances of unparalleled fiscal humiliation
December 1993	Julian Clary uses the British Comedy Awards' national live TV platform to slander former Chancellor of the Exchequer Norman Lamont in an unexpectedly amusing way. The Exchange Rate Mechanism is not mentioned
December 1993	Newman and Baddiel play Wembley Arena. The Exchange Rate Mechanism is still not mentioned
27 December 1993	*Shooting Stars* makes its début as part of a Vic and Bob theme night on BBC2
Winter 1994	First and only series of *The Day Today* kick-starts the Alan Partridge small-screen parabola. Chris Morris's sadistic studio anchor torments Patrick Marber's hapless economics

correspondent Peter O'Hanraha'
Hanrahan over his inability to fully come
to terms with the Exchange Rate
Mechanism

Spring/summer 1994　Tired of grappling with the intricacies of
European Community finance to a
soundtrack of newly corporatized US
grunge-rock, the British public awards
itself a national holiday, as the releases of
Blur's *ParkLife* and Oasis's *Definitely
Maybe* coincide with the launch of
Loaded magazine to inaugurate an era of
rude patriotic vigour and unprecedented
cultural self-satisfaction

December 1994　Spike Milligan uses the British Comedy
Awards' national live TV platform to
bad-mouth the heir to the throne in a
characteristically outrageous manner

Spring/summer 1995　First series of *Father Ted*. The word
'Feck' enters polite vocabulary

December 1995　At the end of his Christmas Special –
Knowing Me, Knowing Yule – Alan
Partridge is inadvertently responsible for
the death of a guest and must
contemplate televisual oblivion

Summer 1996　The Wembley crowd's rendition of
Baddiel, Skinner and Lightning Seeds'
maudlin Euro 96 anthem 'Football's
Coming Home' marks the high point of
the football/comedy/pop/patriotism
interface

August 1996　Something wicked this way comes: first
sighting of The League of Gentlemen at
the Edinburgh Festival

1 May 1997　New Labour electoral landslide

August 1997　Princess Diana's death. Among the
endless cultural and political ramifications
of this epoch-making event, the novel

David Baddiel writes about it will pass inexplicably unnoticed

Autumn 1997   *I'm Alan Partridge.* Swimming boldly against the tide of increasing linguistic diversity, Alan stigmatizes the speech of his well-meaning Geordie retainer as 'just noise'

Summer 1998   Frank Skinner marks the low point of the football/ill-suppressed homoerotic hysteria interface by claiming (on a World Cup edition of *Fantasy Football League*) to have rubbed the bulbous head of the Jules Rimet Trophy against the tip of his penis

31 August 1998   Reeves and Mortimer's *Families at War* pilot picks up the baton of televisual home invasion from *Noel's House Party*'s 'Gotcha Oscar', but – as if inspired by antics of UK 4 × 100m relay team – drops it before the actual series starts

Autumn/winter 1998   First series of *The Royle Family.* In a season of good omen for comedic hyper-realism, *The Johnny Vegas Television Show* also makes an inspired one-off début

Christmas 1999   Ali G's *Alternative Christmas Message* proves the unexpected highlight of Britain's millennium celebrations

Winter 2000   First series of *The League of Gentlemen.* Still a year to wait until Papa Lazarou's Pandemonium Carnival, though

Easter 2000   *The Royle Family*'s Caroline Aherne and Craig Cash unveil their *Back Passage to India.* The reaction of E. M. Forster's living relatives can only be guessed at

Early summer 2000   'Nasty' Nick Bateman expelled from *Big Brother* house for breaking 'rules'

Autumn 2000   Brazenly unenvironmental petrol tax protests segue seamlessly but with tragic aptness into the Foot and Mouth crisis. *Brass Eye*'s 'Animals' episode proves horribly prophetic

Christmas 2000 BBC2 screens 'last *Fast Shows* ever'

Spring 2001 First *Celebrity Big Brother*. Jack Dee breaks out of house and wanders aimlessly in East London post-industrial wilderness before returning, chastened, to fortified televisual enclave

May 2001 Tony Blair wins second term

February 2002 Death of Spike Milligan

June 2002 Brian May plays 'God Save the Queen' on top of Buckingham Palace to commemorate Elizabeth II's Golden Jubilee. Ben Elton compères

Summer 2002 *The Fast Show* announces extensive live 'Farewell' tour

Autumn 2002 *I'm A Celebrity Get Me Out Of Here!* consummates mainstream TV's ten-year flirtation with the Reevesian entertainment ethic

Autumn 2002 Ricky Gervais – appearing on *Parkinson* to publicize the second series of *The Office* – suggests that the recent tragic death of Rod Hull in a roof-top fall might in some way have been due to hand injuries sustained in the course of his puppet Emu's much-celebrated onscreen tussle with the veteran Yorkshire chat-show host

Winter 2002–3 Almost ten years after its first screening, *The Day Today* 'War Special' inspires the second Gulf War
Ben Elton and Lenny Henry sighted in Vic Reeves's wedding photos in *OK* magazine
Ricky Gervais announces Christmas 2003 editions of *The Office* will be the last

Part One

1
On the Launchpad

The Reeves and Mortimer despot/democrat
trajectory is about to commence

*'The present time, together with the past, shall be judged by a great
jovialist'*

Nostradamus

*'You'll never guess what I just saw backstage . . . Nicholas Witchell
with a barrage balloon Sellotaped onto his back, trying to convince
all these termites that he was their queen'*

Vic Reeves

In a late-nineties BBC TV documentary about Steve Martin, the
stadium-filling stand-up balloon-folder turned Hollywood leading
man recalls looking around him at the angry political comedy which
prevailed in his homeland in the immediate aftermath of the Vietnam protest era. 'Hmm,' Martin remembers his mid-seventies self
thinking, 'all that's gonna be over soon . . . and when it is, I'm
gonna be right there. And I'm gonna be *silly*.'

It would not be the act of a madman to imagine Vic Reeves
and Bob Mortimer making a similar plan in downtown south-east
London a decade or so later, with Margaret Thatcher as their
Richard Nixon and Ben Elton as their Richard Pryor. If you hadn't
ever spoken to them. But once you've listened to them talking about
what they do (in this instance, over tea and biscuits at the BBC,
at around the same time the Steve Martin documentary goes out)
it's hard to conceive how the massive cultural impact Reeves and

Mortimer have had on this country in the past decade or so could possibly have been a matter of prior calculation.

They have always been endearingly incapable of guessing which of their ideas will go down well and which won't ('You imagine everyone will like everything when you first think it up,' Vic muses, 'then when you actually do it, you think "Oh, maybe not"'), seeming to clutch to their hearts with especial tenderness those comedic sallies which are greeted with total incomprehension on the part of their audience.

Vic remembers an infamous early appearance at the Montreal Comedy Festival: 'There were 7,000 people, one of the biggest crowds we've ever had, and it was absolute silence for twelve minutes. We went out and we had the lucky carpet with us. The basic joke is Bob comes on and says, "I've been having some bad luck." And I say, "Well, have you got a lucky charm?" And I turn out to have a lucky charm which is too big to carry . . .'

Vic shakes his head contentedly: 'You could hear people in the audience saying, "That carpet's too big" – they just couldn't accept someone having a twenty-foot roll of carpet for a lucky charm.'[18]

Bob has similarly fond memories of 1998's notoriously impenetrable BBC2 series *Bang Bang . . . It's Reeves & Mortimer*. 'We have this hope,' Mortimer insists, rather poignantly, 'that if there's anyone left bothered about us in fifty years' time, that will be the one they'll remember.'[19]

It seems jokes nobody understands are like pop stars who die young. They never get the chance to let you down.

[18.] 'It's a very English thing to make an arse of yourself,' Vic notes later, with regard to the transatlantic comedic divide whose existence was confirmed by this Canadian communications breakdown. 'American comics tend to say, "We're the same as you". Whereas with us, it's more likely to be "We're not the same as you – we wear bad shoes and we're completely thick."'

[19.] 'In fact,' Bob recalls poignantly on another occasion, '*Bang Bang . . .* was our real attempt at making something commercial: our official, formal show to be something everyone would like!' 'Fucking hell,' Vic shakes his head. 'We never explained what the humunculus was, or why he was in the desk.' For those boiled eggs that kept coming out of dead people's mouths, though, an explanation is eventually forthcoming: 'That was their souls.'

'There's such a thin line between what works and what doesn't,' argues long-time Vic and Bob associate and *Vic Reeves Big Night Out* catalyst Jonathan Ross (while pretending not to care whether any fellow customers have registered his presence in a Soho Starbucks in the early summer of 2002). 'It's all delivery and perception and context. And I think they understand that better than anyone. That's why they never get beaten down – because *they* find what they do genuinely funny. That's what makes them different from what you might call more workmanlike comedians, or some of the sort of stuff I do,' Ross grins.

'You sit down and write material which you think people might find funny,' he continues. 'Then you try and hone it so they definitely will do, but you're not living life for yourself. It's purely work. It was never like that for Vic and Bob, though. They're not a service industry: even when they're doing things to pay the rent, they're still enjoying themselves. And something like that time in Montreal – where they were doing stuff with a miniature Elvis and some monkeys on a plate to a bemused bilingual audience – they just enjoyed the whole experience. For them, it doesn't represent the death of an act or a step back in a possible career plan, it's just another funny moment in an already amusing day.'

Reeves and Mortimer used to commemorate the jokes which no one got with a weekly memorial service in the 'tumbleweed moment' running gag on *Shooting Stars*. Now that they themselves are verging on institutional status, it's hard to remember just how roughly they once rubbed against the comic grain. But when the *Big Night Out* first appeared – in a succession of (to use Vic's characteristically art-history-informed adjective) 'Hogarthian' south-east London pubs, in the second half of the 1980s – the ideological tyranny of alternative comedy was still at its height.

'It just didn't interest me,' Vic remembers scornfully. 'I hate being preached to. I can make my own mind up: tell me something new.' In Vic's case, something new meant a potent blend of old-fashioned vaudeville and a spirit of the purest comic anarchy.

Consider for a moment the *Big Night Out*'s warped talent contest 'Novelty Island' (in which Mortimer's increasingly poignant *alter ego* Graham Lister strives to impress the unfeeling Reeves with a series of doomed variety acts, such as pushing lard through the mouth and nostrils of a picture of Mickey Rourke). Now cast your mind back to its most obvious comedic precursor, 'Alan Whicker Island' – a vintage Monty Python sketch about an archipelago inhabited entirely by people who look and behave just like the abrasive TV travel-show presenter turned spokesman for American Express. The fundamental difference between these two comic conceits is that the latter addresses the entertainment apparatus it is attempting to deconstruct from the top down, while the former does so from the bottom up.

This levelling tendency in Vic and Bob's work is balanced from the first (for example, in the marvellously arbitrary adjudications of the terrifying Judge Nutmeg) with a healthy respect for the comic potential of absolute rule. Their unique ability to combine the insurrectionary fury of the eighteenth-century mob with the icy *hauteur* of the pre-revolutionary aristocrat is the basis of what rocket scientists of the future will term 'The Reeves and Mortimer despot/democrat trajectory'.

3. Primary Ross/Reeves interface

As with the initial encounter between Lorenzo de' Medici and Michelangelo – to which it has often been compared – the bare physical facts of the first meeting between Jonathan Ross and Vic Reeves are a matter of historical record. It was the start of the second series of *The Last Resort* in the autumn of 1987, and after the runaway success of his début season, Jonathan Ross was looking around for fresh inspiration in the midst of a 'horrible second album moment'.

His brother Adam, who was running a club called The Swag at Gossips in Soho at the time, had mentioned a 'slightly crazy DJ guy . . . the only person he knew who admitted to liking prog-rock when no one else would even acknowledge that stuff. He'd put on a record like "Alright Now" by Free and mime to it while wearing a horse-brass round his neck.'

When Ross senior discovered that this individual also did 'strange paintings of Elvis', his curiosity was definitely piqued. A meeting was set up at a Japanese restaurant in Brewer Street, where Reeves would bring his pictures and Ross would pick up the tab. Fifteen years later, the latter remembers the occasion in tones endearingly reminiscent of one of those scenes in a TV dating show where someone goes to the toilet between the starter and the main course to tell the cameras how it's going.

'I liked the way he looked,' Ross remembers. 'I liked what he'd done with his hair – he was the first person I'd seen with what was sort of the George Clooney cut. I'd always been interested in the evolution of male style but never really had the courage to do anything about it. Jim [it is a tribute to the power of the Vic Reeves persona that even people who know him really well seem slightly uneasy about using the name on his birth certificate] certainly led the way there.[20]

'I'd never seen anyone who was quite so comfortable about looking ridiculous for the sake of style,' Ross continues, 'which is something I deeply admire in people – that almost complete sublimation of the ego in pursuit of "the look". He was wearing all black, and he had his hair done very short. He looked great and very unusual – kind of like a mod, but those early ones who were inspired by the American beats. Anyway, it was a very interesting look and I knew he'd done it consciously, so that really impressed me.'

What was the atmosphere like between the two of them? 'It was reasonably friendly, but a little awkward. I was slightly embarrassed at the time about the way people might perceive me as being the epitome of Thatcher's young man. I suppose it was because of the shoulder pads – shoulder pads equating in a post-*Dynasty* kind of way with flash and success. Anyway, I was very conscious of going out of my way not to seem like that person.'

And yet Ross felt comfortable buying two paintings (for a hundred pounds each, though Vic only asked for ten) on the spot – one of which featured Elvis ironing Tommy Trinder's trousers?

'I do remember thinking immediately afterwards, I hope I haven't offended him in some way. I was always concerned about the north–south thing as well . . . especially back then. It was very important at that stage for any vaguely sensitive southerner not to act like a

---

[20.] Though Jonathan Ross's fashion sense must surely rank quite highly on any list of things one wouldn't want to be credited with inspiring.

prick in any way to do with money or status or feeling proud of being brought up in the nation's capital city when in the company of northern gentlemen.'

Vic and Bob seem to have had a talent for reflecting this feeling back at people. 'Yes, but very *nicely*, never in an anti-southern kind of way . . . It was almost a casual acknowledgement of who they were. One of the things that always really attracted me to them was that they were clearly from the north-east, yet it wasn't like "Hello, we're northerners, look at us". Their unapologetic use of phrases and terms that either were peculiar to their region, or seemed like they might be to people from the south, made the whole thing feel kind of true, even when it was anything but.'

Ross first encountered the two of them together a few months after the Brewer Street meeting, when he went down to see Vic DJ-ing at Gossips. 'There were about three people in the audience and some bloke pretending to be a playboy singing "I'm the man who broke the bank at Monte Carlo". Bob turned up afterwards and I assumed he and Vic were a gay couple, because they seemed quite tender with each other. Bob was concerned that it hadn't gone well and I didn't understand that they worked together, I just thought, Oh, he's gay and this is his little partner. So when Vic said "I'm doing a thing with Bob" I just thought "Oh fuck, it's a Linda McCartney situation". But of course, it wasn't.'

Right from the start of his own TV career, Ross seemed keen to rehabilitate British comedy's old guard – the Frankie Howerds and Sid Jameses – who had fallen by the ideological wayside in the 1980s.[21] Was one of the things that impressed him about Vic Reeves the way he seemed to be referring to a pre-alternative tradition?

'I think early on I was just struck by his originality and his fearlessness . . . the way he presented himself as an exotic figure, not so much in terms of being from the north-east, just in a kind of "Hello,

---

[21.] 'Sometimes I wasn't sure if I *was* actually championing things,' Ross remembers, 'or just enjoying the idea of saying I was. Coming out for Frankie Howerd, for instance, was something I was really pleased to have done, but with, say, *On The Buses*, I would probably have said "Wow this is great", where actually it wasn't.'

I'm Spike Milligan's illegitimate son" sort of way. It's just that unique manner Vic has of observing things and presenting himself ... It's not so much courage, because courage is when you know that you might fail. It's more like an insane confidence in his own world view.'

2. Seven days in the sitcom wilderness: 'Listen very carefully, I will say this only once'

There's a great bit in Graham McCann's 1998 biography of Morecambe and Wise where, as a means of establishing the weight of expectation resting upon his subjects' disastrous 1954 small-screen début *Running Wild* (the one which caused the *People's* television critic to pen the somewhat premature epitaph 'Definition of the week. "TV": the box in which they buried Eric and Ernie'), the author outlines the other entertainment on offer on Britain's only small-screen channel on the night Morecambe and Wise staked their first claim on the medium. Bear in mind that this was a time when, in McCann's suitably austere phrase, 'Hours of viewing, like public drinking, were limited in the interests of temperance'. Thus, the early evening newsreel was followed by the rather Reevesian-sounding *Coracle Carnival* (with its exciting coverage of people paddling up and down a river in Roman-style boats). Then came that eternal televisual staple, 'Association Football' (Aldershot versus the Army), followed by *Gravelhanger*, a drama so bad it made *Heartbeat* look like a mouth-watering prospect. The ill-fated *Running Wild* was next up, before the evening reached a somewhat anti-climactic conclusion with a discussion of the situation in Indo-China, followed by the national anthem.

There would seem to be plenty of ammunition here for those who claim that the now unthinkably large audiences often cited as evidence of the superiority of previous generations of TV were actually just a result of there not being anything else on. Yet *Running Wild* got dreadful viewing figures with no competition, while more than half the nation would watch *Morecambe and Wise* Christmas shows a couple of decades later when it had two (count them, two) other channels to choose from.

Anyway, to extend the reach of McCann's licensed-premises-based viewing metaphor, British TV at the start of the 1990s had left behind the old Scottish Highlands and Islands Keep the Lord's Day Special scenario, but was still a long way shy of the non-stop twenty-four-hour lock-in that would be the digital epoch. In short, this was an era of limited Sunday opening and the occasional late-night extension.

What we really need to help us understand the dramatic impact of *Vic Reeves Big Night Out* is some kind of contemporary record of 1990's primitive entertainment landscape. A diary, say, of a whole week's worth of British sitcoms in that last grim Thatcherite winter . . . Thank goodness I kept one![22]

Friday, 21 February

'Allo 'Allo

This failsafe blend of *Carry On*-style innuendo and hoary World War II stereotype has entered the national subconscious at such a high level that it's hard to know what to think about it. Except that the catch-phrase 'Listen very carefully, I will say this only once' will be remembered long after *'Allo 'Allo*'s source material – late-seventies BBC drama series *Secret Army* – has faded from the collective memory. And that the only way to truly grasp this show's ethical daring is to imagine the likely tabloid reaction to a French TV network essaying a comedy series about the humorous experiences of British prisoners in a Japanese POW camp.

Watching

Once the impact of its punkily downbeat theme tune ('It was boredom at first sight, he was no one's Mr Right') has worn off, this amiable chunk of Scouse whimsy actually puts together its clichéd ingredients (interfering mother and put-upon only son) in a modestly charming way. Tonight, chirpy Brenda and her lovably gormless motor mechanic boyfriend Malcolm indulged in a bit of furtive courting aboard a friend's beached pleasure

---

[22.] I was getting paid to do this by a magazine. I'm not mad or anything.

10

craft, and were surprised when the tide came in and they had to be rescucd by a lifeboat. Malcolm's last line – 'Nothing ever happens' – made the influence of Samuel Beckett even more explicit than it was already.

Home To Roost
It's hard to believe that this depressing rubbish with John Thaw and Reece Dinsdale in it is actually churned out by the same writer (Eric Chappell) who brought us the immortal *Rising Damp*. And yet, it is.

Colin's Sandwich
Even those who have never previously harboured warm feelings towards Mel Smith have to admit that this is quite good. The prevailing mood of world-weary cynicism recalls the great early days of *Shelley*, and by working through its desire to use the word 'buttocks' in its opening few moments, tonight's edition freed itself from that perennial concern to become genuinely humane. The man whose attempts to take control of his own life are constantly thwarted by his own essential decency, yet he can't help speaking his mind however horrific the situation he has become enmeshed in, is a perennial theme of all great drama, from *Hamlet* to *Ever Decreasing Circles*.

Saturday, 22 February

Not traditionally a big night for sitcoms. Luckily, Keith Barron will soon be back on our screens in *Haggard*.

Sunday, 23 February

You Rang, Milord
Jimmy Perry and David Croft generously stage a benefit night for all their old characters. Lord George and the Honourable Teddy are the same as they were in *It Ain't Half Hot Mum*, but in different clothes. Paul Shane, Su Pollard and the other one are the same as they were in *Hi-de-Hi* but in different clothes. The air raid warden in *Dad's Army* is the same as he was in *Dad's*

Army but in different clothes. The story is *Upstairs Downstairs*-style class war but played for laughs, which ought to have been a winning formula, but unaccountably – despite the plentiful opportunities for whisky watering and chamber pots – the whole thing looks a bit tired. In a footnote of modest historical interest, the comedy lesbian is played by one Katherine Rabett, who – had the cookie of royal libido crumbled a little differently – could quite easily have ended up as the Duchess of York.

The Two Of Us

Disgusting piece of Thatcherite slop in which 'Ashley' and 'Elaine' (played by Nicholas Lyndhurst – unwisely striving to shrug off the sacred mantle of Rodney in *Only Fools and Horses* – and the evocatively named Janet Dibley) are a wildly unappealing upwardly mobile couple, currently endeavouring to become entrepreneurs by running a pizza joint in the evenings. Any kind of manual work in a sitcom like this is, it must be remembered, side-splittingly hilarious. 'I wanted a leather-topped desk and a BMW, not a tin of olives and a moped,' Ashley moaned tonight to great audience hilarity. As if all this, another interfering mother and (this is the modern world after all) a businessman with a mobile phone weren't enough, this week's episode also found room for a cameo appearance from Simon Schatzberger, deeply loathed star of the 'French polisher? . . . It's just possible you could save my life' *Yellow Pages* ad.

Monday, 24 February

Desmond's

The fact that the only other non-white character in this entire week of British sitcom is a woman in the dentist's waiting room in Thursday's début edition of *One Foot in the Grave* gives some indication of the burden of representation Trix Worrell's Peckham Rye barber's shop comedy has to carry. In these circumstances, occasional lapses into the all-singing all-dancing tendencies of *The Cosby Show* are probably understandable. The comedy African is quite funny, too.

Tuesday, 25 February

Chelmsford 123

In which Jimmy Mulville shows that he still has some way to go before he can truly be considered the Tim Brooke Taylor of his generation.

After Henry

For reasons known only to themselves, ITV considered the return of *After Henry* an event of sufficient significance to merit the front page of the *TV Times*.[23] In truth it *is* slightly better scripted than most of its rivals in the hegemonic middle-class-parents-cope-with-grown-up-children-and-demanding-mother genre, but when Prunella Scales says '*After Henry* confirms my theory that all the best comedy is based on pain', she really is not kidding.

Porridge

Manna from heaven. In tonight's repeated episode, 'Poetic Justice', the magistrate responsible for Fletcher's incarceration found himself behind bars for bribery and corruption and sharing a cell with the man he sentenced. 'How do you think I feel,' he demands in a fine example of the celebrated Dick Clement and Ian La Frenais technique of natural justice through paradox, 'being sent down by a crook like me?'

Wednesday, 26 February

By some completely unprecedented scheduling oversight, there are at present no British sitcoms on a Wednesday evening, but it cannot be very long before someone chooses a common saying in everyday use, cuts off its second half (*Too Many Cooks . . . A Stitch in Time . . . It's an Ill Wind . . .*), finds a comedy location – motorway service station, taxidermists, baked bean factory – adds an interfering mother, someone with a car phone, and three

---

[23] And this was in the days when being on the front cover of the *TV Times* really meant something: when home-entertainment listings were as tightly controlled as the colour coding of Henry Ford's cars.

grown-up children, and remembers that trousers are funny, and there we'll have it. ITV, 8.30 p.m., and June Whitfield's our uncle.

Thursday, 27 February

May To December

Anton Rodgers, the poor man's William Gaunt, plays the middle-aged solicitor who is – horror of horrors, call out the militia and phone D. H. Lawrence – *going out with someone quite a lot younger than him.* Worse still, her name is Zoe Angel . . . and as for the comedy cockney secretary and her hilarious marijuana plant, let us draw a discreet veil over her (and it). It would be all too easy at this point to lament the passing of a halcyon epoch of situation comedy, but the harsh truth is that for every *Steptoe* . . . there has probably always been a *Mind Your Language.*

One Foot in the Grave

David Renwick's suburban revenge comedy is the rarest of contemporary phenomena – an entertaining new sitcom with funny jokes in it. Victor Meldrew (played by the excellent Richard Wilson of *Only When I Laugh* and *Tutti Frutti* renown) is an irascible retired security guard who vents his considerable spleen on children, men with walking sticks, and toilet rolls whose perforations don't coincide. Tonight he was in hospital with unexplained stomach pains and found himself having his pubic hair shaved by an escaped lunatic called Mr Brocklebank. Later on, when asked by a passing Conservative candidate for his vote in a forthcoming by-election, he gestured towards his genital region and proclaimed 'I'd sooner stick it in a pan of boiling chip fat'. Last, and perhaps best of all, came this explanation for chronic insomnia: 'How can I go to sleep?' Meldrew wonders. 'Every time I nod off, I have this hideous dream that I'm imprisoned in a lunatic asylum and Arthur Askey is singing underneath the window.'

At this point, the journal ends. But as well as showing just how desperately *Vic Reeves Big Night Out* was needed, and beyond the eerily prophetic resonance of Victor Meldrew's dream,[24] this grainy snapshot of life before reality TV can also – with the aid of hindsight's high-powered microscope – be seen to reveal a small-screen comedy world in a fascinating state of flux.

The exhaustion of the classic British sitcom form is made all the more apparent by the grisly spectacle of seventies behemoths trading on past glories. And the advent of *One Foot in the Grave* – arguably the last in the *Dad's Army/Fawlty Towers/Only Fools and Horses* family line of generation-crossing mass-audience sitcoms[25] – only further reinforces this sense of transience and impending extinction.

Meanwhile, at the other end of the demographic scale, a lot of the bright young things of what someone with no regard for mythic nomenclature might term the *Not the Nine O'Clock News* generation were finding that their own performing careers were running out of steam a little earlier than might have been expected. By cunningly diverting their substantial remaining energies into the brave new world of independent production, the Jimmy Mulvilles, Mel Smiths (no one else liked *Colin's Sandwich* as much as I did) and Gryff Rhys Joneses of the world would snatch success from the jaws of failure via the new empires of Talkback and Hat Trick.[26]

1. Getting Chiggy with it

'I remember going down and seeing them at the Deptford Albany,' says Reeves and Mortimer's manager Caroline Chignell – universally known as 'Chiggy' – of her first sighting of her future clients, 'and thinking, Oh my God! It was just so different from anything

---

[24.] The lunatic asylum is John Major's 'classless' Britain, the window is Channel 4, Reeves is Askey.

[25.] While *The Vicar Of Dibley* and *My Family* also achieve this rare feat, they have been excluded from this élite lineage because I don't like them.

[26.] The extent to which their creative frustrations might have paved the way for the greater artistic achievements of a subsequent era is a matter of conjecture. Simon *Spaced* Pegg does speak warmly (if vaguely) of a preceding generation of performers-turned-producers who 'had had their own stuff messed around with, and wanted to make sure it didn't happen to anyone else', but that's about as far as the hard evidence for this proposition goes.

else . . . Vic and Bob didn't really come out of the comedy world: what they were doing seemed to be referring more to art and pop traditions. There was a real feeling of a community of artists around them. Yet at the same time, their act seemed to involve all the sorts of things that would make your dad laugh, but done in a really contemporary way.'

In manned space flight, the last-minute pre-launch stages are always especially fraught. And so it proved with the Reeves and Mortimer despot/democrat trajectory, as the little matter of success-fully translating their uniquely deranged equilibrium to TV was very far from being a done deal.

'There was obviously some irony involved when Vic claimed to be "Britain's top light entertainer",' Chiggy remembers, 'but he believed it too – and he looked it when he wore a white suit.'

Vic's early televisual forays on Jonathan Ross's *Last Resort* were greeted with a reaction most fairly characterized as general bemusement, but looking back now, there were portents of the greatness to come. When he painted pictures of guests (including punk svengali Malcolm McLaren) on china plates as 'Lesley Cooper, street artist', a couple of prescient reprobates ran down out of the audience to steal them. And Vic's attempts at adding a much-needed touch of class to an ill-fated village-fête-themed show as the bucolic Silas Cloudharvest elicited at least one memorable reaction. ('I was talking to one of the prop guys afterwards,' Jona-than Ross remembers fondly, 'and he said "That farmer was shit: if he hadn't had that cucumber flute, he'd have died on his arse".')

There were, Chiggy remembers, 'a lot of people sniffing about' in south-east London in the very late eighties. Whether or not BBC2's Alan Yentob and Channel 4's Michael Grade actually did go and see the *Big Night Out* at Deptford Albany on the same evening in an epic battle for control of the future of British comedy,[27] it was the latter (via Ross's production company, Channel X) who ended up signing the deal.

After an embarrassing episode when Ross and Reeves went to the BBC boss's house only to find out that he actually wanted Vic

---

[27.] 'I'm sure I remember that they did,' insists Jonathan Ross, 'though every-one else tells me that story is apocryphal.'

to be the host of a new series of *Juke Box Jury* (a job which his friend and fellow scion of the South London biker underground Jools Holland was happy to take in his stead), it was never really going to be otherwise. The demon Yentob would get his man in the end. But for the moment, everything had turned out for the best. When the *Big Night Out* finally transferred to TV, the particular circumstances of a newly established independent production company making a show for a young channel would facilitate a level of freedom that a more firmly established institution could never have permitted.[28]

'The thing that set the tone,' Chiggy remembers, 'was Jim's absolute control of the visual aspect. Something like that would never be allowed to happen now, but it was his and Bob's vision entirely – all the sets, all the props, all the costumes . . . The scripts were all drawings [preserved for posterity in the Penguin book *Big Night In*] – "shell/bottle lamp with patchwork shade", "Kleenex/ticker tape". And it was amazing how literally the people making the props took everything: they were so terrified of accidentally putting down an aubergine rather than a cucumber, or making something blue when it needed to be white.'

Vic and Bob seem to have been quite an intimidating proposition at this stage. 'They had a very small, close-knit group of friends, and you would not dare ever to even guess what was funny and what wasn't, or you would land yourself in terrible trouble,' Chiggy concedes. 'I don't think it was just me . . . I think everyone felt that way.'

. . . Lift off! 'Twisted movements . . . little puppets . . . light breezes blowing gently across the floor'

The cover of the 26 May 1990 issue of the *NME* has a historic look about it few others of that epoch can match. The music paper (which had adopted Vic and Bob at a time when rock 'n' roll

---

28. 'The early days of Channel 4 was a lovely time to be making shows,' Jonathan Ross recalls fondly. 'Because we were groping towards a way of making things work for a different audience, and there was so little in the way of hierarchy or show-business structure – you could find someone you liked in the street and have them on TV within the week.'

hopefuls of a similarly charismatic stamp were distressingly thin on the ground)[29] looks forward to the first episode of *Vic Reeves Big Night Out* on the coming Friday night with a properly inflated sense of occasion.

'People may well anticipate some jokes of the type normally associated with alternative comedy,' Vic warns, portentously, 'but they are going to be disappointed.' What comes instead will be, he promises, 'very visual and very aesthetically attractive'. Among the featured attractions, the viewers at home can look forward to 'twisted movements . . . little puppets . . . light breezes blowing gently across the floor', safe in the assurance that 'except for sex and politics, everything is covered'.

The big night finally comes. And from the moment Vic walks on with Bob dressed as Isambard Kingdom Brunel and carrying a stuffed alsatian, it's clear this isn't going to be your everyday TV comedy experience.

Beginning and ending with a song, the show incorporates not only the marvellous 'Novelty Island' talent contest, but also the fearsome and arbitrary Judge Nutmeg, whose Wheel of Justice is the centre of an elaborate ritual of care ('What do we do with the wheel of justice? Comb its hair!') and generates a centrifugal force unparalleled in the history of jurisprudence ('Spin, spin, spin the wheel of justice – see how fast the bastard turns!').

Reeves, modestly hailed in the opening credits as 'Britain's top light entertainer . . . and singer', vainly endeavours to keep a grip on the proceedings in his multifarious roles as baffled continuity announcer, lecherous game-show host and super-confident master of ceremonies. The proceedings also benefit from regular interventions by Vic's bald assistant, Les, who loves spirit levels but has a terrible fear of chives, and top turns such as the astonishing performance-art group, Action Image Exchange. And then there's the enigmatic Man with the Stick, whose amusing helmet is decorated with cartoons of 'Spandau Ballet laughing at an orphan who's

---

[29.] Reeves and Mortimer's most vociferous champion at the paper was James Brown, the future founder of *Loaded*, whose debauched lifestyle would later be a source of some anxiety to Vic, when he briefly became his landlord.

fallen off his bike' or 'Milli Vanilli trying to create negative gravity in their tights'.

As with The Goons and Monty Python before them, the affection in which Reeves and Mortimer would come to be held by those who find them funny is rivalled only by the confusion and irritation they inspire in those who don't.[30] And this fact of course only serves to intensify the joy of the former happy grouping.

It's not long before people in every town in Britain are yelping at each other in hurriedly fabricated Darlington accents (slightly softer than conventional Geordie): 'You wouldn't! You wouldn't! You wouldn't . . . let it lie.' Other catch-phrases prove equally infectious – the all-purpose 'Very poor', the trip-to-the-barber's-inspired 'It's not what I asked for', and best of all, with its pay-off delivered in an appropriately gormless voice not a million miles away from Keith Harris's Orville: 'I'm naïve, me . . . but happy.'

With characteristic perversity, Vic seems to have been most willing to talk straightforwardly about what he was doing before anyone else knew what he was up to. Certainly he would rarely again be as explicit as he had been over that first Japanese meal with Jonathan Ross. ('He explained the loose idea of Vic Reeves being simultaneously him and not him,' Ross remembers wistfully, 'but I'm sad to say that at the time I didn't really pay as much attention as I should've.')

Speaking to Vic over the phone at his Deptford office in the middle of the first series, there is certainly no sign of his head being turned by success. Asked as a test of his artistic integrity whether he would ever consider doing a building-society advert, his response is heartwarmingly straightforward: 'If they're paying me, I'll do 'owt. I'm shameless.'

He is happy to talk about his tailor – Sidney Charles of Deptford High Street ('I've always gone to him, and I will continue to go to him as well') – but reluctant to be drawn on Jack Hargreaves, Frank

---

[30.] 'It is a national split,' Vic notes of the sharply divergent reactions inspired by his comedy, 'but I think that's a good thing.'

(I remember reading something written about Vic and Bob around this time by the eminent American showbiz authority John Lahr – son of the man who played the cowardly lion in *The Wizard of Oz* – in which his determination to misunderstand them seems to border on clinical mania.)

Randall, Will Hay, or any of the other big names of bygone variety eras to whom his *Big Night Out* persona seems to be paying implicit tribute. 'If I mentioned anyone, I'd be speaking out of turn really, wouldn't I?' he demurs, sneakily.

But aren't he and Bob bored of being compared to Morecambe and Wise all the time?

'It's been said. And I suppose if people have spotted it, there must be something there, but without being modest, I think we're very unique . . . I don't think you can really say that we're like anyone else, or want to be – we just make it up as we go along really.'

Perhaps a little taken aback by the warmth with which the *Big Night Out* is received, Vic and Bob subsequently seem to delight in erecting a wall of wilful obfuscation between themselves and the outside world. It's a wall that large sections of the British public seem to delight in swarming over – maybe inspired by the crowds picking up souvenir bits of demolished masonry on the freshly unified streets of Berlin.[31]

Either way, in the first flush of his fame, Vic Reeves can often be seen riding an antique motorbike round his old Greenwich haunts on scorching summer days, dressed in full biker's leathers. Within a matter of months, he almost needs a police escort to protect him from the hordes of impressionable teenagers begging him to autograph cooked meat products or pieces of celery.

'Their popularity rose absolutely from the north,' Chiggy explains. 'When they went out on tour after the TV show had been on, they were initially doing pretty small, university-only type gigs, but when they got to the north-east, we literally had to get security.'[32]

[31.] Or maybe (on more sober reflection) not.

[32.] Much of the legwork for this triumphant regional uprising had been done by the unlikely vanguard of *Viz* comic. From its inception in 1979 as a humble photocopied sheet flogged in Newcastle pubs to its late-eighties/early-nineties heyday with a bi-monthly circulation of over a million, this unlikely paragon of Thatcherite enterprise culture alternated trenchant satire of corporate and political hypocrisy ('The twelve water authorities of England and Wales . . . Taking your shit away and putting it in the sea') with some of the most puerile sexism and scatology ever committed to print.

When I arrived at *Viz*'s Tyneside nerve-centre in the summer of 1989,

At a less expansive cultural moment, this cult following in their ancestral homeland might have kept itself to itself. But this was the Madchester epoch, and with the rest of the country unprecedentedly susceptible to the charms of northerly enunciation, Vic and Bob soon found themselves exciting – on a national basis – the sort of intense, personally focused teen adulation that the pop stars of that baggily collective pre-Britpop musical moment seemed to have given up a right to.

By December of 1991, in the wake of an autumn repeat, a fantastic New Year special and a second series, a live *Big Night Out* fills Hammersmith Odeon for weeks on end. As in all the best games of Chinese whispers, a double transfer – from cult, localized live attraction to TV series to big-budget nationwide roadshow – had been enough to completely garble the original message.

If Reeves and Mortimer's act can fairly be said to be 'about' anything (and however sniffy they get when anyone accuses them of being surrealists, Dalí and Buñuel's manifesto that 'nothing should submit to rational explanation' sometimes seems to have been written for them), it is about celebrity.

It's one thing to unravel the macramé of minor television faces, pop stars and brand names in which we all find ourselves entangled and then mix them up again into ever more delicious confusion, but what happens when your own fame becomes a strand of that macramé? The moment of bewilderment which precedes recognition and laughter is one of Vic and Bob's most precious comedic assets, which is why familiarity could be fatal to them.

At Hammersmith Odeon, Vic and Bob seem rather bored with the Les Facts and the 'You wouldn't let it lie' and 'What's on the end of your stick?' routines, and the parts of the show which are less concerned with ritual and more concerned with invention are by far the most enjoyable. With the *Big Night Out* now established

---

in the hope of asking comics mastermind Chris Donald a series of penetrating, nay prophetic, questions on these very subjects, it seemed strangely appropriate that the man behind the publishing sensation of the decade – the man whose 'crisps world cup' would be (alongside the Beastie Boys' *Grand Royal* magazine) a template not only for *Loaded*, but also for pretty much the entire media mindset of the mid-nineties – should be temporarily indisposed, fast asleep on the toilet.

as perhaps the most original and inspiring of all the generation-welding TV comedies, its perpetrators would have to move on if they wanted to stop their talents congealing like old Ready Brek in the chipped breakfast bowl of the folk memory.

2
'Don't Mention the War'

Conflict aftermath and comedic rebirth, from The Goons to Richard and Judy

'I died for the England I dreamed of, not for the England I know'
Spike Milligan, in anticipation of imminent death
under enemy fire, Italy, 1943

'With our circuit, people at the beginning tried to separate them-
selves from the mainstream history of comedy, but in truth, if you go
back, there have always been little clumps of young performers who
appeared to be different but actually weren't'
Alan Davies, in his manager's West End office,
fifty years later

Vic and Bob's first appearance on *This Morning . . . with Richard and Judy*, in the autumn of 1991, is not a huge success. After a few conversational false starts, Vic (to whom the institutional acceptance represented by the booking means a great deal) is finally getting into his stride with an impassioned discourse about his love for *Dad's Army*, when Judy interrupts him with an exasperated – and characteristically curt – expostulation of 'I can't take any more of this'.

Both parties plainly consider this a very unsatisfactory piece of interaction – referring back to it in anxious tones on subsequent meetings – but for the watcher at home, it is actually much more fun than later, superficially more successful, encounters.

The idea that an up-and-coming Channel 4 comedian should

be able to speak sincerely about his love for Captain Mainwaring and Private Pike is simply beyond Finnegan's comprehension at this point. A couple of years later, she would probably have found it easier to grasp, but life is much more fun when she still doesn't get it. The excitement of two different worlds colliding with (at least) one side unaware of how much they actually have in common is always far greater than a formal meeting of minds.

One of the distressing side-effects of British TV's ever-increasing self-awareness in the 1990s is a steady decline in the number of arenas in which people can make a joke that everyone isn't in on. Like school playing fields (also steadily diminishing in number), such open spaces supply a vital service to the community, and certain technical forms of virtuosity cannot be mastered without them.

What concerns us at the moment is the thing that Vic and Judy have in common. Beyond a fondness for *Dad's Army* itself, it's a shared appreciation of what the success of the show was based on, which was the folk memory of a moment (well, a six-year span of extraordinary hardship and heroism) when Britain found itself to be – in the words of J. B. Priestley – 'the hope of all that's best in the world'.

The Second World War was the beginning of modern British comedy. If you got a frigate every time you heard someone say that, then we'd all be admirals. But from Spike Milligan's war memoirs to Freddie Starr doing his Hitler impression, to old-school Scouse reprobate Stan Boardman wittering on about 'The Germans' and their 'Fokkers', to Basil Fawlty's celebrated over-reaction to the presence in his hotel of guests from the land of Beethoven and Goethe, the shadow of that great conflict certainly loomed pretty large over the seventies and eighties comedy land-scape.

This was why when Martin Amis said in his book *Koba The Dread* that people in Britain were happy to laugh at Soviet Commu-nism but not happy to laugh at the Nazis, it seemed as if he must have gone to bed too soon after eating a large portion of strong cheese. A recollection of that spirit of cheery defiance so touchingly embodied in the *Dad's Army* theme tune, 'Who do you think you are kidding, Mr Hitler?',[33] would persist throughout all sections of British society to the very end of the century,[34] despite the best attempts of disreputable right-wing forces (from Margaret Thatcher and her Winston Churchill fetish to Fascist groups trying to collect funds by pretending they were intended for war veterans' hospitals) to co-opt it as their own.[35]

Gavin Hills – journalistic avatar of that upsurge of compensatory masculinity widely termed 'New Lad' – described himself as being part of 'The Airfix Generation': 'Boys who grew up seeing war as something distant and glorious, a playground game'. To be strictly accurate, this was not just *one* generation (Hills's considerably older fellow *Loaded* contributor Vic Reeves recalls growing up making models from kits and painting all the uniforms in paisley colours, and in any case, the ability to see war as something distant and glorious has been a vital weapon in the armoury of recruiting sergeants from the dawn of time) but it is the legitimate province of youth to fancy its own experiences to be unique.

Anyway, Hills was so moved by those images of wartime Britain which were so prevalent ('like the flickering shadows of a former,

---

[33] As recorded specially for the show by music-hall veteran Bud Flanagan, this inaugurated the tradition of getting a comedy legend of a previous generation to sing your theme song which would culminate in Eric Idle singing 'One Foot in the Grave'. Graham McCann's meticulous history of *Dad's Army* reveals that the show's original title sequence contained actual combat footage (rather than the more light-hearted sequence of the platoon on manœuvres which was ultimately settled upon), a creative decision which – had Jimmy Perry and David Croft won the battle they fought over it with the BBC – would now appear as an uncharacteristic (albeit well-intentioned) lapse in taste.

[34] It's worth remembering in this context that the heroic home guard of Walmington-on-Sea were first brought to the screen not in the patriotic post-war aftermath, but in that most determinedly forward-looking of decades, the 1960s (in fact, in the supposedly revolutionary year of 1968).

[35] I remember standing on Hackney Downs at a public celebration of the fiftieth anniversary of VE Day in the summer of 1995, listening to the Bangladeshi mayor of the borough make a sincere speech in very broken English. Looking around at the genial multifariousness of the crowd – drawn away from its TV screens and out into the park by a surprisingly impressive sound and light display – there was no other option than to be temporarily overwhelmed by a profound sense of patriotic pride.

more honourable world') amid the VE Day anniversary celebrations, that he decided to join the Territorial Army.[36] Even without being able to consider (as they hadn't been on TV yet) the alarming examples of Simon Pegg's crazy friend Mike in *Spaced* and *The Office*'s notorious killing machine Gareth Keenan, this seemed a somewhat extreme reaction.

As a first step to getting to grips with the enduring legacy of the Second World War and its long lost sense of common purpose, I felt that going to see two showbiz combat-zone veterans go through their paces looked like a safer bet.

Where there's armed conflict and the imminent threat of violent death, there's hope

In the course of about an hour onstage at the Royal Albert Hall in the early nineties, Eltham-born nonagenarian Bob Hope tells approximately twelve jokes. A shorter version of one of them ('Me, George Burns and a couple of older fellas, we get together every Saturday night and try to get in touch with the living') will turn up a decade or so later in the course of the first single to be taken from Robbie Williams's fourth solo album *Escapology*, but that is not the end of the elder Bob's contribution to modern show business.

Learning lines was never a priority for this godfather of the autocue ('What comedian', Hope is once reported to have asked, 'is going to give up playing golf for a script?') and as befits a man who hit puberty before the Russian revolution, most of his material on this occasion has to be fed to him by his piano player. But when he does 'It's Delovely', with his long-suffering wife Dolores singing the first word of each line, there is a flash of that effortless mid-song repartee that once made him and Bing Crosby the coolest men in the world.

[36.] In the wake of Hills's early death in a Cornish fishing accident in 1997, the determination of his many friends in the media establishment to apply the gloss paint of martyrdom directly on to the rough grain of that sad and senseless demise (without waiting for posterity to supply an undercoat) would testify poignantly to the very same yearning for heroism and moral significance which he himself had earlier identified.

Bob Hope was always older than he had a right to be – playing the romantic lead with Natalie Wood and Eva Marie Saint when he should have been their dad – but his audience is younger than anyone would have dreamed. Some are here to see Britain's own old-fashioned song-and-dance funnyman Brian Conley, who does a lovely turn from *Me and My Girl*, but then falls victim to a heckler of rare acuity. When Brian asks the audience to suggest impressions for him to do, a mighty voice booms down from the balcony with the following crushing proposal: 'a comedian'.

Most of the people, however, have come to pay tribute to a pioneer postmodernist, perhaps sensing that without Bob Hope's *Road to* . . . movies (and *Son of Paleface*), there would have been no Bob Monkhouse and maybe no Farrelly Brothers. Hope's short, sprightly bursts of stand-up (and sometimes sit-down) comedy are punctuated with long film-clip compilations of past career highlights, projected on to a large screen above the heads of the New Squadronaires Orchestra. His commentary on these is recorded, not live, so there is a weird reality lapse where the real Hope rasp fades into the taped Hope rasp.

Goon, but not forgotten

Using the Beatles (upon whom Milligan, Sellers, Secombe and the man we are about to meet were such a crucial, if neglected, influence) as a template, posterity cut fourth Goon Michael Bentine a deal midway between Ringo Starr's and Pete Best's. His substantial contribution to the first three *Goon Show* radio series might have been largely overlooked, but his 1970s children's TV series *Michael Bentine's Potty Time* would introduce many an impressionable child of a later generation to the madness and grandeur of war (albeit at a comfortably surreal remove, via epic battle scene reconstructions starring a clan of small imaginary creatures called The Potties, and with little bits of sand blown into the air to signify explosions).

In 'From the Ridiculous to the Paranormal', an autobiographical one-man show he puts on at the Shaftesbury Avenue Lyric Theatre in the same week as Hope's Royal Albert Hall date, Bentine refers to being born English as 'first prize in the lottery of life'. His wartime experiences – after being refused entry to the RAF eleven times on account of his half-Peruvian parentage, Bentine was arrested as a deserter; he then contracted typhoid, typhus and tetanus as a result of a bungled inoculation – suggest otherwise in the strongest possible terms. But Bentine's capacity for laughing in the face of adversity seems to be more or less infinite. Now suffering from cancer, he describes this as his farewell appearance (which it ultimately turns out to be), yet still leaves the stage with a grin. Goon, but not forgotten.

For those who have grown up thinking of *The Goon Show* as something Prince Charles likes which has a lot of silly voices in it, the idea that it actually represented a revolutionary overturning of the established order will necessarily take a bit of getting to grips with. But when the historian Peter Hennessy called The Goons 'a kind of decade-long "other ranks" revenge on the Empire and its officer class', he was not talking out of his hat. And *Observer* jazz critic Dave Gelly's analogy between the impact of Milligan, Bentine and co. and that of the 1951 Festival of Britain was not far off the mark either: 'The festival laid out the future pattern for architecture, town planning and design . . . while the Goons set about reducing to rubble the redundant edifice of British imperial smugness.'[37]

As ex-servicemen united in their hatred of bureaucracy and time-wasting officialdom, the four men honing their act after hours at the Grafton Arms in Victoria's Strutton Ground in the aftermath of the war had more than just bad memories of unfeeling superior officers in common. First off, being forced to do things you don't want to do, in a confined space, in company you would not necessarily have chosen, has always been one of the most fertile breeding grounds for comedy (and would continue to be so long after The Goons were demobbed, from *Porridge* to *Father Ted* to *The Office*).

But beyond that, Spike Milligan's personal experience of wartime as an expansion of mental as well as physical horizons does not seem to have been an isolated one. 'Going abroad was a bonus in their lives,' he wrote fondly of his fellow Gunners, 'even though it took a war to give it to them.'

Spike Milligan, Pauline Scudamore's fascinating biography,

[37.] In Peter Hennessy's *Never Again (Britain 1945–51)*.

describes the impact of his first wartime posting to Bexhill-on-Sea. Far from alarm at being snatched from home and hearth and prepared for the possibility of violent death, Milligan's chief response seems to have been one of exultation at unexpectedly rediscovering those senses of space and creative possibility which had been steadily closing down since late adolescence, when his family returned from Burma (where his father had been a non-commissioned officer in the colonial army) to the grim, grey world of pre-war Catford.

Escaping from the pettiness of 1940s south-east London[38] into a life of endless new experiences and constant physical danger, he found himself blessed with a dramatically heightened awareness of the world around him. 'His sense of the ridiculous began to bubble in earnest,' writes Scudamore of Milligan's experiences in the North African campaign (so memorably detailed in war memoirs such as *Rommel: Gunner Who?* and *Monty: His Part In My Victory*): 'what had war to do with all this beauty?'

Having got into the battalion concert party by means of his facility with a jazz trumpet, Milligan found himself expanding the element of knockabout banter in his musical performances into anarchic full-scale revue shows such as *Stand Easy*. In much the same way that Dadaist art had been underpinned by the horrors of the First World War trenches, these early comedic forays were inspired by the madness unfolding around him. 'It was pure lunacy, no rhyme or reason in it,' Spike later observed to Scudamore, 'it was meant to be pointless, just like the war.'

The traumatic experiences under fire which would haunt him for the rest of his life would find a clear therapeutic echo in the regular bomb blasts and deranged sound effects of *The Goon Show*. 'By creating a world where explosions hurt no one,' *Goon Show Companion* compiler Roger Wilmut wrote sympathetically, 'he made his own memories of the reality more bearable.'

The impact of wartime experience was not always so explicit. *Hancock's Half Hour* and *Steptoe & Son* writers Galton and Simpson

---

38. Strangely adjacent to the Deptford badlands in which Vic Reeves's *Big Night Out* first put down roots. Given that Eddie Izzard grew up in Bexhill-on-Sea, it is reasonable to assume that the young Milligan left spores.

were originally recruited to the septic ranks of professional comedy scribes from a pneumonia ward. But Tony Hancock, a.k.a. The Lad Himself – the fellow 'NAAFI comedian' with whom Spike Milligan would later share a disastrous barge holiday (they couldn't agree on which pubs to stop at) – never saw any action scarier than the concert party in Bournemouth.

Back in Civvy Street, the ex-soldiers' battle-hardened irreverence would often rub up uneasily against those stuffy institutions – most notably the BBC – which had yet to reflect the impact of post-war social changes. The Goons, in Milligan's subsequent assessment, were 'trying to break into satire'. (They 'could have beaten the fringe by ten years', he insisted to Pauline Scudamore, had the producers of the time not 'all been frightened out of their fucking jobs'.)

Peter Sellers 'could do any voice of any politician in the land', Milligan boasted, 'the Queen included . . . and that made us lethal'. Yet archaic restrictions on the representation of living people forced them to hide behind such diplomatic formulations as Dinglebee for the prime minister and Lady Bold De Speedswell for the Queen.

The unsympathetic attitude of BBC bureaucrats would drive Milligan up to and, eventually (when the pressure of writing all the *Goon Show* scripts on his own caused him to attack Peter Sellers with a kitchen knife), over the brink of nervous collapse. However, the next generation of would-be TV satirists would be able to rely – at least in one case – on more sympathetic treatment from the corporation's top brass. And in this instance, the lapse into military terminology is not inappropriate.

Hugh Greene was their valet

Mary Whitehouse used to credit Graham Greene's brother, Sir Hugh Greene (Director General of the BBC from 1960 to 1969), with being 'more responsible than any other single individual' for what she perceived as the moral decline of that decade. Needless to say, Greene saw things differently. As a foreign correspondent for the *Daily Telegraph* he had reported of Hitler's consolidation of power in 1930s Germany, and his personal experience of the ensuing moral abyss was the foundation of his own vision of the BBC as 'a symbol of the liberation of the individual imagination'.

He took over determined to 'clear away a certain amount of accumulated dust from what seemed . . . at the end of the fifties a rather stuffy institution, out of touch with the young and the rebellious, appealing to a rather narrow section of the public'. But Greene's conviction that 'To keep pace with the values of a changing world you have in fact to keep a bit ahead'[39] was not going to endear him to everyone. And while it's one thing to set an agenda, it's another thing to keep to it.

When daring new programmes like *That Was The Week That Was* and *Till Death Us Do Part* prompted howls of protest from the same sections of society that would later fail to be amused by Chris Morris and his very brassy eye, Greene might easily have bowed to public pressure and taken them off the air. The fact that he didn't[40] would have far-reaching consequences. In fact, it is probably fair to say that without Sir Hugh's steadfast refusal to countenance the objections of West Midlands primary-school teacher Mary Whitehouse and her 'Clean Up TV' campaign, the swinging sixties might never have got off the ground.

Describing Whitehouse and her 'moral reformers' as 'dangerous to the whole quality of life in this country', Greene did not just regard their activities as inimical to British traditions of freedom, tolerance and adventure. As someone determined to be 'positively and actively on the side of the values [he] had seen being attacked and turned upside down in the previous decades in so many parts of the world, with the establishment either on the side of reaction against liberal values or too weak to resist their overthrow', he saw born-again Christian campaigners like the Festival of Light as one step away from the Nazis.

The impact of the 1939–45 conflict on the history of comedy

[39.] In *Whitehouse*, by Michael Tracey and David Morrison

[40.] *That Was The Week That Was* did vanish from the screens in the run-up to the 1964 election – on the transcendentally bogus grounds that it might affect the result – but by that time the damage was done. And in any case, Ned Sherrin and David Frost's band of fearless TV revolutionaries had already shown their new establishment colours with their heartfelt eulogy to JFK.

reached far beyond such celebrated post-war landmarks as *The Goon Show* and *Hancock's Half Hour* and into the brave new world of the 1960s. But once you reach a generation of performers who are too young to remember the war at first hand, the situation inevitably changes.

With a very few honourable exceptions (notable alongside *Dad's Army* in the annals of comedic self-respect is the last episode of *Blackadder Goes Forth*), most comedy about wartime written by people who didn't live through it leaves the viewer with an uncomfortable suspicion that what is really being laughed about is the happy accident of birth which prevented those who are getting the laughs from having to go through this awful experience in real life.

In 2001, the strangely bitter and twisted second series of sketch show *Big Train* (which left Arthur Mathews – the milder-mannered half of the usually inspired scriptwriting duo Linehan and Mathews – holding the baby after his comedy compadre Graham Linehan decided to strike out on his own) contains a disproportionate amount of this sort of material. Nothing makes even the most left-leaning person yearn for the return of national service[41] quite like the sight of a load of easy-living peacetime comic actors getting cheap laughs at the expense of people who risked their lives to fight evil.

What comedians generally say when subjected to this kind of accusation (taking their lead from the much-discussed *Beyond The Fringe* sketch 'The Aftermyth of War') is 'it's not actually about the war, it's about the way the war has been represented'. But this defence is just as specious as Monty Python's claims that *The Life of Brian* wasn't actually taking the piss out of the Bible – 'Brian was another prophet we made up . . . blah blah blah . . . You can see Jesus's arm in scene 76 and it is treated very respectfully . . . blah blah blah' – when everyone knows *the fact that it was is the reason why it was funny.*

[41.] After all, they used to have it in Communist countries too.

The amazing *Let The People Sing* dead cow prophecy

Let The People Sing is not one of celebrated *Dad's Army* fan J. B. Priestley's better-known novels. Written to be serialized over the air by BBC radio before its first publication in book form, it was originally broadcast in instalments, beginning in early 1939 and with later episodes increasingly overshadowed by what someone on a History Channel documentary would probably refer to as 'the darkening storm-clouds of war'.

The book's protagonist is an out-of-work English comedian called Tommy Tiverton.[42] Looking back nostalgically to the halcyon days of 'the vast smoky-coloured caverns of the packed Empires and Palaces', Tommy yearns for 'a simple audience, not bedazzled by American speed, sharpness and cynicism, and blind to the richer English drollery of character'. At this stage, the threat to traditional variety is not TV, but that other little box in the corner of the front room, the radio. 'I like my public to see me,' Tiverton sniffs poignantly, confronted with the undeniable ascendancy of the catch-phrase-toting warriors of the wireless who will one day inspire some of Paul Whitehouse and *The Fast Show* team's least amusing material.

By a set of circumstances too serpentine to go into but involving an IRA bomb and an equestrian statue, Tommy Tiverton finds himself on the run across middle England with Professor Ernst Kronak, an intellectual asylum-seeker from central Europe with a happy knack for working high-flown political and philosophical theories into day-to-day conversation. ('In a certain limited sense all the English may be said to be anarchist,' he observes at one point,

---

42. In their autobiography *Eric & Ernie*, Morecambe and Wise blamed the war for the death of old-fashioned variety (which they would later be credited, like Reeves and Mortimer after them, with resurrecting for a televisual age) on the grounds that it killed off lots of good acts, and was the cue for the London Palladium to start booking only American bill-toppers. The fact that Tommy Tiverton is already, before the war has even begun, casting envious sidelong glances at 'all these new acts, all alike, crooning away into mikes, pretending to be Americans' suggests that Eric and Ernie's chronology is not quite as reliable as their comic timing.

later ascribing the relative weakness of the English revolutionary tradition to 'this limited and natural anarchy of the national soul'.)

Priestley, who had talked about the need to shore up morale in the face of the possibility of an imminent conflict (and accordingly seems to have designed the latter stages of *Let The People Sing* as an explicit call to arms), already seems to be looking to the kind of country that people would want to live in afterwards. 'Plenty of nice lads ready to go and be killed,' someone says grimly at one point – of Britain in 1939 – 'But . . . that's being ready to die, not being ready to live.'

The book's narrative climax hinges on the fate of an underused small-town variety hall which the snobbish local establishment want to turn into a museum ('Too much of England, I think, is a museum,' observes Professor Kronak, sternly) and which incoming American-based multinational United Plastics want to incorporate into their sinister mass-production facility. The debate about whether the townsfolk will stand up for their birthright of good spirits and inane singalongs in the face of this twin threat looks forward not only to the war that is about to begin,[43] but also to subsequent debates about globalization and American cultural imperialism.

Things look bad for a while, but in the end the necessary stiffening of communal resolve is effected by that apparently most placid and parochial of domestic institutions: Sunday lunch. Destiny mobilizes 'the revolutionary force of women who have spent a warmish morning in an undersized kitchen cooking a dinner they do not particularly want to eat themselves'. In these circumstances, the author notes, 'husbands and children, like so many idiotic passengers invading the engine room, are apt to hear something unpleasant about themselves'.

When the after-effects of such savage tongue-lashings are intensified by digestive disturbance – occasioned by 'a consignment of badly refrigerated Argentinian beef' – the menfolk are finally shaken out of their complacent reverie. 'Vast edifices of masculine sham' are seen to crumble, and the town comes together in a patriotic

---

43. 'Take this lying down,' someone warns with grisly prescience, 'and before long they'll be making ashtrays out of you.'

fervour to defend and cherish its heritage of communal entertainment. 'Like the nation waking from a long sleep' is how the book's
author describes it.

'What did you do in the comedy war, Daddy?'

More than four decades later, the Falklands conflict (itself the result
of a badly refrigerated Argentinian beef) would be responsible – at
least in the fevered minds of Margaret Thatcher and her tabloid-
running dogs – for a similar national awakening. But by this time,
the heritage of collective jollity in which J. B. Priestley placed such
touching faith would have been subject to a dramatic bifurcation.

'Alternative comedy grew out of punk,' Jonathan Ross explains,
'with the same determination to show an older generation "our
values are different from yours". And once you've taken a step
down that road, there's really nowhere else to go but to end up
saying you don't respect *any* of your predecessors' values, even
though in a way that's unfair.'

Just as John Lydon got in trouble with Malcolm McLaren for
admitting he liked Neil Young, so in the pre-Vic-and-Bob era it
was very much not the done thing for up-and-coming alternative
comics to allude respectfully to their professional forebears. 'The
older comedians became outcasts,' remembers Ross (who, in his
role as honest broker between the generations, would subsequently
do as much as any other individual to bridge the ideological and
demographic chasm), 'but they only had themselves to blame.
Because, with a few honourable exceptions such as Bob Monkhouse
and Des O'Connor, they were very scathing towards the new
generation when they should have welcomed it.'

By the time of Ben Elton's appearance at the 1987 Royal Variety
Performance, the new comedy establishment's take-over seemed
to be more or less complete. 'Five years after the first series of
The Young Ones,' wrote Mick Middles in *When You're Smiling*,
his excellent short biography of Les Dawson, 'the walls of an old
order seemed to be crumbling.' And yet the fact that on this particular occasion an old pre-alternative warhorse like Dawson
could win one of the best receptions of the night gave a far surer

indication of the way things were heading than many a more obvious portent.

Just as the apparent ideological climax that was the introduction of Margaret Thatcher's poll tax eventually proved to be the beginning of the Iron Lady's end, so the Comic Strip planting its standard on the ramparts of *ancien régime* showbiz actually signalled a rearguard action by the battered survivors of earlier times. And not just in terms of influence. (Les Dawson's magnificently sardonic hosting of mid-period *Blankety Blank* would later be cited by Vic Reeves as a model for his own demeanour on the *Big Night Out*.) In the late eighties, northern theatrical impresario Larry Price told *Middles*, 'the people who had been all but wiped away by alternative comedy suddenly started coming back . . . We'd all been told they'd gone for good, but the audiences wouldn't have it.'

Pantomime bookings went through the roof, and some of those who'd grown fat and lazy on the rich pickings of pre-alternative TV came back with a point to prove. There was something inspiring about the spectacle of battle-scarred comedy campaigners scrapping their way back to social respectability.

Take Bob Monkhouse, for example. (And anyone whose response is 'I wish you would' has not read Bob's fantastic autobiography, *Crying with Laughter*.) There was no height to which he would not stoop to reclaim his rightful place in the comedic spotlight: going head to head with Frank Skinner on *Gag Tag*, wiping the floor with his rival panellists on *Have I Got News for You*, even delivering the following unforgettable killer blow to the unfortunate Bobby Davro on ITV's *An Audience with Bob Monkhouse*: 'You'll be remembered after Robin Williams has been forgotten . . . But not until then.'

This rehabilitation of the old-school comic would culminate, a decade or so later, in *Phoenix Nights*, Peter Kay's elegiac love-letter to the working men's club. And in the not-so-edifying spectacle of Bernard Manning's return to prime-time TV, eating his tea in his Y-fronts on *The Entertainers* (then, a year or so later – even less edifyingly – being sent to India with a camera crew in tow).

From the easy-going vantage point of the early twenty-first century, the idea of an ideological divide in comedy which actually meant something might seem somewhat elusive. But you wouldn't have to spend very long in Manning's Embassy Club to rediscover it.[44]

Another way in which Margaret Thatcher was the mother-in-law of alternative comedy, besides the obvious one

In the preface to his second fictional endeavour, *Whatever Love Means*, David Baddiel refers to a special 1990 *Time Out* magazine screening of the film *Henry: Portrait of a Serial Killer*. At the question and answer session afterwards, a woman put her hand up and observed that she felt 'shocked, soiled even' by the film's graphic violence, eliciting the harsh if not entirely unmerited reproof from elsewhere in the audience: 'For fuck's sake, it's not called *Henry the Elephant*, is it?'

Most people would have appreciated the cruel irony of this exchange and then got on with their lives, but David Baddiel decided to make it the cornerstone of a new moral (or, more accurately, *a*moral) scheme. 'It was at that point', he writes, 'that the 80s fell away, or at least that seriousness fell away.'

The comedian's initial reaction to this moment of satori – he claims to have 'laughed for 15 minutes' – might seem somewhat hysterical, but presumably something about the spectacle of a man humiliating a woman in public must have been especially gratifying to him. Especially following hard on the heels of ninety minutes spent sitting in the dark watching other women being gruesomely murdered.

As such self-consciously uncaring voices as Baddiel's have grown ever more dominant, it has become increasingly easy to overestimate the height of the intellectual barricades erected during the 1980s. No decade which provided a lucky few with the opportunity to see Jerry Sadowitz at his majestically offensive best can fairly be judged

---

44. As final confirmation of his passage out of the political wilderness, in January 2003 Bernard Manning gets a review in the *Guardian* – and more in a 'we're welcoming him back into a broad church' than a 'shame on this heinous individual' kind of way. As he leaves the stage, Manning's cheery sign-off line is 'Keep your friends white'.

an era of unalloyed moral priggishness. Indeed, far from being an oasis of non-sexist rectitude, the Comedy Store at this time was often little more than, to borrow Jeremy Hardy's gruesomely memorable phrase, 'a roomful of people baying to hear the word "cunt"'.

While sympathetic observers such as William Cook have tended to portray alternative comedy as a reaction – or, most neutrally, a counterpoint – to Thatcherism, in fact the relationship between the two was a good deal more complicated than that. For example, Margaret Thatcher was the mother-in-law of alternative comedy not only in providing it with a necessary object of antipathy, but also (further echoing the historic tension between working-class men and their wives' mothers) by giving it a house to live in.

While her obsession with the deregulation of broadcasting might have originally been designed to intimidate the BBC and open the way for her (then) ally Rupert Murdoch to colonize people's homes with *The Simpsons* and Granada Men and Motors, its other end results were the creation of Channel 4 (a place where ambitious young satirists could get together to make a good living by taking the piss out of her) and a changed TV power structure in which competing production companies would compete to satisfy egotistical comedians' every artistic whim.

It would obviously be foolish to make too explicit a historical comparison between the Second World War and the three governments of Margaret Thatcher (apart from anything else, in the Second World War the good guys won). But in the same way as the traumas and hardships of 1939–45 would underpin the comedic triumphs of Spike Milligan and Tony Hancock, so – by undermining pre-existing social structures and leaving people with a profound sense of cataclysm – the distinctly unfunny Tory governments of the 1980s had also prepared the ground for a rich comedic harvest.

'For many people,' wrote Ian Jack, on travelling through northern England in 1987, 'their link with history – the functions and behaviour, morality and religion of their recent ancestors – has been snapped.'[45] It is against this desolate backdrop that many of the most vital cultural manifestations of the late 1980s – from the re-

---

45. Reprinted in Ian Jack's *Before the Oil Ran Out: Britain in the Brutal Years.*

embrace of pre-alternative comedic traditions at one end of the entertainment spectrum to the Acid House movement at the other – can most easily be understood.

What better way to disprove the depressing Thatcherite contention that there was 'no such thing as society' than by coming together in a gleeful ecstasy (or lager-fuelled fug) to savour some form of communal jollification? Apart from anything else, it's what J. B. Priestley would have wanted.[46]

'This used to be a picture house,' says Lee Evans – with his South London showbiz heritage hat on – to a packed Lewisham Odeon in the early nineties. 'You don't give a shit, do you?' Evans's personification of his audience as a dangerous beast, ready to turn on him at any moment, is not entirely fanciful. Before the alternative circuit began to find his modesty and innocence beguiling, he died a thousand deaths in holiday camps and working men's clubs. He used to box when he was younger, too, and now he seems to think if he stays in one place for too long – or messes about and tries anything too fancy – the crowd might flatten him.

One shoulder slightly raised in a perpetual half-flinch, Evans doesn't so much deliver his lines as let them escape, like compressed air released from an over-pumped bike tyre. Perpetually poised just beyond the brink of hysteria, he must duck and dive or die. His comedy is the product of a harsh Thatcherite world, a world entirely without safety nets, which is perhaps one reason why people find watching him simultaneously plummet into the abyss onstage and soar ever skywards in career terms so strangely reassuring.

Like Norman Wisdom (at this point enjoying cult status in Albania) before him, Evans is a highly skilled celebrant of incapacity. And Evans's awareness that the bottom can call again at any moment is – if anti-scatological pun laws will permit – fundamental to his act. Hence his unusually pointed (and grateful) observation that the unfortunate butts of his jokes – bystanders,

---

[46]. Reprising Priestley's own journeys across the UK in the above volume, Jack went to meet the veteran author at his home in the Cotswolds, but Priestley's only interest in their encounter was to claim for himself the rare edition of one of his books which Jack had hoped to get him to sign.

burger-eaters and toilet-sweepers – are 'always the same guy'. Evans pauses. 'And that was me once.'

'If there are tears in my eyes, you put them there.' So says Des O'Connor to Loughton's ambassador of laughter Alan Davies, who has not punched him in the kidneys, but told him some jokes. If there is a comedy equivalent – in terms of instantaneous constituency broadening – to a band's first appearance on *Top of the Pops*, initiation to the fraternity of Des's sofa is probably it.[47] And Davies certainly looks at home there. His nasal vocal delivery has a hint of Kenneth Williams about it, his eyes dart beneath a curly fringe, picking out the audience's weak points, and the cackles rise off them like steam from a herd of wet cattle.

A few weeks on from his O'Connor début, the bleary-eyed and unassuming Davies is chain-smoking in his manager's Regent Street office. There is an old-fashioned show-business ambience, as opposed to the thrusting combativeness of the new comedy establishment: Tony Hancock's former agent still has an office here, and sitting in another room is *Blockbusters*' Bob Holness.

Having graduated from Kent University with a degree in drama in 1988, Davies belongs – alongside Steve Coogan – to that section of the comedy fraternity respectfully referred to by the softly spoken agent Addison Cresswell as 'fucking wannabe actors who couldn't get it together to get an Equity card any other way'. Alan's first steps into the stand-up spotlight coincided with the explosion of

---

[47.] Alan Davies supplies the following first-hand account of what goes on behind the scenes at the O'Connor ritual. You sit 'like a first-year in the staff room' with veteran scriptwriters such as Neil Shand. They 'encourage you to use your best stuff, help you put it in some kind of order, and work out what Des is going to say. You do an audio tape for Des [always Des, never Mr O'Connor] to listen to, but you don't actually meet him until you go out on the set and shake hands under the lights. Then you do your bit in one take.'

If all this sounds a bit regimented (and Eddie Izzard plainly thought so, as in his hoity-toity early nineties incarnation he refused to submit to such Shandite strictures, causing what his agent Caroline Chignell terms 'a terrible hoo-ha'), Davies, for one, has no complaints. 'As you sit there under the lights,' Davies admits, shamefacedly, 'you're just thinking, Thank God I know roughly what I'm supposed to be doing.'

comedy clubs in London. And his preference for personal rather than news-based material (belying his background as a teenage Labour Party member – 'marching and all that')[48] harmonized usefully with a general depoliticization of the UK comedy scene.

'With our circuit,' Davies insists cheerfully, 'people at the beginning tried to separate themselves from the mainstream history of comedy. But in truth, if you go back, there have always been little clumps of young performers who appeared to be different but actually weren't.' Whether or not this will also turn out to be true for the next generation – hatching out, even as he speaks, in a scary *Aliens*-style spawning room – only a daredevil would hazard a guess.

[48.] In the eighties, when it really meant something.

3
Morris, Ianucci, Coogan, Lee, Herring and Marber

a.k.a. The new school of linguistic exactitude

'Prose consists less and less of words chosen for the sake of their meaning, and more and more of phrases tacked together like the sections of a prefabricated henhouse'

George Orwell

'His one real regret was that he had saved David Frost from drowning . . .'

Alan Bennett on Peter Cook, at the latter's funeral

In his justly celebrated post-World War II essay 'Politics and the English Language', George Orwell subjects a series of badly written paragraphs to in-depth analysis. Some are academic in origin, some are propagandist in intent, but most blur the boundaries between these two supposedly separate fields of human endeavour, contributing to an environment wherein (to repeat the above quote for maximum rhetorical impact) 'Prose consists less and less of words chosen for the sake of their meaning, and more and more of phrases tacked together like the sections of a prefabricated henhouse'.

Orwell's aim in highlighting the widespread use of clichés and jargon[49] is not only to highlight the poverty of linguistic expression

---

[49]. The Latin-rooted terminology which, in Orwell's rather poetic estimation, 'falls upon the facts like soft snow, blurring the outlines and covering up all the details'.

involved, but also to reveal a more sinister subtext. 'Such phraseology', he maintains, 'is needed if one wants to name things without calling up mental pictures.' He goes on to establish this degraded form of language – saying things in such a way as to conceal the reality behind the words – as a vital component of totalitarianisms of both left and right.

In outlining his response to those who express themselves in such a way, Orwell uses an image which will be familiar to readers of Henri Bergson. When he writes of 'a curious feeling that one is not watching a live human being but some kind of dummy', he overlaps with the latter's idea of the fundamental basis of all human hilarity. But much as George Orwell loved a laugh in his private life, he does not exploit the shortcomings of his linguistic inferiors for specifically comic effect.

On The Hour: because fact into News(s)peak won't go

By the early nineties, however, the time was right for a group of pushy young showbiz up-and-comers to apply Orwell's critical vision with merciless rigour, albeit with no higher goal than the provision of top-flight radio entertainment. Needless to say, things have changed a great deal since George's day. The arbitrary[50] dystopian rubicon of 1984 has been crossed with no apparent ill-effects, and with the once forbidding edifice of Soviet Communism lying in ruins, the future of parliamentary democracy seems about as secure as it can be.

Yet the shadow of Newspeak – the wilfully obfuscatory language which Orwell imagined in *1984* as the intellectual mechanism of a coercive state – stalks the airwaves of John Major's Britain as threateningly as ever before. It does so not in the form of governmental decree, but in the crisply presented guise of contemporary current-affairs journalism.

The unseemly combination of euphemism and self-aggrandizement, the ignorance masquerading as knowledge, the inflation of non-stories into headlines, the prurience disguised as

---

[50.] In all senses other than being 1948 backwards.

moral concern, the wilful compression of human suffering into unrecognizable shapes: it is these all too familiar features of modern-day factual programming that the guerilla radio show *On The Hour* gets to work on. And by the end of the first five-episode series, in the autumn of 1991, the entire amoral apparatus of contemporary news-gathering has been pretty much dismantled.

The glee with which *On The Hour* sets about doing this is entirely infectious. Listening to the edition in the second series where Chris Morris hawks a faked tape of Neil Kinnock losing his rag at the Labour Party conference around various tabloid newsdesks, there's a sense of being part of something genuinely outrageous. Not just because there is swearing involved and it's on Radio 4, but because Morris's combination of intellectual audacity and technical mastery of his medium seems so much more than equal to the task in hand.

The impact of this sudden rush of surplus capacity is all the more dramatic, emerging as it does from the butt-end of an apparently unbroken tradition of toothless and self-satisfied radio 'satire'.

'If you were reasonably intelligent and starting out your career in '89 to '90,' *On The Hour* writer Stewart Lee remembers, 'it took about two months to crack the formula of topical comedy as it was then.'

What was it about the established formats of *Spitting Image* and *Weekending* (within which Lee and his writing partner Richard Herring had cut their comedic teeth) that seemed so tired?

'It was just so mechanical – if you'd have called it formulaic, they'd have gone "Yeah, so, what's your problem?" . . . We did quite a good parody for *On The Hour* once about a Radio 4 programme called "It's Satire Day", where the characters were trying to compress everything that happened in the world into a Robin Hood sketch format.'

Presumably after ten years or so of Conservative government, there was a strong sense for those – like Lee – who also plied their wares out on the stand-up circuit of attacking things that had already been thoroughly savaged?

'A lot of the people involved in Radio 4 satire probably voted Tory anyway,' Lee observes sardonically. 'But beyond that, a lot of the language available to us had just been really debased – to the point where even the word "satire" had started to really annoy me.

Satire just seemed like replacing one thing with another, until after a while you start thinking, Why don't you just say what the thing itself is?'

Saying what the thing itself is

The original impetus for *On The Hour* came from producer Armando Ianucci, a slicked-back BBC insider who, having already worked on *The Mary Whitehouse Experience* and *Weekending*, presumably knew a thing or two about what he *didn't* want. Chris Morris – hell-bent on destroying the radio establishment from within like some fearful computer virus – supplied the maverick element.

Having started out as a news trainee in the not so illustrious surroundings of BBC Radio Cambridge, Morris worked his way up the ladder by unorthodox means. These included a series of legend-building stunts (such as filling a studio with helium in the midst of a live broadcast) and increasingly high-profile sackings and walk-outs from local stations in Bristol, Cambridge and London.[51]

With the exception of the mercurial Morris, who – then as now – operated more or less as an autonomous city state ('He sent in completed packages,' a still-impressed Stewart Lee remembers. 'We barely ever saw him'), there appeared to be a clear divide between the writers and the performers. Ianucci acted as go-between, fulcrum and pivot, while simultaneously exercising some degree of control over both groupings, and the resulting creative tension seemed to give everyone involved the incentive to stay on top of their respective games.

On The Hour's calling card is the bracing precision of its language. The way this holds good throughout all the writing – from Chris Morris's one-man Jesuit comedy suicide mission to the milder-

---

[51.] For someone less well-connected than Morris, such a devil-may-care attitude might have been a fast-track to career oblivion. 'He normally works a long-term contract,' Ianucci noted to Andy Beckett in the *Independent on Sunday* ('Prank Master' in the *IoS Sunday Review*, 21 August 1994), 'the sackings break it up and they keep hiring him back', concluding, somewhat bitchily, 'One of the governors probably went to his public school.'

mannered interjections of Lee and Herring ('our favourite comedy at the time was *Spinal Tap*,' Lee remembers, 'and we just copied that by imparting lots of really dense information'), to the occasional trenchant contributions of grizzled *NME* veterans Steven Wells and David Quantick – allied with innovative use of editing and sound, creates an almost overwhelming effect.

A further vital factor in the overall impact of the show, and one all too easily overlooked by insiders as well as outsiders, is the consistency of the performances. 'I was very conscious that Armando knew exactly what he wanted from us,' remembers Patrick Marber, one of a six-strong cast alongside Morris, Jewish drama expert David Schneider, Steve Coogan, Doon MacKichan and Rebecca Front (the last two 'fresh' from the somewhat debilitating experience of playing the female parts in *The Mary Whitehouse Experience)*. 'We did have to learn a different way of performing sketches.'

And what was different about it exactly? 'Armando told us "You're not allowed to be too funny".' For Marber in particular – a somewhat obtrusive presence as co-presenter of Radio 1's little-lamented first venture into comedy, *Hey Rrradio* – this simple instruction opened the ivy-covered door to a secret garden of comedic understatement.

Having largely given up on his rather declamatory (nay Eltonian) stand-up persona, Marber was 'arsing around in Paris, trying to write a novel and failing' when he got the call from Ianucci (with whom he'd worked previously on *Weekending*) in the summer of 1991. Recognizing a good thing when he heard about it, he wasted no time in coming back to London on the coach.

'I just think he [Ianucci] cast it brilliantly,' Marber asserts. 'We all knew each other a little bit, but not too much. We were people who had been around a bit, but not long enough to be bitter, who were young enough to be hungry, but all at a point in our careers where we really needed it to work.'

Beneath the imposingly monolithic surface which results from this cunning manipulation of human resources, *On The Hour* is riven with intriguing fault-lines. As with its clearest historical parallel – the emergence of the *Beyond The Fringe* quartet of Peter Cook, Dudley Moore, Alan Bennett and Jonathan Miller, and their televisual satellites from *That Was The Week That Was*, way back in the early sixties – the rapid advent of this new comedic generation entails not only a maelstrom of competing egos, but also a grisly wake of hurt feelings, inter-personal complexity and apparently lifelong antipathies.

When Alan Bennett said at Peter Cook's funeral that 'His [Cook's] one real regret was that he had saved David Frost from drowning', it was a mistake to think he was speaking entirely in jest. And while the *On The Hour* story involves nothing quite as inherently dramatic as the moment in 1963 where the talented man who could swim (Cook) prevented the not so talented but very ambitious man (Frost, who had persuaded the BBC to let him star in just the sort of epoch-making TV series which the former individual might have made, had he not been away opening on Broadway) from meeting his end in an American swimming-pool, there is no shortage of human conflict there, either.

Remembering the formative experience of *On The Hour* ten years afterwards, Steve Coogan says: 'I'll never forget the first day I walked in to work on that show . . . I really felt like I'd found my home.'[52] The impression Coogan means to give by saying that he felt at ease with *On The Hour* in a way that he never had before is that this was the point at which the yearning to produce high-quality work (which had so far remained implicit rather than explicit in his career) finally found the chance to express itself. 'I didn't remember him ever having done anything much good before' is how Stewart Lee puts it, somewhat more bluntly. And if Coogan had some cause to feel intimidated on finding himself in such acerbic company, he also had his own ways of establishing his status with the group.

'We were all children at that stage really,' says Patrick Marber. 'We certainly didn't have much experience of success. But Steve was really rich and knew a lot about money – he was just so flash and cool. He had a Mazda MX-5! I realize now that's a hairdresser's car, but it didn't seem that way at the time.'

[52.] This is the first point in this book at which an apparently straightforward statement from Steve Coogan ultimately turns out to be slightly less straightforward than it initially seems, but it will not be the last.

'Steve Coogan was earning tens of thousands of pounds from adverts,' recalls a slightly less bowled-over Stewart Lee, 'and I remember him saying things like "It's really nice to be able to do this, as I get loads of money from my voice-over work and this will bring me a new level of respect".' A phlegmatic pause ensues. 'For me and Rich [Herring], it was what we'd always wanted to do and it was also the bulk of our living. For him with his bad Ronnie Corbett impressions, it was the peanuts on top of his Ferrari advertising life!'

Before we can proceed any deeper along the Coogan trail into the *On The Hour* jungle of behavioural complexity, we need to find out why those particular peanuts meant so much to him.

Steve Coogan in flashback

'I remember thinking very rationally,' says Steve Coogan of his fiercely ambitious younger self, 'I'm eighteen years old now, and all the people in show business who I find entertaining – Rowan Atkinson, John Cleese – they will get older, and there will have to be new people. There are people in sixth forms now who in ten years' time will be successful and they're just like me, so why can't I be one of them?'

No one could accuse this man of lacking focus. As an adolescent, Coogan would drag schoolfriends off the bus to his home in the Manchester suburb of Middleton to force them to enjoy his *Monty Python* and *Not the Nine O'Clock News* records. ' "No, Steve," they would say, "I don't want to listen to comedy, I want to go home." '

Diverting from an apparently pre-ordained course to 'an all-right sort of white-collar job', and having been rejected by several fancy London drama schools, Steve Coogan went to Manchester Poly and launched himself into show business. Doing live gigs as an impressionist as a means of getting an Equity card – 'I just thought, What can I do that other people can't? and I knew I could do voices' – Coogan, in his own words, 'achieved mediocrity very quickly'. He got on TV, did Neil Kinnock and Jeremy Paxman for *Spitting Image*, sat on Des O'Connor's sofa and even shook hands with Jimmy Tarbuck on *Sunday Night at the London Palladium.*[53]

His voice was – if a momentary slip into the Partridge-esque idiom can be forgiven before Norwich's most eloquent ambassador has even had a proper name-check – quite literally his fortune. Coogan's knack for modulating his tone of address to send out just the kind of confident, thrusting message advertisers liked to deliver meant that alongside his straight comedy work there was also a good living to be had from voice-overs, corporate training videos and presentations. While this work brought substantial material rewards, it nevertheless intensified the young Coogan's apprehension that as quickly as his career was progressing, it was not necessarily moving in the direction he would have wanted.

His fear that he might be becoming, in his own damning phrase, 'a cut-price Bobby Davro' was intensified by a harrowing experience at the Edinburgh Festival in 1990. Sharing a flat and a nightly bill with the as yet largely unheralded Frank Skinner, Coogan found himself horribly eclipsed by the latter's easy way with the crowd.

'He was very hard-working and very good,' Coogan remembers. 'He did twenty minutes at the top of his act unscripted, just chatting to the audience, and I couldn't do that – I'm someone that has to craft what I do, but Frank can busk it: he's a natural.'

One year later, Coogan – having opted not to return to the scene of his Edinburgh humiliation – was in a hotel in Rhodes in Greece, 'doing a sort of holiday rep entertainment for families and getting told off for swearing'. He picked up a newspaper in a hotel box room and read that Skinner had won the festival's prestigious Perrier Award. 'It was', Coogan admits with engaging frankness, 'probably the most depressing moment of my life.'

At this point, he had already started work on *On The Hour* and by the time a further twelve months had passed, Coogan would be back in Edinburgh, winning the same award for himself with a new show (performed in conjunction with future *Fast Show* mainstay John Thomson) featuring more developed comic characters, rather

---

[53.] At this stage, Coogan related to the broader community of impressionists in the same slightly tangential manner that Pat Nevin (who liked Joy Division and was rumoured to have an A-level) related to the average eighties footballer.

than throwaway impressions. A key influence on this happy reversal of fortune would be Patrick Marber, who not only directed and co-wrote Coogan's Perrier Award-winning 1992 show, but seems to have played a role in the successful overall redirection of his career not dissimilar to that of Noriyuki 'Pat' Morita in the *Karate Kid* films.

'For a while it was kind of like a big brother/little brother relationship,' Coogan remembers. 'I wouldn't do anything without asking Patrick what he thought.'

They first met properly in Edinburgh in 1990.

'Steve was depressed because he was getting annihilated by Frank,' says Marber, 'but I did my best to reassure him that he was a funny guy who would have his day.'

On this sympathetic foundation, a friendship was built and Marber soon found himself acting as a 'kind of mentor . . . I think at that time I had more confidence in Steve's talent than he did'.

To say that the high-earning but as yet critically unacclaimed Coogan had a chip on his shoulder at this point might be putting it a little strongly, but there was certainly a salt and vinegar crisp or two up there. And presumably, in terms of *On The Hour*, his burgeoning alliance with the Oxford-educated Marber must have made for a reassuring buffer zone against an intimidating group of cooler-than-thou, non-mainstream writer–performers from more illustrious educational backgrounds than Manchester Poly? Coogan smiles. 'I think that's a fair summation.'

Similarly for Marber, snatched from comedic oblivion and plunged into a very competitive arena wherein people were liable at any moment to bring up the fact that he had 'once done an act with a panda', it is easy to see how a friendship with the brazenly successful Coogan made sense. What no one could really have predicted was that the complex personal and professional dynamic which developed between the two men would produce some of the boldest and most enduring comedy of the nineties.

The *On The Hour* ice pack commences its break-up

Before *On The Hour* makes its triumphant transfer to the small screen as *The Day Today*, internal tensions within the group ensure that there is already a breakaway faction. Exactly what happened to cause this split has been the source of much speculation, and hopefully the following account will clear up any misunderstandings. (While these events lack the gory trappings of Jacobean tragedy, the extent to which they still loom large in the minds of the participants – a full decade later – confirms that wounded pride can take longer to heal than all but the most savage dagger scar.)

Stewart Lee's side of the story

'The reason we ended up not being involved in the TV series,' Lee explains, 'is that we didn't think we were being offered a fair deal. We wrote about 20 per cent of the first series. I don't think that would be an exaggeration – probably someone on the internet would know what the exact proportion was. And when it went to telly we were offered thirteen minutes a week, but as we felt we'd set the tone for some of the characters, we asked for less money and less minutes, but a share in the future of the show.'

With Ianucci reluctant to give up this degree of control, a stalemate rapidly develops. Lee and Herring go off to make their own Radio 4 and Radio 1 shows, *Lionel Nimrod's Inexplicable World* and *Fist of Fun*, and when *On The Hour* is released as a BBC audiocassette (and later on CD), their contributions have been surgically removed by Ianucci.

'There might have been an argument about us wanting to get paid three hundred pounds instead of two hundred for it going to CD,' Lee says phlegmatically, 'but basically Armando edited us out to prove a point. I don't hold it against him, really.'

Like a pair of latter-day Trotskys, snipped out of the photo of triumphant Bolshevik revolutionaries on the balcony with Ianucci's Stalinist Stanley knife, there is little Lee and Herring can do but

51

put a brave face on life in comedic exile (and keep an eye out for shifty-looking individuals carrying ice-picks).

'I was about twenty-three at the time,' Lee remembers, affecting an indulgent air. 'Most of the other people involved in *On The Hour* were in their late twenties and I remember feeling quite sympathetic and thinking, They've got to take what they're offered because otherwise they've missed the boat.'

So why do his and Herring's live shows at the Edinburgh Festival a year or so later feature the latter delivering repeated savage blows to the head of a balloon likeness of 'the playwright Patrick Marber'?

Lee laughs: 'We were only annoyed with Marber because he came to the whole thing quite late, and he seemed to be the most delighted of anyone at the idea of us being forced out of the picture.'

Patrick Marber's side of the story

'I've been under siege by them for years, really,' Marber says, rather forlornly, of his erstwhile colleagues, 'but I've never responded up to now.' He pauses. 'I think they're of the view that I plotted to get them sacked.'

Presumably he doesn't intend to take this opportunity to confirm the truth of that accusation?

Marber laughs, perhaps a little nervously. 'In the summer of '92, me, Lee and Herring, Steve and Simon Munnery did a show in Edinburgh called *The Dumb Show*, which didn't really work. When we all got in a room together, we just didn't hit it off. And some time after that, they fell out with Armando, and that was it, really. The irony of it is that I thought their material was absolutely fantastic – you would always feel excited on *On The Hour* when something they had written came in . . .' Marber pauses. 'I suppose they're maintaining that on some level they invented Alan Partridge?'

He sounds slightly surprised at the news that they haven't done this – at least not in my hearing.

'They *did* write the first piece of material,' Marber explains. 'Armando asked Steve to perform it and this generic sports voice came out – sort of Elton Welsby, sort of Jim Rosenthal. Then Steve came up with the name and Alan was born, but I think it would definitely be fair to say that Alan Partridge wouldn't have happened had Lee and Herring not written the original sketch.' As to the scale and grandeur of the oak that will grow from this particular comedic acorn, though, only destiny can decree it.

Knowing him, knowing them

In its original Radio 4 incarnation, the *On The Hour* offshoot *Knowing Me, Knowing You* – wherein Alan Partridge, sports-desk incompetent and all-round loose cannon, is misguidedly given his own chat show – is an instant comedy landmark. As inhabited by Coogan, the hapless but ever emphatic Partridge goes beyond straightforward caricature into the realms of immortal comic characterization.

Alan will pursue a metaphor until it turns and fights like a wild animal at bay, and in his own freedom from shame there can sometimes be discerned a form of primal innocence. When he hits a child prodigy, or informs a recently freed hostage that their time in captivity was equivalent to watching 9,000 episodes of *Inspector Morse* – 'it doesn't sound so bad when you put it that way' – he seems in some strange way to strike a blow for everyone who has ever felt hemmed in by the constraints of conventional etiquette.[54]

Part of what makes *Knowing Me, Knowing You* special is the precision of its cultural references. 'It's about fine judgements,' Coogan insists, 'making the right choice of a name or a word without being obvious, but also without disappearing up your own arse.' While the time and trouble Coogan and his writing partners invest in getting details right – from Alan's car (a Ford Scorpio) to the exact layout of his East Anglian home turf – pay off on their own account, the laughs which accompany brand recognition are easily come by. The real greatness of the show comes in achieving a level of emotional acuity that matches and even surpasses that of the product placement.

It would not be unreasonable to assume that a good deal of

[54.] In this respect, he is an illustrious forebear of Ricky Gervais's David Brent.

Alan Partridge's remarkable intensity comes from Coogan's own pre-Partridge fears that his life might be vanishing down the toilet of middle-rank showbiz.

'It *was* that,' admits an impassioned Coogan, 'it was . . . Impressions are just a facility – something I can do . . . I hated being a known quantity. If people really want to annoy me, they still say, "Oh look, it's Steve Coogan – top TV impressionist".'

There's a great moment in a radio episode of *Knowing Me, Knowing You*, where Alan encounters top TV impressionist Steve Thomson, played by Marber (who while he modestly insists that he is 'not in the same league as Steve as a performer' contributes a series of beautifully judged supporting characters to radio and TV series alike). 'I want to be funny, but with dignity,' begs Steve. 'Do your Frank Spencer,' Alan whispers malevolently.

No disrespect is intended to Marber's later career as an award-winning dramatist in saying that nothing in his subsequent canon surpasses the acuity of some of these exchanges. The happy knack of translating your own personal anxieties and hang-ups into subtle but brilliantly accessible comedy is given to very few comedy writing partnerships, and at this point Coogan and Marber seem to have it in spades.

'Certainly in *Knowing Me, Knowing You* in general, I tend to play the characters who try to usurp Alan's status,' Marber admits. 'I'd like to write something one day about what it's like to be "the man behind the man",' he continues. 'When you start off, it's great – the other guy takes all the pressure – but eventually it's just not enough. Your ego gets bigger and you want to go and get some of the glory for yourself.'

One of the strange features of this kind of partnership is that (as the career trajectory of Paul Whitehouse will demonstrate even more dramatically) however successfully the person in the subordinate role subsequently defines themselves as a creative individual, they can never quite escape the shadow of their former incarnation.

Watching Marber on TV, winning an *Evening Standard* Laurence Olivier drama award for his play *Dealer's Choice*, the look on his face when he finds out they've got Coogan to present it to him might well be described as 'a picture'. He can laugh at the memory now, though: 'I think one part of me was thinking it was lovely to be standing there with Steve and it being me getting a prize, and the other part of me was thinking "Couldn't I have someone legit?"'

A boot of non-fact grinding into the face of news for ever – *The Day Today* hits the ground running

Remarkably for the work of an ensemble with so little experience of the medium, *The Day Today* – the exquisitely realized small-screen version of *On The Hour* which finally reaches BBC2 screens in January 1994 – manages to create a televisual language every bit as perfectly adapted to its target as the radio prototype had been. Ianucci, Morris, Coogan, Marber et al. inflate the familiar visual and verbal tics of the TV newsroom into such magnificently grotesque shapes that they hang in the air above every subsequent 'legitimate' broadcast in the manner of gigantic barrage balloons.

Morris's all-powerful studio overlord presides like some puffed-up Paxmanesque nabob over a sumptuous array of courtiers. As well as Coogan's marvellous roving sports buffoon, there's Doon MacKichan's doyenne of the money markets, Collaterlie Sisters, Schneider's physically mutable weatherman, Marber's hapless political correspondent, Peter O'Hanraha'Hanrahan (forever struggling to come to terms with the intricacies of the European Union in the face of Morris's withering scepticism) and Rebecca Front's intimidatingly eco-friendly Rosie May, purveyor of that archetypal 1990s informa-hybrid, 'Enviro-mation'.

It's the success with which these individual embodiments are cradled within an appropriate stylistic whole that makes *The Day Today* so devastating. The caffeine-crazed fast-cutting, the invasive close-ups, the ransacked sock-drawer of different film stocks, the priapic graphics; this is the infrastructure of televisual deceit, and to watch it being taken apart piece by piece is at once utterly liberating and a little scary.

But what are the consequences of this act of premeditated destruction? In *Mrs Slocombe's Pussy*, his not terribly provocatively entitled memoir of half a lifetime's television watching, *Guardian* journalist Stuart Jeffries asserts that *The Day Today* 'blew up the

TV news and the fragments descended into exactly the same place as before the explosion'. But this is very far from being the truth.

If anyone has any doubts about the way the surreal extrapolations of *The Day Today* feed back into the mainstream of official news-gathering, there's a 1995 BBC Learning Zone documentary about TV current affairs which can swiftly dispel them. Footage of arrogant young trainees learning to parcel up their partial interpretations of the world into easily digestible one-minute packages is smoothly intercut with *The Day Today*'s Rebecca Front analysing the cosmetic rituals of her inspired US reporter, Barbara Wintergreen ('Your make-up is so thick that you can't really move your head'). When you factor in a series of anonymous talking heads saying things like 'the editing is the way you apply the grammar' in such a way as to leave it unclear whether they're talking about *The Day Today* or the actual news (of course the answer is they're talking about both), it's hard to believe that the whole programme isn't a prank devised by Chris Morris himself. Nor is this the end of the overlap between *The Day Today*'s fiction and TV actuality's fact.

A whole host of those – from Alan Titchmarsh to Richard Madeley – who might have been expected to look to their laurels in the wake of Partridge et al.'s brutally well-observed mockery, instead respond by moving in the opposite direction and absorbing it into their day-to-day demeanour.

The idea of an object of satire embracing the more baroque extremities of their own comedic portrayal did not make its début in the nineties. Three decades earlier, in the wake of Peter Cook's celebrated impression of Harold Macmillan (a tacit relaxation of previously stringent rules regarding the representation of living persons having made the satirically motivated impersonation a much less perilous business than it was in *The Goon Show*'s day), it was maintained by many that the prime minister began to behave more and more like Cook's take-off and less and less like his actual self. In this context, the apparent severity of Peter Cook's oft-quoted response to finding out that Macmillan was in the audience as he performed at his Establishment Club actually cut both ways.

Cook's apparently rather discourteous (in-character) proclamation – 'There is nothing I like better than to wander over to Soho and sit there listening to a group of sappy, urgent, vibrant, young satirists with a stupid great grin spread all over my face' – was an admission of defeat as much as a display of aggression. If the prime minister would actually cross town to hear Cook's impression of him, that didn't say much for the amount of pain it caused him.

Accordingly, when the home secretary Henry Brooke – the subject of some of the programme's most savage attacks – wanted to get *That Was The Week That Was* taken off the air, Macmillan argued against this precipitate course on the shrewd grounds that it was probably better to be satirized than ignored. In his appreciation of how crucial an attribute being seen to be able to take a joke would become in British public life, the supposedly out-of-step-with-the-times Macmillan actually seems to have been quite a forward-thinker.[55]

As anyone who has ever laughed at a cruel remark made at their own expense knows, a show of imperviousness to such slights does not guarantee a diminution of their impact. Often – for example, in the poignant and disturbing case of Sammy Davis Jr – it will have quite the opposite effect. While *The Day Today*'s well-aimed barbs initially seem to bounce straight off the gnarly hide of the British body politic, some of them find their target, causing strange and unforeseen infections of the blood.

Far from confirming the inability of satirical endeavour to affect the way people think, *The Day Today*'s calculated inhumanity seems to impact upon not only the way world events are presented to us, but also the actual nature of the events themselves. For instance, Tony Blair and George Bush's campaign to mobilize support for a multilateral attack on Iraq in 2002–3 seems to reflect the long-term influence of *The Day Today* 'War Special' (in which Chris Morris's demonic anchorman systematically orchestrates the beginning of a global conflict with the help of some snappy editing and a series of provocative effects) at a *policy* level.

It would be a misunderstanding of the true nature of satire to

---

[55.] As with the supposedly clear divide between the dynamic, modernizing Tony Blair and his bumbling, old-fashioned predecessor John Major, with hindsight the question as to which of the bumbling old-world Macmillan or his dynamic thrusting successor (ignoring the brief Sir Alec Douglas-Home interregnum) Harold Wilson was actually more in tune with the way the country was going is intriguingly moot.

think that its success or otherwise is measured by the achievement of meaningful change. (As Peter Cook was fond of pointing out, the art form was defined in the cabaret clubs of Weimar Berlin, 'and see how they stopped the Nazis'.) But even if it was, inspiring the leaders of the Western military–industrial complex to new heights of bellicosity would probably not be the kind of meaningful change those responsible had in mind.

The *Day Today* diaspora

Perhaps inevitably – given the radical nature of the programme itself and the delicate balance of power within it – there was only one series of *The Day Today*. But by the end of it, the genie was well and truly out of the bottle. Subsequently, old boys and girls of the New School of Linguistic Exactitude swarmed out into the world like graduation day celebrants in an American teen movie, carrying the lessons they'd learned securely in their knapsacks.

For Ianucci, the huge extent of his managerial and catalytic achievements in the course of this three-year period have hobbled some of his later endeavours with a rather disabling sense of self-regard. Furthermore, his decision to venture in front of the camera in the patchy but occasionally revelatory satirical vehicle *Friday* [then *Saturday*] *Night Armistice* is not entirely vindicated (if only because the collective screen presence of the remorselessly untelegenic trio of Ianucci, Schneider and one-time Lee and Herring bit player turned Alan Partridge co-writer Peter Baynham underlines a little too clearly the innate truth behind the programme's admittedly prophetic style-is-triumphing-over-substance message).

On the upside, his poorly received solo venture *The Armando Ianucci Show* does contain – in an extended sketch about impoverished Africans getting together to raise money for the British showbiz establishment – perhaps the most devilishly effective reversal of conventional comedic pieties ever seen on TV. And there's always Alan Partridge to keep him busy.

For MacKichan and Front, life is considerably more difficult. Eleven years with a woman prime minister do not seem to have brought any notable extension of employment possibilities to the distaff component of groundbreaking TV topical revue ensembles. As with *That Was The Week That Was*'s Eleanor Bron and *Not the Nine O'Clock News*'s Pamela Stephenson before them, opportunity does not knock as loudly as it might have, and while MacKichan can sometimes[56] be seen presenting teaching-baby-to-swim segments on *This Morning*, or taking the female supporting role in comedies about vets who don't really like animals, Front struggles even harder to get out of the background.[57]

Stewart Lee and Richard Herring shoehorn their penchant for cerebral juvenilia into a classic odd-couple double act. The chain-smoking Lee ruthlessly exploits the sort of dangerous good looks most university-common-room existentialists can only dream about, while his comedy partner – a self-confessed 'small, fat, middle-class white bloke from Cheddar in Somerset' – struggles to come to terms with the fact that though he may idolize Ice-T, Ice-T's dad was not a caravan-owning headmaster called Keith.

The roots of their comedy lie in gentle mockery – 'Today in Somerset electricity arouses only suspicion, not fear' – but a high degree of self-awareness is another vital ingredient. 'You've mis-understood the art of simile, haven't you?' they chide each other gleefully: 'What you've done is mix up being *like* something, with being what it actually is.'

It is in one of Lee's solo routines that the work of the School of Linguistic Exactitude finds arguably its most complete expression. Billing himself as 'the third most theoretically rigorous comedian in Britain' (heaven knows who numbers one and two are), he analy-ses the body language of a picture postcard featuring two kittens and a dog playing the piano. 'Perhaps', he surmises, 'that kitten had a much more formal musical training.'

Meanwhile, on the opposite side of the *On The Hour* barricades, the Coogan–Marber relationship finds another vehicle for self-exploration (as if *Knowing Me, Knowing You* was not sufficient

---

[56.] Before *Celebrity Fame Academy* calls her out of the *Smack the Pony* showbiz wilderness as a last-minute replacement.

[57.] Though she often shines in this capacity – especially as Jilly Goolden in *The Smell of Reeves and Mortimer*'s memorable tribute to BBC2's *Food and Drink*.

outlet) in the form of Paul and Pauline, a.k.a The Sacred Calfs. It is a measure of Marber's moderating influence on Coogan's occasional cheeseball tendencies that when the duo first met, the latter was already doing a Paul Calf-type character, but at that stage he was called 'Duncan Disorderly'.

Leading psychoanalysts have inevitably looked to Coogan's childhood for the roots of the meticulously observed Mancunian brother and sister – he the hard-drinking, student-phobic City fan, she the indomitable slapper – who would eventually become Alan Partridge's main rivals in his character pantheon. Coogan himself has done nothing to dissuade them: 'Do you remember those football colouring books?' he asks in 1995. 'I remember colouring in George Best and Bobby Charlton and then getting to the Manchester City players and putting lipstick and earrings on them to make them look like girls.'

The way the characters actually develop (Paul having made his TV début on a show Coogan recorded for Granada with John Thomson and Caroline Aherne) is defined by Jonathan Ross's *Saturday Zoo*, where Coogan, Marber and soon to be *Fast Show* luminary Simon Day are employed to be 'sketch actors'. Having had a sketch cut in the first week, 'because it was crap', and seen Marber summarily fired (though retained by him in a vague directorial capacity) Coogan decides to go 'for his big gun'.

'There was no intention of having Paul Calf on *Saturday Zoo* at first,' Marber remembers. 'Steve was saving him for his own special.' After a few weeks, when the rough-as-dogs-and-proud-of-it Calf is obviously going down a storm, his shy and retiring sister Pauline follows him into the spotlight. However happy – 'disturbingly sexy' even, in Marber's words – he ultimately looks as Pauline Calf, Coogan still 'takes some persuading' that this is the right direction for him to move in on TV. 'It'll work,' Marber remembers himself arguing. 'You *can* be a woman.'

With her dirty laugh and all-consuming desire to have sex with Patrick Swayze, Pauline is a comic creation so exuberant that she positively juts out of the screen. 'Tits first,' she counsels potential suitors, 'I'm not a slag.'

The relationship between her gruffly genial philistine of a brother and his slightly pretentious but basically well-meaning student friend Roland – played, with a suitably apologetic air, by Marber – is such an inch-perfect representation of the class-based complexities of the Coogan–Marber friendship (with both parties moved one rung down the social ladder) that when Pauline and Roland tie the knot, well, it's almost *too* perfect.

One of the most significant if rarely remembered segments of *The Day Today* (in fact, with hindsight you might say that it sets the pattern for most of the next decade's most popular and influential shows) is 'The Bureau', a pioneering docusoap-style mini-drama set in the emotionally overheated surroundings of a tiny *bureau de change*. Paul and Pauline Calf pick up this prophetic marker and their subsequent starring vehicles – a *Video Diary* and the aforementioned *Wedding Video* respectively – prove to be the ideal means for Coogan and co-writers Marber and Henry Normal to explore the nascent phenomenon of reality TV.[58]

Even in its formative *Video Diary* stage, what people will one day call Factual Entertainment Programming is already having an invigorating effect on the schedules. Watching someone you don't know moaning about the day they've had for a couple of minutes before *Newsnight* can be informative as well as therapeutic. And even if sometimes it's neither, well, maybe the tedium is the message.

As if appreciating this, Coogan and co.'s use of the video-diary format is all the more deft for not being explicitly satirical. They opt instead to exploit the medium's huge potential for richness of character development and well-observed detail (Paul Calf's diagonally striped sheet and duvet set springs to mind) to reflect the way the ever-increasing likelihood of seeing our lives replayed on the small screen might change the way we live them.

⋆   ⋆   ⋆

[58.] Debate continues to rage among cognoscenti as to which of these two TV landmarks is the better. 'I do think the Pauline Calf one is funnier,' Coogan maintains. But isn't the difference between the two that while the first (Paul Calf) video diary is actually about something, the *Wedding Video* is about a *version* of something? 'The second might not be purer,' Coogan concedes, 'but it *is* funnier. I remember watching the other one for the first time at the production office – sitting in deathly silence and thinking, this has less laughs in it than anything I've ever done.'

Last but definitely not least among *The Day Today* diaspora, how does Chris Morris, the Dark Lord Sauron of the *On The Hour* saga, fare out on his own in the world? Having already emphasized the self-contained nature of his contribution by letting the surviving cast members make *Knowing Me, Knowing You* without him, it's no surprise that he continues to plough his own furrow with singular intensity.

The development of what tomorrow's media-studies students will no doubt refer to as The Chris Morris Method – cloaking oneself in the robes of broadcasting authority, then leading unwitting accomplices into a nightmare world of absurdist humiliation – continues at breakneck pace.

'The first thing you do is try and decontextualize everything so you make nonsense,' observes the usually reclusive Morris in the aforementioned *Independent on Sunday* interview. 'But then I just started thinking it would be a bit more of a challenge to get people to talk this rubbish *without* actually editing . . . The risk of somebody just saying "You're talking bollocks" is huge . . . but it really gets your adrenalin going.'

While Morris's quest for new stimuli to his adrenal gland will lead him down ever more dangerous pathways – not least shouting 'Christ's fat cock' at Cliff Richard and announcing the death of a still very much alive Michael Heseltine on his understandably short-lived Radio 1 show – his most significant moment prior to the protracted unveiling of *Brass Eye* in 1996–7 comes in a much more low-key setting. The five ten-minute interviews Morris records with an ailing Peter Cook under the rather off-putting title of *Why Bother?* sidle on to the Radio 4 airwaves with a minimum of fuss in 1994, but they contain some of the finest work either man has ever produced.

These almost entirely improvised encounters between Morris (in his cocksure interviewer guise) and Cook's patrician *alter ego* Sir Arthur Streeb-Greebling work brilliantly on several different levels: as a clash of comedy titans, a passing on of the baton and a strangely touching farewell. 'The next time we'll want to interview you,' Morris snarls with a superficial abruptness which stomps off around the houses and comes back as tender regret, 'you'll probably be dead.'

There's often an edge of sadism to the Chris Morris Method: 'If somebody knows there's something awful going on but doesn't know how to escape and is constricted from doing so by good manners,' he has been heard to exult, 'it degenerates into a siege, whereby you fling ghastly suggestion after ghastly suggestion at them.' When Morris is pitted against a worthy adversary such as Cook, however, real fireworks can result. Listening to this sublimely well-matched pairing discuss the discovery of a fossilized nine-month-old Christ, it is sometimes hard to believe what you are hearing.

As Streeb-Greebling dissembles magisterially in response to Morris's increasingly malign sallies – 'I've been distorted, I've been misrepresented and I've been quoted accurately, which is worst of all' – deeper historical connections between the generations begin to reveal themselves. Literally *minutes* of innocent amusement can be had from assigning each of *On The Hour*'s leading lights to a suitable counterpart from the early sixties satire boom. (Morris is Cook, Coogan is Dudley Moore, Marber is Jonathan Miller, Ianucci is David Frost and . . . *Oh dear Lord, please make it stop.*)

Still more intriguingly, the overweening arrogance of Morris's preening media archetype actually has its roots in Cook and co.'s pioneering experiment with irreverence. That supercilious, know-it-all demeanour – you might call it the all-seeing sneer – so prevalent in the British media of the late twentieth century, from the *Guardian*'s 'Pass Notes' column to Kirsty Wark's attitude to the arts, was originally defined by that first wave of bold young satirists, tweaking the nose of the early sixties powers that were.

Who was notorious *That Was The Week That Was* provocateur Bernard Levin (being rude to diplomats or addressing an audience of farmers as 'peasants'), if not the spiritual father of Morris's *Day Today* anchorman? And once the traditions of social and political deference which so deadened British cultural life prior to the sixties had been broken down, what was to stop those who had achieved that goal becoming a new ruling class, every bit as entrenched and invulnerable as their predecessors?

By a choice irony, the satirists themselves were among the first to notice this happening. Especially when pop's unwashed hordes – The Beatles, David Bailey, Jean Shrimpton, *people who hadn't even been to university* – barged rudely through behind them, widening the modest breach they'd made in the walls of public propriety into a yawning chasm, and treading on quite a few elegantly shod toes in the process. In his impassioned 1969 tract *The Neophiliacs*, *Private Eye* founder Christopher Booker fulminated loud and long against 'this new aristocracy' of 'photographers, dress-designers and Beat Musicians', which was a bit like a former member of The Clash writing a book about the pernicious impact of Two Tone.

Whether the graduates of the New School of Linguistic Exactitude will ever have cause to make similarly curmudgeonly expressions of regret about those who follow in their wake, only time will tell. One thing that *is* certain is that the Cook–Frost generation had to stretch their own canvases. Away from the rarefied world of groundbreaking BBC satire, the comedians of the nineties work in a white space of pretty much unrestricted magnitude. And liberty on such a grand scale can sometimes be its own limitation.

4
The Great Mythological Armour Shortage of 1993–4

Parts One to Five

One

'Comedy naturally wears itself out – destroys the very food on which it lives'

William Hazlitt

What must it feel like to be a comedian on national television telling a joke which you know that not all, but a good proportion of the audience will have heard before? Not just because it's an old joke – after all, jokes, like tunes, are something there can only be a certain number of – but because you yourself told it on a different show a couple of weeks previously. Maybe twice.

Paul Merton is on Des O'Connor's couch in the autumn of 1993. For many comics, Des is the perfect foil – not so much a sympathetic interrogator as a craven one – but the antagonism upon which Merton thrives is not a part of his repertoire. So Merton is telling the joke about someone going into a newsagent's and asking if they've got a copy of *Psychic News*. The punchline – 'You tell me' – has already been a palpable hit on *Have I Got News for You*, on Merton's own television show and throughout his successful live tour.

But this evening Merton doesn't look as if he has the stomach for the delivery. Trying to say the line as if it's just come to him seems to be making him miserable. Not showbiz Paul Merton

65

miserable – grouchy, curmudgeonly and all those other '-lys' that make him so entertaining on the radio – just the plain, common or garden kind. He forces the punchline out eventually, but his body seems to be trying to stop him. The message in his eyes reads: 'Why me?'

This might not have been exactly what William Hazlitt, the nineteenth-century stand-up essayist, meant when he wrote: 'Comedy naturally wears itself out – destroys the very food on which it lives', but the point still stands. When the occupation of 'joke-teller' was on a par with, say, 'juggler' or 'optometrist' in terms of social significance, the issue was simple: the only imperative in the recycling of your own or other people's material was not to get caught.

There is a perfectly respectable comic tradition of unapologetic repetition.[59] It dates back beyond Morecambe and Wise (who learned their trade in the variety halls at a time when 'an original joke was a rare treat') to Sigmund Freud, who was so sympathetic to the old joke transaction that he even designed an equation to represent it in a therapeutic light.[60]

For the new breed of TV-career-driven, magazine-cover, advert-icon comedians which emerged in the 1980s and 1990s, things were much more complicated. The same medium that brought them success changed the very nature of their calling.

Everybody thinks of comedy as essentially a 'live' phenomenon, but all too often seeing favourite performers in the flesh is now less of an experience than seeing them on television. You've seen the show, you've heard the jokes, now shell out to experience them all over again without being able to make yourself a cup of tea. And then buy the live video.

An unprecedentedly large phalanx of big-name, alternative-gone-mainstream comedians set off around the Civics and Regals of the land in the autumn of 1993. In Paul Merton's footsteps followed

---

[59.] There has been no more delightfully brazen exponent of this tradition than Quentin Crisp. 'I need a constantly changing audience,' the self-styled 'stately homo' has been known to observe of his move to America in the twilight of his years, 'because I say the same things over and over again.'

[60.] 'One probably recovers from the impression the joke makes on a newcomer some of the possibility of enjoyment that has been lost owing to its lack of novelty.'

Steve Coogan, Lenny Henry, Rik Mayall and Ade Edmondson, Ben Elton, Jack Dee, Newman and Baddiel. All had to face the recycling dilemma, and it wouldn't really be fair to blame them for taking the easy way out. They are, after all, only human.

New material takes months to write. And comedy agents are renowned for their heroic efforts to make boxing promoters look scrupulous, forcing wet-behind-the-ears comedy novices out on two-hundred-date tours before they've had a chance to drink their Perrier Awards.

The mass live audience which television brings makes different demands anyway; if you don't recycle your greatest hits onstage, you might get lynched. It must be a bizarre and perversely unsettling sensation for those who learned their trade fighting for survival on small stages in front of demanding crowds, to find themselves suddenly in front of several thousand people and able to do no wrong. The air of unreality which so often hangs over large-scale live comedy events stems from the fact that a large section of the crowd have come to pay tribute to an established TV persona rather than to watch someone push back the outer envelope of their art.

Jack Dee's Channel 4 television show (first broadcast in 1992) complicates things still further by being a stylish distillation of an idealized live comedy experience. Suavely suited professional arrives at club in classic car, scythes through the crowd, is extremely amusing for about twenty-five minutes and then leaves, gracefully acknowledging the applause of the crowd with a modest nod of the head. The idea behind the show's 'Bohemia Club' setting, Dee explains, 'was to be somewhere Simon Templar might take his best girl for a night out'.[61]

An actual tour, though, is a different matter. Dee himself is fine – a tidy bundle of compressed malice – but the Hammersmith Apollo, a venue so cavernous that many a seventeen-piece soul orchestra has looked lost in it, is not the best place to see him. There is something fundamentally depressing about the experience of such well-ordered mass sniggering. As if in acknowledgement of

---

[61.] The venue refers not only to an idealized British televisual past, but also to 'the American tradition of supper rooms, where cabaret is quite a sophisticated event'.

this, the crowd's biggest laugh is reserved for some witless heckler's oh-so-amusing reference to Dee's role in a television advertising campaign. Jack's contempt for this runs deeper even than usual. He seems almost, well, bitter.[62]

'It's not good enough just to be getting a laugh,' he frets, a few months later. 'After a while, you start to be fussy about the kind you're getting . . . There's a particular laugh which I really hate,[63] which is the one that belongs to people watching television shows.' What does that mean exactly? 'That "Ooh no, missus" kind of thing – *Carry On*-type comedy where you only have to mention knickers and you get this awful "Yo ho ho". I would do anything to stop that. I'd rather people didn't laugh at all.'

Two. Variety is the spice of life . . . except when it isn't

'My hair's got a life of its own,' says Paul Merton, taking up residence at the London Palladium, in the winter of 1993–4. 'Last week, I found it in the kitchen making itself an omelette.'

'Oh excellent,' exclaims the man in the row behind me, 'excellent.' He is still repeating the second half of this (admittedly excellent) joke to himself as Merton, ursine as ever even in a low-slung double-breasted suit, ambles on to the next. The question of why it is that comedy audiences are so easily satisfied has long troubled the philosophers, but Merton's presence at the top of the bill at this illustrious venue does send out some intriguing signals.

---

62. Things go better at the Southend Cliffs on a Bank Holiday Monday during the same tour, which is a good job, because that's not a time and a place at which a comedian can afford to leave anything to chance.

63. Reacting to the quality of an audience's laughter is a dangerous road to go down. (I remember seeing Mark Lamarr once punish a crowd for the alleged parsimony of their response by remaining onstage at the interval, until they felt obliged to slope off one by one, authentically embarrassed: 'You've not made it easy for me,' crowed the Swindon spiv, 'so I'm not going to make it easy for you.') This deviation from good showbiz practice is seen at its most distressing in the phenomenon of comedians performing to small crowds at the Edinburgh Festival who opt to berate the three people who have bought tickets to see them for (a) not being more numerous and (b) not laughing enough.

First, Merton – like Jack Dee and Reeves and Mortimer – is trying to clamber over the social and demographic barriers erected around comedy in the 'alternative' era. Second, he is cocking a snook at the sense of social inferiority which has always been near the heart of his act – right down to his stage name, taken from the defiantly unfashionable London borough from which he originates – by reconnecting it to the grand variety tradition Tommy Trinder used to embody as the host of *Saturday Night at the London Palladium*, before he took the piss out of Michael Grade's scary uncle, Lew, once too often and got consigned to showbiz oblivion.

Early on, the tone – set by the earnest 'Shhh' that goes up when the lights go down – is rather too reverent. Merton is at his best when not tied to a script: setting up funny little antipathies and then pursuing them to the ends of the earth. In this grandiose setting, though, his regular stand-up material sounds rather laboured: some of the jokes have been round the block too many times and their deliveryman seems nervous. Merton's sidekicks – Richard Vranch, unappetizingly (if accurately) billed as 'the bloke who plays the piano on *Whose Line Is It Anyway?*' and Lee Simpson, Julian Clary's flatmate in *Terry and Julian* – work hard to bring him out of himself, even to the extent of pulling 'Hey! What-a-crazy-guy!'-type faces, but can't quite pull it off.

To make matters worse, a pair of particularly aggressive and unfunny front-row hecklers have been struggling throughout to impair everyone's enjoyment. Early in the second half of the show, the standard stock reproaches – 'What paper are you reviewing this for, *Exchange & Mart?*' – having failed to secure the compliant silence promised by the wholesale suppliers, Paul Merton suddenly and unexpectedly loses his temper. Not just a flash of cold fury, but a full-scale, eye-popping, forehead-vein-bulge scenario, as he rounds on the would-be scene-stealers with real venom, telling them in no uncertain terms to get out of his face or to expect severe physical consequences.

There's a moment when this confrontation could go either way, but then the disruptive elements stand up and slink off with the crowd's jeers ringing in their ears. Merton is plainly embarrassed by his outburst, speaking shamefacedly of 'having created a marvellous mood for comedy', but the hecklers' witlessness has given him something to define himself against, and from that point on, the show never looks back.

There are flashes of real verbal inspiration, but rather unexpectedly, the real highlights of the performance are moments of visual comedy which incorporate the scale and opulence of the venue. When Merton descends from the ceiling on a recalcitrant platform, or contrives an awe-inspiring reconstruction of the Dam Busters using just six fluffy rabbits, you can almost feel the old place relaxing.

Watching Merton present his BBC1 history of the London Palladium (timed, with that rather wearying synchronicity which is such a hallmark of the nineties comedian, to coincide with his shows there), nodding with exaggerated reverence at the feet of great ventriloquists and strong men, some words commonly attributed to the great curmudgeon Alexei Sayle spring to mind. These words are roughly to the effect that the reason music-hall (which bears the same relation to variety as rhythm and blues did to rock and roll: it was fundamentally the same, it just happened first) died out in the first place was that it was rubbish.

The moral force of this statement does not come so much from disrespect for such great acts of yesteryear as Arthur Henderson and His Dancing Combs, as an understanding of the basic principles of evolution. Appreciating the amusing things dinosaurs used to do with their tails should not stop us acknowledging the fact that they are unlikely to stage a successful comeback.

So when, in 1994, the Perrier Award goes to unknown (and horribly unfunny) Australian duo Lano and Woodley for their 'classical clowning' and people who think this is a good thing say that variety is coming back and it's good to see comedy rediscovering its music-hall roots, something is rotten in the state of Edinburgh. Certainly there are very few things more boring than bad stand-up, but one of them is bad variety.

What's more, comedy has *already* rediscovered its music-hall roots, and in ways that this brace of Antipodean chancers whose act has its origins in a field of human endeavour whose name must never be spoken (it begins with an 'm' and rhymes with 'crime') can scarcely even conceive of.

The uncritical embrace of pratfalls and arm-waving is one thing, but comedy which takes into account the reality of the culture it comes from is quite another. When Vic Reeves and Bob Mortimer reopened the lines of communication between comedy and vaudeville in the late eighties, they did so in a way that reflected the changes in our entertainment landscape. And most of those who follow through the old showbiz-shaped breach Reeves and Mortimer had made in the national subconscious – Tommy 'Great days, great days' Cockles, John Shuttleworth with his Yamaha organ and sole agent Ken Worthington, twenty-year-old Matt Lucas and his monstrous theatrical creation Sir Bernard Chumley – add at least a twist of their own to such blue-plaque heritage source material.

But a passing reacquaintance with the legends of showbiz antiquity will not, in itself, be enough to sustain the comedy newcomer of the nineties. A supplementary form of iconic nutrition is going to be required.

At this point in our story, a grisly shadow is waiting in the wings. It's one we have done well to ignore until now, but the time has come to call it out into the open.

Three. That whole 'comedy is the new rock 'n' roll' farrago

It's not just onstage that the comedian's ever-increasing cultural visibility is causing problems by late 1993. On *The South Bank Show*'s 'A to Z of Comedy', Jim Davidson, Billy Connolly and Harry Enfield all agree that one of the hardest things about their job is the lack of a line between who you are and what you do. Facing your audience with just a microphone for protection raises other spectres beyond being bombarded with your own catchphrases on family walks.

It also makes it hard to maintain the requisite multimedia career assault without feeling somehow personally diminished by it. As public figures, comedians lack the layers of mythological armour which protect actors or pop stars. Their struggles are not embedded in our consciousness in the same way. In short, they suffer from an acute lack of mystique; Dustin Hoffman as Lenny Bruce, Sir Laurence Olivier as Archie Rice, Sally Field in *Punchlines* – none of these quite make it as role models.[64] And it's hard to have faith in your own showbiz myth when no one really cares about that tricky time you had on your Open Mike début at the Comedy Store.

At this juncture, the nearest thing the post-alternative circuit can boast to an iconic figure is probably Deptford reprobate Malcolm Hardee – formerly promoter of the infamous Tunnel Club in the carbon-monoxide-choked badlands of the Blackwall Tunnel Approach Road – whose autobiography, *I Stole Freddie Mercury's Birthday Cake*, published around this time, is as sorry a collection of ill-informed prejudice and warmed-over apocrypha as you could ever wish to read.[65]

Other than the fact that he once launched an unprovoked physical attack on the comedy critic of the *Observer*, it is hard to see what Hardee has ever done to earn the seemingly genuine respect and admiration of so many of his peers. Only an art form in pretty bad shape, living legend-wise, would choose to doff its collective cap to a performer whose main claim to fame is his willingness (nay, compulsion) to show off his prodigious testicles in public.

Here[66] lie the roots of that other rapidly decaying chestnut – the one about comedy being the new rock and roll. It's not just ill-informed media commentators who have tended to look to pop stars for their understanding of comedy fame. Comedians do it too. The first visible concession to celebrity made by most up-and-coming laughter-makers is to hang around with as many low-rent indie bands as possible. First Vic and Bob, then Rob Newman, then Mark Lamarr and Sean Hughes; all colonized the music-press gossip columns in the hope of discovering some kind of celebrity structure. The strange thing about this transaction is that, regardless of relative earning power, success of own TV show, etc., it still tends to be the comedians' eyes that have stars in them.

How many of today's comic superstars wouldn't really – in their heart of hearts – prefer to be in a mildly successful rock group?

[64.] Perhaps the closest thing to a real cinematic role model for nineties comedy is Robert De Niro's Rupert Pupkin in Martin Scorsese's *The King of Comedy*, and he's a dangerous lunatic.

[65.] It is also, coincidentally, quite fun.

[66.] In the arid soil of iconic deficit.

Only a gifted psychic could answer this question. But even the fearsomely focused Eddie Izzard loses sight of the big picture when it comes to music. While Izzard's willingness to spurn the siren lure of television has played a vital role in establishing him as most people's idea of the coolest comedian in Britain, if there's a chance to plug The Wasp Factory (the distinctly not-epoch-making band he manages at this juncture), he'll be in front of the camera before you can say Andrew Loog Oldham.

Those in the know might point out that he is dating the lead singer, but that's not all there is to this. It's as if comedians know that however famous and successful they become, they can never have a pop star's aura; that ability to create an event simply by their very presence.

When Newman and Baddiel finally emerge from a blizzard of hyperbole to perform to a nearly full Wembley Arena in December of 1993, there *is* a real sense of a big event. It comes not just from the fans, but from the other comedians in disguise checking out the lay of the land for future engagements (in fact, it is eight years before another dares to attempt it, but then both Eddie Izzard and Lee Evans carry it off in quick succession).

The show itself, with its giant video screens, motorized skateboards and 'flying' in a safety harness, works hard to make a virtue of its exaggerated scale. Whether or not Newman and Baddiel's Wembley Arena performance is the logical culmination of a masterplan to take comedy to the next commercial level, or just a spectacle designed to look big on video,[67] it's certainly a lot more fun than watching them on TV. (In person, even David Baddiel's compulsive unpleasantness becomes mildly compelling, if only in the context of more than ten thousand people considering it to be entertainment.)

The fact that not many people over twenty-five seem to find them funny makes Newman and Baddiel more interesting rather than less. And the eagerness with which the duo's younger admirers

---

[67.] 'To be honest, we did it because we could,' their manager Jon Thoday remembers, a decade later. 'We thought it would be exciting and it was – when they came on and picked up the chairs to do "History Today" and everything went crazy, well, *I've* never seen anything like that.'

have taken them to their hearts is not explicable solely in terms of Rob Newman's sex-god status.

There is something very paternalistic about Newman and Baddiel's comedy of recognition – all the 'you know how it feels when . . .'s, and the self-conscious youth-cultural name-dropping (Baddiel's impersonation of Brett Anderson from Suede, for example, is the sort of thing you might expect from an embarrassing supply teacher who is trying too hard to be down with the kids) – and the goodwill it engenders from those a couple of steps down the age ladder is startling. Supportive whoops and cheers greet the end of each sketch, and even portentous extracts from forthcoming novels are roundly cheered.

Several of the wordier sallies seem calculated to go over people's heads, but in some ways this is the point of them. Rob and David do not need to be as coy about their Cambridge University educations now as they would have had to have been even two or three years before.[68]

They can flaunt their learning safe in the knowledge that their fans want them to succeed, despite all their obvious advantages. (It's no accident that their best-loved routine gently mocks the childishness at the heart of so much academic disputation, as the warring academics of *History Today* descend in the blink of an ear from the lofty heights of intellectual debate to playground taunts of 'that's you, that is'.) To a generation raised to see a career as an impossible dream, Newman and Baddiel offer the rare and even inspiring spectacle of young men using their educations to make a living.

[68.] When Stewart Lee had won the Hackney Empire New Act of the Year competition in the winter of 1990, one of the judges – a leading comedy promoter of the time – congratulated him in the following abrasive terms: 'Good, now you can show those Oxbridge wankers like David Baddiel what real comedy is . . .'

Lee felt duty bound to confirm that while he had won the competition 'fair and square', he too ('As a student in the eighties, it was the last thing you would mention') bore the stain of education at one of Britain's two supposedly élite universities. 'But you're not like them, are you?' the promoter demanded. 'Well,' he replied, 'I don't know . . . Am I?' When a number of promised bookings subsequently failed to materialize, he was able to ponder at leisure the novelty of being a victim of Oxbridge-education-based employment discrimination.

Four

'He lays himself on the line, and we're not much used to that sort of honesty'
Sean Hughes tour programme, January 1994

There is an armchair centre-stage at Brighton's Dome Theatre, as Sean Hughes begins a tour that will last the best part of three months. But Hughes – a rheumy-eyed Stan Laurel lookalike with an appealing London-Irish brogue – rarely sits in it, preferring to pace back and forth like an expectant father who would rather not have kept the baby.

His coat-hanger frame is slightly bent, as if his chin were glued to his left shoulder. His jokes have a twist in them, too – turning back to have a gentle smirk at themselves before the punchline is even out of sight. 'I'm buying a house at the moment so I've just had a survey done: 80 per cent of people said I should go ahead' is a line Steve Martin would not have kicked out of bed at his late-seventies peak.

As Sean forsakes the amiable Garry Shandling-inspired metatextual footling of his *Sean's Show* television series for a bombardment of quick-fire gags in the style of Frank Carson, the odd cheap shot does get through. (Why waste time trying to wring laughs out of Linford Christie's genitalia when you could just as easily join the BNP?)

Hughes's return to comedy basics must be doubly surprising to anyone devoted enough to have stumped up five pounds for the programme, which presents him as a cardigan-clad visionary of our era. It describes Sean's battles with Catholicism and his search for his true identity, culminating in a change of name (from John, which is not all that far from Sean, when you stop to think about it). 'He lays himself on the line,' apparently, 'and we're not much used to that sort of honesty.'

Poetry is a new direction for Sean and, judging by the reception accorded to his recent book *The Grey Area* – which has sold 20,000 copies in hardback alone – a successful one. But that doesn't mean he is any good at it. In fact, as a writer of verse (and later prose),

Sean Hughes has a seemingly unattainable ambition: to make Sandi Toksvig look like a significant literary figure.

How can someone be so perceptive one minute and so totally blind to their own limitations the next? In the broader show-business world, this is known as the Clive James Conundrum.

Taking yourself too seriously is a common flaw among comedians. It only becomes a real problem when it makes you hate your audience. Hughes once threatened to play over-eighteens' venues only – on tonight's evidence, he would need to book a bus shelter if he did – and yet at this point seems to maintain an easy, avuncular rapport with his much younger fans.

There's no reason why he shouldn't, either, as teenage self-absorption is his major comic staple anyway.[69] And the extension of adolescence from a seven- to a twenty-year span which mysteriously takes place at some point around the turn of the decade[70] only renders Hughes's distinctive brand of late-twenties bachelor angst ('How am I ever going to have a kid when I still wake up in the foetal position?') all the more à la mode.

A year or so later at the London Comedy Festival, however, things seem to have gone a bit sour. Hughes looks increasingly uncomfortable with the tender years of his constituency. His attitude at times seems almost disdainful, as he veers uneasily between talking down to his audience (heaven preserve us from bad impersonations of Damon Albarn – the real thing is difficult enough to cope with) and going wilfully over their heads. One Winston Churchill and Nancy Astor reference is so reluctant to give itself up that a passing police detective inspector has to be called in to talk it down off the roof.

What makes Hughes's increasingly compulsive underachievement so frustrating is that at his funniest – dissecting dysfunctional family relationships or Dublin lounge décor, for example – he is a truly challenging performer. He has a real talent for undermining the assumptions of shared experience on which so much second-rate

---

[69.] And ten years later, it still is.
[70.] 'Between the Westland Affair and the release of Blur's *Parklife*', is how Philip Larkin might have put it, had he not been otherwise engaged at a Happy Mondays gig.

comedy is based. 'Did you ever do that thing', he asks at one point, in the casual vernacular of a thousand arrested-adolescence nostalgia gags, 'of feigning serious injury when your dad hit you?'

In happy contrast to Hughes's ever grouchier generational rank-pulling, Lee and Herring – the mid-nineties' fifth-form (or even year 10) comedians of choice – prefer to make the most of the youth and supposed impressionability of their target audience.[71] In the course of three series of their *Fist of Fun* Radio 1 show (one of the few artistic successes of the early years of Matthew Bannister's regime at what was then Britain's most-listened-to radio station),[72] this mischievous double act develop a uniquely participatory style of comedy which involves mobilizing listeners *en masse* to scour the UK for the charity event that raises the least money.

'The Lee and Herring child army' – *Fist of Fun*'s core audience of young people with time on their hands – are also encouraged to deluge unsuspecting local radio personalities with sacks of motiveless fan mail. So how do the twenty-seven-year-old generals of this deadly teenage guerilla force think their footsoldiers feel about them?

'We've got some stalwart fans who are impressed by us,' insists Richard Herring proudly, 'but not all that many of them . . . Mostly, we send people stuff we've got lying around in the office and they write back in a slightly ironic way and say, "Oh thanks – I've got a piece of rubbish that you've touched".'

Five. Bill Hicks in the afterlife, a.k.a. that whole 'comedian as martyr' delusion

As Bob Hope was to Bob Monkhouse, as Mort Sahl and Tom Lehrer and Lenny Bruce were to the *Beyond The Fringe* generation (i.e. both icons of American otherness, and an object lesson in just

---

71. 'A lot of good things are found by teenagers first,' insists an older but no more or less wise Stewart Lee in 2002, 'because they have the spare time and the enthusiasm and they can't go out and drink yet. When I was twelve or thirteen in a suburb of Birmingham, waiting for *The Young Ones* to come on – there was a thing that you felt was for you.'

72. It never quite worked on TV though. There was something about the physical positioning of the audience which seemed to undermine the bed-

how much might be achieved by British comedians who were willing to study them hard enough), so were Denis Leary and Bill Hicks to the people who saw them at the Edinburgh Festival in 1990–1.[73]

There were some similarities between the two – both were gravel-dry iconoclasts with beguilingly rough-and-tumble sensibilities – but a fairly general feeling prevailed that had Hicks not hit the ground running first with the cancer material, Leary might have thought twice about following him out of the low-flying helicopter. And even while Hicks was still alive, some people were buffing up a pernicious duality.

Hicks, the story went, was chiselling nobly away at a Platonic ideal of comic integrity, while Leary was 'just an opportunist' (like that's not what all comedians are meant to be). And then, a few years afterwards, Bill Hicks died. Which was tragic. Worse still – in terms of his subsequent apotheosis by comedians (and indie bands) in search of a higher purpose – he died at approximately the same age as Jesus. Denis Leary, meanwhile, bought shares in the MTV version of himself, made some OK films and was seen about town with Liz Hurley a lot.

In a year (1994) when death cast an abnormally long shadow over what are sometimes called the lively arts, Hicks – with River Phoenix and Kurt Cobain – made up a trio of prematurely departed icons who proved that whatever else you might think of the Grim Reaper, he certainly has taste. Their passing left a spiritual hole in the middle of each of their respective fields that was too big to walk around.

While for both Cobain and Phoenix the end was – purposely or otherwise – self-administered, Hicks was different. His act celebrated hedonism; he spoke out in favour of recreational drug use and was a fanatical defender of the right to smoke. Early on in his

---

situationist premise. 'I think it was about six months ahead of its time,' Lee reflects. 'Looking back now, it all seems a bit precocious . . . I wonder if we painted ourselves into a corner.'

73. Leary was the first of the pair to make a splash when he came over in 1990, with Hicks following twelve months later – initially marketed (somewhat ironically, in view of subsequent events) as 'this year's Denis Leary'. A widespread eagerness to atone for this minor aesthetic injustice probably accounted for the excessive adjustment which followed.

career, his profligate lifestyle seemed to court the kind of excess-fuelled, rock-star-style premature death which eventually befell his fellow Texan 'outlaw comic' Sam Kinison. Yet he finally died of natural causes in the ugly form of pancreatic cancer, having long since given up not only drink and drugs but cigarettes too.

'The comic is a flame – like Shiva the destroyer,' Hicks had told the *New Yorker* critic John Lahr (the same man who made such a meal out of not getting Reeves and Mortimer) in a rather vainglorious moment in 1992. 'He keeps cutting everything back to the moment.'

Comics are so much of the moment that it is difficult enough to capture what is good about them on TV when they are alive, and harder still for them to sustain an afterlife. Even when they do – as, say, Lenny Bruce has – anyone who didn't see them perform will often find it hard to remember what was funny about them.

The only hope, as so often, lies in commercial exploitation. 'It's Just a Ride', the tribute film which makes up the first part of the hastily patched-together Channel 4 video *Totally Bill Hicks*, offers some fascinating insights into Hicks's life and work. There are revealing interviews with his parents – God-fearing Southerners who 'couldn't understand why Bill used the f-word so much' – and with the geeky friends with whom he used to sneak off to perform at a rough-and-tumble Houston comedy club at the tender age of fifteen.

The affection and envy mingling in the eyes of his fellow professionals speaks volumes about Hicks's talents (comedians are competitive people after all, not usually given to abasing themselves at the feet of their peers). Eddie Izzard and Sean Hughes represent Hicks's UK fan club – it could just as easily have been any number of other people – but the most illuminating insight comes from the American comedian, Brett Butler. Hicks's treacle-voiced fellow Southerner, star of Channel 4's *Grace Under Fire* (which was quite funny for a while, until it got all syrupy), observes astutely that 'For all the talk about Bill being like Hendrix or Dylan or Jim Morrison, it was Jesus he wanted to be'.

These Messianic tendencies are all too apparent as Hicks emerges from tongues of fire on to the Dominion Theatre stage on the last night of his 1992 *Revelations* tour. But it's the ordinariness of his appearance which is striking once he's taken his cowboy hat off – slicked-back hair, button eyes, face like a potato in a stocking – and which throws the brilliance of his performance into even sharper relief.

Bill Hicks's command of the stage and of his material is so complete that it sometimes seems like he's using a sledgehammer to crack a nut, even when he isn't. His intensity – especially when personifying his own libido as the demonic Goat-boy (motto: 'Let me wear you like a feed bag') – is almost frightening. Like the preacher he often fancied himself to be, Hicks could be self-righteous and he could hector, but he could also be devastating.

'Ever noticed', he muses, 'how creationists look really unevolved?' The industrial-strength sarcasm which went down so well in Britain sometimes landed him in trouble in his less sarcastically minded homeland, especially when applied to such notoriously humour-resistant targets as fundamentalist Christianity. In October 1993, when Hicks turned his scorn on anti-abortionists in a routine being recorded for *The David Letterman Show* – 'These pro-lifers . . . You ever look at their faces? . . . [screws up face and assumes bitter, pinched voice] "I'm pro-life" . . . Boy, they look it, don't they?' – he became too hot for even the supposedly cutting-edge Letterman to handle.

The fact that the cancelled slot had been recorded in the same theatre where Elvis's rotating pelvis was deemed unsuitable for *The Ed Sullivan Show* did nothing to lessen its mythic significance. And when the ensuing censorship furore spurred Hicks on through the rigours of chemotherapy to a final epic bout of creativity – 'It was like Bill to the tenth power,' said friend and producer Kevin Booth. 'He couldn't be involved in any kind of mundane situation for even a second' – the foundations of his martyr cult were firmly in place.

It does not diminish what was special about Bill Hicks (in fact it rather underlines it) to say that comedians, as a rule, are *meant* to be involved in mundane situations. That is what encourages them to think up funny things to say.

'Two options are open to him,' Harry Secombe wrote of the aspiring laughter-maker in his preface to Roger Wilmut's *Tony Hancock: Artiste*: 'either he gives them [the crowd] what he wants, or he provides them with what they want. If he takes up the former he is liable to finish up returning to the rice pudding factory from which Hughie Green plucked him.'

You don't have to subscribe fully to this extreme mechanistic view of the comedian's proper relationship with his or her audience (after all, as Vic and Bob have shown us, many of their art form's richest possibilities are bound up in the utter bemusement and confounding of the paying customer) to think that the whole Shiva the Destroyer thing is a bit of a blind alley.[74]

What the legend of Bill Hicks offers is an *excess* of mythological armour. And, just as later English monarchs would struggle with the weighty chain-mail of Richard the Lionheart, so other comedians who tried to put on Bill's heavy suit would generally end up blundering around, bumping into the antique furniture. Take Rob Newman, for instance, cruelly sustained by Hicksian example in the delusion that his post-Newman-and-Baddiel career was actually a heroic one-man struggle against the evils of capitalism.

Denis Leary meanwhile – blessed by destiny with the chance to go on living, with all the failures and compromises that entails – has had a different kind of afterlife. While the bones of Hicks's *œuvre* have subsequently been picked clean by well-meaning vultures, and the endless slew of commemorative videos and live CDs have inevitably become subject to the law of diminishing returns, Leary's 1992 A&M album, *No Cure For Cancer*, now stands – from its savage assault on the culture of complaint (built around the healing mantra 'Shut the fuck up') to its rabble-rousing redneck anthem, '(I'm An) Asshole' – as a gleaming comic monument.

Untarnished by the oxide of sainthood, it's both the perfect refutation of late-eighties bullshit and a brutally ironic reversal of the pop culture myth-making's founding principle of living fast, dying young and leaving a beautiful corpse.

[74.] Though the enduring validity of a Hicks quote on a T-shirt on the Stop The War march on 15 February 2003 ('How do we know Iraq has weapons of mass destruction? We looked at the receipt') suggests there might be something in it after all.

5
Constructing the Citadel

The comedy edifice needs bricks and mortar, just like any other (in five more parts)

1. The Management

> 'They get blamed for things I've done'
> Stewart Lee

Amid the remorseless expansion of the comedy industry in the late eighties and early nineties, the basic business of just being funny or not being funny gets pushed ever more to one side. A comedy career tends to be publicly defined in terms of material – rather than creative – advance: how much you got paid for your video, how many series you've had on Channel 4, how many nights you can sell out at which West End theatre. It is in this context that the small amount of coverage given to the complex art of comedy management will generally be encountered.

Which of us has not felt an involuntary contraction of the bowel muscles on watching some pointless TV showbiz news report and hearing the halfwit holding the microphone say 'and [insert name of pop-culture phenomenon X, from bingo to pigeon-racing] has become *big business*'? While such in-depth reportage has probably ensured that at least the names of the three main corporate players in British comedy – Avalon, Off The Kerb and PBJ – will be vaguely familiar to anyone with a passing interest in the field, the extent of the impact they've had on their various clienteles may well come as something of a shock.

The contrasting ways in which the workplace cultures of different management companies evolve has had a crucial influence on developing social, creative and ideological divides in the British body comedic. To such an extent that at times you start to wonder if comedy management is an exoskeleton or an endoskeleton.

Like record company bosses and film producers, comedy managers tend to get a very bad press. This is because everyone else – from critics to fans to the artistes themselves – has a vested interest in blaming them for anything that might go wrong in their clients' careers. As false as the notional opposition between the unsullied innocence of the artist and the deceiving greed of the agent undoubtedly is, people find clinging on to it much easier than asking themselves awkward questions about exactly whose idea it was to do that dreadful advert.

It is much to the managers' and agents' credit that you will rarely hear them complain about the resultant sullying of their reputations. Whatever their other differences, they seem to share an innate understanding that it is chiefly by means of this process of 'automatic guilt by association' (succinctly formulated by Stewart Lee as 'They get blamed for things I've done') that they earn their percentage. Thus one form of formal buck acceptance begets another.

Speaking to comedians[75] about their agents, there is very little of the bitching which might be conspicuous in discussions of a similar nature with an actor or author. Perhaps because comedy is such a lonely and competitive business – Off The Kerb boss Addison Cresswell describes its practitioners as 'the most paranoid group of people I've ever met' – the very existence of an advocate and mentor, however fallible, is something to be grateful for.

(a) Avalon's testosterone vale

The turning-point in Jenny Eclair's long slog from waitress to resting comedy actress to Perrier Award-winning comedian seems to have been the moment she moved from the sisterly agency she shared

---

[75.] Successful ones, that is: the things the ones who don't make it have to say about the people who help them not quite make it are not suitable for publication in a book – such as this one – with a broad family readership.

with French and Saunders, Ruby Wax and Sandi Toksvig to the testosterone vale of Avalon (home to Frank Skinner and David Baddiel among others). Talking to her about them in 1995, she seems quite happy to be the lone female on the books of an organization for whose profile the word 'muscular' is widely deemed to be an understatement.

'I adore them,' she says, 'because they play the game so well – the reality of going up and down the motorway playing to six people is very mundane, but when the pantomime is done properly ... *well*, I can almost believe the car which is taking me to Manchester this afternoon will be a bullet-proof limo, even though it'll actually be a Ford Orion.'

For corporate gigs (the dark underbelly of a good comedic living), Avalon even supply her with a bodyguard. 'The companies concerned are paying quite a lot of money,' Eclair explains cheerfully, 'so they want to take your skin off and hang it behind the door.' This is exactly the sort of malevolent impulse people who have done business with Avalon in the television or publishing industries can sometimes be heard to accuse *them* of.

Having just lost his proverbial shirt (and quite possibly his actual shirt, too) in a disastrous foray into producing West End musicals, Jon Thoday founded Avalon with former Woolwich Poly entertainments secretary Richard Allen-Turner in 1988. On the basis of Thoday's experience that 'theatrical agents always blamed the talent and failed to take responsibility for their own mistakes', they decided to build up a comedy-management stable based on a very different principle. They set out to be '100 per cent on the side of their clients'.

This is the sort of nebulous thing snidey Jay Mohr says in *Jerry Maguire* when he's trying to tempt Rod Tidwell away from Tom Cruise, but in Avalon's case it does actually seem to mean something. 'There is a kind of ethic that "the act is always right",' agrees Stewart Lee, 'which in one sense is reassuring, but can occasionally be unhelpful ... Because the act' – Lee continues feelingly – 'is sometimes wrong.'

'Traditionally,' Thoday explains, 'the agent stands in between the artist and whoever they're making the deal with, but we tend to stand more *with* our client. We've never really worried about the people on the other side of the table, because it's not them we have a relationship with.'

Is this why the name of Avalon has been known to inspire loathing as well as love? 'Right from when we first started in 1988, we've been very good at spotting talent,' Thoday insists. 'The more talented clients you work with, the more often you need to say no to people, and if you're saying no, there's no real difference whether you shout or tell them nicely – no one likes to hear it. So I think a certain amount of the bad feeling we've experienced over the years has come from the people who would have liked to work with us, but haven't been able to.'

If you think of British pop's abundant managerial mythology – from arch teen manipulator Larry Parnes, through Brian Epstein and Led Zeppelin's Peter Grant, to Malcolm McLaren's *Great Rock 'n' Roll Swindle* – the relative paucity of human interest in the annals of comedic career guidance was in urgent need of rectification by the late 1980s. And the oft-overlooked sense of mischief embedded in such cornerstones of Avalonian folklore as Thoday enlivening a bad night out at the Hackney Empire by persuading a rival agent to sign a third-rate act ('I thought it might be funny to recommend the person who was rubbish,' Thoday remembers unrepentantly, 'and they were signed the next day') was at least a first step towards making good that deficit.

The flipside of the gang mentality which Avalon are often accused of fostering is an impressive record of loyalty to such maverick left-field performers as Simon Munnery. The company's sense of collective embattlement probably dates back to the size of the initial splash they made in the complacent duckpond of the late-eighties UK comedy scene. Even though – or perhaps more accurately, because – the bulk of Avalon's early signings (Skinner excepted) came from Oxford or Cambridge University backgrounds, they were sufficiently out of step with prevailing alternative dogmas to excite alarm and despondency amongst the doormen of socio-political righteousness.

'Someone like Frank Skinner, who might now be perceived as a cash cow,' Stewart Lee remembers, 'signing him was a bold decision when they did it, because no one else wanted to. There was a definite perception when Avalon was starting off that they were the barbarians at the gates. I remember [celebrated pillar of ideological rectitude] Jeremy Hardy writing a column in the *Guardian* accusing Simon Munnery of being a neo-Nazi,' he smiles, 'which was a much less popular option comedically then than it is now.'

Avalon's institutional machismo is not to everyone's tastes – the co-ordinated windcheaters traditionally worn by their employees at the Edinburgh Festival causing even the famously mild-mannered Addison Cresswell to mutter darkly about 'muppets in matching jackets'. And their aggressive style of management has undoubtedly had its casualties on both sides of the deal-making fence, but no one can deny that they have an aesthetic. And British comedy needs as many of those as it can get.

For legal reasons, it seems best to confirm at first hand the veracity of the following anecdote about an Avalon Christmas company outing on the Eurostar. Is it true that on one particular mid-nineties occasion, an enraged Jon Thoday was obliged to complete his journey in the guards van after narrow-minded French officialdom thwarted his attempt to buy a second complete drinks trolley?

'It wasn't a trolley,' growls an affronted Thoday, 'it was the entire bar.'

(b) Off The Kerb: Mr Cresswell remembers when all this were nobbut fields

Self-confessed Millwall fan Addison Cresswell[76] founded his operation – the longest-established of the three main management empires – in the early eighties. He did it initially 'for a laugh' on the grounds that 'it was better than signing on'. The Comic Strip were touring with French and Saunders at the time, and he put together a rival package for about a fifth of the money under a name thought up by John Hegley.

---

76. Cresswell's own hard-man-of-comedy credentials come under savage attack from Malcolm Hardee in *I Stole Freddie Mercury's Birthday Cake*, but Hardee is hardly the most reliable witness. And the fact that in the midst of one of the numerous cheerily profane mobile conversations from which I will be quoting, Cresswell reveals that he is actually in a hospital bed awaiting a major stomach operation, certainly puts him a few places above Emo Phillips in the hard-man-of-comedy league table.

Off The Kerb's off-the-cuff beginnings were a long way from today's multi-million-pound concern. Cresswell 'ran the business for three years with one phone in a basement in Peckham . . . There were no answering machines, let alone mobiles – it was all 10p's and phonecards in those days – and it'd take you a couple of days to track anyone down, because whenever you phoned them up they'd always be out . . . but then it all got serious, and now every fucker has four agents and a style guru to hold their mobile phone for them.'

He seemed to adjust successfully enough to the expansion of commercial opportunities which transformed the industry he had initially got involved with in the hope of 'drinking himself silly, getting laid and not starting work till one o'clock the next afternoon', into the bloated careerist enclave that it is today. In fact, in self-consciously presenting his acts as a stable by schooling people like Jack Dee and Lee Evans in the benefits of wearing 'a fucking smart suit' made by his own tailor (Eddie in Berwick Street, Soho), Cresswell might be said to have played as big a part as anyone in the professionalization of the unwashed comedy hordes.

'I've always been a bit more rock 'n' roll,' he observes, when asked about the difference between his approach and that of his two rival agencies (though given his acts' allegiance to the well-cut whistle, perhaps Motown would be a better analogy). 'I like people who work hard instead of sitting around moaning and waiting for the phone to ring. I never took on acts that didn't have any bollocks[77] . . . Mark [Lamarr] is no angel and Lee [Evans] is a bit of a nutter too, on his night.'

There's a telling moment in William Cook's *Ha Bloody Ha*, where Cresswell says that the thing he most disliked about the comedy scene in the early eighties was that it reminded him of 'everything I hated about college'. He still exudes that peculiarly refined hatred for the products of this country's higher education system which can only come from years spent within it.

However much the pre-celebrity CVs of his roster might suggest

---

[77.] This is not as gender-specific a dividing line as it sounds: Cresswell did take on Jo Brand, after all, who by common consent has more bollocks than most.

otherwise, the boss of Off The Kerb insists that he does not consider forswearing a university education to be an *essential* prerequisite for comedic validity.

'I just feel that if people want to be comedians, they should do their foundation course,' maintains this diehard advocate of the school of hard knocks, 'have some glasses thrown at them on a Monday night in Sheffield or something . . . The amount of fucking arseholes who've just come out of Oxford or Cambridge and straight away they're waltzing round the BBC – honestly, you can't move up there for those cunts . . . I think they should be burned at the stake.'

As if realizing that his own eloquence might've got the better of him at this point, Cresswell flirts momentarily with the language of conciliation. 'Don't get me wrong,' he qualifies subtly, 'comedy can come from anywhere.'

(c) All the way with PBJ

Encountering each other in the corridor of their management company's Soho Square office, Vic Reeves and Armando Ianucci exchange wary acknowledgements. They do this in the manner of two jungle creatures who don't explicitly eat each other, but who feel they have to be wary just in case the other one decides to give it a try.

'You never quite know what to say to them,' Vic observes afterwards of these chance meetings with his comedy peers and fellow PBJ clients. 'It's like the office above the shopfloor where people from various departments bump into each other.' The idea that they might have a workplace culture of their own is one which takes a bit of getting used to for nineties comedians, most of whom probably grew up in times when the phrase 'a proper job' still meant something.

The secret of PBJ's success – and with a client list including Rowan Atkinson, Lenny Henry and Harry Enfield from the alternative *ancien régime*, and Vic and Bob, Chris Morris and Eddie Izzard from the next generation, they must be doing something right – seems to lie in offering a respite from the relentless push and pull of the comedy marketplace. In contrast to the sharp-suited hustle and bustle of the other two main agencies, PBJ founder Peter Bennett-Jones cultivates the aura of a mildly eccentric English gentleman. And in so far as the enterprise which shares his initials has a mythology, it's for not having one.

'Peter had been looking after Rowan [Atkinson] for a couple of years,' remembers Caroline Chignell of the late-eighties expansion which brought her into the company. 'There was a real sense of a next generation coming through, but unless we had some kind of definite structure, no one would want to join us.' She had been out on the road promoting a tour with Harry Enfield when Bennett-Jones asked her to join him. When she expressed doubts about whether she had what it took to make it in comedy management, he described the key attribute necessary as 'a sense of fair play', which would probably be some distance away from most people's best guess, *sine qua non*-wise.

'I'm probably not like most agents,' she admits apologetically, 'in that I don't tend to shout and scream, and I'm not particularly rude. My idea of a good deal is one that gets the best for your client but also makes the person who's paying you want to come back for more – as that's the only way you can take other people forward with you in the relationship.'

While this softly-softly approach might sound a bit dull compared with the more frontiersmanlike approach of PBJ's rival agencies, it's worth remembering that it's helped nurture some of the most extreme TV comedy ever produced in this country – from *The Day Today* and *Brass Eye* to The League of Gentlemen (who join PBJ after the Edinburgh Festival in 1996). 'We actively encourage people to take as much time as possible to get things right,' insists Chiggy, 'but we are at the behest of the clients. If they turn around and say we need to make some money because we've got an enormous tax bill or an expensive divorce to pay for – which does happen sometimes – then there's not really very much we can do about it.'

2. Diversification

There are two main forms of creative diversification available to the modern comedian, and these will be addressed in alphabetical order.

(a) Acting

As beguiling as Addison Cresswell's vision (outlined at the end of chapter 2) of a plague of would-be thespians diminishing the purity of the comedic bloodline undoubtedly is, it is not strictly accurate. For one thing, there is a perfectly respectable tradition of successful comedic career cross-overs. It dates back to Queen Elizabeth 1's favourite jester Dick Tarleton (who moonlighted as a comic actor at James Burbage's theatre in Shoreditch) and forward to Max Wall's inspired inhabitation of the plays of Samuel Beckett and Les Dawson's unforgettable 1990 appearance in *La Nona*, a thought-provoking TV film (based on an allegorical Argentinian novel of the same title) about a hundred-year-old woman so greedy that she eats her family's furniture.

Comedians – like rappers – often make very good actors, because their day-job already entails presenting an idealized version of themselves. In the aforementioned Wall and Dawson examples, the genius of the casting was that it referred to attributes they already had – in the former's case, a certain stone-faced stoicism; in the latter's, a penchant for appearing in public dressed as a lady and a well-established liking for his dinners – while taking them to places they would never have gone of their own accord.

The challenge for a later generation – constantly besieged as they are by casting agents trying to pep up their callback lists – is to get the balance exactly right between something they are already and something that they definitely aren't. In the case of Cresswell's client Lee Evans, this means parlaying his bumbling stage act into a crisply marketable international big-screen persona. In the light of the rejection letter from *Opportunity Knocks* (which as far as starting at the bottom goes, just about takes the cake) thoughtfully reprinted in the programme for Lee Evans's West End run at the Lyric Theatre,

Shaftesbury Avenue in 1995, the effective and occasionally inspired big-screen performances Evans delivers in Peter Chesholm's *Funny Bones*, the excellent *Mouse Hunt* and *There's Something About Mary* – one of the biggest (and best) Hollywood comedies of the decade – must surely rank as game-raising of the very highest order.[78]

The comic/thespian transition does not go as smoothly for everyone.[79] But for those who realize that there's more to establishing your dramatic credentials than doing a couple of months in *Art*, acting can provide an outside chance of creative rehabilitation, even for those who seem wholly out of the running.

Take Paul Kaye, for example. Just when the damage his celebrity-stalker persona Dennis Pennis had done to standards of behaviour in British public life might seem to have rendered him utterly beyond the pale of respectable society, along comes BBC1's Friday-night drama *Two Thousand Acres Of Sky*. In which, by exploiting his eerie resemblance to Marilyn Manson to superbly benign effect as the philosophically inclined new-age wastrel Kenny, Kaye secures an unexpected but entirely heartwarming form of redemption (as well as a series of Woolworths ads and his own entertaining game show).

As for those thespian wannabes so rudely fingered by Addison Cresswell, the case of Steve Coogan's acting career is a complicated one, which will be dealt with in the fullness of time. As for Alan Davies, after a couple of false starts – notably that thing where he plays a disillusioned timeshare salesman sending home video postcards about his romantic conquests – his performances in *Jonathan Creek* and especially *Bob and Rose* eventually mark him out as a first-class comic (and even straight, dramatic) actor.

There is a clip of the younger Davies which always inspires high

---

[78.] About his own six-part BBC sitcom, however, the less said the better.

[79.] When Vic Reeves appeared on celebrity *Mastermind* in early 2003 and described his profession as 'comic actor', Magnus Magnusson nearly choked on his sugar-free gum: if he hadn't seen Vic's transcendently wooden performance in the sadly uncommissioned 1991 pilot *The Weekenders*, he must at least have caught a couple of episodes of *Randall and Hopkirk (Deceased)*. Then again, on reflection, I suppose the commitment Jim Moir has invested in the part of Vic Reeves over the years would put Robert De Niro to shame.

levels of hilarity when it gets shown on *Before They Were Famous* programmes. It's an embarrassing 'experimental' student film he made while wearing a long Echo and the Bunnymen-style raincoat. And when you stop and think about what happened to the artistic aspirations of the mid-eighties as they were passed through the mangle of Thatcherite enterprise culture, it *is* hard to suppress a wry chuckle.

When the acting jobs didn't come through straight away on first leaving drama college, Davies followed Norman Tebbitt's advice, got on his bike and looked for work as a stand-up comedian, subsequently earning six-figure sums by making adverts depicting the Abbey National building society as a safe haven from the rigours of capitalism. In this context, the words 'because life's complicated enough' could hardly be more apt.

(b) Writing novels

There is an honourable tradition of comedian turned novelist, too. Yet while it would be quicker to name the nineties comedians who *haven't* had novels published than the ones who have, if you were to ask yourself if any of them have written a book anywhere near as wild and personal as Spike Milligan's *Puckoon* (which, by some strange and gratifying quirk of popular taste, has somehow sold several million copies) or as grainily insightful as Les Dawson's *A Card for the Clubs*, you would have to conclude – regretfully – that they have not.

It is very easy to see what appeals to comedians about the idea of writing fiction. It brings a new brand of kudos (every comedy professional's favourite aftershave) and demonstrates – once and for all – to your parents and peers that you have made something of yourself. On the downside, if it's going to be done properly, it involves long months – and ideally years – of solitary toil, with very few breaks for everyone to gather around and tell you how talented you are.

Ben Elton has cunningly circumnavigated this problem by designing a computer program which enables you to write a 'novel' in three and a half hours, with the help of a copy of the *Mail on Sunday* and a specially trained marmoset. But for those of his profession who are too conscientious to use this demonic piece of software, there are still, it seems, almost insurmountable obstacles to be overcome.

Sometimes, people who work in the publishing industry get together over a frugal lunch of dry crackers and Sunny D to discuss what their reaction would be if a comedy agent ever approached them to see if they were interested in a client's forthcoming fictional endeavour, and then revealed that the comedian concerned was planning to actually complete the book *before* signing the big money deal. All are agreed that they would be very surprised.

In short, trying to get a comedian to go about writing a novel in the right spirit of speculative humility is like using a teasmade to make toast. It's just not something their mental circuits are wired up for.

At this point, the example of Rob Newman modestly presents itself.

'It's good to see a graduate making something of himself for a change,' observes a rough and ready individual in the queue for complimentary tickets outside the Royal Festival Hall in October 1994. 'Normally they just do fuck all and live off the state.'

The most interesting thing about Newman and Baddiel as a double act (which continues to be interesting about them long after their ways have parted) is that they have never been ashamed to wear their educations on their sleeves in front of a mass audience (Gary Bushell is in the audience tonight, and it takes a powerful cultural force to get *him* into the Royal Festival Hall).

In this context, writing a novel was the perfect next step for Robert (né Rob) Newman. While his début literary effort, *Dependence Day*, is never going to be taught in schools, it's not nearly as embarrassing as his detractors might have wished it. And if, in Newman's attempt to cultivate a literary mien on a promotional budget of Naomi Campbell proportions, there is a hint of having his cake and eating it, well, what would you want to do with a cake *other* than to eat it?

There is a slightly awkward moment just before he dances onstage at the South Bank, however, when it looks as if the scrum of people trying to get autographs from his former comedy partner (now in the audience) aren't going to sit down in time. But as soon as they do, it quickly becomes clear that Newman's gone-to-bed eyes have not lost the power to bore into young women's – *uh* – hearts. Few other performers in the distinguished history of this venue can have had 'There's a bra on the stage for you' shouted at them.

Everything seems to be in place for the whole enterprise to be a huge success before it even starts – the launch party for the video of the show will take place immediately afterwards – and that, in terms of Newman's attempt to rebrand himself as a literary figure, is really the problem. The dividing line between a recycled stand-up set, supposedly spontaneous chat-show patter and long-laboured-over literary conceit is simply not clear enough. The temptation to drift from one to the other just seems too strong for the star of tonight's show to resist.[80]

When Newman repeats a routine that he did, pretty much word for word, on *The Danny Baker Show* the Saturday before [historical note: for a brief period in the mid-1990s, Danny Baker had his own chat show on BBC1], there is some uneasy shifting in the crowd. It's a typically convoluted flight of fancy (at least I hope it's a flight of fancy) about walking the streets of London as a woman in order to write a book about it. This story deconstructs itself so thoroughly that by the end virtually nothing remains, and the audience is left with the sort of profound feeling of dissatisfaction which will be familiar to anyone who has read Eric Morecambe's *Mr Lonely*.

Morecambe's novel – first published in 1979 – is the story of Sid Lewis, a popular northern comedian 'whose Christmas shows are watched by thirty five million people'. Its cover is illustrated with a photo of someone who is presumably meant to be Sid, holding his NHS specs in a disturbingly Eric Morecambe-like manner. Its contents will come as a rude shock to anyone who thought the novel-as-thinly-veiled-semi-autobiographical-vanity-project was a cultural innovation of the 1990s.

[80.] Newman subsequently makes more strenuous efforts than anyone to shed his comedy skin, but somehow nothing he does – leaving Avalon, writing hard-bitten sub-Irvine Welsh police procedural novels about corrupt Stoke Newington-based police detectives, not saying anything funny in public between 1996 and 1999 – can quite enable him to break free.

Mr Lonely's hero – a none too subtle amalgam of Morecambe himself and his own inspiration, Birmingham comedy legend Sid Field – has 'the gentle approach of the late Arthur Haynes, yet, at times, the coarseness and strength of Jimmy Wheeler'. Only the book's absurd ending strikes a perversely resonant note (if anyone is reading it currently, please look away, as the surprise is about to be ruined) when disaster strikes for the unfortunate Mr Lewis at his moment of ultimate validation. Making a drunken but triumphant exit from the big showbiz award ceremony which has just proclaimed him the people's favourite light entertainer, he is involved in a fatal collision with a skidding taxi and impaled on his own newly won trophy.[81]

3. The Edinburgh Festival: Homage to Caledonia

'It's like a Butlins for comedians'
Addison Cresswell

The Edinburgh Festival's Perrier Award is sometimes dubbed 'The Comedy Oscar' – perhaps because the people who deserve to win one don't always seem to do so. But behind the annual carbonated product-placement hoopla lurks a unique and fascinating institution, where creative and not-so-creative currents come together in a manner reminiscent of the different tidal streams merging beneath southern Africa's Cape Point.

On the one hand there is a prodigious bacchanal – 'It's like a Butlins for comedians,' exults Addison Cresswell. 'Three weeks with your own people!' – degenerate enough to make even the

---

[81.] Morecambe seems to have been prompted to write this book by his admiration (which he expressed publicly in the most glowing terms) for an earlier volume: 1970's *The Comic*, by *Sunday Times* football writer and occasional *That Was The Week That Was* contributor Brian Glanville. One of the reasons this astute study of a comedian in the midst of a nervous breakdown was so unusually well observed was that Glanville's dad was a dentist who used to count Frankie Howerd and Max Wall among the clients at his West End surgery, giving his son exclusive access to comedians under conditions of unusual stress.

diehard hedonists of the rock 'n' roll circuit jealous. To those in that decadent sphere who have never experienced it, you might say: 'Imagine if Glastonbury lasted a month . . . And it was indoors. With no Healing Field.'

At the same time, the Edinburgh Festival also provides an unprecedented opportunity for career advancement. Highly polished London club sets which no one might see in a year will suddenly be scrutinized by every parasite in the sordid world of TV production – up north on expenses to pay their annual homage to Caledonia. This unique compression of the national media also offers immense creative possibilities to those who are bold enough to take them.

Steve Coogan is happy to admit to 'quite cynically using Edinburgh as a showcase' for his Patrick Marber-assisted change of direction, when winning the Perrier Award in 1992. But for others whose talents would prove less easily susceptible to commercial application, the festival's semi-captive audience makes it the ideal arena in which to try to imagine themselves a career in the most creative way possible.[82]

Those who were lucky enough to experience the full-scale Cecil B. De Mille version of Simon Munnery's Nietzschean cabaret *Club Zarathustra* in August 1996 – a show dedicated to the cause of insulting not so much its audience's intelligence as the very fibre of their being – will never forget the majesty of what they saw.[83] The yoke of shame lying upon the shoulders of whichever Channel 4 executive it was who decided not to commission a

---

[82.] This facility has – sadly – been somewhat undermined in recent years by a combination of escalating advertising costs (pushed up by the war between rival promoters) and declining TV revenue potential. 'You could lose 13 grand in Edinburgh, get a Channel 5 series and make 11,' Stewart Lee notes poignantly . . . 'It's like the arms race – nobody's going to win.'

[83.] Munnery tells one lucky punter 'You have the anagram of a good face', and amid the relentless barrage of eerie music, weird poetry and men in hoods, *Club Zarathustra* never loses sight of its central objectives of linguistic exactitude and existential severity. 'Cleanliness is next to godliness, you say? The chip shop is next to the hairdresser's, but that does not persuade me to visit either.'

series from the TV pilot which ensued will be just as hard to shake off.[84]

By throwing together performers and audience in a confined space in an atmosphere of barely suppressed hysteria, the Edinburgh Festival churns up some fascinating etiquette quandaries, such as how to behave when the person who elbows you sharply to one side in their eagerness to get to the bar turns out to be the same person you just paid to make you laugh. Most people seem to handle this quite well, and if comedians are troubled by the knowledge that for the price of listening to them for an hour, their audience could have experienced not one but two troupes of Clydeside puppeteers, they manage not to show it.

It's not just the barriers which traditionally separate performers from their audience that Edinburgh breaks down. It's also the ones that keep them apart from each other, and perhaps even more importantly, from their critics. As exhilarating as these new-found proximities are, they can also be dangerous.

Inevitably when a group of already competitive people are thrown together in such pressurized circumstances, the odd fist-fight will result. (The memorable moment when self-destructive Walthamstow-based misanthrope Ian Cognito decided to launch one verbal tirade too many against erstwhile getaway driver Ricky Grover, and was summarily knocked unconscious for his pains, is just one incident in a rich heritage of drunken feuding.)

Still more poignant is the tragic spectacle of media pundits who go native and – in the erroneous belief that some of Edinburgh's magic dust will have rubbed off on them – start presenting their own shows about their festival experiences, or the vital role they have played in the evolution of rock journalism.

[84.] On further investigation, things turn out to be somewhat more complicated than that, Munnery having actually been given the go-ahead to produce scripts for the series 'on the condition that he didn't disappear up his own arse'. Unfortunately, the pressure of keeping within these guidelines ultimately proved too great, and the scripts were never completed. Although Munnery's League Against Tedium *alter ego* did eventually make it on to BBC2 some years later – in the Stewart Lee-directed misanthrope's travelogue *Attention Scum* – by that time the character's moment somehow seemed to have passed.

As incestuous and self-indulgent as all this undoubtedly is, if the Edinburgh deterrent – that you might at any moment have to justify anything you've written, in person, to whoever you've just written about – could be applied to every corner of the national press, there can be no doubt that standards of accuracy and politeness would greatly improve. (In this connection, it is always instructive to see how uptight London-based features journalists become when their attempts to use the festival as a one-stop shop for a swingeing attack on the apolitical complacency of the comedy circuit are momentarily frustrated by someone like Al Murray or Frank Skinner snatching their notebook and reading out to the crowd all the sarcastic things they have been writing in it.)

To the broader national culture at large, the Edinburgh Festival (especially as mediated through an annual fiesta of nauseatingly self-satisfied BBC2 TV coverage) remains a blight, exuding exactly the same flatulent aura of insulated smugness which London was so notorious for in the pre-Madchester eighties.[85] To anyone lucky enough to be in the seat of Scottish government for the magic month of August, however, it feels like the centre of the world.

Which makes it all the more of a shame when, as the bank holiday weekend draws nearer, the Perrier Award – referred to with wry deference in some comedic circles as 'The Little Bottle of Water' – casts an ever-longer shadow over the festivities. Especially as the Perrier is no Delphic oracle; it's just the collective opinion of a couple of people who have won competitions in magazines, the odd resting TV producer and a handful of ambitious journalists (usually with one of Alan Coren's children prominent among them).

The comedy awards which really matter are the ones on ITV on the first Saturday in December.

---

85. The pre-lapsarian metropolitan pomposity which Radio 1 DJ's Mark and Lard send up so effectively (if a decade after the fact) by referring to the nation's capital as 'London village'.

4. The British Comedy Awards

'I've been round the back, fisting Norman Lamont'
Julian Clary, British Comedy Awards, 1993

Most of the ever-proliferating number of showbiz prize-giving ceremonies prefer to stay as far away as possible from the essence of
the art form they are supposed to be celebrating. But the British
Comedy Awards – in its heady blend of acerbic wit, rampant egotism and breath-taking cruelty – is just about as complete a reflection
of the world it was created to celebrate as can be contained in a
small box in the corner of your living-room.[86] And all this at the
behest of London Weekend Television, a station renowned – in
recent years at least – for its almost complete inability to produce
anything like a functional TV comedy programme.

So how did this unlikely paragon of verisimilitude come about?

'The first year [1990],' remembers host Jonathan Ross, 'Michael
Parkinson presented the show from the London Palladium, and it
died on its arse. The next year . . .' he continues, gulping modestly,
'I guess I needed the money.'

It should be remembered at this point that the Jonathan Ross of
the early nineties was a long way from the all-conquering career
behemoth of the early years of the twenty-first century. In fact, as
things went increasingly awry for him, the Comedy Awards would
gradually end up as the only time in the year when – with a little
help from its hugely influential scriptwriter Danny Baker[87] – you
could see Ross on TV at his best.

[86.] Those lucky enough to attend the party afterwards have borne witness to
scenes of decadence which would make W. C. Fields, if not Fellini, blush.
Ulrika Jonsson trampling people in her urgency to escort Roland Rivron to the
lift was only the start of it. 'In the mid-nineties,' Jonathan Ross remembers,
'the place was awash with cocaine, though obviously I have no evidence to
substantiate that, other than going into the toilet and seeing all the male cast
members from a very successful US sitcom coming out of the same cubicle.'

[87.] One of the British Comedy Awards' most memorable moments of pure
anarchy came when Michael Barrymore – in early-nineties loose-cannon
mode – forcibly unplugged Ross's autocue, as if to say 'Let's see how
good you are without it'. Needless to say, he pulled through.

'ITV were a little nervous about it,' he remembers of the show in the first year he took it over, 'and if you looked at what they did the year before, you could see why. Danny Baker had written this script and it was really verbose but also really bold. I stuck my neck out and insisted we use it, and it sort of snowballed from there. Whenever anyone complains about getting a hard time, we just say "It's the spirit of the roast" [the roast being an American tradition where everyone gets slagged off and has to pretend they don't mind] and coming out into that kind of atmosphere seems to help everyone rise to their best potential.'

Why does he think it works so well?

'It's quite an interesting thing to do to comedians – to have them coming out for a minute and a half, not knowing what I'm going to be saying to them. They're kind of a bit on edge and they all want to make an impression, so inevitably they end up pushing things a bit further.'

Sometimes, as in the semi-legendary 1993 case of Julian Clary, they go a little too far. (Clary's famously outrageous response to Ross's innocent enquiry as to what he had been up to was that he had been 'out the back, fisting [fellow awards presenter and former Chancellor of the Exchequer] Norman Lamont'.) While Clary's *coup de théâtre* earned him the undying respect of 99 per cent of those watching, it certainly didn't do his chances of filling Bruce Forsyth's shoes as host of a revitalized *Generation Game* any favours.

'But with some people,' Ross insists (Ricky Gervais and Johnny Vegas in 2001 would presumably be prime examples), 'you could identify their appearance at the Comedy Awards as the moment where they stepped forward to claim a wider audience.' Whether or not it's true that, as Ross contends, 'you can basically predict how someone's year's going to go from the kind of impression they make in that minute and a half', there is no denying that the British Comedy Awards offer the ambitious comedian a stage unlike any other.

From the risky but ultimately triumphant (Gervais making comic capital out of his producer's wheelchair, or Spike Milligan calling the heir to the throne a 'little grovelling bastard' while accepting a lifetime achievement award) to the just plain disastrous (Jerry Springer trying to make a move on Rachel Weisz without knowing that she was someone he was meant to have heard of springs to mind at this point),[88] there is an authentic sense of spontaneous high drama about the British Comedy Awards' most memorable moments. And that is something the Oscars – never mind the BAFTAs – would do well to emulate.

5. Back at comedy base camp

By the mid-1990s, the London Comedy Store – once the spiritual home of alternative comedy – is firmly re-established in new, college-bar-style premises on the other side of Leicester Square. Going there on a random Thursday night at this point is a bit like going to The Cavern three years after The Beatles left, except that in this case the old stars still turn up to perform at the drop of a benefit-collecting hat.

The sense of being part of a living heritage attraction is hardly dispelled by the discovery that half the front row are students from Middlesex University completing their comedy module. Though it is sometimes hard to avoid the feeling that the waters of the London comedy scene have been drastically over-fished, two out of six acts on this particular evening have got something special about them, and that is a pretty heartening percentage.

It's easy to see how Open Mike contender Ardal O'Hanlon managed to come equal first in the Hackney Empire New Act of the Year contest. Where some Comedy Store regulars just seem to be going through the motions, he is polished and graceful and makes every one of his ten minutes count. There is a beguiling feel of genuine otherworldliness about his reminiscences of a dad who spent all his money on the horses – 'he bought them hats and scarves and everything'.

Harry Hill is a little further down the comedy conveyor belt at

---

[88.] The memory of a brazenly worse for wear Caroline Aherne shouting 'get on with it' at an ailing Nigel Hawthorne – making one of his last public appearances in front of a suitably sycophantic crowd to decorously accept an award on behalf of Alan Bennett – is so painful it has had to be relegated to a footnote.

this stage, with one Radio 4 series behind him and a series of short black-and-white films coming up on BBC2. He's got a distinctive look: rosy cheeks, milk-bottle specs and huge shirt collar sprouting out of the top of his jacket, giving him the appearance of a man with no neck. His act has a lovely rhythm to it. Hill sets up a series of riffs – snatches of Queen lyrics, ways of coping with the lack of services on the M40, his father depriving him of the best cuts of meat by saying they were poisonous – and flits between them with blinking eyes and darting tongue. For now, it's hard to predict where his headlong comic momentum might take him, but there is a definite hint of lizard, as well as Izzard, in this man's demeanour.

6
The Illusion (or Otherwise) of Spontaneity

Eddie Izzard and Phil Kay play different 'danger edges'

'I prefer everyone to know exactly what I'm doing, because that means I'm good at what I can do, rather than what people think I can do'

Eddie Izzard

'I took some MC squared: it's great, it's just like E'

Phil Kay

One of the most striking things about watching Eddie Izzard perform at the Albery Theatre in the winter of 1994, is how much easier it is to keep your mind on his comedy – now that he sports a ruffled shirt and thigh-length Dick Whittington boots – than it used to be when he was crammed into conventionally mannish garb. He just seems so much more physically relaxed for having publicly established himself as a transvestite. Going to see him live a couple of years previously, before the secret of his sartorial leanings was out, Izzard's body seemed to be struggling to escape from a stone-washed denim prison.

The confidence which comes from commercial and critical success (specifically 1993's triumphant residency at another West End theatre, the Ambassadors) seems to have made him more disciplined, not less. He hasn't curbed his rambling, manic digressive style, just tightened up the rhythm slightly. The freshness of Izzard's comedic menu is remarkable, too, not only for how quickly he rustles it up, but also for the familiarity of its ingredients: advertising; launderettes; the relative suavity of cats and dogs. As served by any other comedian, this would be pretty stale pub fare, but in Eddie's hands, it's Michelin-star material.

Izzard's chief comic gift is the ability to weave vivid mental tapestries out of the dullest strands of quotidian normality: from the infectious rage of a small dog to the joy of turning on in-car heating at exactly the right moment. Only rarely does his fluid wit solidify into quotable shapes (e.g. on the moral dilemmas of supermarket shopping: 'One jam is made by Nazis out of mud and twigs, the other is made by rabbits out of fruit that agreed to be in it'). But sometimes, when he pulls himself up in mid-flow, there is the same sense you used to get with Robin Williams in his (pre-Hollywood) prime, of the audience racing to catch up with a mind that's already two blocks ahead of them.

It's funny talking to Eddie Izzard in person around this time: 'funny' in the sense of being held up in the visa-application queue at the border crossing between the kingdoms of 'Ha Ha' and 'Peculiar'. This is not because of anything particular he himself does. He is very quick and open, and if you find yourself lapsing into one of those embarrassingly complicated questions which starts off asking one thing and ends up asking another, he will probably answer both parts, shrugging off any attempt at interrogatory clarification with a friendly but firm 'I thought I got what you meant'. What hits you about Izzard is just how much those people who really like him – and it's hard to find anyone who's seen him perform who doesn't, at this point – tend to build his speech patterns into their own.

The deliberate pauses that say 'Ah yes, where was I?' (like brief suburban station stops to remind you that your train of thought is heading for the seaside). So many people go in for these now – not just other comedians (although there are plenty of these doing it too) but normal human beings – that when talking to the man with whom they originated, it almost feels like he's been ripped off.

Eddie's sartorial innovations have been less widely imitated. Today's look comprises calf-length leather boots, black leggings (which are almost tights), and an emerald blue sweat-top whose buttons fall open, somewhat distractingly, to reveal a silky white shoulder strap. It would be wrong to pay so much attention to the Izzard wardrobe if it didn't seem expressly designed to be noticed. I saw him in Marks & Spencer on Oxford Street once, wearing a jacket that Tammy Wynette would have thought twice about.

Such chance sightings, or onstage in record-breaking theatrical engagements, are no longer the only way to see Eddie Izzard. He has started to turn up on TV, too, which makes this a crucial passage in his career, as, apart from being a transvestite, the thing he's been best known for is refusing to appear on television.

After a much hyped but almost entirely disastrous start on Comic Relief, there's been a disruptively flirtatious and very funny showing on *Have I Got News for You*, a brisk little star-trip at the British Comedy Awards, a slightly awkward chat show début on *Ruby Wax* ('She said "You can go anywhere you like on the set" and I thought, Oh shit, that's too much choice') and then a brutal perfect six on Clive Anderson. On balance, it would be fair to say that the small screen seems to like him.

'Not being on TV almost became like a religious thing,' Eddie admits, backing this point up with one of his trademark extrapolations in indirect speech – ' "Thou must not go on telly, I will never go on telly, I will kill them all with swords".' This unusual act of self-denial seems to have been based on an almost excessively conscientious approach to the Comedic Diversification Strategy (a) (as expounded in the last chapter).

'My whole position', Izzard explains, 'was that I wanted to do straight acting, and if I went on telly and it worked, then I'd have a whole load of comedy baggage that I couldn't get rid of.[89] If Paul

---

[89.] This way of looking at things receives support from an unlikely quarter in the ebullient person of Kathy Burke, who – despite catching the eye and ear of London's emerging comedy mafia from the moment she first came up with immortal darts-fixated super-slattern Tina Bishop for Rowland Rivron's Raw Sex troupe (a pre-Bob Mortimer Vic Reeves even asked her to be his comedy wife, though she doesn't seem to mind that nothing came of it) – was always wary of going 'too far down that comedy road'.

'I never wanted to be one of that lot who "started out doing cabaret",' she maintains. 'I like it to be known that I was always an actress.' And for all Burke's subsequent comic *coups* – as hardbitten media empress Magda in *Absolutely Fabulous*, tragic teenager Perry (her own creation: 'He was based on this lad I knew called Perry') and iconic bad mother Waynetta

Merton did Hamlet now,' he continues, apparently in all seriousness (I for one, to borrow the immortal words of Paul Calf's student
friend Roland, 'would rather see Dave Lee Travis play Macbeth'),
'people would probably just be going "to be or not to be ...
but in a brown suit" – they'd get all mixed up because his persona is so large. I just thought if I stayed off TV, it might work
better.'

The fact that he's played two major theatrical roles in the past
few months suggests the plan might be working. Izzard's big step
up from spear-carrier in a school play to West End lead in David
Mamet's *The Cryptogram* was, in his own characteristically realistic
assessment, 'Not an unqualified success, but not the complete
embarrassment it might have been, either'. At the very least, it
established 'a certain believability in the fact that I can act'.

He's not at the Robbie Coltrane or Keith Allen level yet [historical
note: in the mid-nineties, Keith Allen was a successful TV actor,
not someone who wasted his time writing pointless plays about
Glastonbury with semi-retired conceptual artists], but he's working
on it. In fact, Izzard is perfectly happy to admit that 'they are where
I want to fucking get to'.

It's not something you'd guess from his amiable, meandering
onstage demeanour, but in person Eddie Izzard is one of the most
fiercely and openly ambitious people you could ever encounter –
the sort of scarily focused individual whose reading is mainly
composed of the autobiographies of film stars and great war leaders,
so he can 'see how they did it'.[90] When you're in a room talking to
him, it's almost as if there are actually three people there: you,
Eddie and Eddie's ambition, and if you had to pick out which of
the trio was calling the shots, you would probably guess it was the
last one.

Slob on *Harry Enfield's Television Programme* – she has steadfastly refused
to jump the thespian ship. This won't stop all those who enjoyed her
brilliant cameo as an egotistical guest star in the second series of *Happiness*
(and a powerhousedly potty-mouthed off-the-cuff display at the 2002
Comedy Awards) from hoping that she might one day forsake *Gimme
Gimme Gimme* for a role in a fully fledged comedy.

[90.] If you hadn't seen him live, you might almost be tempted to think he had
no sense of humour.

The roots of his almost frightening capacity to apply himself run deep: 'There are two types of people,' Izzard insists, 'some who'd quite like to get something going, and others who *have* to . . . and I sort of had to.' The traumatic circumstances of his early life – Eddie was born in Yemen in 1962, and by the time he was six he'd moved from Northern Ireland to Wales to Bexhill-on-Sea, his mother had died and he'd been sent away to boarding-school – seem to have given him an appetite (creatively at least) for running towards the danger.

Izzard's career up to this point has combined ruthless calculation with devil-may-care aplomb (the latter honed over years of sword-fighting, escapology and 'talking bollocks from a unicycle' to the backs of retreating crowds in shopping centres from Peterborough to Worthing). 'The "don't give a damn thing",' he says fondly, 'you need to bottle that . . . they were Hell Gigs, but learning to survive them mentally gave me a safe sheet of ice.'

He seems to refer just about everything he does – from running his own Raging Bull club in the seedy heart of Soho to breaking out of comedy into straight acting – back to these formative years as a street-entertainer. But there is no precedent there for the issue he is currently addressing, which is whether the TV exposure he now feels he can allow himself will tarnish the distinctive Izzard mystique.

The idea of a comedian saying no to any form of self-advancement, even if he's only doing so out of a more evolved form of self-interest, is certainly a beguiling one. Watching Eddie being a TV comedy personality on *Ruby Wax*, there's definitely an extra edge of piquancy to that familiar feeling of disappointment you get when you see someone do part of their act on a chat show as if they've just thought it up.

Izzard insists he is not going to make a habit of doing this, but transvestism – the issue in hand – was too important to take chances with. 'For me to get on there and talk about being TV [he favours this insider abbreviation even though – or perhaps because – it confuses more people than it reassures] in a relaxed way, and be fuck-off about it, that was my whole plan. Somebody watching out there who's TV and just thinks that they're the abominable snowman could maybe use that . . .'

Presumably there aren't an infinite number of ways of saying something that is important to you in an amusing way?

'If I find one that works,' Eddie acknowledges with feeling, 'I'm pretty pleased.'

One of the things that makes Eddie Izzard such an exciting comedian to watch is the sense that his set is evolving as you watch it. It would be a mistake to run too far with this particular baton, though. 'What I do does have a feel of spontaneity because I start out going "right, now . . . fish . . . er . . . fish",' he explains, 'but I always know roughly where I'm going to end up. The unfortunate thing is if people think it's totally improvised, then when they realize it isn't, they'll think I'm letting them down.'

So he's not happy if people think he's making the whole thing up on the spot?

'No, I prefer everyone to know exactly what I'm doing, because that means I'm good at what I can do rather than what people *think* I can do.'

However honest he is about the amount of preparation that goes into what he does, people still seem to have something invested in the idea that he's plucking it all out of the air as he goes along. Eddie's act was recently described in the following (somewhat florid) terms: 'Like the bumblebee who hasn't studied aerodynamics and therefore doesn't know the impossibility of it all, he flies.' But this particular bumblebee has actually studied aerodynamics very hard indeed, as the following full-stop-free statement of comic practice makes abundantly clear.

'When you first come up with some new material,' Eddie explains, 'it tends to be a bit clunky, and then you suddenly click into an angle so that when you're doing it you think "Oh, here comes this bit again" and you really power up to it, and the audience feels excited because you're obviously giving it a whole bunch of energy, and then you find that you can ad-lib it and go off at tangents, adding new bits all the time,[91] so at the beginning the whole

---

[91.] The only first-hand description of what it actually feels like to be a comedian on top of your game I can remember to rival this came from Alan Davies (with whom Eddie Izzard has several things in common, not least childhood trauma, both men having lost their mothers to illness at a very early age).

thing is really loose and unset, but then, after you've done it about twenty or thirty times, it starts getting laid in concrete . . .' He almost pauses for breath at this point, but then thinks better of it. 'So my idea was to artificially keep this beginning period going for as long as possible – constantly twisting the material, coming in backwards and spinning it round until it gets as good as it's going to get – then record it and hopefully move on.'

In the winter of 1995, Eddie embarks upon a nationwide tour every bit as gruelling as that last sentence. Starting out with the final version of his Albery Theatre set, as preserved for posterity on the video *Unrepeatable* ('The point of a video is that it *should* be repeatable, it's the *material* that's unrepeatable'), he hopes by the tour's April close to have a new two-hour show, ready to take into the West End at the conclusion of the following year. By this con-stant process of urbane renewal, Eddie Izzard says he hopes to be able to continue doing stand-up 'until he drops dead'.

Does he draw mental diagrams of his set so he knows which bits to work on? 'No, it's just a vague head thing. I know I've got to change it, and I'm always seeing stuff when I'm on tour. Like last time I saw birds migrating, and I thought, I've got to talk about this, because it is amazing, and it took me ages . . . Normally you work on an idea for about five gigs and if it doesn't work, then you dump it, but I'd held on to this for about twenty shows and in the end I got to this nice thing of them migrating but not actually getting anywhere because this big bird at the front, who's the leader, has got the map blown all over his face by the wind and can't actually see where he's going.'

The thing Eddie Izzard is trying to get to, like a stand-up Gary Larson cartoon or an animated version of a Steven Wright one-liner, often seems to involve stretching nature to the point where it twangs back again. 'People are sitting there, and I'm giving out information

'You're very rarely thinking about what you're actually doing,' Davies admits, 'it's the next thing and the next thing. That line didn't work, so that other one in twenty minutes probably isn't going to go down too well either . . . Why's that person not laughing? I'll go over there for a minute. OK, they're laughing now so I'll come back. The best thing is when a weak line gets a big laugh and you know you've got a really good one coming up and you're thinking, Wait for it.'

to them so they can paint mental pictures,' he explains, 'like the wolves in the car driving along and shouting at antelope – the reason why it works is that I seem able to give out just the right amount of information-glue for the image to stick in your mind.'

The hallmark of his comedy might be identified by someone at the sort of universities where people get paid taxpayers' money to talk about these things in a totally humourless way as a kind of 'hyperactive anthropomorphism'. By this means, characters and voices – ranging from Roger Moore to Stanley Holloway – can be assigned with equal assurance to huskies, flecks of falling fluff or a blue item of underwear in a white wash-load.

Izzard would be the last person to claim a patent on this technique. He is happy to admit to learning from other comedians, freely citing Richard Pryor (especially the second *Live* video and *Live on Sunset Boulevard*, 'when he'd just got back from Africa and had stopped using the word "nigger"') as the fount of his talking-animal routines. Steve Martin and Billy Connolly – 'his stuff is always a story that he's told, as opposed to a gag about two men going into a pub' – are others who get inspirational credit.

But however open he is about his influences, there is still something unique about the dynamic of Eddie Izzard's career. Other comedians use videos as a way of making a bit of extra money at Christmas. For Izzard, they're a means of disciplining himself: a way of making sure he has to keep coming up with new material.

When it comes to using the release of *Unrepeatable* as a spur to construct a completely new show, Eddie Izzard is as good as his word. And it's fascinating to observe the way his act develops between the aforementioned Albery season and his next, extended West End run – a couple of hundred yards away at the Shaftesbury Theatre – twenty months later. Not least because, as the developing myth of his own creativity feeds back into Izzard's perception of himself, his own theories of comedic fluidity almost seem at risk of becoming set in concrete.

Never mind the theories of comedic fluidity, where's the bar?

In his choices of venue, as in many things, Izzard's judgement is on the cunning side of sound. Theatres are better places for comedians to play than rock clubs; not just for their own status, but also for that of their audience, who get to feel cooler than a theatre crowd instead of less cool than a rock one. The only potential drawback is overcome with seven magic words: 'drinks may be taken into the auditorium'.

When Eddie upgrades to the much larger Shaftesbury Theatre, the mid-nineties opening night A-list – from Terry Christian and Mariella Frostrup at the top to Elvis Presley and Lord Lucan at the bottom – turns out in force. Not to be outdone for razzmatazz, the star of the show swaps his usual low-key arrival onstage for what he precisely terms a 'coming-out-of-a-book entrance'.

The covers of a huge fibreglass tome pull apart to reveal a flight of white steps. Atop them sits a blue armchair, in which reclines the resplendent figure of Eddie, the principal boy, a vision in PVC and distressed suede. While Izzard himself glistens like a newly hatched turtle, the whole book business strikes a disturbing note.

The programme introduces us to the great works of literature (the authors include Chekhov, D. H. Lawrence, Lewis Carroll and Spike Milligan) from which pages will be projected on to the open volume behind him. There is something strangely galling about the idea that just because Eddie has chosen – rather late in life, some might argue[92] – to discover the joys of creative reading, we in the audience should automatically wish to hold his hand as he embarks upon this great journey.

Happily, he opts not to offer us a tutorial in practical criticism. Happier still, fears that – amid the excitement of his actually getting some work as an actor – Eddie Izzard might have forgotten to write any new stuff, or that having 'drunk from the big TV-cup' might have diminished his mystique in some way, soon prove groundless.

Some of the tricks of his trade – the chasing himself around the

---

[92.] Though in this connection it should be remembered that he does suffer from dyslexia.

stage, the distracted manner as disguise for ruthless planning and extreme mental agility – are growing familiar. And there is the odd moment (especially when he starts to get on non-linguists' wicks by doing stuff in French) at which the needle starts to flicker fractionally towards 'been there, done that'.

But when he's got a new thing going (as he has for most of this show) – the Corinthians bemoaning their choice of St Paul as a penpal, or a savage assault on the integrity of blacksmiths – he is still in a class of his own. And one piece of speculative comic fluff plucked from the deep orange of Izzard's jacket ('If Buddhists and extreme Protestants live in the same area,' he muses, 'one of them must wear an away strip') turns out to be philosophy in whimsy's clothing. Which is odd, because the search for a subtext in this man's material generally goes unrewarded.

Some might say that in running a non-controversial gamut from the queue at the late-night garage to the relative merits of oranges and satsumas, Izzard embodies the apolitical narcissism of Majorite middle youth. But the fact is that inside this mild-mannered con-sumerist paragon there is an old-fashioned righteous liberal scream-ing to get out. ('Why do these people always go around in groups of five?' Izzard observes of those who hunt in packs on the streets in search of women – or men in women's clothes – to harass and humiliate. 'Perhaps it's because they've only got a fifth of a personal-ity each.')

In extending Izzard the licence to wear, say and be exactly what he wants, his audience are drawing a linc between themselves and the uptight denizens of the 1980s. That's not to say his appeal is time-specific, but the occasional flashes of conceit which are creep-ing into his act by the mid-nineties are an understandable conse-quence of having come to represent (to himself as much as his audience) an ideal of unfettered self-expression.

His fans just love to watch Eddie Izzard pushing his luck, which is why, when a button falls off his jacket early in the second half of his Shaftesbury Theatre opening night, he feels not just able but actively *obliged* to sew it laboriously back on in front of 1,400 people.

'I went out on a limb, and there was no arm there'

'He plays a different danger edge from mine,' Eddie observes generously of mercurial Glaswegian Phil Kay, his surprise – but worthy – successor as Top Live Stand-up at the 1994 Comedy Awards (for all his self-confessed monomania, Eddie is never short of a good word to say about one or other of his contemporaries), 'in that you really don't know what he's going to do next, whereas I always try and have a back-up of prepared material which I can nail to a tree if things start to get ugly.'

When things go well for him, the hyperactive, straggle-headed Kay can run a packed house ragged – harrying them into the pen marked laughter with the same innocent pleasure in his own facility as a champion sheep-dog. Like his fellow Scot, Billy Connolly, he has the ability to take a crowd to a place it didn't expect to go before it even knows it's left. Only at the odd moment – when a runaway train of thought hits the buffers, and Kay looks around, blinks and says, 'Where am I?' – do you realize how fast he has been moving.

Kay's greatest strength lies not so much in his material – a winning blend of observational scatology and high-octane flummery ('In Glasgow, three out of four women . . . is most of them') – as in the strength of his life-force. Whether surfing on an ironing board, or charging back and forth into the audience with heroic disregard for the potentially life-threatening cat's cradle of microphone lead which results, his irrepressible physicality seems to magnify the audience's energy and reflect it back at them.

The first time I see him perform, at the 1994 Edinburgh Festival, the whole room is exhilarated, hanging delightedly on to his every word as he drags them hither and thither with joyful abandon. Towards the end of the show, someone pulls him up, in a friendly way, on a minor factual inconsistency between two rambling reminiscences. For a couple of seconds, Kay is left stranded in mid-air, like a cartoon character who suddenly looks down to see a canyon. Sometimes when this happens he peers down into the abyss, swivels and jauntily scampers back to safety, but on this occasion he plummets, and is only saved from a painful landing by a generous cushion of laughter.

A few weeks later, on a rare promotional trip to London, Kay is already looking back on this moment with fondness. 'I went out on a limb,' he observes cheerfully, 'and there was no arm there.'

'Comedy is not one of the arts,' the denim-clad Kay continues, somewhat controversially. 'It can be as good as anything while it's happening, but moments after, it's gone.' Maybe this very fleetingness explains why so many of this . . . [*well, what is it if it's not an art? Please let it at least be a*] . . . craft's leading practitioners seem to work so hard at making a career out of it.

It's not often you encounter a performer who actually savours that impermanence, but Phil Kay is that elusive beast: a comedian whose eyes do not light up at the idea of a sixty-nine-date tour (the sort of commitment a standard-issue comedy career progression would definitely demand of him). 'Even if someone said it was the last sixty-nine gigs I would ever have to do,' he insists, aghast, 'I *swear to God* I couldn't do it.'

As befits the philosophy graduate that he claims to be, Kay thinks a lot about the things he can't – or won't, or just doesn't – do. 'I'm *very* aware of what I'm not doing,' he says, 'which is a really good, dependable act.'

Having seen him on a less-than-great night too, I can confirm that there is no false modesty involved in this statement. 'I'm not totally in control,' Kay admits brazenly. 'I haven't got much that's solid . . . There aren't many classic jokes.' (The nearest he comes to a traditional Bob Monkhouse-type one-liner is a passing reference to an erotic vision of Marti Pellow – 'my first Wet Wet Wet dream'.) He does have a great way with a disruptive influence, though, when the mood of the room is right. 'You look a bit like me, too,' he muses on one occasion at a young woman with a perm who had the temerity to speak out of turn when he was in full flow, 'I figure maybe you're a method heckler.'

'When it's going well,' Kay explains, 'you can do the things that make people say, "Hey wow, how do you dare do that?", but you can only do it because they were laughing in the first place.' Once that elusive little thrill of almost physical pleasure is set up between himself and a crowd, Kay will try to keep it going for a bit longer and a bit longer – 'like a ping-pong ball on a fountain' is how he describes it – until it feels as if there is no limit to what he can achieve.

On the first of his six nights at the 800-seater Queen's Hall in August 1995, Kay pulls off the most amazing comedic *coup* I have ever seen. A couple of minutes in, a rowdy hen party begins to make its presence felt. Instead of picking them up, wringing a couple of laughs out of them and then dropping them unceremoniously to show who's boss, as most comedians would, Kay sets his intended theme for the evening completely to one side, and devotes his whole performance to staging a fabulous mock wedding.

He painstakingly assembles a groom – 'an honest, poor, working-class, one-armed man' – flowers, best man, bridesmaids, trans-aisle grudges, the whole bit, and fearlessly carries the entire service through to its conclusion, without a hint of anti-climax. Kay's genius is to create a situation in which the entire crowd can participate, and then to remember things about it that everyone else has forgotten. Fifteen minutes after picking on someone upstairs for sitting with their arms crossed, Kay is a priest conducting the marriage service – 'In the sight of the Lord and the strange grumpy man'.

Being more than usually dependent on the goodwill of the people who have come to see you does have its downside, though. 'I never like to judge an audience,' he says warily of an especially painful appearance at Malcolm Hardee's less than indulgent Up The Creek club in Deptford, 'and I don't blame them for not laughing at me, but I think because it was Saturday night and they'd paid ten quid, they expected more conventional gags. Everyone was booing and I just carried on for about twenty minutes thinking I would get through it, but I didn't.'

Happily, the burden of people paying money to see him does not weigh too heavily on Kay's shoulders.

'I like to ignore that responsibility and do really well,' he enthuses. 'Though obviously it's not so good if – as I do regularly – you ignore that responsibility and do really badly.'

Isn't it exhausting though, feeling that he has to come up with something new every time he goes onstage?

'It's not tiring to be creative,' Kay insists. 'It's not tiring to be excited. What's tiring for me is thinking, Oh God, I'll have to go through that certain bit which I have to say first, knowing that at any moment I might find that I just can't be bothered.'

When it comes to stripping the engine of comedy down to its bare spark-plugs, Kay's exasperated onstage expostulation – 'It's like . . . What's it like? Something that's the same' – is right up there with John Peel's immortally pissed-off deconstruction of the essence of pop radio. 'You're listening to Radio 1, I'm John Peel, and you're you.'

The problem with spontaneity is that it's hard to get it to work consistently. And the problem with building the audience into your act is that the chances are they're not as funny as you. That's why your relationship with them is as it is.

But even on a middling night, twelve months after his matrimonial triumph, Kay's mix of occasionally inspired stock jokes ('I took some MC squared: it's great, it's just like E!') and frequent flights of conceptual fancy take him somewhere special. The twinkliest star in the whole Edinburgh firmament, he orbits the stage at a bewildering speed, and there's a routine about the roar of flashbulbs at Olympic medal ceremonies – and everyone taking that shard of time and space home with them and thus crinkling the fabric of the universe – which is worthy of Nobel Prize-winning scientist Andy Kaufman. Or even the great Vegas club act, Bert Einstein.

The curse of impro(v)

On the day I meet him, Phil Kay has just decided not to do a voice-over for a Campbell's soup ad. 'I know it's a lot of money for not very much work,' he grins, his voice (as always) speeding up as it gets to the meat of a sentence, 'but if I did one, I'd end up doing another and then another . . .'

It's strange that the more money people make, the more things they seem to end up doing just for the money.

'*Exactly* . . . It ought to be the other way round.'

Refusing the blandishments of the big London-based agencies, cancelling clutches of live dates so that he can go to Chile to watch a solar eclipse, Phil Kay's is what might respectfully be termed an anti-career.

An attempt to package what he does finally makes it on to Channel 4 in 1997, and while *Phil Kay Feels* . . . has bags more panache than most live comedy on TV, the sense that you are missing out on something by watching from home is not generally the stuff of small-screen ratings smashes. Subsequently, Kay's moment seems to pass, and his comedic achievements go on to become the beautiful memory he probably always meant them to be.

While the legend of the Flying-by-the-seat-of-his-pants Scotsman embodies all the best possibilities of comedic spontaneity, the worst are conveniently contained within one word – 'impro' (or 'improv', for those who think adding a 'v' makes the whole concept sound a little less late-eighties). The eclipse of this gruesome manifestation of collective smugness is one of the most welcome developments of the early nineties, so when Eddie Izzard returns to the Albery Theatre in 1996 with a group show called *One Word Improv*, it seems like a wilful step backwards.

Amid a sensory blizzard of pounding music, revolving back-projections and dazzling arc-lights, a quartet of enigmatic figures emerges from a primal fug of dry ice. What imposing gladiatorial spectacle is it that we are to be offered? Not a full-scale Spandau Ballet reunion, but four comedians making stuff up in response to words shouted out from the audience.

You can see the logic behind *One Word Improv*'s grand opening. If ever a comedic genre has been in need of a glamour injection, improvisation is that genre – the televisual novelty of *Whose Line Is It Anyway?* having now worn off to such an extent that controlled screenings are being used by Special Branch to extract confessions from tight-lipped child criminals. But what of the show itself? Surely it's not so much flogging a dead horse as disinterring its long-buried corpse and parading it through the streets dressed as a clown?

It certainly seems that way at first. As the crowd's painfully unfunny suggestions compete for the improvisers' straining ears, the overall experience feels rather like trying to share a bad joke with a deaf uncle. Once things settle down, however, the quartet of Mark 'Carling Black Label advert' Frost, Neil 'Once worked with Mike Myers' Mullarkey, Suki 'No previous form to speak of' Webster and Eddie 'Never off the bloody TV' Izzard turns out to be quite nicely balanced.

Fears that the Izzard ego has expanded to such an extent that there might be insufficient room on the stage for other performers prove happily unfounded, and each of the four has their moment – Webster exhibiting an unnerving gift for off-the-cuff rhyme, Mullarkey naming eighteenth-century British generals after building societies and Frost belabouring Izzard with a beanbag one more time than the star of the show seems to find amusing. It's certainly the man wearing the metallic blue trousers that everyone has come to see, but Izzard is a surprisingly – and agreeably – unobtrusive presence, almost as if listening to himself do this for a month has helped him get rid of some of the self-regarding mannerisms that were beginning to make him annoying.

The notorious improv audience has sadly made no such adjustment. Observing the foolish expression on the face of the man in the row in front of me as he repeatedly shouts the word 'underpants', it's hard to resist the conclusion that – notwithstanding the sterling efforts of Izzard and co. to render it socially acceptable – this is a form of entertainment which really ought to be outlawed by governmental decree. (Happily, a few months later, the European Parliament steps in, and impro – and, indeed, improv – is banned by law.)

What Eddie did next

'You can be good,' Eddie Izzard has often been heard to aver while pondering his next career move, 'or you can be fast.' No one was going to accuse Eddie of rushing his eternally awaited Channel 4 sitcom, *The Cows*.

'It's now about a group of cows moving into a street, and how they get on with the people there who don't know many cows,' he proclaims boldly in 1995, after the project has been in development for approximately three eons. 'It'll either be great or it'll be a pile of shit . . .'

Unfortunately, when the by-then quasi-mythical bovine enterprise finally limps on to the screen a year and a half later, it's the latter of those two possible eventualities which has come to pass (for a happier resolution of the great/pile-of-shit dichotomy, see Caroline Aherne's *The Royle Family*).

Inside the Henson Corporation-designed cow suits for which Channel 4 commissioning editor Seamus Cassidy has mortgaged his organic almond farm in Andalucia, lurks a veritable who's who of comedy acting talent – Sally Phillips of *Smack the Pony* semi-fame and the legendary Kevin (pronounced, in the Gallic manner, Ke-*van*) Eldon.[93] Sadly no one can see who they are, and the script doesn't have one leg to stand on, let alone four.

'At that stage,' Izzard's agent Caroline Chignell remembers a few years later, 'Eddie was absolutely determined to prove that he had the skills and the application to be a writer.[94] I think as it turned out,' she continues sensibly, 'it [meaning the huge Bronx cheer with which *The Cows* was eventually greeted] was probably the best thing that could possibly have happened.'

Once *The Cows* had been ritually slaughtered, Eddie Izzard was free to concentrate on the things he excelled at. Not by narrowing his horizons – his metabolism seems to require new challenges as regular mortals demand tea and toast – but by expanding his stand-up empire world-wide, to include Paris and Broadway, eventually winning a well-deserved Emmy for a US TV special in 2000. His acting got better, too. Though his thespian excursions do tend to elicit the worryingly uniform response of 'Oh look, there's Eddie Izzard in something else', he was actually quite good as the sleazy manager in *Velvet Goldmine*.

A time would come in the late nineties, however, when grown adults would actually break down in tears at the prospect of seeing Eddie Izzard on one more chat show hotly justifying his perfectly legitimate individual preference for feminine apparel on the grounds that 'women wear trousers'. As if centuries of underground resistance to patriarchal oppression culminating in Katherine Hepburn

---

93. Eldon's career – as demented hobbyist Simon Quinlank and the choleric 'Real' Rod Hull in Lee and Herring's *Fist of Fun*, chief stoker on *Big Train*, Chris Morris's actorly accomplice, and superb bad poet Paul Hamilton in *Club Zarathustra* – deserves a chapter in itself. Unfortunately, it's not going to get one here.
94. In fact, he was having well-founded doubts about this vocation as early as 1995, admitting candidly that he 'sometimes despaired of disciplining himself in that area' and blaming 'the lack of instant response' and 'a problem with creativity without adrenalin'.

wearing a tweed suit to play golf and making it OK for men and women to live as equals somehow correlated exactly with Eddie's desire to go shopping dressed as Julie Goodyear.[95]

By the winter of 2003, with Izzard gearing up inexorably for another gruelling live tour (unpromisingly dubbed 'Sexie') and video interface, and Phil Kay last sighted in the comedy tent at the Reading Festival eighteen months earlier – sniffing an audience member's Poppers 'to see what will happen' – it is hard to resist the conclusion that in the comedy business, a little bit of spontaneity will get you further than a lot.

[95.] Perhaps sensing that this particular routine is running out of steam, Izzard starts appearing on TV in men's clothes again, insisting that just because he is a transvestite, that doesn't mean he has to wear women's clothes *all* the time. While cynics might argue that this is not so much having your cake and eating it, as having your cake, eating it, decorously spitting it out into your cupped palm and then taking it back to the bakery for a refund on the grounds that what you really wanted was a doughnut, others of a more idealistic disposition are inclined to use the stipulation that 'transvestites should not be forced to wear women's clothes all the time' as the benchmark of a truly civilized society.

7
It's Frank's (and Chubby's and Jo's and Jenny's) World

The rest of us just live in it

'There was all sorts of dodgy stuff about me being "the backlash" and "symptomatic of the new right" and I thought "No, this is just what the rest of the country is like"'

Frank Skinner

'I don't use Tampax any more, I just roll up the duvet'

Jenny Eclair

A. The boys

'When I won the Perrier Award in 1991,' Frank Skinner remembers, a few years afterwards, 'either the *Independent* or the *Guardian* described me as the closest thing to Bernard Manning ever to win it . . . Because a lot of people who write about comedy haven't seen those acts, when I turned up, they thought I was one of them. But if they went and saw some proper club comedians, they'd see that I am actually very much at the sweet edge, in fact I'm a million miles away from all those people.'

Before he discovered alternative comedy, in the mid-1980s, Skinner had always thought of comics as 'those blokes in between the strippers I never really took much notice of'. Confronted by these sour individuals in bad suits saying vicious things about their Pakistani next-door neighbours in Smethwick working men's clubs,

Skinner's response had generally been to 'have a piss or go to the bar'. So to find himself being bracketed with them when he began to hit the big time a few years later came as a rude shock.

'People would ask me "How long have you been doing the main-stream northern clubs?"' Skinner remembers, the affront still fresh in his mind. 'And in fact I only ever played two of them. I didn't want to do them. I didn't want to go on and tell old gags or do racist and sexist stuff. There's nothing I say onstage that I'd have any cause to feel bad about. It's just that when I first started doing the London circuit in 1988, it was very much a "Thatcher out" type of atmosphere, and I was doing the sort of material I'd done all my life – dirty jokes, football jokes, the sort of stuff that made people laugh at school or at the factory – and the audiences really liked it. The funny thing was,' he continues, 'I used to get reviews where the crowd got a worse slagging than I did – I remember *Time Out* saying "the audience's response to Frank Skinner at the Comedy Store was a cause for despair". There was all sorts of dodgy stuff about me being "the backlash" and "symptomatic of the new right" and I thought "No, this is just what the rest of the country is like".'

The idea that Skinner was somehow out of step with modern thinking was not confined to the critical establishment. Even after receiving a painful lesson in comic timing at his hands at the Edinburgh Festival in 1990, Steve Coogan still wasn't convinced Skinner would ever be anything more than an unusually talented old-fashioned comic.

'I used to think he was really good,' Coogan remembers wryly, 'but he'd never make it because he was too out of line with contemporary opinion.'

In fact, as events would show, Skinner was not behind the times but ahead of them. What happened in the early to mid-1990s was that the unreconstructed West Midlander's idea of 'what the rest of the country is like' took over the commanding heights of the media as well. Put simply, a heady cocktail of football, sex, drink, drugs and Britpop loosened the nation's morals to the point where it was no longer uncommon to find people saying 'fuck' on ITV.

Looking beyond such everyday indicators to the level of national self-image, it would probably be fair to say that Frank Skinner was a key player – along with Paul Gascoigne and Princess Diana – in a ten-year process (beginning with Acid House and ending with Princess Di's funeral) by which Britain went from being one of the world's most famously uptight countries to one of the most emotionally and behaviourally incontinent. How he came to play this role is a question which takes a fair bit of getting to the bottom of.

Frank Skinner is taller in person than he is on television, but nothing else is different. Nattily turned out in a crisp Ben Sherman shirt, well-ironed trousers and gleaming new trainers, only the occasional quiet sniff disrupts his immaculate exterior. In many other comedians, such nasal disturbance would be a worrying hint of incipient drug addiction. Skinner merely has a cold. 'That's me in microcosm, really,' he grins, 'I'm sniffing in an interview and it's not cocaine, it's a Vicks inhaler.'

One of the visions people have of Frank Skinner (not without a little encouragement from the man himself) is as a stalwart defender of the manly values of working-class middle England against the effete corruptions of the metropolitan chattering classes. Yet in conversation, this illusion is swiftly dispelled by a succession of undeniably liberal opinions. 'I don't think it'll make any difference to his career at all,' he says of Michael Barrymore's coming out, which is all over the papers in the week that I meet him. 'He's too funny and too well-loved, and he won't pretend it hasn't happened: he'll take it on the chin.'

A short pause ensues, after which Skinner – far from supplying the salacious punchline which might have been anticipated (ejaculation is, after all, his bread and butter) – embarks on a thoughtful meditation on the progressive broadening of the British public mind. 'This country's come a long way since the Jeremy Thorpe trial,' he muses. 'I remember my parents being perfectly happy with the idea of a bloke in court charged with hiring a hitman to kill a former male model, but the idea of two men having a sexual relationship they found absolutely outrageous.'

It is this very buttoned-upness – at this juncture still widely, if erroneously, believed to be the essence of his homeland's national character – that Frank Skinner's comedy seeks to undo.

The Billy Graham of anal sex

The bare facts of Frank's first thirty-eight years are already in the public domain: blue-collar, Black Country Catholic born and bred, he was expelled from school at sixteen for trying to establish a black market in recycled dinner tickets. He escaped factory work via night school to do a degree, then an MA, in English literature.[96]

He taught at a further-education college for a while, but not before seeing the Sex Pistols play live (because he was the only one shouting for more, Johnny Rotten shook his hand and said 'Thank you') and briefly singing with a band of his own. It was still some years until the Skinner showbiz odyssey began in earnest, but after an inspirational trip to the Edinburgh Festival in 1986, he finally realized he didn't want to wake up old not having had a go himself, and began to tell jokes in public.

'I still remember it very clearly,' he says, his emotions plainly running high, 'the day I had this strange moment when I thought to myself "What would it be like to be seventy and look back and think, If I'd have tried comedy would I have been any good?" That made me quite unnerved. To look back and think, Remember when I tried doing comedy? I died on my arse and had to give up, is fine. But to look back and think, I wonder what would have happened? is terrible.'

Another performer – 'a dog act' – was already registered with Equity under Frank's real name (Chris Collins), so after a career-threatening flirtation with Wes Bromwich, he borrowed Frank Skinner from a man in his dad's pub dominoes team and started travelling round the country with it.[97]

---

96. Frank has often been struck over the years by the reluctance of interviewers to mention his education: 'They obviously think: "Well, that clouds the issue a bit." '

97. Skinner claims to have done this 'without telling his family'. It's interesting in this context that perhaps his most emotionally engaged work on television should be the early-nineties Channel 4 sitcom *Blue Heaven* – which he wrote and co-starred in with seventies sitcom survivor Paula Wilcox and described as 'a love letter to the Black Country'. A moving reflection of Skinner's feelings for his parents, who both died within a few months of each other at the end of the eighties, *Blue Heaven* was not widely seen and didn't get a second series.

'I didn't start doing stand-up comedy till I was thirty,' Skinner recalls ruefully. 'I think if I'd lived in London and realized what was going on, I would probably have gone into it straight from school . . .' But isn't one of the things people like about him that he's someone who's had a life before comedy, rather than hitting the stand-up circuit straight from college?

'Maybe that's true, but I'd rather have had twelve extra years of being a stand-up comedian. The tabloids could have got some fantastic photos of me if I'd been successful earlier on. I got so absolutely blasted so regularly, goodness knows what sort of messes I'd have got into if I'd been going to places like Stringfellows instead of places like Smethwick British Legion . . . You know, Page Three girls rather than people who worked in heavy industry – it would have been nice. And I sort of missed out on that. In fact, there was a time when I thought I'd wasted about fifteen years of my life drinking, messing about with various women, being on the dole and doing rubbish jobs. And then it turned out I'd actually been researching for my later career! So that was a bit of good news.'

As Frank Skinner's slightly hunched figure scuttles back and forth across the stage on one of his endless early-nineties UK tours, he seems to be conducting a one-to-one conversation with the entire auditorium. Beneath his poacher's anorak, Frank's T-shirt bears the legend 'Rage Against The Machine'. The coupling of this self-confessed apolitical hedonist's name with that of a fiercely puritanical rap-metal group seems somewhat incongruous, but the band he used to be in – an early incarnation of West Midlands punk legends The Prefects – did have a song called 'Bristol Road Leads to Dachau'.

With just a microphone and no overloading amplifier stacks to help him impose himself upon the paying public, Skinner's control over a live audience is quite awesome to behold. In the first part of his show – when he's improvising stuff about the town or the venue in which he happens to find himself – it's almost as if Skinner is establishing a power relationship with the audience. He'll pick out three or four people who he'll keep on coming back to throughout the show, almost as if they're human punctuation marks for the rest of his material.

'This may be hard to believe,' he insists later, 'but I've never been that calculating about it. I just feel so at home onstage doing stand-up – so absolutely where I ought to be. I do talk with the audience, but I never think, I'll pick on these three to get me started. It's just that when you're standing in front of a group of people, you instinctively start saying "All right mate, what are you doing here?" I think that it probably comes from having done a bit of teaching. I never liked the lecture approach, I always preferred it to be more of a seminar – talk for a bit, ask some questions and get them all involved – and that's how I think stand-up comedy should be, too.'

More than any other British comic currently working, Skinner combines the classic broad-church appeal of an old-school saucepot like Max Miller[98] with the alternative club scene's rigorous devotion to new and original material. 'I once asked an old mainstream comic why so many comedians play golf,' Frank remembers, 'and he said "You know when you're on tour, you've got your days free", and I thought, "I haven't got my days free: I spend the days writing jokes."'

Far from resenting the responsibility of constantly coming up with new material, Skinner seems to enjoy the challenge.[99]

'For me personally,' Skinner insists, 'being a comedian is having funny ideas and saying them: it's not just saying them. I need the complete process . . . You squeeze your head for a bit and then they start to come,' he continues fondly. 'You try them out, and the ones people like are in and the ones they don't, you kick up the arse. It's like panning for gold . . . you've got to wade through a lot of shit to get to the nuggets.'

Frank Skinner will wade through more shit than most when the tantalizing scent of a nugget is upon him. Anyone who says there is no cruelty in this man's comedy just hasn't been paying attention. It's not his talent for crowd control that is disturbing – even at his

---

[98.] The cover of an old Max Miller album seems to supply the answer to the question 'Where did Frank Skinner get his wardrobe?' The contents suggest Miller might have also been influential in Frank's notorious fondness for an off-key singalong.

[99.] Running in new material for a marathon autumn tour at Edinburgh in 1995, Skinner allegedly does a different set every night for ten days. I say 'allegedly' because that sort of behaviour could get him into a lot of trouble with his fellow comedians.

most savage, Skinner rarely does more than toy amiably with his victims ('I like to think I can spot pretty early someone who doesn't enjoy it,' he says benignly. 'I don't want anyone to go away squirming') – so much as the darkness that seems to reside somewhere near the core of his act. The question is, where does this darkness come from?

'I read in the paper that part of the problem was that he felt he was being typecast,' Skinner says of the (then recently deceased) dwarf actor David Rappaport. 'Although that *is* tragic, it's surely partly comic as well.' Rappaport's suicide is the jumping-off point for a routine which Frank eventually drops because he can tell it is 'making people uneasy'. And yet making people uneasy is something Frank seems to take a certain amount of delight in.

'Did you hear Frederick West's house is up for sale?' he asks the St Albans crowd in time-honoured and convivial 'set them up to knock them down' fashion. 'What a horrible place that would be to live . . . Gloucester.' Now this is pretty funny, in a slightly callous sort of way, but over the course of a full-length show, the very heartlessness which makes Skinner's wit so devastating can also start to nag a bit.

You start to wonder if he really does think there is nothing more to life than football and one-night stands, and if so, whether his audience actually agrees with him or is just going along with him for the purposes of comedy. Frank Skinner was well ensconced in the New Lad elevator before it had even left the ground (or indeed before anyone had thought of a name for it). Now that he – and it – have reached the top, you sometimes can't help wishing he'd get out and take a look around.

There's such a strong sense in his act of men and women being animals that are implacably opposed to each other – especially in the anal sex material, of which there is a profusion in his mid-nineties live show. As Skinner anatomizes with Proustian attention to detail[100] his predilection for (to adopt a snooker-rooted euphemism) the difficult brown over the easy pink, it sometimes comes across as if the thing that most appeals to him about this particular transaction is that it is designed not to give women pleasure.

[100.] Right down to the particular textural quality of the stains on the bedding.

'But lots of women have told me that they *do* get pleasure from it!' Skinner insists when challenged on this issue. 'I'd hate to think that I sound like some terrible misogynist putting women in their place by not letting them orgasm.'

But he does seem to draw a very dark line between male and female.

'Do I?' Frank asks, soft brown eyes glinting harder for a moment. 'I'm not disputing it. That's a genuine question.' He thinks for a while. 'I suppose the joy for me in the anal sex material,' he continues, pausing to savour the absurdity of this sentence-opening, 'is that I'm not a comic with a message, but I do think that it's a bit tragic that there are so many sexual no-go areas – even in conversation. And I do like to think that if people don't try anal sex on the strength of that material, they will at least talk about it.'

The suggestion that his attitude in this regard is almost evangelistic – that he is, in fact, the Billy Graham of anal sex – seems to amuse Skinner greatly. He tries the allegation on for size, rolling it round his tongue with indecent relish,[101] before pronouncing it a perfect fit.

Thinking about it afterwards, the religious element in the 'Billy Graham of anal sex' formulation seems to give Frank almost as much joy during our exchange as the rude part. Maybe his oft-expressed yen for heterosexual sodomy is actually born out of Catholic guilt. (I know the Bible doesn't formally come out in favour of it, but what more natural means of contraception could there be?)

While Catholicism undoubtedly looms large within the Skinner psyche, no one curious about the pessimistic foundations of his comedic universe can afford to put all their Easter eggs in the Vatican's basket. There's another factor, historically familiar to those on both sides of the confession grille: the demon drink.

[101.] If Skinner ever chooses to market his own condiment, Paul Newman style, it will have to be called 'Frank Skinner's Indecent Relish'.

Frank Skinner's heart of darkness

Asked about the routine in his *Live at the Palladium* video where he describes regaining consciousness after a heavy night on the ale having actually wet the bed,[102] Frank Skinner responds with characteristic candour: 'That is better researched material than anyone might think.'

And yet presumably an actual alcohol dependency on that level would be no laughing matter?

'It was a problem, yes – only the hangovers, not the drinking. But then I found out that the best way to cure a hangover was by drinking some more. And that is one of the great discoveries of life, but not one you actually want to make, because once you cross that line you have truly seen into the heart of darkness.'

Skinner eventually 'got help' and hasn't had a drink since September 1987. But presumably his temperance must create its own problems, given that alcohol is the oxygen of comedy. 'Drinking is a fantastic thing,' Frank laughs. 'There is no doubt that it is impossible to experience true joy without alcohol in your life.'

So he's experienced no true joy since September 1987?

'I definitely think I lost about 15 per cent of my life experience – the joy, but also the horrible end. My dad used to say "none or enough": that was our family motto. At one stage, I was getting up in the morning and having half a bottle of sherry before I got out of bed, and that probably doesn't fit in with most people's fun-loving drinking experiences. You know when people stand around and start swapping drinking anecdotes? As soon as I join in, the laughter turns to "Oh God, that's terrible".'

The moment when the laughter turns to 'Oh God, that's terrible' seems to be the one that Skinner's comedy keeps coming back to.

'I think comedy probably is what's replaced drinking in my life,' he confesses cheerfully, 'because I do get an incredible buzz off it. The walk from stage to dressing-room after a good gig is the best journey you could ever go on: that's the only time in life I feel completely ecstatic – I have to admit to having had the odd Alan

---

[102.] And subsequently attempting to hide this fact from the lucky woman lying next to him.

Shearer moment and punching the air a bit after a really good one.'

Skinner's sheer joy in his own facility ('It sounds a bit tragic to say it, but I do think being a professional comedian is the best job in the world; even saying those words "professional comedian" has made me go all tingly') is the infectious flipside to the darkness we've already delved into.

A moral thing

Frank's cheeky-chappie ancestor Max Miller famously had a red book and a blue book; the former containing those jokes that were suitable for universal consumption, the latter containing those that weren't. It is hard to be sure how Miller might have reacted if someone could have told him that a joke very much from the latter camp – his classic ocular malfunction routine 'every time I see F, you see K' (think about it) – would one day form the basis of an advertising campaign for the French Connection high-street clothing chain. It seems likely, though, that the sort of words which used to be called 'unprintable' would have loomed large in his response.

In helping to erase the boundary between the things people talk about in public and the things they talk about in private, Skinner – alongside other alumni of what might be broadly termed the 'confessional' school (from Tracey Emin at one end of the artistic spectrum to Nick Hornby at the other) – has had a huge impact on the way the British conduct themselves.

'Everything is in the act,' Frank admits. 'I have virtually no private areas of my life at all.' But can't that be painful sometimes for the other people involved?

Skinner shakes his head: 'I never name names,' he replies, 'or only very rarely . . . the woman who was with me the time I wet the bed came to a gig in Leicester. She approached me afterwards and said "I wish you hadn't mentioned my name". But I think that was more because I'd never actually owned up at the time.'

Far from being mortified by the memory of this encounter, Frank seems utterly unfazed by it. Presumably a public confession was less embarrassing than a private one would have been. 'I think people would be very surprised', he nods genially, 'if they knew the percentage of the things I talk about which have actually happened.

I would guess it's at least 95 per cent – I might embroider or add a bit on here and there for the purposes of comedy, but I'm not a person who has ideas out of the blue. What I do is, something happens then I'll think, That was quite funny.'

So it's important that if he says something is a 'true story' (which I always assumed was the comedian's code for 'I made this up in the bar before the show'), everyone should believe him? The apparently unshockable Frank Skinner looks genuinely appalled: 'But I'd *never* say "This is a true story" if it wasn't . . . That's a *moral* thing.'

Royston Vasey interlude: making Priapus blush

Billy Bunter's obscene proletarian uncle, Roy 'Chubby' Brown was born and christened Royston Vasey in wartime Grangetown – a satellite port of Middlesbrough. Once, in the dark and distant 1970s, Chubby appeared on *Opportunity Knocks*. How different things might have been had he not lost to a spoons player. He could now be presenting a daytime quiz on ITV instead of shifting scabrous videos by the hundred thousand.

The dividing line in terms of Brown's popularity is traditionally portrayed as the soft south versus the naughty north. In fact, it's a class barrier, not a geographical one. Chubby has been big in London for years, packing out the Dominion and Hammersmith Apollo (née Odeon) with an ease that many a bigger name would happily trade some status for. And there is a strong hint of the old-fashioned football crowd in the chants which presage the dimming of the Apollo lights in the midst of a lengthy Brown residency in May 1995 – 'Who ate all the pies? Who ate all the pies? You fat bastard! You fat bastard! You ate all the pies!'

The audience's sense of renegade solidarity has been bolstered by the chance to buy some outstanding souvenir merchandise – Chubby Brown polo shirts, Chubby Brown turtleneck sweaters. There is also a rumour that security are checking people's bags to make sure no one has a book with them.

The curtain rises to reveal a lavish backdrop: a huge painting of the London skyline with – nice touch, this – a Polygram Video sign at the centre of it and a cartoon stork flying overhead, bearing an infant Chubby. Snapshots of Brown's life-story flash up on screens at either side of the stage and the man himself finally emerges to a hero's welcome. His bizarre apparel of garish romper suit and flying-helmet-with-goggles-pushed-up is a visual catch-phrase, prompting as quick and happy a flush of instant recognition as any verbal signature.

For a large man, Brown is exceptionally quick on his feet. His wits are not slow, either. When the mood takes him ('Her cordon bleu should be cordoned off'; 'I knew her mother was coming round – I saw the canary throw itself into the cat's mouth'), he is a gifted domestic griper in the Les Dawson mould. He is swift and merciless with hecklers, too – 'If you were that important, the seats would be facing you'. But that is not what the crowd have come for. It's filth they want, so it's filth they get.

Not for nothing is 'Chubby' *Bill-and-Ted*-speak for an erection. Brown's life's work is to make Priapus blush, and with this goal in mind he marshals an endless pudendal parade of motts, minges and bell-ends; licking his fingers, waggling his tongue and scratching his crotch in a grotesque parody of male sexuality.

There's certainly not a great deal of love in the room: one of Chubby's favoured euphemisms (if you can call them that – there ought to be a word for substitute expressions that are uglier than the conventional Anglo-Saxon) for the sexual act is 'snap the bitch in two'.

Brown says a lot of hateful things – not just about women, but about Third World poverty, homosexuality, race, AIDS, the Japanese earthquake, the Pet Shop Boys ... pick a subject – but he somehow does so without finally seeming (as, say, Jim Davidson does) to be full of hate. In terms of relations between the male and female of the human species, Chubby's comedy of nihilism is actually not all that much more disturbing than Frank Skinner's.[103]

Yet the dirty-mouthed north-easterner's under-the-counter image persists throughout the decade as a kind of living embodiment of beyond-the-paleness. Someone (it was either Howard Jacobson or Rabelais, but I am reluctant to give the former credit for the

---

[103.] He's got a better singing voice than Frank's, too, when he chooses to use it.

observation without written proof) once said that Roy 'Chubby' Brown was sent down to earth to 'remind us of the difference between man and God'. Posterity (in the suitably angelic guise of The League of Gentlemen) will eventually reward his years of stalwart service in this connection with a special kind of small-screen immortality. As Larry Vaughn, foul-mouthed mayor of Royston Vasey, Brown gets to play the non-democratically elected figurehead of the town which bears his real name (and to realize what is presumably a long-cherished ambition by saying 'fuck' on BBC2).

Terry Wogan's right-hand man

Frank Skinner, meanwhile, develops his jauntily amoral TV persona in a less celestial fashion – as Terry Wogan's right-hand man, as the devil's advocate on *Do the Right Thing*, as Bob Monkhouse's sparring partner on *Gag Tag*. And then by embarking on a bizarre *Über*bachelor proto-reality TV existence as David Baddiel's on- and offscreen lodger, getting paid large sums of money to talk about footballers' hair.

'*Fantasy Football* stemmed from a time when Frank and David were sharing a flat together,' Avalon co-founder Richard Allen-Turner remembers. 'Neither of them had girlfriends for a while, and they spent quite a lot of time watching TV and making the type of observations that would end up going down so well in the show. The way the set was in the original series, that was just what their flat used to be like: I remember going into the kitchen to make myself some tea there once and struggling to find an empty mug that didn't have green fur in it.'

The reek of unmodified masculine *bonhomie* pervading *Fantasy Football League* reflected not so much the explicit influence of the show's apparent American prototypes (Mike Myers's *Wayne's World* and Mike Judge's *Beavis and Butthead*),[104] as the extent to which those prototypes were actually *arche*types, revealing eternal

---

[104.] In the down-home forms in which they originally appeared on US TV, rather than in their more opulent but equally excellent later cinematic incarnations.

verities about male friendship. Unlike the closed social circle of the traditional football crowd, the doors of Skinner and Baddiel's fetid living-room were open to all.

'It's the same when you see new people coming to grounds,' Skinner notes contemptuously of those who object to *Fantasy Football*'s informal outreach programme to the unapologetically middle-class. 'There's always the miserable bloke who says, "Where were you against Shrewsbury?" But I think, No, let 'em come.'

In the context of a discussion about the extent of the constraints broadcasting necessarily places on his off-the-leash stage persona, Frank Skinner describes the contrasting demands of live and television audiences as follows: 'It's the difference between being funny with your mates in the pub and being funny at your gran's house.' Like the magical room in the Jamiroquai video, this divide is narrowing from both sides simultaneously, even as he speaks.

B. The girls

Jo Brand recognition: 'I wish things didn't have to be like this on every level really'

It would be fascinating to know what Whym Chow's owners Katherine Bradley and Edith Cooper would have made of the first episode in the second series of *Jo Brand Through the Cakehole*. An amateur dramatics society performs a version of Quentin Tarantino's *Reservoir Dogs*. The script is entirely unaltered, and there is something gently and deliciously subversive about the sight of a group of apparently strait-laced elderly women – a real live amateur dramatics group, not professional actresses – enunciating the word 'motherfucker' repeatedly and with obvious enjoyment.

Like much of the best of Jo Brand's material, this is both a simple joke and a clever piece of cultural criticism. At a time when Quentin Tarantino's linguistic *braggadocio* seems to have reached the saturation point beyond which no reference to him or his work could possibly be of any interest, Brand reflects this fact back at itself through a distorting fairground mirror.

'It was a bit of a risk,' she admits, dividing her attention between coffee and cigarettes in an airy Channel 4 conference room, 'but the women really loved doing it. They were all, "Ho ho ho, what's my son going to say?"'

Amid such infectious affability, it is hard to keep a grip on the fact that in the mid-1990s there are people who regard Jo Brand as some kind of cake-fixated Antichrist. She seems to derive great enjoyment from provoking those who are predisposed not to like her, but when, say, she is being slagged off by the *Sun* (as she constantly is), does she on any level wish things didn't have to be like this?

She nods, ardently: 'I wish things didn't have to be like this on *every* level really.'

The strange thing is that (Gary Bushell excepted) the people most likely to be upset by Jo's jovial brand of boisterous anti-machismo generally seem to be liberals, rather than lads.

'A lot of the time,' she says, 'lads will just think it's a bit of a laugh. They know it's not going to change things politically – they're safe in their own kind of laddish kingdom, so it doesn't worry them. In some ways, it's good that they've actually sat down and paid attention. I don't have a grand plan – I'm not that organized a person – but if I did, that would be stage one. Stage two would be to try to take them a bit further than they expected to go.'

Striding into the Bloomsbury Theatre spotlight with her electric-shock hair and sweet-wrapper trousers, she has certainly come a long way from the self-abnegatory figure who used to creep onstage as 'The Sea Monster' on *Friday Night Live*. Jo Brand has made the same progression Lenny Henry just about did after *OTT*:[105] from indulging the preconceptions of the less enlightened members of her audience to throwing them back in their faces. (Though – again as with Henry – this turns out to be one step forward that can all too easily be retracted.)

'I do deliberately keep my weight up,' she tells the evening's tragic token heckler, 'so a tosser like you won't fancy me.' Brand still does a lot of fat jokes – in fact, it would be fair to say that they make up the main body of her set – but fat is now a means rather than an end. Her unabashed celebration of all things supposedly

---

105. The little lamented 'adult' version of *Tiswas* (as if the kids' one on Saturday morning wasn't grown-up enough!) to which Henry contributed a demeaning African chief character who said 'Katanga!' a lot.

unladylike – gluttony, drunkenness, sexual licence, toilet humour, nicotine-dependency, hitting people – is not just fun in itself. It also makes an effective cover for the sort of straightforwardly political observations which a less rambunctious comedian might find it hard to get away with in the post-alternative era.

Pre-showbiz life experience probably helps in this regard. 'You are a bit more normal', Brand admits, 'if you've done a few proper jobs for a bit.' A solid grounding in the grim realities of psychiatric nursing – not to mention pulling the heads off chrysanthemums at a garden centre ('particularly good training for the comedy circuit, that') – helps her steer clear of the kind of limiting, generationally specific routines which straight-from-college comedians tend to fall back on. You won't catch Jo Brand wittering on about *Starsky and Hutch*.

'A lot of people do that kind of nostalgia stuff believing that they were very happy in their teenage years,' Brand observes sagely, 'but that's probably just an illusion.' She seems very happy in the here and now. 'I'm miserable as sin a lot of the time,' she says, 'but I've been much happier in my thirties than I was in my twenties. I like to read my diary occasionally to remind myself what a miserable, alienated old sod I used to be.'

Jo Brand had always nursed comedic ambitions, but her comedy début – at an ill-tempered London benefit – was not overly auspicious. 'I had the seven pints of lager temerity,' she remembers wistfully, 'to think I could go on after everyone else had died and storm it with my sad five minutes about Freud . . .'

The sad five minutes about Freud were soon dropped, but it took Brand some time to develop the barnstorming deadpan of today. Hamstrung by nerves, her delivery used to be such a grim monotone that other comedians could get easy laughs by doing impressions of her. In a successful bid to loosen herself up, she deliberately took on as much arduous compèring work as she could get her hands upon.[106] The accolade of Best Live Act at the 1995

[106.] Frank Skinner also testifies to the benefits of regular compèring work (in his case, four nights a week, two in Birmingham, one in Bristol and one in Cheltenham). 'When you do that, the line between being offstage and being onstage just seems to disappear really – you're neither an act nor a member of the audience, you're some strange kind of bridge in-between.

British Comedy Awards is a well-deserved reflection of the authority of her increasingly imperious live persona. But it is in building a functional televisual chariot for this comedic Boadicea that Brand really moves ahead of the pack.

'I always thought, I'm not going to do any crap sketches,' she says, 'but then, funnily enough, I did . . . By the time you actually get to filming,' she continues in characteristically self-deprecating vein, 'you tend to be so knackered that you don't actually give a toss anyway.' There is the odd jotted-down-on-the-back-of-a-fag-packet moment in *Through the Cakehole*, but that does not stop it riding high in the Channel 4 ratings, or being all the talk on Saturday-morning trains into town. And the domesticated cockney cop-show spoof, 'Drudge Squad', is the stuff of which comedy legends are made.[107]

The series begins with an imposing opening shot of Brand filmed from beneath a glass floor. Does she ever think of not doing jokes about her size?

'You can't build your career on one set of values and then shift to doing jokes about embroidery,' Brand argues.

Now that she is so firmly established, though, surely she must be tempted to leave behind some of the more self-mocking material?

'I know exactly what you mean,' her voice rustles with the beguiling timbre of a freshly opened tobacco pouch, 'and I just don't think I can, because that's the kind of person I am really . . . I was like that before I got into comedy, and I don't think I'm ever going to change.'

Sometimes Jo Brand thinks that what she describes, not quite dismissively, as 'the fat-bird stuff' might be history. 'Then something will just pop out and I'll think, Oh well . . . still doing it.'[108]

That's what made me feel that onstage was just somewhere else to stand in the room, rather than a big dangerous step.'

[107.] Rivalled only by Armstrong and Miller's immortal alcoholic police detective and his not-so-invisible friend 'Chuffy' in the nineties UK TV cop spoof canon.

[108.] The potentially counter-productive impact of Brand's perpetual self-deprecation is demonstrated at the Guildford Civic Hall a couple of years later, when one of the small gang of vociferously drunk women without whom no sit-down, stockbroker-belt comedy night out is complete, suddenly subjects the star of the evening to a volley of vicious personal abuse,

Sometimes, too, she'll set up a joke and you will wonder which way it's going to go, and then she'll almost wilfully bring it back to the obvious – as if that gives her as much pleasure as trying to do something different (a cheap laugh apparently giving her quite as much delight as an expensive one).

'I think there's always been a tradition in England of people being a bit useless,' Brand insists, 'and of that being something which this society thinks is quite lovable. I'd like to think I'm a part of that.'

I can see Jenny Eclair, Lee, now the rain has gone

Unable to find the ashtray in an upmarket café, Jenny Eclair has opted to use a plate. She marvels at how much debris accumulates on it within the space of a few moments – a cigarette stub with lipstick traces, some ash, the tuft of cappuccino froth with some more ash dropped in it which she was just about to ingest when the person interviewing her nervously brought it to her attention.

'It's a good job I put my chewing-gum in the ornamental chimney-breast,' she concedes philosophically, gesturing to the little upstairs enclosure from which her smoking has just got us politely expelled, 'otherwise that'd be there too.'[109]

Jenny Eclair's ideal audience consists of 'transsexuals, runaway teenage slags and gin-sodden divorcees', but if these social groups are unavailable, anyone with a sense of humour will do. On a good night, the crowd will leave not merely entertained, but verbally debauched. On a bad night – and the Perrier Award she wins in August 1995 is no insurance against what all comedians technically term 'dying on your arse' – 'you'll be mentally kicking yourself round the stage; even though the words of the set are coming out, you're saying the most awful things to yourself in your head'.

---

almost as if prompted to do so by the endless, genial, pre-emptive harping from the stage.

[109.] There has always been a thin line between glamour and disarray, and this is one high wire Jenny Eclair delights in walking: 'I am best viewed from a distance,' she observes with melodramatic self-deprecation '. . . and at night.'

Jenny Eclair has got better lately at dealing with people not liking her. Perhaps partly because her rogue female persona – 'An alley-cat with delusions of grandeur' is how she describes it, 'slinking through the dustbins in leopardskin and high heels' – has over the last few years become more and more defined from her everyday self. Her car stereo has 'Eclair' tapes and 'Jenny' tapes; her wardrobe has 'PVC pants at one end and nice Marks & Spencer's woollen trousers at the other, with a grey area in the middle'.

By her own admission, Eclair has 'a very clichéd view of fame: all marabou feathers and relaxing by the pool'. The charms of her bottle-blonde wild-woman persona might have faded with familiarity, but like a trusty gusset, she seems to get better with age. Self-proclaimed as 'SE5's answer to Dorothy Parker', Eclair's fag-addled voice rasps like sandpaper on a velvet cushion.

Onstage, she is a vision in spandex, swigging Strongbow and continuing to be authentically scabrous even as the undelivered invitations to her daughter's birthday party spill from her hand-bag.[110] And just when you think there is no new depth to which she can stoop, she gleefully lowers the tone another geological stratum or five. High prevailing levels of scatological and gynaecological exactitude ensure that Jenny Eclair is better experienced in live performance,[111] where her finest, filthiest flights of fancy can elicit gasps of admiration and disgust from even the hardiest audience. Readers might like to indulge in a game of Dirty Joke Jeopardy by imagining the set-up to the following punchline: 'I don't use Tampax any more, I just roll up the duvet.'

Eclair seems greatly to relish physical decay, especially female physical decay. At one point in our conversation she refers fondly to 'Mother Nature, pulling strings and knitting stretch-marks over the thighs of women', and she rarely seems happier than when talking about Nembutal overdoses or beautiful blondes drinking themselves to death. 'I think it's because I always wanted to be an actress,' she admits, 'and that's what tends to happen to them.'

[110.] Serves the ungrateful wretch right: giving birth gave her mum 'labia like spaniels' ears'.

[111.] Even in the suitably saucy company of Frank Skinner, her Channel 4 vehicle *Packet Of Three* never quite got on the road.

Is that why she preferred not to unwrap her Perrier Award bouquets?

'Once you take the cellophane off, it's just a bunch of flowers in a vase,' she sighs, 'but if it's still in the cellophane – even if it is rotting – it's still a bouquet.'

If you say the unsayable for long enough, it will eventually become commonplace. The idea (most explicitly posited in Eclair's *Bad Behaviour Show*) of women behaving as badly as men in the interests of sexual equality is not necessarily a recipe for a kinder, gentler world. But that's hardly the point here. Less influenced by the teachings of Gandhi and Martin Luther King than the gospel of pioneering US skate-punks The Suicidal Tendencies – 'Two Wrongs Don't Make A Right, But They Make Me Feel A Whole Lot Better' – Jo Brand and Jenny Eclair still manage to be non-gender-specific hedonism's answer to the suffragettes. Whereas their forebears chained themselves to railings and threw themselves under the king's horse in the Derby, Jenny Eclair writes a column for *Loaded* and Jo Brand enjoys a romantic entanglement with Malcolm Hardee (hmm, maybe that king's horse option wasn't such a bad idea after all).

There are times in the mid-nineties when it feels as if Brand and Eclair's willingness to engage with the spirit of the moment might be legitimizing something which doesn't necessarily merit such validation, but by the turn of the millennium it's clear that in holding their own at this crucial juncture, they were actually elbowing themselves – and by implication, others – vital room to manœuvre. As well as instituting the grim tyranny of the 'geezer-bird', Jo and Jenny's firm grasp on the sceptre of phallocentric authority also made it easier for other women to be geeks and nerds and all sorts of other culturally worthwhile things (see chapter 19 for further details).

It is interesting to observe the choices they themselves make in the years that follow. Jenny Eclair gets in touch with her inner blue-stocking and does a lot of highly paid voice-overs for adverts and TV shows about people renovating houses in the south of France. Jo Brand, having previously described herself as being 'at that age where if I don't have a baby soon, I'm going to have to get one from outside the supermarket', eventually reproduces by more socially acceptable means and goes into semi-retirement.

She ventures out occasionally, but only to fill Jasper Carrott's shoes presenting lacklustre TV advert compilation shows, before re-emerging into public life in the spring of 2003, with characterically spirited showings alongside Doon MacKichan on *Celebrity Fame Academy* and under the merciless makeover microscope of Trinny and Susannah.

In some respects, this seems a waste of Jo's talents. In another way, it's the ultimate confirmation of her uncanny knack for mixing up those pleasures which are licensed with those which are frowned upon. This gift is perhaps best encapsulated in her routine about the notorious sexual practice known as 'the biscuit game', wherein groups of men masturbate competitively on to a wheat cracker. Brand's dispassionate account of this gruesome ritual culminates in the triumphant declaration: 'I managed to sneak in and grab the biscuit.'

8
'Sensation'

or Given that we consume culture with the same hearty appetite with which we might approach a tasty meat or cheese product, why not savour the two pleasures in the same language?

'When I laugh too much, I start off with the hiccups, and if it gets really bad, I'll vomit . . .'

Vic Reeves

'. . . Whereas I urinate freely . . .'
Bob Mortimer

On a cold mid-nineties winter night, the bought-in seats which have been bolted on to the Wolverhampton Civic Hall's wooden floorboards create the sort of formal but festive atmosphere you'd normally associate with a school play. Tonight's entertainment will certainly have a juvenile streak to it, but the crowd is a good deal less student-dominated than your average comedy assembly. Vic Reeves and Bob Mortimer have built a uniquely democratic world of laughter: transcending social and economic divisions, and appealing equally to all who live in thrall to showbiz.

As usual, the duo are impeccably turned out (in dashing blue and yellow suits), and the former's hair looks much classier now that he's stopped dying it. *The Smell of Reeves and Mortimer* live experience begins with a raucous but still plaintive heavy rock number about a cliff-top tragedy involving a former magician's assistant called Carol-Anne. 'Don't blame the clergyman', Vic wails, 'for leaving muesli all around him.' The comic potential of muesli might seem to be on the brink of exhaustion, but Reeves and Mortimer's interest in particular foods, like their obsession with the nuances of microcelebrity, goes beyond routine laugh-getting.

By yoking together the most specific physical and entertainment sensations – the touch of lard, the voice of Lovejoy – they lead us to a deeper understanding of the strange and complex beauty of everyday life. In this respect, Vic and Bob are the yin to *The Day Today*'s yang (or it might be the other way round, I can never quite remember).

Next to Reeves and Mortimer's instinctive grasp of the niceties of popular culture, their most potent weapon is a delight in the possibilities of the English language. When Bob falls, his injuries include 'multi-directional sock roll and cancellation of favourite concert memory'.

One minute, Vic is giving us disturbing vision of the apocalypse – 'Cats will turn into butter, and that, ladies and gentlemen, will be that.' The next, Bob is presenting us with an old-school northern-club gag that Bernard Manning would be proud of. 'I'm seeing a new lass,' he boasts. 'Works at Marks & Spencer's . . . won't let me try nowt on.'

The rough-and-ready nature of a stage show suits some of their more extravagant recent conceits: for instance, Otis Redding and Marvin Gaye, the Punch and Judy agony uncles, are easier to find funny when not blacked up. The welcome return of the *Big Night Out*'s staple talent contest, 'Novelty Island', heralds an unsettling descent into complete gibbering madness. (For the record, the winner is Mr Wobbly Hand: 'currently in dispute with the Tango corporation over the theft of his act'.)

The encore is stranger still. When Vic starts to belt out his chart-topping version of Tommy Roe's 'Dizzy', all members of the audience with hair longer than Michael Heseltine's jump up from their seats as if by prearranged signal, run to the front and start dancing wildly. The only other time I've seen this happen in quite the same regimented way is in response to an encore of 'Green Door' at a Shakin' Stevens gig (it is a little known but very pertinent fact that a pre-fame Vic Reeves in mid-eighties pop-wannabe mode once appeared as an extra in a Shaky video). Perhaps dimly aware that he has somehow come full circle, Vic's blankly expressive face hovers for a moment between pride and embarrassment, eventually opting – quite rightly – for the former.

Seated opposite each other at a long, biscuit-laden table in a Groucho Club meeting-room in the spring of 1995, Vic and Bob are talking about handwriting. 'I was taught Marion Richardson writing,' says Bob, 'which is partly joined and partly not, then I poo-pahed the joined bit and now I print like a child.'

'So Marion Richardson's claim', Vic muses, impressed, 'was, "I've thought of a new form of writing where you don't join up all the letters".'

His partner's charter flight of fancy will not be rerouted. 'Girls who went to school in the late seventies', Bob continues, 'have been taught to write with very large letters. I think David Cassidy is responsible for that.'

On TV, the oblique wit which fuels such conversational flights of fancy is filtered through production values worthy of Heath Robinson . . . as reimagined by Hieronymous Bosch. The second series of *The Smell of Reeves and Mortimer* (Vic and Bob's fourth multi-part TV excursion) is about to confirm that none of the magic has been lost in the potentially perilous slow-motion leap sideways from Channel 4 to BBC2.[112] 'In show two, we've got a big organ that's got a pub inside,' Bob says proudly, 'and actually seeing that sort of thing realized is a joy.'

The duo are full of praise for the BBC props and costumes people who rise to the challenge of translating Vic's drawings into three dimensions. And a challenge it undeniably is. The first episode begins thus: 'August 1831. Bank Holiday Monday at the banqueting hall of King Henry VIII'. The furious monarch curses the head-waiter over the minute portion of cheese on which he is expected to dine, before a series of poignant historical tableaux outline the history of the dairy product in question. A pulsating calypso/voodoo number then conclusively establishes 'the link between cottage

---

[112.] The only reason *The Smell of* . . . isn't included alongside *Vic Reeves Big Night Out* and *Shooting Stars* in the top ten (well, fifteen) in the introduction is to give everyone else a chance.

cheese and evil'. 'Edam', Vic adds, by way of an afterthought, 'has long been associated with necromancy.'

This archetypal Vic and Bob routine might no longer have the novelty value that made the duo teen idols five years before, but its underlying thrust is as sharp as ever. Given that culture is a thing we consume with the same hearty appetite with which we might approach a tasty meat or cheese product, why not savour the two pleasures in the same language?

'Nicholas Parsons, Jim Bowen, Bob Holness – they've gone into a strange, untouchable area now,' Bob observes.

'Fish you can't really mention any more,' adds Vic, 'but cucumbers and melons are coming back.'

The key to Reeves and Mortimer's enduring appeal, now that the days of number-one singles are probably behind them, will be knowing when to move on. But before this all-important next step can be contemplated, it's time to consider their legacy. From Harry Hill's *Pub Internationale* (which they like) to *Noel's House Party* (which they're not so sure about), the impact of Vic and Bob's first two TV series is still being felt. The strangest and most mischievous entertainers ever to attain mass popularity in this (and possibly any other) country, Vic and Bob have warped the brain patterns of an entire generation, somehow transcending the media-saturated knowingness of the age to recapture the lost innocence of vaudeville.

So are they proud of being responsible for a turning-point in British comedy history?

'I don't know whether that's true,' Bob says wistfully, 'but it's a lovely thought. We enjoyed doing it and it would be nice if it wasn't just a forgotten moment. The one thing it has definitely done is make people be a bit daft again.'

Could there ever come a point where silliness might become as oppressive as ideological rigour (or at least the appearance of it) used to be?

'Yes,' Bob confirms. 'I think it's on its way now.'

This concern seems to have prompted a subtle rethink in the Reeves and Mortimer camp. Where they used to resist any attempt at analysis of what they do, they are now willing at least to entertain the possibility of rational inquiry.

'We've never really done mad for the sake of mad,' Bob insists.

'If we say something which might on the face of it appear completely insane, there's usually something at the tail end of it.'

What kind of something?

'People always quote us saying, "About this time of night I like to put a Caramac under a rabbit",' Vic says. 'But that was a way of saying, "This is how dreary my life is".'

As with all great double acts, Vic and Bob's relationship is the rock on which their best comedy is built: 'You've got to have a bond,' Reeves says. 'You've got to know what the other person's thinking.' While offscreen, things seem to be fairly constant (in flagrant contravention of the double-acts' charter, the pair are the best of friends, and Bob is the only person who seems to be able to call Vic Jim without feeling slightly weird about it), the comedic balance of power in their act – in contrast to historic role models such as Laurel and Hardy and Morecambe and Wise – is constantly shifting.

'It's smart to switch it round,' Bob beams, 'and from a selfish point of view, it keeps things interesting for us.' And if the best way to mark these changes is by hitting each other over the head with giant saucepans, then so be it. *The Smell of Reeves and Mortimer*'s increasingly frequent recourse to straightforward slapstick is one of two flagrant attempts at broadening Reeves and Mortimer's comedic base, the other being flatulent Jacques Tati cast-offs, 'Le Corbusier et Papin', inspired – if that is the right word – by infamous turn-of-the-century French farting phenomenon Le Petomane.

'Originally,' Bob explains, 'the noises were our way of appreciating our environment, but the director saw an opportunity for explosive gags with a fart connection, and we thought, Well, it's a cheap laugh . . . we'll have it.'

Vic and Bob's comedy is more tightly bound up with their bodily functions than even their sternest critics might have imagined.

'When I laugh too much,' Vic confesses matter-of-factly, 'I start off with the hiccups, and if it gets really bad, I'll vomit.'

'Whereas I', says Bob, pausing to let the previous bombshell sink in, 'urinate freely. The eagle-eyed might have seen it happen,' he continues informatively, 'when we were doing the Stotts [falsetto-talking Scots brothers Donald and Davey] in the last series. I had to ask Jim whether he happened to have a car and he said yes he

146

had a green sports car.[113] I knew it was going to crack me and it did – you can see a great stain spreading down my legs.'

Vic sighs. 'I suppose that *is* an accolade.'

A year or so later, Reeves and Mortimer have received an accolade of a different and even more fragrant nature. The first series of their BBC2 celebrity quiz *Shooting Stars* has miraculously won a Silver Rose of Montreux. I say 'miraculously' not because they didn't deserve it (the judging panels of coked-up TV executives traditionally hand out awards to some fearful old rubbish anyway, and besides a Golden Rose would have been much more appropriate), or even on account of the history of disastrous live appearances on foreign soil recounted in chapter 1, but because of the problems presented by subjecting their peculiarly British sensibility to judging by an international jury.

Presumably something about the idea of semi-famous people competing to answer questions from categories written on the back of a huge descending pigeon – the legendary 'Dove from above' – must have transcended the language barrier, because *Shooting Stars* was not made for subtitles. Bob remembers a typically taxing question, shaking his head in mock sorrow: '"Will Carling takes his name from a refreshing pint of lager . . . Can you name any other sports stars who take their name from lagers and beers?" And the answer is "Fatima Whitbread". That sort of thing doesn't really translate particularly well.'

'We'd say "Mark Lamarr – fifties throwback",' Vic adds ruefully, 'and on the subtitles it came out as "Mark Lamarr, who is here representing the 1950s period".'

Shooting Stars made its first appearance as a one-off; part of an early BBC2 experiment with themed nights.[114] (The channel was turned over to Vic and Bob for several hours on 27 December

---

[113.] Among the other moments in the Reeves and Mortimer canon that have given rise to involuntary urination is the following exchange between Bob and Paul Whitehouse's bus driver in *The Weekenders*: 'You killed my brother . . . brrrrrutally, mind.'

[114.] 'When it was repeated a little while later, it got quite a big audience,' Bob explains. 'Someone at the BBC spotted that and said "Those are cheap", and then we were away.'

1993, whereupon they also took the opportunity to broadcast Mike Leigh's *Nuts In May*.) The programme's origins went back further than that, however. Asked in 1990 if he would ever consider inviting live guests on the *Big Night Out* instead of making cardboard cut-outs, Vic replied: 'We will do, we just haven't had time yet.' While acknowledging that it was 'a lot easier to use masks', Vic insisted that he'd 'like to have [celebrated Brookside curmudgeon] Paul Collins on, Ian Astbury of The Cult, Phil Oakey – he'd be nice'.

Vic's keenness to impact upon the lives of celebrities dated back even further than this, to his teenage years in the north-east. Bruce Dessau's *Reeves & Mortimer* recounts how Jim Moir and his compadres in their Dadaist Darlington street gang, The Fashionable Five, used to play with the minds of visiting punk rockers (well, Generation X) by arranging themselves in eye-catching formations backstage and then returning to the same positions, dressed identically, the next time the band came to town.[115]

While it would be overstating the case to term Vic a stalker, it is worth noting that two out of the three celebrity interfaces he hoped for in 1990 did eventually come to pass. Phil Oakey produced the groundbreaking version of Deep Purple's 'Black Night' 'in the style of the Human League' which graced Reeves's 1991 album *I Will Cure You*,[116] and Vic's hold over erstwhile members of Ian Astbury's tribalist retro-rock phenomenon eventually became so strong that when he later (after their subsequent reunion) took to describing himself as having been 'responsible for The Cult getting back together', no one felt inclined to contradict him.

The following face-to-face encounter takes first place in the summer of 1996. Vic and Bob are by this time living the lives of country gentlemen with their respective partners and children on the not-quite-neighbouring Kentish farmsteads which seem to cause Alexei Sayle so much grief. The bond between the pair seems closer than ever. They are in high spirits after travelling up to PBJ's Soho Square offices on the train together, and some close questioning is

---

[115.] This crucial formative experience is one of a number described in this meticulously researched biography.

[116.] Oakey also appears in the pilot episode of *The Weekenders*, laughing in a field.

148

going to be called for if the veil of Reevesian obfuscation is to have any chance of being lifted.

ME: *One of the things that was so much fun about the* Big Night Out *was the way it plucked familiar names – seemingly at random – from the distant world of TV and rendered them accessible in a new way by making masks of their faces and pushing animal fat through the eye-holes. Would it be fair to say that* Shooting Stars *is basically doing the same thing, but working on a three-dimensional celebrity canvas?*

VIC: You're quite right – it's doing it for real.

BOB: We've been slightly aware, filming the second series, that we're really just doing a *Big Night Out* with a few guests watching. We did start to worry that perhaps we weren't giving the other people who were on enough scope.

ME: *But the show's not there for their benefit, is it?*

VIC: There should be a bit of give and take though. We can use them for our own purposes, but they've got to be allowed to do their bit.

BOB: It has to be edited with an eye to making sure every guest has their moment, so it isn't just a barrage of piss-taking. I don't think we'd leave anything in if it just seemed like we were laughing at them.[117]

ME: *The show looks very live though . . .*

BOB: We try to keep it very much like that. I don't know if I can speak for Jim, but I have a particular hatred for the - pretend live show.

ME: *Is there any discussion of what's going to happen, apart from between yourselves?*

BOB: The only thing we really discuss is the punishment at the end. Because at the start we don't know who's going to win, they all get warned about it.

VIC: We had Richard E. Grant in a barrel and we rolled him down a slope to knock a load of plums into some Victorian potties. Apparently he'd said he didn't want to

---

[117.] Those who remember the appearance of Lynne Perrie (a.k.a. *Coronation Street*'s Ivy Tilsley) might beg to differ.

do it, but no one had told us, so we ended up forcing him into this barrel against his will. [Vic tries to look remorseful, but can't quite manage it.] There are a few other little bits and pieces where you say 'Well, would you mind doing something like this?' But we won't tell them anything more than that. It's the same thing with Ulrika Jonsson and Mark Lamarr – we won't let them anywhere near the rehearsal.

ME: *There's a very delicate balance of power between the team captains, isn't there? How did you achieve that?*

VIC: We had Ulrika because of her reputation [inscrutable laughter].

ME: *What sort of reputation is that exactly?*

VIC: Her reputation for enjoying herself and not taking things too seriously.

BOB: Have you ever seen the clip of her as a weather girl where she cracks up laughing on *TVAM*? There's something quite genuine about her. I don't think we'd met her till the day of the first show – we just thought she wouldn't mind . . .

ME: *Would it be fair to say that Ulrika's ego has exploded as a consequence of the acclaim and social acceptability that* Shooting Stars *has brought her?*

BOB: People seem to think so, because she's had a bit of coverage. But she's so down to earth, we certainly don't see it . . . She has started getting drunk rather a lot, though.

VIC: She's always wandering round holding a can of lager in her hand.

ME: *What about Mark Lamarr?*

VIC: I saw him have a fight in the street the other week. He had this great big scrap right in the middle of Soho. Afterwards there was a huge grin on his face – I've never seen him happier.

BOB: He drinks, he fights . . .

VIC: We met him – I think it was at *The Word* – and he was saying that he hadn't got any work. So we thought, Oh well, we need a team captain and he'd be good opposite to

Ulrika. But I want to see his hair nicely dry. I'd love it if at some stage he'd wash his hair and allow it to dry freely – just let it flow and see where it goes . . .

ME: *Who would you say has been the best guest?*

BOB: Gordon Burns – the *Krypton Factor* presenter – he was great. He said, 'I really don't mind, do whatever you want, I'm not going to try and be witty.'

VIC: We had him knocking toiletries off the top of a wall of dog food with a trombone. Those sort of people are always the best.

BOB: Darcus Howe was great [assumes suitably stentorian Darcus Howe-style voice]: 'What say you?'

VIC: He's bonkers really. He blurts things out and then tries to retract them – 'I once stole an Austin in 1962 . . . No I didn't.' So I suppose the ideal is a semi-serious current-affairs or quiz-show host. The people you'd imagine would have a lot to say probably do say too much . . . I was watching the rushes of the one with Eric Bristow in and you can hear this 'uh uh uh' all the way through – he has this weird laugh that sounds like it's coming up from an underground mineshaft . . .

BOB: Or a recently chastised monkey.

VIC: And there was a good thing with Simon Bates . . . about him being a bedroom gymnast.

BOB: He suffers from giantism, doesn't he, in his middle area . . .

VIC: He's very protective of his 'Our Tune'. His sincerity is . . . [pauses till he comes up with the right word] *unpardonable.*

BOB: Shall we get [former Radio 1 DJ and pioneer of snooker on the radio] DLT on? That would be tricky, wouldn't it? That's the greyest area . . . but DLT might just work.

VIC: I don't know anything about him, but I'd love to read a biography. Do you remember his *Really Real Video Show* where they had all the old songs from the sixties and they got video-makers to make videos for them that were all completely literal? For 'Tears Of A Clown' they would have a clown weeping, or there'd be someone called Lucy floating in a sky with some diamonds . . .

ME: *Do you find it any easier, now, to predict which of the things you do will give people endless delight and which will leave them as bemused as* The Really Real Video Show?

VIC: We still have absolutely no idea.

BOB: The things that seem to stick in people's minds – like when Vic started rubbing his legs, or I shouted 'Ulrik-ka-ka!' – are always the ones you just do for no apparent reason.

VIC: If you try and manufacture them, they invariably fail . . .
BOB When we used to do 'Novelty Island', there was an old bloke who'd just come on and shout 'You're wasting your time'. It was all right but it was contrived – it didn't really have the natural effect of the things that just come to you on the spur of the moment.

ME: *How did the leg-rubbing thing get off the ground?*

VIC: It wasn't a sexual thing at first. You know those tapes that go around record companies of demos that are really awful? There was one we saw of this old bloke performing a song that sounded very like 'Santa Claus is Coming to Town' [Vic sings the words in a voice not dissimilar to Oliver Reed's Bill Sykes], and by the time he got to the last line, which for some reason was 'and all the children are waiting', he was rubbing his trousers in a very strange manner.[118]

ME: *Presumably you were not unhappy to see Spurs players on* Match of the Day *celebrating a goal by aping this strange and disturbing ritual.*

VIC: [nodding delightedly] I think quite a few of them do it.

BOB: It's because they're all booked into hotels on Friday nights with nothing else to do but watch the telly. Footballers have taken on 'which is nice' from *The Fast Show* as well.

[118.] Confronted with the suggestion that the whole leg-rubbing thing got a bit out of control, and that some people even thought Vic's advances towards female guests in *Shooting Stars*'s second and third series verged on sexual harassment, Bob is appalled: 'But within the character, that was the most he would ever have done: it wasn't a precursor to anything, it was as sexy as he would ever get!'

After Steve McManaman had scored once, he was asked to talk through the goal and he said: 'The ball came over from the far side, and I put it past the goalkeeper and into the top corner . . . which was nice.' He did it brilliantly as well.

ME: *Isn't there a danger that the all-important top entertainer/raw material equilibrium might be destroyed by this type of friendly interplay?*

VIC: There doesn't seem to be . . . I find it very endearing.
[At this point, the gentle rustling of crumpled yellow paper signifies that Bob has pulled a half-eaten Cadbury's Flake from his pocket.]

VIC: Is that your Flake from yesterday?

BOB: Yes.

VIC: How long does it take you to get through one of them then?

BOB: Well, from the look of things . . .

VIC: Have you ever known anybody have a Flake for twenty-four hours and just nibble at it occasionally?

ME: *No.*

VIC: It must take an incredible amount of will power

ME: *Perhaps it's like that thing in* Mean Streets, *where Harvey Keitel burns his hand in the flame to test his courage?*

BOB: [with unaccustomed vehemence] He sounds like a fucking idiot to me.

VIC: Well, what do you think you look like, sat there with a half-eaten Flake?

BOB: [smugly] I look like a man who's looking after his body . . . and thereby his mind.

9
A Class of His Own

Paul Whitehouse, *The Fast Show*, and the poetry
of social insecurity

'When we realize that a sketch doesn't have a joke in it, and we've not got a hope in hell of making it funny, we're not afraid to put a bit of classical music over the end and fade it out, in the hope that someone will think it's quite clever'

Paul Whitehouse

'It's my fault . . . I'm not having a go at anyone'
Paul Whitehouse

The question of whether the body rules the mind or the mind rules the body has detained many of the great philosophers, up to and including Morrissey (the singer turned real-estate tycoon, not the Consumer Monkey of the same name).[119] The message of Bob Mortimer's Cadbury's Flake – and beyond that, of the whole Reevesian comedic gospel – seems to be that it doesn't necessarily have to be an either/or situation.

[119.] Morrissey the Consumer Monkey appeared in *Vic Reeves Big Night Out*. There is no logical explanation for him, but he seems to have put a regrettable end to a burgeoning friendship between Vic and the pennywise primate's illustrious Mancunian namesake (the former having previously sung very professional backing vocals – credited as Jim Moir – on the latter's version of The Jam's 'That's Entertainment'). The real cause of this breach is a matter of pure speculation, but perhaps Reeves made the cardinal error of not taking Morrissey as seriously as he takes himself.

This is not the only long-established intellectual breakwater which seems on the point of being washed away in the floodtide of mid-nineties cultural self-confidence. For example, the idea that footballers' tastes in music or comedy should be the source of anything other than widespread derision would have been heresy in an earlier epoch. But in the heady days of 1995–6 – when Britain cheerfully gave itself credit for finally getting rid of the Tories (before it had actually got around to doing so) – a strange kind of general amnesty is proclaimed.

For all the ridicule deservedly heaped upon John Major's rhetoric about 'classless Britain', his inclusive conservatism seemed to set the agenda for its own demise. The most vibrant and thrusting cultural manifestations of the age – from Britpop to *Loaded* magazine – all appear to hark back rather than forward. The title of Blur's 1992 manifesto *Modern Life Is Rubbish* could just as easily have been the slogan above the podium of that (or any) year's Tory party conference, and from Oasis's Beatles fixation to Suede's seventies suburban degenerate chic, the musical hallmark of the era is a peculiarly energized form of nostalgia.

If you substituted football and ice-cold lager for the warm beer and cricket of John Major's ill-fated 'back-to-basics' crusade, the determinedly no-nonsense fun-seeking of *Loaded*'s editorial line could have come straight from Number 10. But while the self-conscious reconnection with the wellsprings of British cultural vitality which went on in the mid-nineties – from the apotheosis of Michael Caine to the gleefully satirical opening dance sequence of *Austin Powers: International Man of Mystery* – did have its retrogressive elements, that doesn't mean it was entirely conservative in its impact.

The bulk of Britain's most explicitly revolutionary moments – from the Peasants' Revolt to Cromwell's republic to the Glorious Revolution of 1688 – have initially arisen from the urge to preserve or restore historic rights and freedoms (whether those historic rights or freedoms were real or imaginary is a can of worms we don't need to open here), rather than the desire to establish new ones. It doesn't matter whether you see the frenzied cultural consolidation of the mid-nineties as a long overdue reclamation of lost common ground after the divisive radicalism of the Thatcher years, or a continuation of the Iron Lady's sinister project by stealth.[120] Either way, the Labour landslide of 1997 would not have been nearly so dramatic without it.

And yet, when Tony Blair endeavours to institutionalize the vague sense of national self-satisfaction somewhat embarrassingly branded 'Cool Britannia' as an instrument of government policy, disastrous consequences inevitably ensue. Like all cultural phenomena worth their salt (and some that aren't), once someone has gone to the trouble of thinking up a name for it, it's pretty much all over.

Returning to the heady days of pre-Blairite euphoria, the nervousness which lurks just beneath the apparently easy-going surface of that time is all too apparent. From the neurotic (but fun!) mockney mannerisms of Blur's *Parklife* to *Loaded*'s oh-so-valiantly ill-concealed fear of female advancement in the workplace,[121] the ebullient tone of the era covers some pretty profound anxieties.

If you had to pick just one artefact to sum up the complex and contradictory cultural mood of Britain in the mid-nineties, it would be hard to better *The Fast Show* (enshrined alongside *Shooting Stars* as every self-respecting premiership footballer's favourite pre-match TV treat). And even the way the things that seemed most reassuring about this programme at first – specifically, the firm hand of Paul Whitehouse on its moral and intellectual rudder – become less so as the decade progresses, shows how accurately it reflects the uncertainties of its epoch.

'A mate of mine made a fatuous comment about John Major,' Paul Whitehouse remembers in 1995, 'and I went, "Oh shut up Dave,[122] that's rubbish", and he said "Oh yeah, you're right".'

Out of such everyday conversational exchanges, the fabric of

[120.] A somewhat curmudgeonly position this, but what the hell, curmudgeons pay taxes too.

[121.] Challenged as to the escalating nipple count between the first edition of his magazine (in which a flash of Liz Hurley's flesh was the only – admittedly, very prophetic – hint of things to come) and the second (wherein *The Naked Gun*'s Leslie Nielsen presided over a veritable mammarian banquet), James Brown's considered response was 'the art editor is a closet case and he's over-compensating'.

[122.] The 'Dave' in question presumably being *Fast Show* and *Happiness* co-writer Dave Cummings.

TV comedy history is woven. From this humble beginning, Paul Whitehouse fashioned one of the most poignant and enduring characters in the first series of *The Fast Show*: the man who stands at a bar with a couple of male friends, and whatever the issue under discussion – from the proper constituents of an all-time best England football team to the relative merits of different alcoholic drinks – he somehow finds himself condemned to an agony of embarrassing uncertainty by a blizzard of conflicting opinions.

'I'm terrible like that,' Whitehouse admits. 'If someone says "Oh, that's a really good film" before I go and see it, I'll probably think it is, but if someone else says it's crap, then a seed of doubt will be planted.' Peer pressure is a big issue in *The Fast Show*. Another much-loved running gag involves the man who butts into his posher friends' conversation, embarrasses himself completely and then exits, resignedly proclaiming: 'I'll get my coat.'

'I like to think I'm quite cocky, and at home in any company,' Whitehouse affirms. 'But you're not really, are you? However much of a brave face you put on, you sometimes realize: These people are just so much better than me at everything.' The fact that he says 'realize' instead of 'think' suggests that the social anxiety to which he refers is not just a mere show of modesty. As does his asking 'That is the word, isn't it?' a couple of times after using faintly technical TV programme-making vocabulary (before laughing and saying: 'I *know* it's the word, so what do I need to ask *you* for?').

Paul Whitehouse's gradual emergence from the shadow of his better-known partner-in-laughter Harry Enfield has been accompanied by enough testimonials to his humility and general good humour to turn a lesser man's head.

'Oh, I'm such a great bloke, aren't I?' Whitehouse proclaims, with an unexpected hint of self-loathing.

The off-duty Whitehouse speaking voice has a broad London accent – not a million miles away from Lance the market flower-stallholder he still does with Harry Enfield sometimes – but there is a striking richness and flexibility to it, as if it might go anywhere at any moment. His face looks like it has seen a bit of weather, and there is a gentleness about him which belies his formidable powers of observation; the uncanny ear for everyday speech which has enabled Whitehouse (in harness with Enfield and shadowy third man Charlie Higson) to create characters with a direct line to the nation's subconscious.

Appropriately enough, given their in-depth exploration of lounge-bar philosophy, he first met Enfield in a pub. In Well Street, Hackney in the mid-1980s, Whitehouse was working for the council with the odd bit of plastering on the side. Little did he realize that the man in the corner doing the 'passable' Prince of Wales impression would one day – Whitehouse affects a mighty grievance – 'nick my lines and my characters and go on to make millions'.

Apportioning credit for amusing pub conversations is an edgy business, even – perhaps especially – between friends. Cheerfully accepting that had he not hooked up with Enfield, he 'would probably never even have got involved in the wonderful world of show business', Whitehouse is understandably protective of his role in fashioning Stavros, Loadsamoney, Smashie and Nicey et al. He and *Fast Show* co-creator Charlie Higson (whom he first met during a brief and ultimately unconsummated flirtation with higher education at the University of East Anglia) evidently relish the chance to do something without Harry's name on it.

And now (especially as more and more people realize that *The Fast Show*, far from being merely a Harry Enfield spin-off without Harry Enfield, is actually something pretty special) they get the chance to turn on each other.

Whitehouse speaks on several occasions of 'thwarting Charlie', and is flushed with the success of a heroic campaign to stop his colleague incorporating topless women into an Italian TV spoof. It's a good job decency prevailed too,[123] as the simplicity of the best ideas in *The Fast Show*'s rapid-fire sketch attack is classical, not brutish.

'There's not a lot of explanation, set-up, gags, even . . .' Whitehouse explains. 'It's just "Get in, see the character, do the catch-phrase and be gone, before anyone really notices that you haven't actually done anything".'

At the time of this interview, BBC2 have been reshowing *The Fast Show*'s début series before putting on the second one, and it's

---

[123] In fact, a dim mammarian recollection suggests Higson probably got his way in the end.

already hard to remember how baffling the whole thing seemed before viewers had a chance to catch up with the running gags. Whitehouse is 'a bit worried people might see through them – "Hang about, it's the same thing every week!"' But there's not much sign of that happening. The power of catch-phrases such as 'Let's off-road!' and especially 'Suits you, sir' – the calling card of two obscene tailors whose unctuousness is leavened with a prurient and aggressive obsession with their customers' sex lives – only deepens with repetition.

Graciously keen to emphasize that *The Fast Show* is very much a team effort, Whitehouse is not above some innocent fun at his fellow performers' expense. He makes no effort to hide the fact that rosy-cheeked Midlander Mark Williams – 'currently filming John Hughes's *101 Dalmatians* with Glenn Close and Hugh Laurie' – is also the man in the heinous 'We wanna be together' building society adverts. And what of Caroline Hook née Aherne (a.k.a. acerbic chat-show hostess Mrs Merton) – is she really as scary as she seems?

'Hard as nails' is Whitehouse's verdict. 'Peter Hook [Caroline's then-husband, erstwhile New Order bassist and reformed wildman of rock] has got curvature of the spine from the pressure of her thumb.'

Unlike several of his *Fast Show* colleagues, Paul Whitehouse has no dramatic training (unless you count his not-quite legendary stint as 'The Slitherer', rolling around in a black binliner on the first series of *Vic Reeves Big Night Out*). He doesn't seem in the least bit bothered about this, though, and there's no reason why he should be.

Whitehouse has extraordinary facial as well as vocal elasticity – he can look twenty years either side of his actual age with equal ease, not just playing his characters, but inhabiting them. The cheesy grin which once won him the unlikely accolade of 'Baby Smile of the Rhondda Valley' still works for him. But there is something extraordinary – at times even disturbing – about the amount of emotional intensity he can bring to a two-minute comedy sketch.

As Ron, the unhinged football manager, or Ted, the gnarled and honourable old retainer horrified by the depth of his aristocratic employer's affection for him, Whitehouse conjures up levels of pathos that are almost too powerful to bear.

He makes no reference to any formative traumas which might be at the root of this ability. His family – cheerfully pigeonholed as 'Full-on proles with middle-class pretensions' (his dad worked for the coal board, his mum sang for Welsh National Opera 'until she became mum') – moved from South Wales to suburban Enfield when he was four. Whitehouse is now the father of two daughters himself.

'It is good, you know,' he observes, almost evangelically, of parenthood. 'It staves off the excesses of show business apart from anything else.'[124]

There is certainly nothing of the showbiz insider about Paul Whitehouse at this point. 'Because I never actually chose it as a vocation,' he explains, 'I still feel as if I tricked my way in: "We got away with it, the fools have given us money for another series".' He doesn't seem at all intimidated by the BBC. 'We're like naughty little boys at school sitting at the back of the class really, and it's probably best for us that we stay that way.'

Finishing his second cup of tea, and preparing to leave for lunch with his publicist in the corporation restaurant, Paul Whitehouse reaches for his coat. As he pulls it from the back of his chair, he fixes this apparently uncontentious garment with a withering look and proclaims contemptuously: 'Every dad in Islington's got one of these.'

Eighteen months or so later, it's the sort of baking hot, late summer day for which the formal meteorological term would be 'Scorchio'. On the rapidly melting tarmac outside Middlesbrough FC's Riverside Stadium, the cast and crew of *The Fast Show* gather for a regional press photocall. Kids on mountain bikes inscribe predatory arcs around them in the manner prescribed by Eric Cantona (i.e. like hungry seagulls waiting for scraps off a trawler).

Camera-laden local newsmen keep an anxious eye on their equipment and John Thomson goes through his paces as Roger the Nouveau Football Fan – a man so in tune with the squeaky-clean commercialization of his newly adopted sport that at moments of

---

[124.] Sadly, subsequent events suggest this particular paternity dividend does not last for ever.

high drama he is liable to shout out the sponsor's name off his replica shirt. Pictures are taken, the media departs and the action moves inside the ground. The scenes to be shot this morning require Roger to turn to the more traditional supporters seated around him and to offer them Pringles and Aqua Libra from his picnic hamper, while vouchsafing such brazenly revisionist opinion as 'It's a shame to support just one team – it's nice to keep your options open'.

This shooting schedule ought to be simple enough. Unfortunately, just as filming is about to start, someone realizes that the extras' Arsenal shirts have just set off for downtown Middlesbrough in the back of a car. 'It's my fault,' Paul Whitehouse says tautly, 'I'm not having a go at anyone.' It turns out that this is as close as he gets to an executive producer's tantrum.

In the two hours that follow, there are enough annoying interruptions to give Whitehouse's reputation for saintliness a thorough test. A posse of chattering cleaners works its way around the ground with the head-scarved inexorability of a gang of Romanian potato-pickers. Dustmen noisily empty the bins at the corners of the stadium. The grass-cutting tractor-driver struggles to keep control of his vehicle, and two men operating deafeningly loud vacuum cleaners have to be begged to turn them off.

No sooner have they replied with a genial OK than the noise starts up again. Appreciative laughter from the assembled company acknowledges the fact that this feels more like something that would happen in *The Fast Show* than anything actually being filmed does.

It's a sure sign of the programme's encroaching institutional status that there is now such a thing as a '*Fast Show* moment': a certain way of failing, a sudden sense of the individual inadequacy which is the kick-drum at the heart of the rhythm of life. From the tragic saga of the lonely squire obsessed with his gamekeeper to the everyday humiliation of the regular guy condemned to say the wrong thing in front of his more sophisticated friends, *The Fast Show* has repeatedly distilled poetry from the pain of social insecurity and class distinction; something British comedy has traditionally been as much hobbled as energized by.

In the process, the names of Whitehouse, Higson and their supporting cast of seasoned professionals – John 'Don't call me "Fat Bob"' Thomson, Caroline 'Mrs Merton' Aherne, Simon 'Tommy

Cockles' Day, and Mark '*101 Dalmatians*' Williams – have become bywords for comedic perspicacity and top-flight character acting. Arabella 'No offence' Weir was even commissioned to write *Does My Bum Look Big In This?* – a spin-off chick-lit atrocity – from one of the programme's least amusing character scenarios.

The days when *The Fast Show* was a secret people could discover for themselves are now long since past. Everyone knows that Paul Whitehouse's mum used to be an opera singer, that he is very good at swearing, that he has the dirtiest laugh since Sid James and that he was moved to create the incomprehensibly inebriated Sir Rowley Birkin QC after meeting someone very like him on a fishing trip. Everyone also knows that his lower-profile writing, producing and performing partner Charlie Higson writes scary books and was for several years lead singer of The Higsons – Norwich's answer to Pigbag.

So what happens next? Between mouthfuls of lunch-time spaghetti in a trailer that is more 1970s gipsy camp than Hollywood backlot, Paul and Charlie ponder the vital question of how their cheeky street-urchin of a show is going to cope with its elevation to the ranks of TV aristocracy. When the third series comes out, will people finally start to see through the shallow façade of their so-called humour to the aching void beneath?

'That's already happened,' Whitehouse says resignedly. 'We got sent this big pack of press cuttings after the second series came out on video, and they all seemed to agree that *The Fast Show* was brilliant, except right in the middle there was this one little thing from the *Big Issue* that said "Can I be the first to burst the bubble? *The Fast Show* is nowhere near as funny as people,"' he raises a wiry eyebrow, '"*particularly its stars*, seem to think."'

What were they hoping for when they first stepped out from Harry Enfield's shadow?

'In one way it was a continuation of what we used to do with Harry,' Higson explains, 'in that we didn't want to do the traditional things you tend to get in sketch shows – firing squads, Nazi generals, dressing up as the cast of *EastEnders* . . . what are the others?'

'Bandits,' Whitehouse butts in authoritatively, '*banditos*.' He expectorates in character.

Higson ignores him and continues: 'The difference was that we wanted it to be based more on character and style than on jokes.'

They must have had some sort of template in their minds for the kind of thing they wanted to achieve?

'Well, we both grew up loving *Monty Python*,' Higson admits tentatively.

But haven't Cleese, Palin & co. inspired more terrible sketch comedy than anyone else alive?

'Probably, but the great thing that *Monty Python* had was that it was its own world: it didn't look like anything else. It's the same with Vic Reeves [with whom both Charlie – who is still 'series adviser' on *Shooting Stars* – and erstwhile 'Novelty Island' regular Paul go way back]. When you're watching it, you're not watching anything else. That feeling is not something you can sit down and design: it either grows out of what you're doing or it doesn't.'

There's no harm in giving Mother Nature a helping hand, though.

'The traditional way of doing things,' Higson explains, 'was that if you had a little quickie character which needed to be seen three or four times in order to work, you'd put them all in one show, so we'd take a bit of a risk in putting them in three or four different episodes so people would watch and think, What the fuck is that? And then after a few weeks they'd think, Aah, *that's* what it is, and that would make them feel a part of the whole thing.'

Like a supermarket's loyalty bonus scheme?

'Exactly . . .'

'When we realize that a sketch doesn't have a joke in it and we've not got a hope in hell of making it funny,' Paul strikes up informatively, 'we're not afraid to put a bit of classical music over the end and fade it out, in the hope that someone will think it's quite clever.'

Charlie smiles. 'It is nice to be able to put things in, like Ted and Ralph, that are really closer to drama, and get away with them because people are following the characters . . . but you do have to balance that every now and again with a fat bloke falling over.'

They claim to have 'a whole series of poncey rules' about what is allowable and what isn't, but when pressed the only one they can think of is No Political Satire. But surely *The Fast Show* is at the very least political with a small 'p'?

'We do hope that to some extent it reflects what England is like today,' Charlie smiles apologetically. 'I know that sounds very pretentious, but we do like to think there is an element of reality to it.'

But doesn't the sheer unwieldiness of the filming process compromise what Whitehouse, slipping easily into the voice of his trusty DJ *alter ego* Mike Smash, calls 'the reflecting normality, meaning-of-life type stuff'? Wasn't there something slightly awkward about all those people in the football stadium – who just wanted to get on with their jobs – being told to keep the noise down by a load of showbiz parasites up from London determined to make a glib statement about how football has lost touch with its working-class roots?

'You do get very embarrassed sometimes,' Higson nods.

Whitehouse looks pained. 'When we were doing Smashie and Nicey, there was this sketch in a graveyard where he was building a monument to his mother – "She's not actually dead yet, but I think she'll love it when she does go". It was a good idea when we first thought of it, but then we went down to the churchyard on the day and there's this huge sign saying "In loving memory of Mum" with "FROM MIKE SMASH" written underneath it in great big letters, and all these *genuine* mourners were coming to visit their grans' graves . . .'

He tails off for a moment, but his natural equilibrium swiftly reasserts itself. 'The thing is, it does actually take forty people to set up a shot. It looks like everyone's standing around doing nothing, but they're not: I have to have my Winnebago, my food-taster and my personal cocaine supply.' Whitehouse grimaces. 'I remember this builder once shouting "Look at them cunts over there – it takes twenty of them to pick up a camera!" And I thought, I've worked on building sites before, mate, so fuck you – you don't know how this works.'

Making TV sketch shows is what passes for industry in this country now – there are machines for the other stuff.

'Exactly,' Paul agrees, mock-soulfully. 'Our labour does have dignity.'[125]

[125.] Watching the *Fast Show* team on the job, it seemed as if a lot of the people involved had honed their comic gifts in the harsh and bruising world of non-showbiz employment and were doing their best to keep the humili-

Is it hard to keep in mind when you're doing something for the fifth or sixth time that the last version is probably the one people are going to see?

'It's an endless series of up and downs,' says Charlie. 'When you first have an idea, you obviously think it's funny, then you start to think about where you're going to film it and who's going to be in it, and it becomes a technical problem. Then you perform it for the first time in rehearsal and it's funny again, but by the fifth or sixth take you've got tired of it. Then you cut it and show it to an audience and hopefully they laugh, and then you go to the final edit and you have to trim twenty seconds off and it becomes this whole big puzzle of "We can't put that next to this because they're both old men".'

'Or "We can't put one latent homosexual next to another latent homosexual",' Paul adds helpfully. 'That's a big problem for us.' He pauses. 'Then the whole thing goes out and you think, Fuck, I didn't like show three.'

Amid the laughter that follows, Higson and Whitehouse wander off in search of some pudding, the former's pensive gait contrasting perfectly with the latter's long lurching strides.

As Simon Day takes his place in the interview hot-seat, Whitehouse comes charging back in through the door shouting: 'I'm sorry, I can't allow Mr Day to speak without me being in control.' The democratic impulse which demands that all *Fast Show* team members should get a chance to have their say gives rise to a certain amount of tension. The fact that cast members contribute

---

ations and pain of the workplace alive. 'Like when someone new starts and you tell them to go down the ironmonger's and get some glass nails?' Whitehouse asks. 'An outsider can probably see that better than we can. I will certainly do that to Charlie [Higson], because Charlie – as Tony Adams was saying the other day [the occasional mention of a celebrity acquaintance being the only trace of what the tabloids now refer to as Whitehouse's 'showbiz lifestyle'] – likes to think he is Charlie Big Potatoes, and I would never let him get away with it.'

He pauses. 'On reflection, that's probably why he's gone away to do *Randall and Hopkirk (Deceased)* – to get away from me chipping at his self-esteem. If I see a little crack, wahey! I'm in there.' Whitehouse assumes the heckler's demeanour which comes very naturally to him – 'You're shit, Charlie . . . mediocrity will rise to the top.'

their own character ideas, and Paul and Charlie edit them, inevitably gives rise to the odd bruised ego – as John Thomson later demonstrates with a strategically placed grumble about changes to his Deaf Stuntman script.

Day has made the obvious break from editorial control by going on a solo tour in a selection of *Fast Show* guises – renaissance pub bore Billy Bleach having won a particularly devoted following. Is it strange to come back to filming after doing his characters on his own for a live audience?

'It feels easier,' he shrugs. 'For some reason, I'm always a bit disturbed by the fact that people are paying twelve quid to come and see me. I always think it's too much . . . you could have a curry for that.'

This is the kind of agent-unfriendly statement that has won Day his reputation as the maverick conscience of the troupe. 'Charlie and Paul are always very keen to make things commercial, whereas [he assumes the voice of a small-town megalomaniac] *if this were my show*, it would be more like a bad Julian Cope album – very self-indulgent, but true to me.' He later shows his individuality by improvising the immortal line 'Go on, do one' in a Billy Bleach football-ground cameo. Off camera, he is also overheard to observe that last night's hotel dinner has 'really turned him back on to lobster'.

'Everyone always says "Oh, *The Fast Show*'s so modern",' Day muses, 'but I don't think it is really. The two ends of the scale are Russ Abbot and Chris Morris, and we're somewhere between the two. That [Morris's *Brass Eye*] is a brilliant show, but there's a lot of arrogance in it.'

Isn't that because, for all their iconoclasm, the *Day Today* posse were always corporation people – they came through on the inside track – while Whitehouse and Higson have always been outsiders?

Day nods his agreement. 'When *The Fast Show* started, Paul used to waltz off with his carrier bag to meet the top brass and you could imagine them thinking, This one's not come in through the usual channels. But I realize now he's used that to his advantage.'

Paul Whitehouse: the easy-going proletarian genius the men in suits don't understand!

'Something like that, yes.'

Caroline Aherne seems to have pulled off a similar trick. Her time on the set is limited this series (her final contribution is more or less restricted to playing a supermarket checkout *savant* with an unhappy knack for deducing painful truths from the contents of shopping baskets. Sample dialogue: 'Meal for one . . . live alone, do you?'). She's about to start filming *The Royle Family*, a new BBC sitcom set on a Wythenshawe council estate, reuniting Ricky Tomlinson and Sue Johnston – *Brookside*'s Bobby and Sheila Grant, for those too young to remember – in the roles of Caroline's mum and dad.

'Nothing much happens,' she grins. 'It'll either be brilliant or shit.'

What is it about *The Fast Show* that makes it incline so much more towards the former than the latter?

'It'll sound like I'm in love with him, but I do think Paul is the best in Britain . . . He's rude, that's what I love – not dirty, just cheeky in a childish way. I think that's great, especially since Paul's nearly forty, has got two kids and is far too grown-up to be doing trump gags.'

While delivering this impassioned soliloquy, Caroline has got carried away applying the make-up for her next scene. 'Oh look,' she exclaims, 'I'm supposed to be a continuity girl and I've done myself up like an old slapper.'

Back down south at BBC TV Centre, a few weeks later, *everyone* is done up like an old slapper. A Chanel 9 awards ceremony is in full swing at the Academia Republic Sminki-pinki Especiale (it's an acronym waiting to happen), and the mystery of Mark Williams's giant stick-on ears is just about to be solved (one of the prizes for 'Tellywelly et Campagne militarios' has gone to the Chanel 9 version of *Men Behaving Badly*, in which Williams appears in the guise of Martin Clunes).

Chanel 9 is a classic *Fast Show* device in that it manages to be simultaneously a very obvious and old-fashioned joke about foreigners talking funny, an opportunity for inspired piss-taking of rival small-screen attractions and something more besides. Like Simon Day's sublimely ludicrous TV detective Monkfish, it ought to be a prime example of television eating itself, but somehow it isn't, because it is created by people with a profound understanding

167

of the merry-go-round of belonging and not belonging, of the way television is woven into the fabric of our lives – the way we are both inside it and it is inside us.

When the third series finally hits the screens, it's almost as if this precious internal balance has shifted somewhat. There have always been *longueurs* amid *The Fast Show*'s quick-fire assault.[126] And as Confucius once said, 'For every Monkfish there must always be a Naked Couple Having Sex.' But while there are some fine comic characters among the thirty or so new introductions (notably Higson's manic depressive landscape painter and Day's maverick eco-warrior Dave Angel – the illegitimate offspring of legendary *EastEnder* Mike Reid and the Hofmeister Bear), there's some pretty routine stuff as well.

It's almost as if being top dogs doesn't suit Whitehouse, Higson and co. There's a bad moment at the 1998 Comedy Awards when they all stagger up to the podium together, drunk as judges, and John Thomson says something graceless about Rory Bremner (not the hardest person to score points off at the best of times, never mind when you've just beaten him in a popularity contest).[127] And if a crowd-pleasing two-month live double-header with *Shooting Stars* at the Hammersmith Apollo was ever intended as a means to open up new creative avenues, then that is not the way things pan out.

So when *The Fast Show* takes what is theoretically its final televisual bow at Christmas 2000 (provincial tours and future reunion specials excepted), it feels like they've knocked it on the head just in time. As Whitehouse's perennially optimistic beenie-hatted teenager proclaims: 'Goodbyes are brilliant, aren't they?' and the camera pulls away to leave him standing alone in a field next to some railway tracks, all the self-congratulatory BBC big-event overkill falls away and a genuinely bitter-sweet moment is shared by all who've tuned in.

*   *   *

[126.] Having originally got the idea of a speeded-up sketch show format from watching a sampler video of *Harry Enfield* highlights prepared for the lazy eyes of TV previewers, Whitehouse often said the actual *Fast Show* 'seemed a little slower' than he'd imagined it.

[127.] The most brazen example of hubristic awards rudeness since Massive Attack's 3-D dissed Sarah Ferguson at the MTV Europe video awards.

When Johnny Depp (who makes a faintly unsatisfactory cameo appearance in the farewell shows) describes Paul Whitehouse not only as his favourite actor but also as 'the greatest of all time ... greater than Brando', this extravagant testimonial is obviously calculated to raise eyebrows. But for those who've watched Whitehouse develop into one of the nation's finest and best-loved comic performers, the extent of his thespian abilities has never been in doubt.

The Fast Show was the perfect showcase for his special gift for thumbnail characterization. From the nicotine-skinned individual who sidles up to strangers in the pub and affects unconvincing solidarity on the grounds that their shared profession is 'the hardest game in the world' to Ted, the tormented retainer trapped in a nightmare limbo of socio-sexual impropriety by the unrequited love of his aristocratic employer, Whitehouse's creations seem to compress a lifetime of melancholy into just a few seconds of screentime.

The happy flipside of his unerring eye for poignancy used to be a thoroughly boisterous public persona. A professional rough diamond, widely admired as an unusually well-balanced and dependable citizen of TV's republic of overwrought egos, Whitehouse would be the last person you (or he himself, for that matter) would expect to find going in for any of that 'tears of a clown' stuff.

None the less, talking to Paul in early 2001, something definitely seems to be troubling him. Right at the start of the interview, he is bemoaning 'the terrible burden of spreading joy and laughter' in his usual jovially self-deprecating way. He pulls a sad face to illustrate the point – the sort of Dickensian inward droop he might resort to at any point in his working life – and then suddenly he checks himself.

'Did you see that look there?' he demands anxiously. 'That's the real me ...' As Whitehouse goes on to describe a passport picture he had taken last year (in which he looks sufficiently miserable to bring a tear to the eye of the most resolutely unfeeling immigration officer), it becomes clear that he is no longer joking.

Has he always felt this way, or is it a recent development?

Whitehouse shakes his head apologetically: 'I know I've got a lot to feel like this [he essays a cheesily upbeat expression which somehow looks even sadder than the preceding grimace] about as well, but there does seem to be a period in middle age where life is *whack whack whack* – it just keeps coming at you . . .'

The most public of these whacks came in November 2000, when Whitehouse separated from his wife of eight years and moved out of the Highbury home he shared with her and their two daughters. It seems to have been a relatively amicable affair, as celebrity break-ups go. Despite receiving bouquets of flowers from the *News of the World*, accompanied by sympathetic invitations to put her side of the story, Mrs Whitehouse has chosen to maintain a dignified silence, and the BBC publicity department stipulates that even if their splitting up was anyone else's business – which it isn't – Paul still wouldn't be answering questions about it.

The only small blot on this commendably discreet landscape is *Happiness*: a new six-part series for BBC2, which Whitehouse not only co-wrote but also stars in. In his first project since the end of *The Fast Show* (not counting *Jumpers For Goalposts*, a jolly, money-spinning sports quiz spin-off for Sky), he plays a recently widowed children's TV voice-over artist whose industrial-strength mid-life crisis plays itself out in pitiless detail against a backdrop of acute celebrity-status anxiety.

Asked in the run-up to the third series about the origins of a rather depressing new *Fast Show* character called Mid-Life Crisis Man (a fifty-year-old who splits up with his wife, grows his hair long and starts going out with a girl thirty-two years his junior) Paul said: 'we're trying to get it out of our systems before it happens to us'. On the evidence of *Happiness*, that gambit seems to have failed. Is he not concerned that people will inevitably draw parallels between his own situation and that of his benighted lead character?

'I don't think they're going to take my feelings into account on that one, are they?' Whitehouse ripostes, with a real smile this time. 'In a strange way, I think I was more concerned about looking at my saggy old face in close up' – he shouts at an imaginary TV screen: 'Oh get off, you ugly *cunt* . . .' – then his face cracks into an even deeper grin. 'So there you are: shallow to the end.'

There's something quite shocking about how much Whitehouse seems to dislike himself at the moment. And *Happiness* turns out to be as brutal a piece of masculine self-excoriation as has ever darkened our screens in the name of comedy-drama. There's a plastic surgery disaster sequence in episode two that has a Zen brutality Akira Kurosawa would have done well to better.

So how did Whitehouse (and friend and co-writer Dave Cummings) come to delve so deeply into the humiliations middle-aged male vanity visits upon itself?

'We just looked at ourselves and our mates, and thought about how much more preposterous life is when you're at that age than it was twenty years before, if only because there's so much more at stake . . .'

But aren't you supposed to be advancing towards a greater serenity and understanding?

'Yeah.' Whitehouse is grinning again. 'But when you complicate that with alcohol, ego, stupidity, hedonism, lack of spirituality and a failure to grow up,' – he looks himself sceptically up and down – 'this is what you get. Those old Tories who are always going on about the sixties and the age of permissiveness being our downfall are probably right,' he continues, waxing unexpectedly illiberal, before pausing, as if to give the punchline a chance to catch up: '*But who wants to go back now?*'

For all the rather bleak impression it gives of its co-author's state of mind, *Happiness* also represents a bold step forward from the cut-and-paste security of the sketch show into the unknown territory of conventional narrative. On the evidence of a disappointing fifty-minute *Ted and Ralph* special,[128] the question of how White-house's genius as a miniaturist might adapt to working on a larger canvas has yet to be answered.

'If you did something in *The Fast Show* that didn't work,' Whitehouse explains, 'you could always deliberately undermine it, or chop it into three and run it over a series, but *Happiness* is a bit more like real life, in that sometimes there are bits that aren't particularly funny, but you just have to hope that a funny bit will be along in a minute.'

[128.] Whereas the two-dimensional nature of the original sketches enabled Harry Enfield's *ancien régime* Radio 1 DJ spoof 'Smashie and Nicey' to withstand their comparable elongation surprisingly well, there was nothing more to add to *Ted and Ralph*'s exquisitely compressed micro-dramas in a longer format.

This is rather how Whitehouse himself seems at the moment; like a man yearning for a funny bit to be timetabled at some point in the immediate future. I wonder if – for all the recognition that *The Fast Show* has bought him – he was actually happier plugging away in Harry Enfield's shadow?

'In some ways it was an easier situation to deal with,' he admits, 'being "the funny one in the background".'

Something in the British national character that *The Fast Show* really put its finger on was our propensity for social unease. Was it possible that some of its intuitive understanding of this might have come from Whitehouse and co.'s own anxiety about their own solidifying celebrity status?

'Obviously, you lose sight of certain things as you get older,' he acknowledges. 'In some cases – for example, youth culture –' he continues mischievously, 'quite gladly. But by virtue of being successful, you do get slightly removed from everyday reality, and that was something that our comedy initially – with things like Stavros and Loadsamoney – was very much about.'

Then success settled on you, like a strange ethereal dust . . .

'Like a terrible ermine mantle,' Whitehouse extemporizes vividly, 'but a double-edged mantle . . . So on the one hand you're all caught up with how beautiful it is, but then you're thinking, Oh my God, I've killed a mink to get this.' He pauses to consider the effectiveness of his wilfully mixed metaphor. 'Then again, they are vermin, aren't they?'

When Whitehouse feels the fur-trimmed stole of fame beginning to settle upon him, his instinctive response has always been to 'shake it off and go down the pub'. But presumably he can only do that a certain number of times before he starts to feel himself turning into Nigel Kennedy, and going slightly mad?

'So that's what you do,' Whitehouse continues phlegmatically. 'You go slightly mad.'

And is that what *Happiness* is about: going slightly mad?

'I suppose it is really . . . in that my character does have this grim obsession with minor celebrity and yet he is also determined to still be the person who goes down the pub with his mates . . . which is what I do . . .' He gets all pensive again. 'And maybe *I'm* doing it for the wrong reasons too.'

At moments like this, it almost feels as if Whitehouse is heckling himself; as if that very connectedness to what he is and where he comes from has now become a huge source of discomfort to him. Reluctant to set him off on another cruel bout of self-recrimination, I try to rephrase the question with the rather clumsy interrogative formulation 'What I was trying to get to . . .'

'Don't "try and get to something", for fuck's sake,' Whitehouse bellows.[129] 'Can't we just skirt around it?'

[129.] What he actually says is, 'Don't "try and get to something", Ben, for fuck's sake,' but that looks silly in print. Having spoken earlier about using the name of the person he's talking to as a means of building a buffer of phoney confidentiality – a trick he claims to have picked up from politicians being interviewed on Radio 4's *Today* programme – Whitehouse employs the technique with increasing savagery himself.

When he appears on *Desert Island Discs* a couple of years later, he gives a veritable masterclass in it, calling Sue Lawley 'Sue' with such relentless pseudo-jocularity that she is forced to abandon several promising lines of questioning. Whitehouse does say a couple of interesting things too, though, between Maria Callas and the Sex Pistols' 'God Save The Queen'. One of them is: 'When *The Fast Show* started, people always used to ask "Isn't it nice to be in the limelight?" And I would have to say that the truthful answer is "No" ', which seems fairly self-explanatory. The other is: 'To regard everything that happens in your life as a potential means of making other people laugh I don't think is healthy, because it cuts out your own reaction', which picks up the grim theme of something he said in an interview in the *Radio Times* the week before about making people laugh for a living 'ruining what should be a spontaneous expression of joy'.

This is as coherent a statement as can be imagined of anything that could possibly go wrong in a comedian's life. Then again, I remember seeing Paul Whitehouse in Dalston Blockbusters in the early nineties, queuing to return videos when hardly anyone knew who he was, and he had quite a melancholic aura about him even then.

10
Cry Harry for England

Hill, Murray and the absence of empire

'In laughter all that is evil becomes holy, and is absolved by its own bliss'

Friedrich Nietzsche

'Sonia – if you switch round the first two letters of your name and add a "B", it spells Bosnia, so . . . is there a lot of conflict in your life?'

Harry Hill

Moustache luxuriantly twirled, and stick-thin legs encased in skin-tight black hosiery, one-time Bonzo Dog Doo Dah Band mainstay Vivian Stanshall is not what you'd call a reassuring presence. 'It might be rubbish,' he proclaims defiantly in the midst of his fragmentary mish-mash of a one-man show, *Rawlinson's Dog Ends*, at the Blooms-bury Theatre in May 1991, 'but by God, it's *British* rubbish!'

Like Spike Milligan (whom he once followed into the same psy-chiatric hospital bed), Stanshall's work, with its relentless twisting of language – scatological, despairingly pre-feminist and occasionally inspired – sometimes sounds like a doomed attempt to come to terms with the delusions of a lost empire.[130] Stanshall meets a tragic

---

[130.] This theme was also explored at great length in his oddly unforgettable film *Sir Henry At Rawlinson's End*, which contains some of the most exhilarating footage of Trevor Howard playing snooker on horseback in the history of British cinema.

end in a fire on his Bristol houseboat before the year is out, but the tradition of what you might call 'post-imperial humour' does not die with him.

In fact, it's soon flourishing as never before in the jokily patriotic soil of the mid-1990s, first and foremost in the work of Harry Hill. While Stanshall and Milligan (who was raised in India and Burma, after all) were both old enough to have lived through times when large chunks of the map of the world were coloured in red, Hill grew up at a time when the British Empire was barely more than a memory and the only shadows of its former greatness were the rapidly fading recollections of those milder forms of global dominion briefly effected in the 1960s by The Beatles and Bobby Moore.

Britain's nostalgic obsession with these twin totems of cultural virility becomes so all-pervasive at some points in the nineties that it makes a refreshing change to find someone willing to address the actual root cause of our ill-founded sense of national superiority. 'I went to a restaurant the other day called A Taste of the Raj,' Hill boasts in a characteristically aphoristic one-liner. 'The waiter hit me with a stick and got me to build a complicated railway system.'

Glastonbury Festival is famous as a home of alternative lifestyles, and in the context of this epicentre of New Age flummery, few lifestyles are more alternative than that advocated by the man whose TV sidekicks will one day refer to him as Mr Harry. In the finest tradition of British festival-going, many of the unusually large crowd crammed into the comedy marquee to escape an impending storm in June of 1994 already look like survivors of a small-scale nuclear attack. Hill, meanwhile, stalks the stage in his usual crisply pressed blazer and shirt, neck subsumed within the starched folds of an enormous wing-collar, pens protruding officiously from his top pocket. 'You heckle me now,' he tells a recalcitrant hippie in the audience, 'but I'm safe in the knowledge that when I get home, I've got a nice chicken in the oven.'[131]

[131.] Glastonbury would have its revenge the next year, though. About half past eleven on the Saturday night, Hill and fellow trouper Simon Munnery (a.k.a., at that stage, Alan Parker – Urban Warrior) had to leave to drive up to Scotland, but got caught up in the crowd leaving after Pulp.

Meeting Harry Hill face to face offstage at around this time, only
his surgically precise sideburns and (readers of a fragile disposition
should be sure they are seated at this point) sandals worn over
patterned socks hint at the sartorial formality of his stand-up persona. Has he always dressed up to go onstage?

'The first time I wore a tie, and then gradually the shirts got
bigger and bigger . . . but I don't really think of it as dressing up,
because it's quite me, anyway.'

Hill's most obvious comedic reference point at this stage (and
indeed, throughout his career) is undoubtedly Vic Reeves.

'I remember going to see him when I was just starting out,' Harry
confides, 'and thinking that in a way he'd already done everything
that I was setting out to do.'

The Pet Shop Boys felt the same way when they heard New
Order's 'Blue Monday', as did Monty Python when they got their
first glimpse of Spike Milligan's *Q* series, but that didn't stop either
contributing something distinctive of their own to the mix.

It's a great mistake, however, to overestimate the extent of Harry's
debt to Reeves and Mortimer. For all the apparent similarities – the
combination of laser-guided contemporary pop-cultural precision
and a yen for old-school showbiz – the differences between them are
more interesting than the similarities. Vic and Bob's devil-may-care

---

'We couldn't go forward or back, and the crowd was getting really
angry . . .' Hill looks increasingly pained. 'We were just two pathetic men
in this car: a symbol of all that Glastonbury isn't . . .'

Or isn't supposed to be – if you ignore all the hamburger outlets and
the fancy four-by-fours in the car park.

'Exactly. But anyway, they started to rock the car, then someone ran
over the top of it, then someone else started shouting, "Turn it over!" It
was really terrifying – like that IRA thing where they got those soldiers
out of the car and killed them – and the only reason it stopped was that some
people recognized me and said [non-committal voice] "Oh, it's Harry Hill".
And then this rough-house type took control and started getting everyone
out of the way so we could back off the road and sit it out till the crowds had
gone.' Harry shudders. 'It was horrible. I'm never going back there.'

At least being attacked by an angry mob at a CND festival probably
comes under third party on your car insurance.

'That didn't matter,' Hill says, bravado returning. 'It was a hired car
anyway.'

spontaneity grows out of the security of their own comic carapace. They carry this with them wherever they go – whether drunk out of their minds on *Comic Relief*, or sober as dons on Paul Morley's *Arena* documentary.

Hill, meanwhile, must construct his one-man comedy bivouac anew each time he goes onstage. While this might seem rather arduous, the high levels of discipline and structure involved enable him to survive in even apparently hostile environments. Whereas the pre-*Big Night Out* Reeves had to start his own clubs to create a suitable environment for himself, Hill weaves his surreal squiggles and swirls of invention into the fabric of a conventional stand-up act, which he plies fearlessly around the drunken bear-pits of the London circuit.

'I do suffer quite a bit,' he observes, somewhat poignantly, 'because a lot of people don't really get what I do.' The buffoonish elements in the Hill comedy costume – the giant collars, the pens in the top pocket – are not there just for kitsch value, but to establish his identity as an alien presence, while also subtly throwing the freshness and occasional cruelty of his thought processes into ever sharper relief.

His bumbling, mole-like demeanour not only defuses potential hostility, but also acts as a cover for material which – in more aggressive hands – might seem actively disturbing. Just as his audience is congratulating itself on keeping up with his rhythmic roundelay of running jokes and cultural references, Hill will confound them with a story about getting his grandmother to buff his car's paintwork because the skin under her arms has the texture of chamois.

A lot of his comedy – and not just the stuff about 'mingling with the monkeys and gaining their confidence' – appears to have a strongly Darwinian character. While it would not be quite fair to say that Hill is obsessed with the survival of the fittest, many of his sharpest routines ('Why do the squirrels bury the acorns? . . . It's just what the oak trees want!') do have an evolutionary edge to them, and a great deal of what he says in conversation – right down to his description of himself as a 'small, weak man with glasses' – seems to back this theory up.

In an attempt to put his finger on exactly what he is trying to do, Hill quotes another stand-up, alleged kindred spirit Ian Mac-pherson, to the effect that 'If you've got a great long post-office queue, there's one group of comedians who'll say, "Look at that queue; look at them all standing; how ridiculous they look!" Then there's the other group – which is Ian and me and various others – who are in the queue, saying, "Well, we're getting a bit closer to the counter."'

As beguiling as this notional division sounds, it is actually – at least with regard to Hill himself – way off the mark. Where he really stands is in a state-of-the-art lecture facility in which the footage of the people in the post office is being beamed over his head on to a giant screen, and Harry is pointing up at them with one of those scary pensticks that throws out a red laser, proclaiming gleefully, 'Those people queuing are descended from apes.'

The roots of his respect for the food chain presumably lie in his pre-comedy medical training. (Like Graeme Garden and Jonathan Miller before him, Hill is a fully qualified doctor.) But while his performing odyssey started off in med-student revue, he never had any interest in what he scathingly terms 'all that gynaecological stuff'.[132]

And while others go to stand-up classes at Jackson's Lane com-munity centre in the vain hope of scamming themselves a career, Hill turned to comedy as a *respite* from job security. Having qualified as a doctor, he found himself eating solitary meals in hospital can-teens in the middle of the night and thinking there must be more to life. 'I just thought, Let's see what happens to people who do this sort of thing. Can you make a living out of it? What would you do during the day? I know it sounds a bit cheesy, but I just thought I had some kind of . . . of . . . *gift*.'

The clinical cut-and-paste style which is now Hill's trademark took some time to develop, however. He started out on the London circuit at the dawn of the decade, too shy to take the microphone off its stand, trying to be deadpan in the manner of Jack Dee. Compèring one night at a small Soho club, he found himself

---

[132.] He adds – somewhat emphatically for someone who shares management with David Baddiel and Frank Skinner – that 'New Lads need to be punched in the face'.

punctuating his act with snatches of Bryan Adams's 'Theme from *Robin Hood Prince of Thieves*' and ad-libbing around a flowerseller's shout he'd heard earlier that day. Thus the much-imitated – but never bettered – Hill running-gag relay was born.

'I kind of realized what I was on to,' he remembers, 'and I used to come home so excited I couldn't go to sleep – I'd be up all night thinking of new things to do. It was fantastic.'

Far from being riven with guilt at the abandonment of his Hippo-cratic destiny, this was truly a man who had found his vacation.

'It's great when someone asks what I do for a living to be able to say "Oh I'm a comedian",' Hill grins. 'It's such a ridiculous job – "That's what I do, you know, I pull funny faces" – I think it's a noble calling.'

The extent of Hill's commitment to his new line of work is demonstrated at a lavish party thrown for him by Avalon in the autumn of 1995. It's a perfect mid-nineties night out. On the enter-tainment roster is an Oompah band, and a mobile disco whose DJ soon has the entire editorial staff of *Loaded* magazine singing along with desperate urgency to the theme from *The Italian Job*. Then, suddenly, a guest collapses next to one of the heavily laden trestle tables. Perhaps it's a seizure. Perhaps she's choking on a miniature hamburger. Either way, it doesn't look good.

The time-honoured cry of 'Is there a doctor in the house?' goes up. Harry is standing quite near the stricken woman and the look on his face reads quite clearly: *Is this some kind of sick joke: what are you trying to do – get me back on the wards?*

Mercifully, just before Hill is obliged to compromise his new professional identity by going to her assistance (and let's be clear on this point, he really doesn't want to), a tiny figure flies past him . . . It is fellow doctor Matt Bradstock, who plays Hill's 'three-year-old adopted son' in his intoxicating brewery-based theatrical pag-eant, *Pub Internationale*. Bradstock saves the day with some timely first aid, Hill breathes a deep sigh of relief and the party continues, its celebratory atmosphere wholly undiminished.

Watching *Pub Internationale* transfer to the Lyric Theatre in Shaftesbury Avenue, the wisdom – the moral necessity, even – of Harry Hill's career switch is patently apparent. Anyone with good enough A-level results, a burning desire to serve humanity and an unshakeable underlying faith in their own significance, can make it as a doctor, but Hill has the rarer knack of making a whole room happy.

In tonight's audience, Bob Mortimer sits in the row behind Ronnie Corbett. Both have cause to look tense – the former because (for the reasons outlined earlier) a less reasonable man than himself might consider Hill's blend of surrealism and vaudeville a marginal copyright infringement; the latter because Bradstock (cruelly dubbed 'Jockey to the Aphids') is at the centre of a restricted-growth gag repertoire that puts his own in the shade. Yet both are laughing, if not like drains, then at least like urinals.

To see Harry Hill on a good night in 1994–6 is to experience one of the purest and most sophisticated forms of entertainment then available in the UK. The waters get a little muddied from 1997 onwards with the start of Channel 4's *The Harry Hill Show* (the forthcoming University of the Third Age pamphlet *If the Mountain won't come to Mohammed . . .* should contain an exhaustive analysis of the conflict between Harry's stand-up and TV personas, although something tells me that this important issue might inadvertently get overlooked), but as his theatrical manifestation mutates from 1994's *Pub Internationale* to 1995's *Savlon 2000* to 1996's *Comeback Special*, Hill establishes himself pretty incontrovertibly as the most reliably funny and audacious live comedian in Britain.

Hyperbole being the oil in comedy's engine, this is the sort of wild claim you might read about any number of individuals, but in Harry Hill's case it happens to be true. *Savlon 2000* is pretty much the perfect showcase for a man in total command of his craft. Aside from its very funny opening film, the show is pure stand-up, and has no theme other than the tears of a young Jimmy Savile falling on a graze and healing it (thus, the invention of Savlon). Even so, there's enough comedy meat here to feed a pride of lions.

Early on in his career, Hill could sometimes come over as a slightly brittle, closed-off performer, but now you can see him reacting to the quality of individual audience members' laughter while they, in turn, savour the thrill of the Hill comedy chase. As they're being harried, time-honoured question-begging avenues suddenly turn into cul-de-sacs ('Apparently, you can tell a lot about someone . . . from what they're like!') and obvious blind alleys open out into huge imaginative vistas.

Some people misunderstand the pleasure Hill seems to take in closing down comic possibilities. Far from being evidence of a perverse refusal to gratify his audience, it's actually a way of enhancing the elasticity of their responses – just as you'd scrunch up a balloon in your hands before inflating it – thereby enabling them to get their heads around extravagant conceits like the 'Arch-Enemies' Dinner'.

The 'Arch-Enemies' Dinner' is a kind of huge Darwinian kebab wherein all the constituents have eaten each other, until right in the middle there sits a snug and happy spider, still perfectly intact, just comfortably warm. Such death-defying conceptual leaps are all the more dramatic for being punctuated with the familiar hops and skips of consensual stand-up. 'Back me up on this,' Harry urges disingenuously, '. . . what are the chances of *that* happening?'

Hill's idea of the essential business of being a comedian – 'Coming up with ideas that I think are funny, and finding out if other people agree' – sounds about as straightforward as they come. It doesn't always work out that way, though. Would he mind giving an example of the kind of stuff he tries that people *don't* like?

'I had this idea which *I* thought was really funny,' he remembers, without a hint of apology. 'It's about my cousin Robbie. He's working on a building site, singing away, and this guy who drives by and hears the singing gets out of his car and says, "I'm a record producer: I'd like to listen to that voice some more. As a matter of fact, I'm going to the studio right now – why don't I give you a lift?" So he gets into the car and goes off, but when they get to some traffic lights, the guy starts molesting him – basically this guy isn't a record producer at all – and my cousin gets out and runs back to work. The next day, he's working on the building site again and another car pulls up with a different guy in, and the same thing happens. Obviously the first guy had been to some sort of club where molesters go and he's said "This guy who sings on the building site, he's a bit of an easy touch".' Harry pauses, as if to appreciate just how badly this joke is going down at the three-quarters-of-the-way-through stage. '. . . And the song Robbie was singing? . . . "I

181

Want . . .'" – at this point he is all but overcome with hilarity – ' "I Want To Be Loved By You".'

Is it something he particularly enjoys – when the first thing in a joke happens, then the second thing has to be the first thing happening again in order that the third thing can be funny? And the boredom of that second thing is so exquisite, and he's putting people through it in the knowledge that the final line is going to be, well not exactly flimsy . . .

'No, go on, you say it: *flimsy* . . . Yes, I do enjoy that.'

Does he mind if people don't get it?

'As long as *someone*'s laughing, I suppose the temptation is to poke anyone who doesn't get it a bit harder – just throw in something else so they'll incriminate themselves.'

Isn't that a bit cruel, though?

'Yes,' says Harry, as if pondering this possibility for the very first time, 'I suppose it is.'

One TV appearance he remembers with particular fondness is on *This Morning* in 1995, where he persuades Richard and Judy to let him demonstrate some of the ideas from a book of silly Japanese inventions.

'I really liked the bit where I'm showing them a new way of wiping your hands on the back of your trousers, and I've got my arse sticking right in the camera, and I'm going "Have you got that? Can you see that, Judy?" '

There is something delightfully old-fashioned about some of Hill's sillier moments, but for all of his admiration for the Max Walls and Spike Milligans of this world, he does not long for some imaginary golden age of pre-alternative innocence. One of the biggest misconceptions about him is that he is somehow 'lost in the fifties'.

'This sounds like I'm blowing my own trumpet,' Harry admits. 'But I like to think my work is quite timeless.'

Without getting too Anthony Clare about it, does he think his slightly skewed approach to Englishness might have been conditioned by living abroad for a while as a teenager? (Hill moved to Hong Kong for two years in the seventies, when his dad was working for a freight company there.)

He nods. 'I suppose I've always had a sense of being a bit different, even though I probably haven't been. I'm actually very straight, really.' As that chicken-in-the-oven routine at Glastonbury proved, straightness can be its own kind of kinky.

Out of the country at the height of the punk era, Hill was kept in touch with what was going on back home by a regular correspondence with a friend who advised him that ELO were the future of rock 'n' roll.

'It was sad really. He died last year, and I found a whole load of his letters. There it was in black and white, him saying "Jeff Lynne is the new Paul McCartney".'

It can't have been easy making new friends in a school full of kids when you were just passing through?

'I made an effort for a while,' Harry remembers, 'but no one was interested. And I remember thinking after six months, I'm not going to try any more, I'm just going to have *me*. After that, it was OK.'

Hill came back to England – 'tanned and rested, with a beard and a safari suit' – some years before Hong Kong finally reverted to Chinese rule (this belated handover of colonial power being commemorated with the sort of compensatory pomp a devious person might invest in the return of an overdue library book).

While apparently untouched by the course of international relations, Harry's deviantly blimpish persona actually marks him out as a post-imperial paragon – blithely celebrating the decline of Britain's global influence in a cheery miasma of celebrity trivia. On Ned Sherrin's Radio 4 showbiz love-in, *Loose Ends*, Harry interviews former *Bread* star, Eurovision runner-up and *Grease* veteran Sonia. 'If you switch round the first two letters of your name and add a B, it spells Bosnia,' he informs her guilelessly. 'So . . . is there a lot of conflict in your life?'

The Reeves/Hill Nietzsche divergence, *or* nailing your colours to Friedrich's mast

On first coming across Friedrich Nietzsche's observation that 'In laughter all that is evil becomes holy, and is absolved by its own bliss', it seems probable that Vic Reeves will be the comedian to whom it most clearly applies. Yet I once asked Reeves for his interpretation of that statement, and he said, 'I suppose it means that if someone has bug eyes or a particularly goofy tooth, you can't laugh at them in the street . . . but you *can* do if they're onstage.'

This vision of his own role as a kind of safety valve for some of humanity's less acceptable inclinations – of it being almost a performer's *duty* to play up the things about them which people would feel guilty about laughing at had they not paid good money for the privilege – is a surprisingly socially conscious one for such an avowedly apolitical comedian. Harry Hill's idea of what he does, on the other hand (that basically anything you can get away with is OK, so long as it's said in the name of comedy) is much more in line with Nietzschean thinking.

'If you drop a Bible from a great height, you can kill a field-mouse,' Harry muses mischievously, nailing his colours firmly to Friedrich's 'God is dead' mast. 'So maybe the Bible *isn't* all good.'

If the mountain shall not go to Mohammed, Mohammed shall go to the mountain . . .

a.k.a. Harry Hill's TV odyssey

While Vic and Bob achieve a perfect televisual realization of pretty much everything they do on their first attempt, with *Vic Reeves Big Night Out*, it takes Harry Hill nigh on a decade to get things right. This hiatus is especially surprising since his work has such a strong visual element right from the off.

'My friend had a cine camera and we used to make horror films in the woods when I was in my teens,' he remembers wistfully in 1994, 'but as you get older it's harder to persuade people to give up their time for things like that – they think you're being a bit childish.'

The exquisitely heartless cinematic vignette about a 'boy with a big face' which kicks off Harry's 1996 *Comeback Special* shows just how much he can achieve on film. Yet his BBC2 début, *Harry Hill's Fruit Fancies* – a series of black-and-white shorts, filmed at the house in Kent where Hill grew up ('My mum was selling it, so we didn't have to pay her anything') – doesn't quite do him justice.

And, from the Channel 4 executive who considers him 'too minority interest' to a disastrous pilot variety show for the BBC (Hill says: 'It must have been the only pilot ever made that no one who was involved with it wanted to get a series'), none of his early brushes with the medium paint a very promising picture.

In fact, talking to him shortly before the triumphant 1997 appearance on The *David Letterman Show* which marks an early turning-point in his televisual fortunes, the usually jovial Hill seems disillusioned with the whole business.

'TV producers sit in a comedy club and hear everybody laughing and they think "we must get this",' he observes with an uncharacteristic sourness, 'but they don't know what "this" is.'

While Hill's experiences as a badly needed star-turn on ITV's abysmal (relaunched) *Saturday Live* seem to provide further supporting evidence for this jaundiced opinion of television executives, the overwhelming confirmation that he can connect directly with a mass audience actually gives his TV career a much-needed leg-up. The 'wall of inertia' which his manager Richard Allen-Turner had previously encountered is swiftly scaled, and Hill selects Channel 4 from among those clamouring to sign him up.

Since the Radio 4 template *Harry Hill's Fruit Corner* is – in Harry's estimation – 'basically a TV show on the radio with what were originally visual ideas translated into sound effects, anyway', transferring to the small screen should be a doddle. It doesn't quite turn out that way, though, largely because the protective structures *The Harry Hill Show* puts in place around its star end up getting in the way of the very tangential virtuosity they are supposed to be showing off.

'I think Harry sometimes does something a lot of performers do,' Richard Allen-Turner says later, 'which is to set too much store by an unfounded fear that the audience will get tired of them.' While the resulting emphasis on catch-phrases and endlessly recurring supporting characters (the Nanna Hills and Bert Kwouks of this world) may well reflect an engaging modesty, it also prevents Harry's inspired 'multiple gag plate-spinning routine' from ever getting into its stride, and ends up seeming somewhat self-conscious.

As it eventually appears on Channel 4, *The Harry Hill Show* is a gentle, absurdist dust-storm of fantasy shoe-shop advertisements, non-celebrity walk-ons from unlikely sounding members of the Hill family, and Keith Harris and Orville singing The Fugees. Moments of genius such as the opening edition's climactic 'war in the wood-land' sequence (wherein Harry strives in vain to stop the badgers from getting involved in a vicious armed conflict between the barn owls and the tawny owls) are up there with anything in the canon of English TV lunacy – from Spike Milligan to the *Big Night Out*, to the best of Russ Abbot – but while the first series is generally deemed to be a success, it never quite settles into a rhythm.

The show's determination to establish Hill's very off-beat talent firmly in a mainstream light-entertainment setting has a fundamentally disruptive intent,[133] but the disruption cuts both ways. However much Harry appreciates the guidance of battle-hardened TV professionals like director Robin Nash, veteran of *The Two Ronnies* and *The Generation Game* ('He was very good at asking questions like "Did you see them as real guinea pigs, or men dressed in guinea-pig suits?"' Hill beams), the resulting veneer of old-school polish muddies the comedic shine slightly.

The real problem is that *The Harry Hill Show* doesn't seem entirely sure of what it actually wants to be – a late-night cult attraction slotting in between *Frasier* and *Eurotrash*, or something more suited to the high plains of BBC1 at Saturday teatime. And after a Channel 4 reshuffle replaces Harry's champions with a less sympathetic new regime, no one at the station seems quite sure what they want it to be, either.

In the ensuing confusion, some very entertaining things happen. An increasingly frustrated Harry embarks on a heroic campaign of nibbling the hand that feeds him, with a series of sketches about Channel 4 which make the things Spike Milligan used to say about the BBC look positively complimentary. And a third and final series uses the collapse of Hill's relationship with the network as a platform for some of the most outrageous material ever seen on British TV, particularly the 'naughty horses' routine about equine deviants in

---

[133.] 'Because it's a very cosy, familiar format,' Harry explains, 'that makes it all the stranger when you see Matt [Bradstock, Hill's diminutive sidekick, a.k.a. 'the party lifesaver'] in his best friend's mother's bra.'

the royal stables deriving unseemly pleasure from their positioning between the Queen's thighs.

In the next thrilling instalment of Harry Hill's televisual odyssey, far from being locked in the tower like what he should have been, Harry escapes captivity in a small-screen cell of his own design via the unlikely rope-ladder of tabloid TV journalism . . .

'Harry got asked to write some TV review columns in the *Sun*,' Richard Allen-Turner explains, 'and what he did was very funny and very refreshing.' Far from hiding his light under Gary Bushell, Hill eschewed the illiberal gruntings of his Oi-loving patron for a sophisticated and free-wheeling approach which combined his tried and tested knack for pop-cultural detail with a beguiling and (in those surroundings) unusually gentle sense of mischief.

Initially sceptical when Allen-Turner suggested that his new-found critical acumen might transfer well to the very medium at which it was initially directed, Harry eventually offers a pilot to Channel 4 in fulfilment of the last stage of his contract with them. When they turn it down, ITV pick it up, and the resulting show – unappetizingly titled *Harry Hill's TV Burp* – not only paves the way for an *All New Harry Hill Show* on the same channel, but also wins a well-deserved Silver Rose of Montreux, just like *Shooting Stars* before it.

While it ought to be a shocking example of television eating itself, *Harry Hill's TV Burp* is actually an eructation more in the grand and satisfying post-prandial manner traditionally believed to be good manners in certain Eastern cultures. It is also a concept perfectly adapted to the slightly cheap-and-cheerful look which has often been the hallmark of Avalon TV productions (the production arm founded by Jon Thoday and Richard Allen-Turner in response to the realization that 'quite a lot of people were preying on comedians' ideas and not remunerating them successfully').

TV Burp seems to have overcome a lot of the structural problems of the old Channel 4 show, largely via the practical realization that, as Allen-Turner puts it, 'Harry doesn't need to surround himself with characters, or clutter things up with complex threadlines'. There is something strangely transcendent about the sight of Hill cropping up on the set of *Emmerdale* (a post-industrial Harry Worth with his warehouseman's coat and clipboard), dispensing much-needed health and safety advice to the cast of that most disaster-prone of soaps. Shorn of some of the kitschy accoutrements (take a bow, Gareth Southgate Badger) which were causing more problems than they solved, Harry is at last set free to realize his full malevolent potential, in the process earning the apt soubriquet[134] 'comedy's worrying uncle'.

bing bing bing . . . Satellite of pub

Step back in time again, now, to the opening night of Harry Hill's *Pub Internationale* at the Edinburgh Pleasance in 1994.[135] Consider the historic moment at which genial landlord Al Murray first introduces the underlying theme of 'tavern etiquette as metaphor for world affairs': 'When will Guinness and Murphy's be served side by side? This madness has got to end!'

No one in the room at this point – least of all Murray himself – realizes that he is establishing the template for at least the next ten years of his professional life. Having lurked around benignly on the fringes of the Avalon community for some time without giving much sign of imminent greatness, he'd come up with the character of the Pub Landlord in the final stages of rehearsals, but had no fixed idea of how he might develop.

'Harry had heard lots of bright ideas from me before,' Murray admits ruefully, some years later, 'and nothing much had ever come of them.'[136] This one was different, though. A profoundly conflicted

---

[134.] In an unusually well-observed *Guardian* TV preview.

[135.] The moment at the end of the show when his Pub Band, 'genetically engineered pub musicians who drink from the lager of life' (i.e. Hill in pompadour wig, his 'adopted son' Alan on keyboards and a beat-perfect Murray on drums) bring the proceedings to a rousing climax with a telling Chas'n Dave-style assault on Blur's popular hit song 'Girls and Boys' – complete with Hill on spoons – might reasonably be described as 'The Bayeux Tapestry of Britpop'.

[136.] Before the Pub Landlord, Al Murray's most reliable comic staple was doing impressions of different kinds of gun.

xenophobe with a nice line in spurious rationalization – 'I'm not saying it's right, I'm not saying it's wrong, it's just the way things are' – the Pub Landlord plainly had legs from the first moment he stepped out on the stage.

Beginning with little more than a catch-phrase (albeit one worthy of Judas Iscariot), Murray spends several months carefully buffing the character, until by the time he's back in Edinburgh again a year later, with *The Landlord's Late Lock In*, he has dropped the rather gratuitous *Star Trek* top and is delivering an object lesson in how to make the unpalatable delicious. In just a few months of extremely hard work, Murray's creation has progressed from an above-average club turn to a brilliantly rounded piece of social and political observation.

Alternately belligerent and lachrymose, a veritable Gazza of the pumps, the Pub Landlord philosophizes eloquently on every topic under the sun – from his love and admiration for the fathers of English nationhood ('Churchill, Nelson, Ray Davies of the Kinks') to the possibility that some exaggeration might have been involved in the writing of the Gospels. 'Bear in mind,' Murray counsels sagely, 'they were fishermen.'

The Pub Landlord is a much richer characterization than his most obvious comedic forebear, Harry Enfield's Loadsamoney.[137] Where Enfield's crest-of-a-wave Thatcherite plasterer was something of a one-trick pony, Murray builds his embattled Little Englander into a springboard for real intellectual debate. And to watch him provoke a live audience into thinking more deeply than they want to about serious issues which they actually have no real interest in is one of the big treats of nineties comedy.

'All he is really,' Al confesses in 2002, 'is an excuse to start talking . . . I don't even see him as a character any more, just as a way of performing that interests me.'[138] It's as a means of enabling his creator to manipulate a live crowd – something he does better than

[137.] Daniel Defoe's 'true-born Englishman' is probably a bit nearer the mark in ancestral terms.
[138.] No wonder Murray takes it amiss when people ask (as they sometimes do, comedy being the cut-throat business that it is) when he's going to ditch the Landlord: 'That's like asking Harry "When are you going to do some blue jokes?" or telling Mark Thomas to "drop the politics".'

almost any other comedian (with the possible exception of Frank Skinner) at work in this period – that the Pub Landlord really sets Murray free.

While admitting to a feeling of mild unease when strangers greet him with a cheery 'Oh, you're spot on about the French, mate', he suffers nothing like the agonies of conscience Warren Mitchell used to in Alf Garnett's heyday – when people would come up and pat him on the back for 'having a go at the darkies' and he would have to say 'I'm not having a go at them, I'm having a go at *you*'.

If you watch *Till Death Us Do Part* now, you can't help wondering if Mitchell's unwanted admirers didn't actually have a point, as the bigotry itself comes through more vigorously than the satire of that bigotry which is supposedly the point of the whole exercise. It seems unlikely that anyone – except the most devout Europhile – will ever feel that way about Al Murray's creation.

'There's obviously a big divide between what I myself think and what I say as the Landlord,' Murray insists, 'but the things he says are so loony and hallucinatory that if anyone agrees with them, that just takes the joke to another level really.'

So what is it about the Pub Landlord that stops Murray getting bored with him?

'I think it's the fact that even when he's completely wrong – which he usually is – the conviction and the energy behind the *way* he's wrong are strangely admirable. I'm not really convinced of all that much, but he's convinced that *everything* he says is right. And he wants to convince you that it is, too, however strong the evidence to the contrary.'

Watching the Landlord in full flood on BBC Scotland's *Live Floor Show* on Saturday nights in early 2003, two realizations hit home. One is just how flexible this superficially brittle character has turned out to be (when he's not just wittering on about the French, that is) – equally well-adapted to the Suez-style post-imperial nuances of the second Gulf Crisis as he was to the intricacies of the Exchange Rate Mechanism. The other is what a shame it seems that no one has ever just pointed a camera at the Pub Landlord in front of a live audience and put the results straight out on to the airwaves as a prime-time TV show.

Prior to the start of what is hopefully a long and fruitful new association with BBC2, Murray's large-scale TV exposure is restricted to a couple of series for Sky.

'I suppose it has the same vaguely fringe cachet as appearing in Edinburgh,' Murray notes wryly, 'in that if you want to see me, you have to subscribe to a Murdoch channel.'

'We wanted to do something that went against the current comedy fashion,' Murray explains, 'that whole kind of low-key, mumbling thing. So we decided to make an old-fashioned American-style sitcom, performed comically and clearly in front of an audience, and somehow to be doing that on Sky made complete sense.' The only problem with *Time Gentlemen Please* is that it feels like it's been made in the hope of being the sort of show its lead character would want to watch.

There has been one very positive side-effect to the somewhat half-arsed nature of the Landlord's TV exposure to date, which is that it's kept Murray's live work on its mettle, rather than encouraging him to pander to the reduced audience expectations that inevitably come with a successful small-screen incarnation. Given that it's when bouncing off a slightly drunk crowd like a Francophobe pinball that the Pub Landlord is seen at his best (and the sort of extended West End run he embarks on in the winter of 2003 would not have seemed like such a big event had he been all over the box as well), maybe his low TV profile has been a sacrifice worth making.

In a strange kind of comedic Russian-doll scenario, Al Murray's tribulations in finding an appropriate TV vehicle seem to echo Harry Hill's. It had always seemed that he was prevented from getting the terrestrial slot he so richly deserved by fallout from Avalon's big tussle with the BBC (which will be dealt with in due course), but that turns out not to have been the case.

'BBC2 had the script for eighteen months and never got round to giving it a proper look,' Murray remembers, apparently without bitterness. 'Then, when I won the Perrier Award [in 1999, at the third time of nomination], they suddenly got all excited and wanted to make the show, but by that time I'd signed up with Sky.'

Radio 4 then had the brass neck to commission a radio programme with the actionably derivative title of *World of Pub*, which somehow won itself an instant transfer to TV. Murray doesn't actually mention this himself. I just wanted to have it down in black and white, as without written evidence it's almost hard to believe it really happened.

11
'That Would Be an Ecumenical Matter'

Father Ted answers the Irish Question

'It would be nice if we could say that we were influenced by Patrick Kavanagh or some great Irish comic tradition, but really it's just Reggie Perrin, Fawlty Towers, The Young Ones – stuff like that'

Arthur Mathews

'I've only been Irish since I moved to England last October. Back home, there didn't seem to be much point'

Dermot Carmody

'A child has been lodged in the tunnel of goats.' By the time these immortal words bring the first episode of *Father Ted* to a close, it's abundantly clear that the similarly overcrowded Annals Of Sitcom Greatness are going to have to make room for a new initiate. Not only is this the finest comedy ever made about three disgraced Catholic priests and their housekeeper,[139] living on a tiny island off the west coast of Ireland, it also establishes its writers Graham Linehan and Arthur Mathews as a potential Galton and Simpson for the millennium's end.

On meeting the lanky, mercurial Linehan and the amiable, soft-spoken Mathews, the first question which needs to be asked is

---

[139.] 'There have been a lot of housekeepers in priest-based comedies,' says Arthur Mathews proudly, 'but ours [Mrs 'Ah, ye will, ye will' Doyle] is the housekeeper other housekeepers call "guv'nor".'

whether the two men who have single-handedly revived the mori-
bund British sitcom tradition are *happy* for their work to be regarded
as British, given that its writers, actors and director Declan Lowney
all hail from what Terry Wogan is still wont to refer to as 'The
Emerald Isle'.

'I like *Father Ted* to be thought of that way,' Mathews nods, 'in
that it comes from the British tradition of TV comedy, which is
the one we've always loved and grown up with. And we'd hate it
to be regarded as some kind of "ethnic"-type show ... I mean
Ireland doesn't bear the same relation to Britain as, say, India does:
I don't think there's that much of a difference between the two,
really, culturally.'

This last point might come as a surprise to those of a more
self-consciously Gaelic persuasion, but at a time when – from
Angela's Ashes to *Riverdance* – an Irish accent threatens to become
the global currency of unexamined sentiment, *Father Ted*'s brilliantly witty vision of Anglo-Irish cultural interaction represents a
bracing and hilarious corrective.

Like most aesthetic revelations that seem to come from nowhere, *Father Ted* has a complex prehistory. Graham Linehan
and Arthur Mathews first met while working for the Irish rock
magazine *Hot Press*, and their comedy partnership began with a
group called The Joshua Trio. 'We'd re-enact moments from U2's
career onstage – like Adam Clayton's drug bust or a nativity play
for the birth of Bono,' Mathews remembers fondly. 'That was our
Footlights.'

Having proceeded from performing their own U2-based sketches
onstage to 'writing stuff and sending it in to TV people', Linehan
and Mathews soon found themselves writing *Stuff* in a more formal
sense, as leading contributors to Alexei Sayle's BBC2 series of the
same name. It was from this connection that their sitcom début –
1994's rather creaky Sayle vehicle, *Paris* – proceeded.

Looking back now, it is hard to see how a comedy series starring
Alexei Sayle as a grumpy impressionist painter could possibly have
been anything other than an instant critical and commercial success.
Yet somehow *Paris* never quite cut the mustard. For all its manifest
failings, the series did demonstrate the breadth of cultural reference
and willingness to go out on a limb which – allied with the lessons

they would learn from this painful formative experience – would help to make Linehan and Mathews's next project something really special. Their contributions to the first series of *The Fast Show* (especially 'Ted and Ralph', the hilarious celibate–gay rewrite of *Lady Chatterley's Lover*, which they initially devised but then ended up handing over to Whitehouse and Higson) gave a clearer indication of what they were capable of. As did their occasional additional writing credits on *The Day Today*.

'We had a meeting with them and sent over a couple of ideas for sketches,' Mathews remembers. 'And we were so excited to be associated with it in any way that we used to mention it on our CV, but then people started giving us credit for stuff we hadn't done, so we had to take it off.'

'Our contribution', says Linehan proudly, 'was like getting a letter published in the letters page of a really great magazine.'

As with *The Day Today*, it's the attention to detail – both cultural and emotional – that makes *Father Ted* such a delight to watch, but whereas the former show makes its own mould, the latter achieves the – if anything – even more impressive feat of reviving a dying art form. The fairground scene at the end of the first episode contains more comic invention than you'd expect in an entire series of most of its rival sitcoms. And the writing blends originality and structural daring with a real respect for form, in that the three main characters – in the classic tradition of *Porridge* and *Steptoe & Son* – are trapped somewhere with people they don't necessarily like.

The causes of their collective exile are, Arthur Mathews explains, 'deliberately vague'. For long-suffering Father Ted Crilly, it's some kind of financial irregularity (although as Ted is at constant pains to emphasize, the money was 'just resting' in his account); for childlike, angel-faced Father Dougal, it was a baptism that went wrong. Very wrong. What about the venal old wino, Father Jack? 'His crime is so big they can't even talk about it.'

'The great thing about priests', Graham Linehan observes clinically, 'is that when someone comes into a room and they've got a dog collar on, there's no exposition needed. All you need to write about is what's above the collar.'

'The other great thing about priests', Mathews butts in, 'is that they prefer to talk about almost anything other than religion.[140] And of course they all *know* each other, too.' It's this combination of factors that makes men of the cloth – in Linehan's words – 'ideal for a sitcom'.

'One thing we learned very early on,' Linehan continues, 'is that whatever you do with the characters, they have to be in – I never know how to pronounce this word – stasis. Every show is a circle that begins and ends in the same situation. That makes it very easy to structure, because all you have to do is figure out how to get these people back into exactly the same position they were in at the start.'

If the characters have to be fully formed from the beginning, that means there's no room for the sort of self-conscious personal growth you might get in an American sitcom.

'The great thing about British sitcoms,' Linehan confirms, 'is that the sadness has always been implicit, whereas American sitcoms have to *stop* and do the sad bit.'

Stopping and doing the American bit

At this point, it is necessary to instigate what those of a basketball-playing disposition sometimes refer to as a 'Time Out'. Not for one of those periodic lapses into maudlin sentiment for which US sitcoms are still – at the time of Linehan's observation about 'stopping and doing the sad bit' – justly notorious, but to consider the impact that seismic creative shifts in American TV have had on *Father Ted* itself. For it's in acting as a kind of prism – refracting shafts of light from the other side of the Atlantic so as to illuminate the British sitcom tradition in an entirely new way – that *Father Ted* has had its most lasting and inspirational impact.

Consider first the race of saccharine aliens which seemed to inhabit most of the shows in Channel 4's 6.30 p.m. US comedy strand in the late eighties and early nineties (and by that I don't just

---

140. 'Arthur has an uncle who is a priest,' Linehan explains later on, 'and he'll come into a room and say things like "I see Madonna's at the top of the charts".'

mean Robin Williams's Mork). Neither the Cunninghams nor the Cosbys, nor the insufferable Kate and Allie, ever uttered a cross word without instantly regretting it. They spent all their time 'relating to each other' and learning to 'work things through' within the family group, prompting all self-respecting emotionally repressed, class-fixated UK viewers to ask themselves the question, 'What on earth is *wrong* with these people?'

So when Roseanne's sister Jackie slammed the door and stomped off shouting 'Oh, go to hell' and Roseanne responded 'This *is* hell', something very unusual and exciting was going on in the world of American sitcoms. The Sartre-inspired contention that hell is other people – or, more specifically, other people in your own family unit – has been a staple feature of British sitcoms since the year dot, but it had not previously been an idea your average American TV network was all that keen to take on board. And yet at some points in the early nineties, it began to feel as if one of the only things that could bring the archetypal American family together was the celebration of its own dysfunction.

The virtuoso opening sequence of *The Simpsons*, wherein the family runs home from shopping, school (where Bart is writing lines on the board to the effect that he 'must not waste chalk') and work at the nuclear power plant, to settle down in front of the TV and watch themselves, proved entirely prophetic (and not just of the way so many people would come to build their daily or weekly routines around events in Springfield).

When it first appeared, *The Simpsons* – alongside similarly subversive, live-action blue-collar sitcoms, such as *Roseanne* and (to a lesser but still significant extent) *Married With Children* – was part of an unexpected shift towards realism in US TV. With the Reagan era drawing to an end, no one could deny that this trend had a political dimension. Sensing a rejection of the apple-pie family values fantasies which had underpinned the Reaganite orgy of greed and fiscal irresponsibility, George Bush (Sr) famously said he wanted the average American family to be 'more like The Waltons and less like The Simpsons'.

Producer James L. Brooks, on the other hand, or perhaps on the same hand (looking at the self-confessed alcoholic jailbird George Sr raised, you can see how any realistic depiction of family life as it is actually lived would be intensely distressing to him), insisted that *The Simpsons* 'shows the normal American family in all its beauty and all its horror'. As the man behind such shameless Hollywood schmaltz as *Terms of Endearment,* Brooks's views on this subject were not necessarily to be trusted either, but *The Simpsons'* creator Matt Groening certainly intended the show to turn out that way. Why else would he have named all the main characters except the angelic brat Bart (anag.) – father Homer, mother Marge and daughters Lisa and Maggie – after members of his own family?

Their newly realistic depiction of family life was just one way in which *The Simpsons* and *Roseanne* extended the sitcom envelope. Another was in emphasizing that (except in Homer's case, obviously) a blue collar does not automatically cut off the flow of blood to the brain.

The possibility that large proportions of the world's inhabitants might not actually be doctors or bank managers is one that rarely seems to occur to the people who make British sitcoms in the early nineties. I certainly can't think of many home-grown efforts – with the honourable exceptions of *Only Fools and Horses* and *One Foot in the Grave* – in which the main character failing to get a job at the meat-packing factory would be exploited for anything other than a cheap laugh. Roseanne even watches things on *Oprah,* and few British comedies at this stage pitch themselves near enough to reality to admit that people actually watch TV.

By the time Linehan and Mathews write *Father Ted,* the *Roseanne/Simpsons* virus of emotional acuity and metatextual mischief has spread – as comedy viruses (and musical ones too, come to that) often do – up the socio-economic food chain. *Seinfeld* and *The Larry Sanders Show* extend this new freedom of thought and expression from the middle-American proletariat to the metropolitan middle class, in the process connecting them up with the urbane heritage of *Cheers* and *Frasier.* It's in establishing a worthy domestic counterpart to the playfulness and sophistication of these great American shows that *Father Ted* registers its most vital breakthrough.

In a bid to gain a deeper understanding of *Father Ted*'s transatlantic antecedents, a further flirtation with the controversial Q&A format has now been authorized.

ME: *This is going to be one of those question-and-answer things, is that OK?*

GL: I love those kind of interviews, there's none of that 'he says indulgently, stuff.

AM: 'For a moment he falters as if ashamed of what he's just done . . .'

GL: 'He stands up on the table and pisses on to the floor. We are both embarrassed, but I carry on as if nothing has happened' . . . [Laughter.]

ME: *I know you're both big fans of* Seinfeld, *and can sometimes be heard joining in the nationwide chorus of outrage about BBC2 never giving it an appropriate time-slot and only showing old episodes from 1992* [an issue which excites more agitation among sections of the cul-turally literate middle classes in the mid to late nineties than the plight of the Kurds or deforestation in the Amazon basin]. *What is it about it that you like so much?*

AM: [with a shrug, as if aware of how mild-mannered and ineffectual this judgement is going to look on paper] It's just very well-written and the characters are really good.

GL: I think it does something me and Arthur have always wanted to see, which is that the people in it just talk about things that you talk about. One of my favourite ever *Seinfeld* jokes is when they say they're going to the flea market and George Costanza asks 'What goes on there, exactly?' and Seinfeld says 'You think fleas are somehow involved, don't you?' [More laughter.] Unless it's a parodic moment or something, the jokes are not landed on very heavily. And because Larry David and Jerry Seinfeld do most of the writing, they manage to give the show a really distinct personality. Sitcoms that are written by factory just don't have that.[141] As good as *Roseanne*

[141.] Admirers of, say, *Friends* have good grounds to dispute this, but a fair compromise between the pro- and anti-factory positions would probably be that while it can sometimes produce great work, ensemble comedy writing can also generate a strange kind of collective hysteria, as the tubby full-backs and headless centre-forwards of the team struggle to show that

was at its best, there was always something a little bit . . . well . . . the word 'factory' is the perfect way to describe it.

ME: *And yet when people write articles about why American sitcoms are better than British ones, they always tend to say it's because Americans usually use a team of writers . . .*

GL: That's a ridiculous argument. We were on holiday in the States recently and the vast amount of sitcoms there were rubbish – we only get to see the one or two good ones here. That's why when you see something like *Seinfeld* or *The Larry Sanders Show*[142] in America, amongst all the other things that are on, it's just wonderful.

ME: *It's strange, though, given the low opinion people generally have of American TV, the way* Seinfeld *and* Roseanne *and* Frasier *are not only the most intelligent shows, but they also tend to top the ratings as well, whereas here it's* Noel's House Party *and* Blind Date . . .

AM: You have to remember that in America the big ratings wars are fought over the sitcoms – they're the flagship shows – whereas here it's the soaps . . .

GL: I do think that the American acting tends to have a more kind of energetic, throwaway style, which I like. I think the problem with British sitcom acting is people queuing up to say the line. In *Seinfeld*, for instance, you feel that everything's just *happening*, and it's wonderful in that sense. I think it would greatly improve the more kind of naturalistic – or supposedly naturalistic – British sitcoms if they borrowed a bit from the *Seinfeld* style of acting; for

---

they're worth their places by playing to what they perceive to be the strengths of the enterprise as a whole.

[142.] The reason that the brilliant *The Larry Sanders Show* doesn't loom quite as large in this discussion as it should do is that it had only just started being shown on British TV at the time, and one of the participants in the conversation (Oh all right then, it was me) hadn't at this point got over his irrational hatred of Shandling's previous *It's Garry Shandling Show* enough to realize how great Larry is. What a big fool he (Oh, all right then, I) must be.

example, if actors did things while other people were doing things.

ME: *Are there any other senses in which the distinction between British and American sitcoms is particularly meaningful to you?*

AM: I suppose American sitcoms tend to be shot on film, and they all seem to be set in the modern day in the real world, whereas British sitcoms – at least the kind we like, such as *Blackadder* and *Reggie Perrin* – tend to be more surreal. Their sketch shows are weirder than ours, though. I love that thing in *Saturday Night Live* where this guy is at work, standing by the photocopier, and he's so bored he just says nothing except variations on people's names.

GL: 'Steve! Steveooo! The Stevemeister!'

Looking back on this conversation a few years later, it's intriguing to see how the things that Graham and Arthur say they'd like to see more of in British sitcoms – 'actors doing things while other people are doing things', guys at work standing by photocopiers experimenting with different ways of saying their colleagues' names – all end up happening in *The Office*. There's a further flash forward to that illustrious twenty-first-century sitcom landmark in Linehan and Mathews's intermittently excellent 1996 sketch show *Big Train*, where an anonymous white-collar workplace set-up very similar (in all respects other than the litter-bins overflowing with suspiciously soggy tissues) to *The Office*'s is riven with an epidemic of uncontrolled public masturbation.

Before we get too caught up in that disturbing onanistic tableau, it's time to turn our attention back to *Father Ted*, hopefully making this transition in the same seamless way that Father Dougal's mind segues back and forth between 'dreams' and 'reality'.

Returning to that pre-interlude discussion of implicit and explicit sadness as if nothing out of the ordinary has happened . . .

The suggestion that there doesn't seem to be all that much real melancholy in *Father Ted* – apart from the married couple who are always fighting but then stop to put on a show of domestic harmony in front of the priests – provokes a burst of anguished laughter from Mathews.

'Yes there is,' Linehan exclaims. 'Ted's situation is *terrible*: he's quite an intelligent man, and he's stuck in the arse-end of nowhere with these two awful people!'

Awful people they may be, but there's no doubt that the dominant tone of Father Ted with regard to the Church is affectionate rather than vituperative.

'There's no way you could call either of us practising Catholics,' Mathews admits, 'but we didn't want to make a Sinead O'Connor album.'

Hard-hitting anti-clerical satire is not really on *Father Ted*'s agenda. Except for the occasional endearing moment of priestly uncertainty from Ted Crilly himself – 'When you actually sit down and think about religion . . . It's one big Roswell Incident' – there's little to offend even the wariest of believers.

'If you look at it in social terms,' says Linehan, 'which you shouldn't really, I think we're probably doing more of a service by not attacking the church but just being a little bit silly about it . . . There's one moment I'm really proud of, when Ted is talking about Jesus. Dougal says "God, he was fantastic, wasn't he?" And Ted goes "Ah, he was brilliant!" There's no way anyone could look at that and say it's offensive.'

'I think it's very innocent,' says Mathews. 'Like that bit when the bishop gets a relic shoved up his arse,' he laughs, 'in the great British tradition of people getting things shoved up their arses – that's lovely gentle humour.'

'We'd be self-censorious more than anything,' Mathews continues, pointing to an episode in the second series which is set at Easter and concerns giving things up for Lent. The producer wanted it broadcast on Good Friday, a mildly provocative course which the writers resisted – 'Myself and Graham are hardly regular churchgoers,' Mathews reiterates, 'but we instinctively didn't want to do that.'

'I was just worried about my parents,' Linehan admits afterwards. 'I knew they would break with convention by actually watching it, and that would be a big step for them, because Good Friday is a very solemn day in Ireland.'

Mathews nods vehemently: 'It's the only day of the year apart from Christmas when you can't get a drink.'

Devotees of the great (and bibulous) Irish humorist Flann O'Brien – also known as Myles Na Gopaleen – may delight at a kindred tone in some of *Father Ted*'s most elegant moments. Yet the series's authors insist they only read him after they'd finished writing it, to see why his name kept coming up.

'It would be nice if we could say that we were influenced by Patrick Kavanagh or some great Irish comic tradition,' says Mathews, 'but really it's just *Reggie Perrin, Fawlty Towers, The Young Ones* – stuff like that.'

'One thing we did want to illustrate with the show', Linehan says in a rare didactic moment, 'is that there's definitely a one-way thing, which is that the English know nothing about the Irish, but the Irish know everything about the English, because they watch British TV, read British newspapers and follow British football teams. We just wanted to make it clear that people in Ireland are paying attention.'

So if *Father Ted* can be said to have a goal – beyond the provision of classic sitcom entertainment – that goal would be 'to show the English how much the Irish know about them'?

'Absolutely,' beams Linehan. 'I think ours is probably the only sitcom on British TV at the moment to mention *Byker Grove* or Blur and Oasis – I'm amazed that more people aren't doing it.'

The thing is that when they do start to do this – as they inevitably will – those references probably won't grow out of character and context in the marvellously organic way they do in *Father Ted* (as in the brilliant episode where the 'bad priest' leads Dougal from the way of righteousness with his renegade Oasis-liking ways, or the fantastic 'all-priest *Stars in Their Eyes* lookalike competition'), they'll just be there to show how marvellously in tune the writers are with the *Zeitgeist*.

'You're right there actually,' Linehan concedes. 'It'll be a bit painful when the kid in *2.4 Children* comes on and says "I've got the new Oasis album". Especially if there's no new Oasis album out at the time.'

Ardal O'Hanlon, the London-based Irish comedian who gives Father Dougal a holy fool innocence worthy of James Stewart, has already cropped up at the end of chapter 5.[143] But the unfamiliarity to British audiences of the actors playing the elder two thirds of *Father Ted*'s priestly trio, Dermot Morgan (Ireland's answer to Rory Bremner) and veteran radio comic Frank Kelly, seems to illustrate Linehan's 'one-way' point perfectly. And emphasizing the informed, outward-looking nature of rural Irish culture ('Everyone's got satellite dishes,' Linehan insists, 'so a much higher proportion of people watch *Seinfeld* and *Larry Sanders*') is just one of a number of ways in which *Father Ted* flips conventional wisdom on its head.

[143.] While the child-in-a-man's-body role of Dougal was written specially for him, O'Hanlon is not one of those comedians who couldn't wait to use their stand-up act as a stepping stone to other careers. 'I always had it in for actors,' he confesses, as *Father Ted* begins its first series. 'I never understood why anyone would want to be one.'

By the time he appears in Edinburgh a year and a bit later, in a larger venue than his intimate stand-up style can really cope with, the awesome pulling power of *Father Ted* ensures that people are queuing half-way to Aberdeen to see him. O'Hanlon is too modest and well-balanced an individual not to find this deeply disturbing. Like Jane Austen's ghost chancing upon a copy of *Pride and Prejudice* with Colin Firth on the cover, he is forced to ask himself some very difficult questions. As a consequence, he, too, ends up writing a novel, not to mention starring in the abysmal BBC ratings-topper *My Hero*.

Another one of those weird flashback-type incidents involving *Roseanne*, *The Simpsons* and *Seinfeld*. If this was happening in *Wayne's World*, Mike Myers and Dana Carvey would be wiggling all twenty fingers while raising and lowering their hands and intoning 'Biddley-do, Biddley-do, Biddley-do'

The only way to understand *Father Ted*'s place in the broader reversal of traditional intellectual polarity which takes place in the early nineties[144] – a time when two dimensions can offer more depth than three, and satellite dishes are bringers of enlightenment rather than totems of cultural degradation – is to go back to the origins of *The Simpsons*. Matt Groening's first family of US cartoon fun began life in America in 1987 as part of *The Tracey Ullman Show*. The BBC snapped up the heinous Ullman but not the 'too American' *Simpsons* (which is a bit like picking a ripe peach and only eating the stone) and the supposed barbarians of Sky TV were then able to use the subtle multi-faceted comedy of Bart, Homer and co. as their main non-footballing selling point.

Questions are asked in the House about preserving Wimbledon tennis for the terrestrial TV nation, but no one ever says anything about the BBC's non-purchase of *The Simpsons* being a vital stage in the breakdown of a shared national culture (those parsimonious souls still determined not to shell out for a satellite dish just have to hire *The Simpsons* from the video shop).

In the years that follow, perhaps the cruellest of all the privations visited upon those who seek to resist the lure of Sky's magic dinner-plate is the cartoon comedy time-lag. While the smugly dished and cabled-up are able to savour the latest developments in what is at this (pre-*Angel* and *Roswell High*) stage the most highly evolved form of US televisual endeavour, those without satellite have to wait around for years in the cultural wilderness, their lives horribly

---

[144.] As embodied in the perplexing phenomenon of the *Modern Review*, which starts off as a perfectly worthwhile initiative to encourage people to write and read about how great *Beavis and Butthead* is, without anyone having to feel guilty about it, but ends up as vehicle for its editor to stalk Liz Hurley in print.

impoverished by the gaping void where *The Simpsons*, *Ren & Stimpy*, *Beavis and Butthead* or Paramount's irresistible Jungian kickaround *Dr Katz* ought to be.

Gradually, the terrestrial channels get their act together and bring the broader population up to date. In 1997, when Channel 4 begins screening the first series of *King of the Hill* – *Beavis and Butthead* creator Mike Judge's poignant exploration of family values and Texan angst – it's actually the first time this excellent show has been seen on UK screens.

Set in the imaginary small town of Arlen,[145] *King of the Hill* focuses on the family life of a lovable propane salesman called Hank Hill, his wife Peggy and their twelve-year-old son Bobby. Unlike most boys of his age, Bobby's face has the spiritual intensity of a Greek Orthodox icon. Sensitive to other worlds beyond the perception of most of us, he can communicate with ant queens.

The look of the show is pitched midway between *Beavis and Butthead*'s blasted suburbia and *The Simpsons'* slightly more comforting round edges, but the feel of it recalls a programme primitive enough to feature actual flesh-and-blood actors. *King of the Hill* has the same exhilarating sense of resistance to stereotype and narrative constraint that made *Roseanne*'s Conner family so compelling in their prime. It also has a beautifully written script and a gallery of precisely observed characters.

It seems likely that the reason animators have been able to do so much great work on TV in the States in recent years is that the cartoon genre acts as camouflage.

'We get a lot of people telling us that *King of the Hill* is more realistic than most live-action comedies,' Judge's colleague, series co-creator and erstwhile *Simpsons* scribe Greg Daniels, says proudly. 'And we think that's because animation sets you free from a lot of the restrictions that tend, in America at least, to hobble your creative development. First off, you don't have to please a star, which is a huge deal, because actors never want to do stuff that makes their characters look bad. Second, you don't have to have

---

145. The name is a phonetic hybrid of Garland and Arlington – in the same way as *EastEnders'* Walford suggests the theoretical progeny of Walthamstow and Ilford.

an annoying laughter track to tell everyone where the jokes are, and third, you're not restricted to just a few stage sets in front of a live audience. Also,' he adds, almost as an afterthought, 'the person whose idea it is can control every single aspect of the production.'

Before the opening credits have even rolled on *King of the Hill*'s pilot episode, Hank and his friends are drinking beer in their yard and discussing the previous night's episode of *Seinfeld*. 'Them dang old New York boys,' observes the endearingly deranged reactionary Boomhauer – a character whose impenetrable accent Judge took from an answering-machine message left by a crazed *Beavis and Butthead* fan – 'it's the show about nothing.'

This might seem like a comedy writer's élitist in-joke ('it's the show about nothing' being the description fans of the show like to quote as if they thought it up themselves, when it's actually George Costanza's specification for *Seinfeld*'s sitcom within a sitcom) but it actually turns out to be quite the opposite. 'I think what we really wanted to do', Daniels explains, 'was to announce to people that we weren't doing stereotypes, but realistic modern Southerners who don't just go to the hay-ride in their carts.'

Judge agrees: 'When you do something about the South, especially in Hollywood, the obvious way to go is with that whole "yee-haw" type of thing. But you can be in a trailer park in the middle of the most rural part of Alabama and everyone has satellite dishes and watches *Seinfeld* and everything that people in New York watch.'

Returning once more to *Father Ted*, having learned an important lesson about the universal comedic significance of people in non-metropolitan areas watching *Seinfeld*

The sad early death of Dermot Morgan in early 1997, shortly after he finished filming the third series,[146] seals up *Father Ted* in the Tupperware container of comedy legend with unasked-for rapidity.

[146.] Morgan's horribly premature demise makes this rather too poignant viewing for comfort on first screening, but subsequent repeat showings prove it to be every bit the equal of its predecessors.

The show stays really fresh in there, though, with any number of classic episodes enduring in the memory well into the next century.

There's the unforgettable encounter between Bishop Brennan and the rabbits, for example, in that provocatively titled episode, 'Kicking Bishop Brennan up the Arse'. Or the brilliant translation of the basic storyline of Mel Brooks's *The Producers* to the seemingly alien terrain of the Eurovision Song Contest (where Ted and Dougal are selected to represent Ireland in a desperate attempt to stop RTE having to stage the contest again, and inevitably triumph with their classic original song, 'My Lovely Horse'). Or the one where the all-purpose clerical formulation 'That would be an ecumenical matter' seems for a poignant moment to offer hope of a solution to Irish problems beyond those of Craggy Island.

The last word on *Father Ted* should go to the writers, though. So, what's the difference between a stereotype and an archetype?

'Basically,' replies Linehan, 'stereotypes aren't funny.'

'The comedy answer', Mathews explains helpfully, 'is that an archetype makes buildings . . . Oh no, that's an architect.'

His colleague fixes him with a stern look: 'I don't think you needed to explain that.'

Postscript: Linehan and Mathews in the comedy afterlife

The shadow of *Father Ted*'s memory might be expected to fall heavily over Linehan and Mathews's subsequent endeavours (especially after the duo drift apart in the late nineties). But somehow – from the magnetically atavistic spectacle of 'Jockeys hunting Prince' on *Big Train* to Mathews's theoretically redemptive return to *Paris*'s costume-drama *milieu* with *Hippies*, to Linehan's often excellent *Black Books* (of which more in a moment) – it doesn't seem to.

The show's most visible legacy is the endless wave of Irish comedians which seems to break upon the rocky shores of the London circuit over the next few years, many of them holding true to the adage first coined by reptilian guitar picker Dermot Carmody: 'I've only been Irish since I moved to England last October. Back home, there didn't seem to be much point.'

'That Would Be an Ecumenical Matter'

Graham Norton's uncharacteristically amusing *Father Ted* cameo as a maddeningly hearty priest prefigures the later subjugation of the entire Channel 4 evening schedule to his gospel of inclusive smut. But it's with *Black Books*, the acerbic collaboration between Graham Linehan and Perrier Award-winner Dylan Moran, that the Craggy Island Midas Touch is seen again to its best effect.

In order to fully appreciate the extent of *Black Books*'s achievement in finding a suitable setting for the uncut gem of Moran's talent, a little bit of historical background is called for . . .

The sun rose once more over that dingy boarding-house in the heart of County Meath – the place where the comedians stayed when they were passing through, the place where the net curtains had been partially rotted by the condensation on the windows. There was one room that the predatory, wart-encrusted proprietress was particularly proud of. She called it 'The Extemporizers' Suite'.

Dave Allen and Eddie Izzard were the only people that had ever stayed there. Their old skin had been swept into neat piles at each end of the room, and the room was kept empty as a shrine to their talents. So where were those unearthly groans coming from that morning? Surely . . . the skin-piles couldn't have merged to create a new living being?

Snapping out of a daydream at Her Majesty's Theatre, Haymarket to see the whey-faced form of 1996 Perrier Award-winner Dylan Moran sidle into view, it seems like they might have. Allen's tipsy roguishness and Izzard's spiralling digressions are so much to the fore in Dylan's hour upon the stage that at times you feel they must be hiding behind the curtain, operating him by remote control. Thankfully, things are not as cut and dried as they seem, and there are other moments when the progress Moran has made over the past year or so is dramatic enough to banish all thoughts of his act's comedic provenance.

He's lost some of the sixth-form sexism, for a start. And Moran now seems to have the stagecraft to back up his natural arrogance. The transition from packed cupboard-under-the-stairs Edinburgh sweatbox-type venues to the wide-open spaces of the West End stage is often a painful one, but Moran makes it look easy. In fact, his rumpled demeanour and *faux*-inebriate teetering acquire a new grandeur in front of a velvet backdrop. And there are times when his creative dream of Wildean epigrams hissed through clenched teeth almost comes true.

At his sharpest – in the burst of comic invention which culminates in the words 'drowned in a dentist's piss', or when a group of men living together proceed in a couple of twists of the tongue from being 'hygiene-conscious' to being uncomfortably aware that their 'lack of hygiene had created things that *were* conscious' – Moran's wordplay is deft in the extreme. Early attempts to find a suitable televisual vehicle for Moran's cynical intelligence don't get very far. But in grounding the eloquent hyperbolic parabolas inscribed by his best stand-up routines – from claiming he feels 'fine' to admitting that he lives underground with an old woman he barely knows and sucks stones for money – in the nurturing environment of a first-class ensemble, *Black Books* achieves a number of real distinctions.

Not only is its embittered bookshop proprietor, Bernard Black, the perfect embodiment of Moran's flair for vinous misanthropy, he also forges – alongside Tamsin Greig's distinctively brittle Fran and Bill Bailey's angelic Manny – a triangular core of problematic co-existence which parallels *Seinfeld*'s central troika of Jerry, George and Elaine, without paying it slavish obeisance. The ever-escalating tension within this group is sufficient to hold it together without any breach of *Seinfeld*'s 'no hugging' rule being necessitated, thereby rendering *Black Books* arguably the closest British TV has ever come to its own 'show about nothing'.

Admittedly, Bernard Black and co.'s literary *milieu* also paves the way for the dispiriting *The Book Group*.[147] But to hold Linehan and Moran responsible for that would be as foolish as blaming Take That for Westlife, or Nietszche for the Nazis.

[147.] A sitcom about people who don't really like books for an audience which doesn't really like sitcoms.

12
The Chat Nexus

'Correct me if I'm wrong, but you're not officially a comedian'
Eddie Izzard to the host on
Friday Night With Jonathan Ross, 2002

'So, Debbie McGee, what was it that first attracted you to the millionaire Paul Daniels?'
Caroline Aherne as Mrs Merton, to Debbie McGee

'The cash nexus' is a rather cold-blooded eventuality, identified by Karl Marx as being integral to the development of a capitalist economy. It comes to pass when all other transactions – barter, dowries, tied accommodation, a goose at Christmas – are gradually superseded by the exchange of coins and folding-stuff, until a monetary imperative rules all social relationships.

'The chat nexus' refers to a point in British TV history at which all spheres of comedic activity (and perhaps even some other forms of human social interaction not explicitly designed to get laughs) seem to intersect in the medium of the chat show.

Why was David Letterman put on this earth? Scientists and philosophers have suggested many answers to this riddle, and the most persuasive is 'To make people who claim Americans don't understand irony look really stupid'. The cigar-smoking Indiana weatherman turned chat-show host seems to have evolved to a point where not just what he says – especially the familiar cycle of nonsensical semi-catch-phrases ('Looking good, looking around' is a big favourite in 1996, horribly familiar to all those lucky enough to have access to Letterman nightly on Sky 2) – but his *whole body* is perfectly attuned to the expression of irony.

It's certainly significant that such an unrepentantly quick-witted man should be at work anywhere in the supposedly dumb-ass world of American TV. That he should have spent many years as the USA's top-rated chat-show host (and remains a key figure in the war between the networks) is little short of miraculous.

Watching Letterman film his show in a New York studio in 1996, what comes through most strongly is the extent to which he is not merely popular, but actively revered. In the middle of the most severe snowstorms in living memory, people have driven half-way across the country to see him throw snowballs[148] at his iconically annoying band-leader and stooge, Paul Shaffer. You might almost say Letterman's audience look up to him as if he were royalty, if their respectfulness weren't a little too whole-hearted for that.

Small wonder, then, that a succession of televisual Sir Walter Raleighs should have endeavoured to import the fragrant (and crinkly) tobacco leaf of the American's hyperironic style. Jonathan Ross is the first to try, in the mid to late eighties, and even if – in his own estimation at least – he doesn't quite pull it off, he still gives Vic Reeves his first big break and alters the course of British TV history in the process. Some years later, Ross's Comedy Awards scriptwriter Danny Baker also gets to give it a go, and – with the full weight of BBC boss John Birt's authority behind him – fails so horribly that the chat show becomes too difficult a prospect to contemplate other than through a protective screen of satire.

[148.] If these retain their solidity surprisingly well under the studio lights (which they do), that's because Letterman keeps his studio unusually cold so that the audience will have to clap and cheer to stay alive.

Phase 1: Comedians as hosts

If someone were to bottle the essence of Mrs Merton, the imperious raised-eyebrow quality that makes her the queen of mid-nineties TV, with Alan Partridge (the ice-white-socked *alter ego* of Caroline Aherne's friend and fellow Manchester Poly drama graduate Steve Coogan) as her doughty prince consort, 'acerbic disingenuity' would be the main ingredient they'd have to list on the label. Butter might not melt in this sweet old lady's mouth as she asks Debbie McGee what it was that first attracted her to the millionaire Paul Daniels, or George Best whether he would have been so thirsty had he not done all that running around, but those beady eyes might freeze her victims in their seats.

The apparent cosiness of Mrs Merton's studio set-up – a prim and properly made-up Aherne surrounded by an audience of real-life pensioners, including her own mother, Maureen – makes the conceit even more deadly. And, as if she needed to make herself any more of a proposition at this point, Caroline Aherne has just married Peter Hook (New Order's famously hard-living bass guitarist, seven years her senior) in an Elvis Presley-themed wedding chapel in Las Vegas. This temporarily reformed wild man now finds himself elevated to unheard-of heights of domesticity as 'Hooky', put-upon leader of his new wife's onscreen house band.

Mrs Merton rules her own small-screen world with a rod of iron. Talking to Aherne some years later, I wonder if she agrees – looking back at her sharp-tongued creation – that compassion hardly seems to have been her main motivating force?

She looks shocked but unabashed. 'I don't think Mrs Merton was *ever* not compassionate . . . it was always done tongue in cheek.' But – as anyone who has ever been the butt of a joke (which must be pretty much all of us) will tell you – just because something's done tongue in cheek doesn't mean there's no pain involved.

At the height of Mrs Merton's fame, a spin-off book was commissioned called *Mrs Merton's World of Television*. It looks like one of those cheap cash-ins publishers try to convince the world and its mum to buy for difficult nephews at Christmas, and that, in fact – at least on one level – is exactly what it is. On another level, however, it is actually a masterclass in the art of controlled sadism, the like of which has not been seen since the early works of Yukio Mishima.

There's a friendly bikers' café just off the A259 in Rye, East Sussex which used to have a copy sitting on the sideboard alongside the free ad sheets and old copies of *Motorcycle News*. Sometimes you'd see leather-clad warriors of the road picking this book up with their asphalt-hardened hands while waiting for their Big Tart's Breakfasts. Invariably they'd put it down within thirty seconds, wincing, as if they'd just seen a friend blind-sided by a recreational vehicle.

'Tell me one person that would've been hurt by Mrs Merton, *ever*?' Aherne demands, still not sounding as affronted as she might be.

Anyone featured in that book, I answer.

'Give me one example.'

Lesley Joseph . . . there's something written about her which is so harsh that I have actually repressed the memory of it.

'Oh yeah,' Aherne shrugs. 'Now *she's* the exception [Laughter.] . . . Perhaps we let the bitterness come through too much with Lesley Joseph.'

The BBC2 version of Alan Partridge's chat show seems to maintain a slightly more even balance between compassion and cruelty. Yet while no other TV programme has quite so thoroughly and tenderly understood the moment when Richard Madeley falls off his stool and tries to make a joke of it, there's still a vengeful edge to a lot of Partridge's most piquant exchanges. The difference between picking on made-up guests (Alan's speciality) and real ones (Mrs Merton's stock-in-trade) is never having to say you're sorry.

'Sometimes we are motivated by petty spite,' Coogan admits. '"I don't like this person, so let's create a character a bit like them".' In the midst of the *Knowing Me, Knowing You . . . with Alan Partridge* writing process, Steve can be seen brandishing the first edition of *Loaded* and fulminating about the absurd fantasy version of machismo it – and especially its cover-star Gary Oldman – seems to embody. A suitably Oldmanesque character (played of course by Patrick Marber) is duly humiliated on Alan's sofa. And Coogan is duly photographed, a couple of months later, at a *Loaded* party.

'I know,' he concedes a few months afterwards, 'it is terrible.' Coogan's accent broadens Pauline Calf-wards. 'But I am a dichotomy.'

If there are times when the fake-chat-show format looks like an easy – perhaps even *too* easy – means of settling cultural scores, karmic payback is just around the corner.

While Alan Partridge is so convincing on the radio that the BBC often receives complaints about him as if he's a real person, it takes a while to get used to the surprisingly youthful face behind the voice (Coogan is seven years younger than Partridge is meant to be) when he first moves to TV. Gradually, however, skilful writing and carefully judged performances tug at the character's newly visible seams to expose the poignant stuffing of his inner life.

Sitting in the audience for the recording of the last episode of *Knowing Me, Knowing You . . . with Alan Partridge*, it becomes very clear how much people appreciate the effort that has been gone to. In a break in the filming, there is a quiz offering someone the chance to win an Alan Partridge tie-and-blazer-crest presentation box, and the man who wins plainly knows more about Partridge than Coogan does himself. (The show later cocks a snook at this same anal-retentive element as Alan proudly brandishes a mask of his own face. 'They are', he understands, 'very popular with students.')

Phase 2: Complications ensue, *or* the biters bit

Caroline Aherne first came to fame by dressing as an old woman in order to ambush people better known than herself with questions which they would never have dreamed of answering in a different context. As if in Catholic penance for washing others' dirty linen in public, she is subsequently subjected to levels of public mortification which Mrs Merton's victims could only begin to imagine.

Distractedly picking the crusts off a ham sandwich in a high-rise TV press office, Aherne ponders her ordeal by publicity. 'I was a bit naïve,' she reflects ruefully. 'I never thought that because I played an old lady, anything I did that *wasn't* old-ladylike would be so much more newsworthy. I can't do anything like I used to – I can't vomit in public . . . not that I ever used to, but I could've if I wanted to' – she grins – 'in the good old days . . .'

From tabloid trivia – brouhahas at restaurant openings, French-kissing Eurovision Song Contest winner Katrina Leskanich on the steps of a radio awards ceremony – to the alarming seriousness of a suicide attempt and subsequent admission to The Priory, her indiscretions have some unexpected consequences. They transform Aherne into a rather old-fashioned kind of star, a Diana Dors or a Pat Phoenix for the postmodern era: someone who becomes more intriguing for revealing their weaknesses, rather than less.

When her marriage to Peter Hook breaks up in 1996, there is genuine pathos in Aherne's declaration that she had 'married for life' and would 'never find another like him'. Shortly afterwards – in an early foretaste of the kind of celebrity horse-trading which will become so prevalent in British culture in the late 1990s and early 2000s that at some points it will actually threaten to undermine the cash nexus – Caroline is pictured in the pages of an early issue of *OK* (at that point still struggling to establish itself as a serious rival to *Hello* in the showbiz sycophancy stakes)[149] on a holiday in Mustique for which the magazine seems to be picking up the tab.

'They take pictures of you all the time anyway,' Caroline explains matter-of-factly, 'so they may as well take them somewhere nice they've paid for you to go. And it was a lovely holiday . . . Everything was free. The only problem was, they expected me to go with a man, and they didn't want the friend I'd actually taken with me in the pictures because they thought everyone would think I was a lesbian. So they just took photos of me on my own – driving a motor boat or "relaxing on the beach" – and it all came over a bit desperate. You know the sort of thing: "After a troubled year, here is lonely Caroline, finally coming to terms with life . . . on her own."'

[149.] *OK* soon begins to overhaul that longer-established rival by the cunning expedient of extending the constituency of its fawning demeanour beyond minor scions of the Belgian aristocracy to the massed ranks of soap stars and daytime TV presenters. When French and Saunders used to do those sketches where they'd sit around in an empty room talking about their friendship with Lulu, no one realized this was a prophetic vision of every-day life in the twenty-first century.

While for Aherne it's the obvious differences between herself and her *alter ego* that cause the problems, with Coogan it's the similarities. The increasingly troublesome overlap between comic persona and offscreen reality begins with journalists labouring cheerfully under the delusion that Alan's walk – stiff-legged, bandy and wholly in character with his 'Elephant Man' haircut – is actually Coogan's own, and expands from there.

'I'll tell you something funny,' says Coogan affably in the first flush of Alan's success. 'I've got a Gucci watch, right. It was given to me as a present. It's pretty understated, I think [he holds out his wrist for confirmation] – it doesn't look too flash, does it? The make-up artist was making me up as Alan a few weeks ago and she said, "Oh, nice touch. That is perfect. A Gucci watch – that's so tacky." I said [hurt pause], "That's *my* watch." And she said [nastily], "Oh, I didn't think *you*'d have a watch like that."'

At the press launch for his 1995 series *Coogan's Run*, the naturally diffident Coogan plays the unaccustomed role of his celebrity self with commendable *élan*. Given the accuracy with which Alan Partridge pinpoints the inanity of the media, you might expect the assembled representatives of the fourth estate to be on their best behaviour. This would be a grave error. 'So, Steve, who rides in the passenger seat of your Ferrari?' is just a random sample of the kind of thought-provoking enquiry to which the star of the proceedings finds himself subject.

At Coogan's side during the Q&A session is Henry Normal – Mancunian stand-up poet and co-writer of Paul and Pauline Calf, as well as Mrs Merton (after a brief custody battle with Caroline Aherne, Coogan eventually lures Normal away from her as co-founder of his Brighton-based Baby Cow production company). Someone asks if Henry Normal is his real name.

'No,' Normal replies. He made it up to preserve his privacy.

Without a trace of irony, the follow-up question shoots back. 'Well, what *is* your real name, then?'

The press pack having finally folded itself away, Steve Coogan allows himself a moment's anxiety. 'With Alan Partridge we get to explore all these fictitious personalities that represent real ones. For the whole thing to work, we've got to try to be above it all.'

But how far above it all is it possible to be when you yourself are an increasingly celebrated participant in the very process you're supposed to be satirizing?

'It is a very difficult game to play,' Coogan concedes. 'Ultimately,' – he eases, grinning, into Partridge-esque metaphoric overkill – 'I'm King Canute . . . but I'm King Canute with armbands on. I've got a fighting chance, if not of pushing back the tide, at least of staying afloat for a while.'

Late for an appointment with Ianucci and Marber (the trio are hard at work on the keenly awaited Alan Partridge Christmas Special, *Knowing Me, Knowing Yule*), Coogan kindly offers me a ride back into town in his Ferrari. It is a ludicrously flashy and impractical vehicle – huge and brazenly scarlet, with *Thunderbirds*-style gull-wing doors – which takes ages to manœuvre out of the car park. He's only had it a few weeks, but he's already been pulled over several times by the police.

'They follow you all the time,' he grumbles. 'You have to drive like a district nurse.' He noses his way forcefully out into the traffic. 'People think there's no way you'll pull out because you'll be too scared of denting your Ferrari, so you have to say "No I'm not, I don't care if I dent my Ferrari".' The demonic look on Steve Coogan's face as he flings the car into a tiny gap reveals a shocking truth: he is not doing this for the purposes of comedy.

When he is driving this car, does he ever see people looking at him with hatred in their eyes and forget why it's there?

'Oh no,' Coogan smiles, 'I always know why it's there.'

Phase 3: Shrugging off irony's shackles

Slicing through the West End traffic in the midst of another unrepentantly macho overtaking exploit, Coogan reiterates his concern about the damage success might do to his most celebrated *alter ego*. Alan Partridge's total disregard for the feelings of others has combined with an acute sensitivity to every nuance of his own celebrity status to make him a peerless lightning rod for the egotism and vacuity of his epoch. But if his creator were ever to join him in the full glare of the media spotlight, Alan's integrity as a comic character might be horribly compromised.

Within a few weeks, Steve Coogan's private life is all over the front pages in a series of salacious tabloid exposés (the one with the lapdancer frolicking on a bed strewn with banknotes would have brought a blush to the cheek of even the seemingly shameless Partridge). Far from being the potentially fatal setback he had anticipated, this ordeal by scandal seems to spur Coogan on to new creative heights.

1997's *I'm Alan Partridge* finds its hero in magnificent exile: like Napoleon on the isle of Elba, but transposed to a Norfolk 'Travel Tavern'. Having lost his BBC contract after the unfortunate death of a guest at the end of the 1995 Christmas Special, Alan's valiant – if doomed – struggle to hang on to his dignity banishes the memory of some of his creator's more hubristic recent career moves (the less said about that album released in the guise of Portuguese night-club singer Tony Ferrino, for example, the better) and gives rise to some of the most harrowing local-radio-based comedy sequences ever seen on British TV.

It also marks the end of Coogan's professional association with Patrick Marber. The latter is heavily involved in the planning and research stages, and still has happy memories of a 'fantastic night' with Coogan and Ianucci in an A12 Travelodge, enjoying such luxurious facilities as the Sebastian Coe Health Club and the carvery which serves 'devils on horseback'. But his second play, *Closer,* is about to open at the National Theatre, and Marber in his own phrase (and if you ever feel inclined to use this word about yourself, the chances are you've got some grounds) realizes he's a 'luvvie' and flies the coop just before the writing process begins.

Peter Baynham is recruited as a last-minute writing replacement and is treated from the outset with his new employer's characteristic courtesy to collaborators. 'A lot of the funniest things Alan says,' Coogan confesses, shortly after the series airs, 'come out of Peter's mouth first.' He can afford to be generous.

From the poignantly claustrophobic setting of the Travel Tavern (wherein, as the motel's only long-term resident, Alan strives in vain to evade the satirical attentions of the staff while taking his own extra-large plate to the buffet) to the unforgettable *King of Comedy* tribute episode (wherein Alan is kidnapped by a crazed fan),[150] Coogan's superb performance sets the tone perfectly for a faultless production. *I'm Alan Partridge* is a triumph of subtle characterization and finely observed socio-cultural detail which belongs in the very front rank of the British sitcom canon.

Caroline Aherne has two potential means of shrugging off irony's shackles. The one which works triumphantly (*The Royle Family*) will receive due consideration shortly. The one which doesn't will have to take its chance here and now.

Audaciously – and as it turns out, ruinously – scheduled on prime-time, pre-watershed BBC1, *Mrs Merton and Malcolm* is developed (perhaps not the best omen this) from a scenario first devised for a British Gas advert. The show takes Mrs Merton out of her TV studio and into the suburban Manchester terrace that was always her spiritual home. For company she has no hapless celebrities, only her slow-witted thirty-seven-year-old son, Malcolm – Craig Cash, exploiting what Caroline calls his 'silent film face' – and a bedridden husband upstairs.

It's always rather uncomfortable watching people's work in their presence, but in these circumstances (sitting opposite Caroline Aherne on an ugly brown sofa while the afternoon sunlight floods through the dirty press office window behind her) the words 'Do you want to see some of the new show?' are particularly daunting. A sampler tape is placed in the video recorder and Caroline says that she will be 'dead interested' to get a reaction.

The short playback – punctuated with apologetic interjections such as 'It's so disjointed, you won't be able to get a feel of it' and 'Have you had enough yet?' – reveals a claustrophobic and unsettling hybrid of Nick Park's Wallace and Gromit, an Alan Bennett *Talking Heads* monologue and Ronnie Corbett in *Sorry*. There are flashes of Aherne's trademark dry wit – 'That's not a swastika,' says Mrs Merton, explaining her husband's signature on his son's birthday card, 'it's your dad's cross' – but it's Cash's Malcolm, with his repeated interjections of 'tremendous' (the last syllable

---

[150.] The brace of Irish documentary-makers who witness these disturbing scenes are played by *Father Ted* creators Linehan and Mathews.

pronounced to rhyme with 'mouse') who leaves the deepest and most disturbing impression.

'You haven't got a clue what to make of it, have you?' Caroline says sympathetically, reclaiming the video from the machine. 'You're probably thinking, My nanna would like it.'

This doesn't seem like the right moment to admit to having no surviving grandparents. As a substitute response, 'It has the quality of a nightmare, but in a good way' is perhaps not all that might've been hoped for, but Caroline seems quite happy with it.

'I love the innocence of their world,' she smiles gently. 'When I'm watching it, I think, I'd like to live there.'

It's hard to find people who agree with this assessment when *Mrs Merton and Malcolm* is actually broadcast, but this time it's not Caroline's savagery that's upsetting them, it's her sincerity. No one (including a succession of aggrieved mental-health charities) can quite believe that Cash's character is intended affectionately rather than being a vile slur on those whose proverbial picnics are a couple of sandwiches short.

'Obviously Malcolm is a boy who is too big to be living with his mum,' Aherne concedes, 'but they get on so well – they really love each other. It's the same with *The Royle Family*,' she continues, deftly changing the subject to irony escape route B (which seems by far the riskier of the two ventures before they both hit the screens). 'The Royles never say a nice word about each other when they're together, but if anyone else said anything bad about any of them, they'd go mad.'

Phase 4: Hosts as hosts

It would be overstating the case to claim that the passing of the Mrs Merton and Alan Partridge era brings an end to the age of parodic mischief. Especially as the format which no one has ever been quite foolish enough to call the 'mockuchat show' flourishes well into the twenty-first century (which, on the evidence of *The Kumars at Number 42* and *This Is Dom Joly*, is long after the last drop of comedic juice has been squeezed from it).

There is, however, a definite sea change in the winter of 1996–7.

With the pain of the Gaby Roslin chat-show experience still fresh in their minds (let's not reopen old wounds by going into it too deeply), Channel 4 courageously shuffles two new heavyweight chat contenders on to the screen. Both acknowledge transatlantic inspiration – Johnny Vaughan's nattily roguish *Here's Johnny* in its titular nod to Johnny Carson's old introduction, and Bob Mills's bizarre *The Show* in its crazed determination to be a live-action *Larry Sanders*.

But it's Channel 5's plans for a new nightly chat show that seem to signal a genuine outbreak of Lettermania. Unable to get their hands on surviving relatives of Adolf Hitler, or an actual talking shark – and with the obvious candidate, Melinda Messenger, yet to present herself – the embryonic network picks *Absolutely* veteran Jack Docherty as its late-night figurehead. Docherty's set might be a postcard-sized version of Letterman's sweeping city-scape, but his *modus operandi* is somewhat different.

He starts out with the encouraging if somewhat (in view of Letterman's annoying tendency to chase his own tail at guests' expense) heretical assumption that 'the people watching might actually have some interest in whoever it is that I am talking to'. But won't the success of Mrs Merton and Alan Partridge make it difficult for people to take *The Jack Docherty Show* seriously?

'These things co-exist,' Docherty insists. 'I don't think Larry Sanders emasculates David Letterman at all – they feed off each other.'

He's right in one way; parody both cocks a snook at and ultimately reinforces the institutional credibility of its subject. And he's right in another way, too – perhaps without even realizing it – in that the acidic spoofing of Mrs Merton and Alan Partridge seems to have cleansed the palate of the British viewing public (like a refreshing sorbet after years of Woganite stodge) and restored their appetite for the real thing.

Like all truly successful satires, they have rendered themselves redundant in the process. What people enjoy about the real thing is the artifice, while the spoof makes fun of the emotional reality that underpins that artifice. You can't have those two pleasures at the same time – that's why the Bob Mills experiment doesn't quite come off, and nobody buys Tony Ferrino records: it's the buffer at the end of the tracks of postmodern TV entertainment.

The next stage in the rebirth of the British chat show is the return of seventies behemoth Michael Parkinson. He might as well have been dead for the previous decade or so (he's actually been writing about cricket in the *Daily Mail*, which amounts to virtually the same thing), but as the crusty veteran's long-overdue late-nineties comeback proceeds, it's nice to see those who helped clear away the dead wood for his return getting the chance to bask in his limelight.

A confident-looking Steve Coogan tells what is actually quite a revealing anecdote about having a summer job in a factory as a drama student – presumably in pre-voice-over days – and being made a fool of by the people who worked there all year round. It's Caroline Aherne who is the real surprise package, though (and not just because, outside periodic big nights out at award shows, the only other times anyone has seen her on TV as herself are in the course of an awkward but compelling solo stand-up experiment on BBC1's *The Stand-Up Show* and an amusing appearance on a schedule-filling late-night ITV comedy documentary series, where she is interviewed by long-term colleague and one-time boyfriend Cash while trying to pretend she doesn't know him).

Sharing top billing with Prince Naseem and Gary Barlow, Caroline talks about her time at The Priory, where – after checking herself in, the day after her suicide attempt – she thought she was going to be making pots in the depression group, but then got reassigned to the alcoholics (Caroline had been drinking champagne to help her sleep, which is rather like eating three-month-old Stilton to stop yourself having nightmares). Parkinson responds sympathetically enough to this admission, but devout Muslim Prince Naseem is especially understanding. Caroline's flirtatious demeanour and faint air of Julie Christie in *Billy Liar* have done something no opponent has yet managed: brought out his inner gentleman.

On this particular Parkinsonian occasion, Caroline thinks, in retrospect, she came across as 'a slight bit simple . . . I was so nervous when I first went on, my lip was stuck to my teeth'. She normally refuses invitations to appear on other people's chat shows – being, by her own admission 'no good at telling anecdotes' – but she was never going to turn down Michael Parkinson.

'I used to love Parky' – she stretches the nickname out, lingering over the 'ar' syllable like it's the most exotic thing in the world. 'Don't you remember staying up late to watch him? The next thing you know, you hear the music and you're on!'

What was it that most stayed with her from watching the show as a child?

'I think it was seeing Les Patterson [Australia's cultural attaché and foul-mouthed foil to Barry Humphries's better-known *alter ego* Dame Edna Everage] and being madly excited that somebody could be so rude and be on telly.' After giving the matter further consideration – perhaps in the light of the influence Patterson and Everage would later exert over her own comedic trajectory – Caroline says: 'In my whole career, that's probably been the main thing, the biggest highlight: to be on *Parky*.' From anyone else, this would be pure showbiz flannel, but Caroline Aherne really seems to mean it. 'Prince Naseem was lovely, too,' she continues. 'He said on the show "Do you want to come and see me fight?" and I just thought it was something you'd say on the telly. But then afterwards Parky said "Do you *really* want to come and see Prince Naseem?" And I said "Ooh, yeah!" I thought he meant a big night out with me and him . . .' Caroline's face falls, as if the disappointment is still fresh . . . 'But I think he actually meant he'd be bringing his wife as well.'

Phase 5: Hosts as comedians

Appearing on BBC1's *Friday Night with Jonathan Ross* in 2002, Eddie Izzard gives the host a straight look. 'Correct me if I'm wrong,' he notes archly, 'but you're not *officially* a comedian.' Izzard's increasingly confrontational approach to chat-show appearances can go either way (he inadvertently provokes an ugly little spat with Nigella Lawson on *Parkinson* around this time from which none of the three participants emerges entirely unscathed), but in this particular instance he has hit the nail on the head. The basis of Ross's amazing career revitalization – from the multifarious lowpoints of the mid-nineties to the felicitous omnipresence of the early 2000s – has basically been a distillation of the essence of stand-up comedy.

The arts of chat-show host and comic have always been closely connected. Not only do many masters of the former art come from a stand-up background – from David Letterman and Jay Leno in the US to quick-witted Northern Irishman Patrick Kielty, whose *Patrick Kielty Almost Live* gives Ross some much-needed competition in the early 2000s – but the all-important opening monologue (as practised with such exemplary skill by Kielty) is the perfect showcase for the comedian's art.

In Ross's case, the relationship has several additional layers of complexity. His multifarious roles – as patron of new talent and frustrated performer ('I always wanted to be more actively involved,' he admits of his early contacts with Vic and Bob, 'I got very jealous that I couldn't be part of the act'),[151] media-savvy operator and honest broker between the comedic generations – intertwine in a curiously dramatic saga of underachievement and redemption, which runs both in parallel and in the opposite direction to the Coogan–Aherne dynamic outlined above.

Talking to Ross in 2002, at the height of his BBC1 Friday/Radio 2 Saturday second coming, he is understandably happy about the way things have turned out.

'If we'd been sitting here eight years ago,' he admits, 'this would have been a terribly sad interview. There would have been things you didn't want to say to my face, and things I felt bitter about and didn't want to reveal.'

What sort of things?

'I think for many years people were giving me a greater benefit of the doubt than I deserved ... I was too easily pulled by the market forces around me. I formed a production company merely so I could do this show that I really wanted to do, but just as with the history of socialism [at this point Ross changes gear from conversational into performance mode], noble early ambitions begin

---

[151.] 'When you try to be on their wavelength, like I did,' Ross admits in 2002, 'you always end up looking a bit desperate.' He recalls with evident unease a 1988 AIDS benefit when he took to the stage as Reeves's straight man: 'Normally everyone is very supportive when you go back to the green room, even if you've gone down really badly, but on this occasion they all just backed away.'

to serve the mechanical needs of the bureaucratic machine that's grown up around you . . . And that', Ross concludes, not all that helpfully, 'is why there's a tendency towards oligarchy in every mass democratic party.'

Exactly how did this tendency express itself in relation to Ross's production company, Channel X?

'I suddenly had this company which employed a lot of people, all of whom wanted to keep working. I wanted to earn more money, and I wanted to carry on being a celebrity, because I've always enjoyed being famous. And in that mix we forgot to make the kind of shows we wanted to watch. I can only blame myself really. I could have made better programmes, but I didn't know how – I suppose I didn't have anything I really wanted to say.'

So how was the transformation effected whereby Ross, having forsaken his late-night chat homeland for a sometime-*Wogan*-stand-in-and-occasional-*This-Morning*-guest-presenter's-slot type exile of his own making, returned to claim his crown with a *great deal* that he needed to communicate?

'There wasn't one particular moment of epiphany . . . For a few years I was drinking too much and doing all those other recreational things people in showbiz get involved in, and then I got tired of that and started doing good work again.

'Chris Evans was something of a catalyst,' Ross continues (and it's not often that you hear those three words spoken in the same sentence), 'in that he both occupied the role I'd had and started doing shows that were much more fun. Early *TFI Friday*, for example, was a very good show . . . He originally came up with that idea for me, and we spent a few summer evenings planning it together, but then I bailed out because I didn't really see how I could sit there and interview All Saints.

'At that point,' Ross remembers ruefully, 'Chris said "There's a whole generation now who only think of you as that big bloated bloke who does *The Big Big Talent Show*", and he was right. It was a great shame – not a tragedy in the Greek sense, but on a small scale, definitely a pity . . .'

At Evans's instigation, Ross started doing a radio show for the former's pet station Virgin, which he 'very much enjoyed'.

'I suppose because I couldn't see the audience and wasn't worried

Darlington Brando: Vic Reeves demonstrates the natural affinity for the leather which made him a pillar of the South-East London motorcycling establishment

Two paragons of broadcasting virtue
(*Above*) *The Day Today*'s sportsdesk-jockey Alan Partridge, in halcyon pre chat show days
(*Below*) Chris Morris: totalitarian anchorman

Two visions of civic authority
(*Above*) Vic Reeves and Bob Mortimer as councillors Cox & Evans (note reassuring mayoral presence of Matt "He's a baby!" Lucas)
(*Below*) Roy 'Chubby' Brown as Royston Vasey's mayor Larry Vaughn: establishing links with the creative community, in the form of hard-working local theatre-in-education troupe Legz Akimbo

1970's reality TV pioneers, the Wilkins family of Reading

1990's social-realist sitcom overlords, the Royle family of Wythenshawe

(*Above*) At home with Slade: entertaining a distinguished guest, in the form of Wizzard's Roy Wood (note Paul Whitehouse enjoying himself in a supportive capacity)
(*Below*) Ted Crilly prepares to launch an ill advised diversionary attack on the episcopal posterior in the classic *Father Ted* episode 'Kicking Bishop Brennan Up The Arse'

(*Above*) The League of Gentlemen's Edward and Tubbs: a marriage made in hell
(*Below*) The drag trade: Eddie Izzard out-glams his comedic heroes in a strategic
publicity shot for BBC 2's Monty Python night

As Brent flails around... daring anyone to break the spell, he becomes a kind of human Catherine Wheel, illuminating the Slough of despond

about their response, I just thought, Fuck it, just do what you think is funny.'

In the process, Ross hit on 'a kind of performance mode where it's not really you: it's more this kind of overly confident, brazenly ego-driven character who finds every minute detail of his daily life inherently interesting and amusing'.

At around the same time as he was transferring this new gospel of enlightened self-obsession to a wider audience, courtesy of a high-profile transfer to the up-and-coming Radio 2 network, Ross was offered a regular slot on the post-*Fantasy Football* sports panel game *They Think It's All Over*. While not, on the face of it, the stuff that career resurrections are made of, it was unlikely that Ross (or, indeed, any sentient being) would emerge with anything but credit from a battle of wits with Rory McGrath and David Gower.

Furthermore, being obliged to extemporize at length on a subject – sport – about which he knew virtually nothing, encouraged Ross to 'hone a new persona for myself, which is actually quite similar to what I am like'. What Ross calls his 'seedy Pan' guise is a semi-domesticated pan-sexual adventurer – in his creator's own words, 'bumbling, slightly mad, fairly fearless . . . a bit of a cunt as well, really'.

Before he knew it, Ross had a protective suit which could see him safely through almost any televisual ordeal. Even being enthroned as 'the new Barry Norman'.

'Previously, I was trying to be something I wasn't,' Ross admits. 'Which was David Letterman, really. Or if not exactly Letterman, then at least a smarter person than I actually am.' If he's still not, in Izzard's caustic formulation, 'officially' one of the comedic brotherhood, Ross now hopes at the very least to give people 'the same feeling you get from a good comedian, which is that they might say anything at any point . . . In actual fact, people *should* feel that with me, because when I open my mouth now, I often don't know what's going to come out.'

Small wonder that, in the wake of this hard-won triumph of acquired spontaneity, Jonathan Ross should experience 'a sort of giddy pleasure' in his almost Thatcheresque work schedule.

'In a strange way, I feel like I've vindicated all the faith people once had in me,' he says, looking back proudly to the bad old days of the early to mid-nineties, 'which is great because it must have been horribly disappointing for them to watch me doing dreadful TV for all those years.'

Johnny Vaughan's career develops along different lines. As the inheritor of Chris Evans's mantle (as *Big Breakfast* patriarch), former *Moviewatch* presenter Vaughan expands his gobby predecessor's penchant for reaching out to the audience at home via the subjugation of a studio full of flunkeys into a comedic style all his own. And it's one that echoes the totalitarian room-control of comedians such as Frank Skinner or Jo Brand to potent effect.

In the more-dayglo-than-thou surroundings of early morning Channel 4, there is even something about Vaughan's fogeyish demeanour which seems perversely radical. His delighted engagement with the commercial weft and weave of everyday life, fearsome appetite for arcane points of detail and overriding concern with masculine propriety (few other daytime TV presenters claim Tolstoy's *What Men Live By* as an inspirational text) make Vaughan's three-year spell in the *Big Breakfast* hot-seat a landmark in televised eloquence. Changing gear in an instant from innuendo so end-of-the-pier it's virtually in the sea to clinical dissections of the hypocrisy of the *Daily Mail*, the relentless acuity of his quicksilver mind sometimes verges on ESP.

Never one to overstate the extent of his own abilities, Vaughan describes himself as a 'mnemonist'. It's a word he picked up from Hermann Hesse's novel, *The Glass Bead Game*. Mnemonists are, Vaughan explains, 'Guys who you might think are highly intelligent but actually just have a good selection of freakish memories'. 'I read that,' Vaughan remembers, 'and I just thought, Oh dear . . . And the worst thing is, I remembered it.' He shrugs ruefully, 'And if I remembered it, I *definitely* am it.'

So why should someone who identifies his own gifts as 'the ability to foster a gang mentality' and 'talking vaguely humorous drivel without a script' suddenly – in the wake of *The Big Breakfast* and a seven-figure golden-handcuffs deal with the BBC – be battling to tailor these talents to the stop-start rhythm of delivering lines, albeit ones he wrote himself?

The funny thing about observing Vaughan on the set of his

ill-fated sticom[152] writing and acting début, *'Orrible*, is that it's the stuff he does *between* takes – the banter, the casual erudition, the shameless playing to the gallery – that feels like it ought to end up on the screen. Constantly bouncing obscure facts and ideas-in-progress off cast, crew and visiting journalists, he's a Tasmanian devil of idle diversion. In the course of a five-minute break in shooting, he holds forth on topics varying from the salesman's short cut round the back of the M3 motorway services known as 'The Fleet Cheat' to the fact that Inspector Morse's Jag was the only one of its kind painted Rolls Royce red, to an impassioned meditation on the inexcusability of a flashy lining in a tailor-made suit.

'Things like that should be done so people who know, know,' Vaughan evangelizes. 'Emphasizing to everyone that it's tailored undermines the whole effect. It's like saying "establishment . . ."' – he scornfully turns an imaginary lapel – ' "rebel".'

By an ironic quirk of fate, it is between these very same two stools that Vaughan seems to fall in making what should have been an auspicious move to the BBC. The reactionary impulses which seemed so refreshing in the early morning on Channel 4 don't respond well to their new institutional setting.[153] Rather than adjusting his intellectual thermostat to complement his new surroundings, Vaughan's initial response to finding himself on the BBC seems to be to embrace the politics of the golf-club lounge.

The first BBC1 series of *Johnny Vaughan Tonight* finds the show's host apparently hell-bent on biting the anti-establishment hand that fed him. Testing his guests for any sign of non-comformity with the same predatory aspect a hyena might adopt towards a pregnant antelope, Vaughan seems to have lost his moral centre completely.

Where Jonathan Ross manages to weave the trappings of his domestic life into a colourful and inclusive tableau, and follows a

---

[152.] You can tell it's ill-fated by the fact that in the interlude between commissioning and broadcast, the name of its main character – Paul Clark – had acquired a mythic resonance beyond any Vaughan could have hoped to inculcate by virtue of belonging to the *Big Brother* contestant who claims to have 'lived his adult life like an international pop star'.

[153.] Which is why it's a good job BBC3 comes along to offer him a timely escape route.

questioning routine (ask the guest how old they are, say they look good for their age, ask them when they last had sex) which for all its formulaic nature generally solicits entertaining answers, Vaughan's increasingly neurotic devotion to the ideal of the nuclear family starts to make him sound like one of those *Daily Mail* editorializers he used to lambaste so effectively.

The (hopefully temporary) eclipse of Vaughan's star casts one of only two shadows on the unprecedentedly glittering 2002–3 late-night conversational firmament.[154] It would be nice to be able to portray the British chat show's dramatic renaissance as emblematic of a broader cultural renewal . . . but such a conclusion would – sadly – be entirely inaccurate.

Before we can find out why, there is one distinctively shaped piece still missing from our celestial chat jigsaw.

Comedians as hosts (slight return)

As befits someone who believes that full disclosure is the surest form of discretion, Frank Skinner is at his most forthcoming in front of an audience. Here are three of the things he says into a clump of whirring tape-recorders at the champagne and bacon sandwich press launch for 1995's *The Frank Skinner Show*, in the appropriately old showbiz surroundings of the London Palladium bar. On the drink problem he shrugged off in his late twenties: 'Alcoholic is a big word, but I'd have a hard time defending myself against it in court.' On forsaking his working-class roots for the Hampstead high life: 'I'd rather be looked down on than beaten up.' On his short-lived marriage to a student at one of the colleges he taught at in the early eighties: 'I should have known it wouldn't work out when I discovered the wedding was on the same day as Jerry Lewis's birthday.'

In the face of such a talent for speaking his mind, what option did the BBC have but to give Frank Skinner his own chat show? Skinner repays their initiative by introducing serial killer's spouse

---

[154.] The ever more disingenuous personality of Graham Norton being the other one.

Rose West as a bogus guest on his first show. 'It was making a point about what real bad taste is,' Frank explains afterwards. 'The fact that people clapped was funny. I didn't expect them to clap – that cracked me up, actually.'[155]

The Frank Skinner Show never looks quite at home on BBC1. It's hard to be sure exactly why – it might be something to do with a certain 'bussed-in' quality the audiences of Avalon TV productions always seem to have – but when it eventually moves to ITV in a blaze of fiscally centred publicity,[156] the show really starts to find its feet.

In the age of independent production companies, a change of channels is not the epoch-making event it once used to be.

'It's only a matter of delivering the tape to a different address,' insists Avalon's Jon Thoday, somewhat unromantically. 'The reason, say, *Morecambe and Wise* got crap after it moved to ITV,' he continues, 'was that they tried to make it with a different team of people, but that wouldn't apply now.'

The fact remains that the identities of particular channels suit

---

[155.] 'We did have some problems with the taste thing,' Skinner admits of the first series's teething problems. 'About half-way through the series, the papers got hold of this thing – the headlines are on the box of the *Uncut* video – that I'd got my wrists slapped for the show being a bit near the knuckle. Some weeks it actually *was* the knuckle. You'd think it would be jokes about sex that would cause all the trouble, but it wasn't. They had this *Biteback* programme on the BBC and one of the main things that was cited on that was a joke where a representative of the deaf had complained that they weren't getting enough money from the lottery, and I'd said a spokesman for the lottery replied "What do people expect if they don't answer the phone?" I thought that was like an old music-hall gag that no one would have a problem with, but it got loads of complaints.'

[156.] 'These things are never just about money,' insists Avalon's Jon Thoday. 'We negotiated with the BBC for over a year, and in the end we went to ITV to find out what the show was worth. Then I gave the BBC a chance to match it because I thought I owed it to them, and at that point they took the moral high ground and told the press we'd demanded twenty-six million.'

Does the fact that Avalon productions seemed to mysteriously disappear from the BBC schedules at that point suggest that the corporation threw all their toys out of the pram in response?

'We're getting into an area here which would obviously be a fantastic exclusive,' Thoday confides, 'but I'm not going to give it to you.'

particular people, and the reassuringly irreverent presence of Skinner is a factor of considerable importance in the ITV networks' bold attempts to modernize their output in the late nineties. By 2002, when he finally ditches the comedy Hawaiian shirts for a nice smart suit (unfortunately insisting on keeping the dreadful song at the end of the show, for old times' sake), Frank has refined his interrogative approach to a fearsome alloy of mischievousness and empathy.

There are still times – for instance, his somewhat cringe-making encounter with Britney Spears – when his inner lascivious uncle gets the better of him, but these are far outnumbered by occasions where the unique quality of his, well, *frankness*, enables him to get things out of people no one else could. To watch Skinner prise the priapic reality of those wild nights with Prince Edward out of an unusually tight-lipped Ulrika Jonsson, or offering a sympathetic shoulder for *Popstars* martyr Myleene Klass to cry on, is to see the chat nexus operating at its most socially beneficial: enabling parties on both sides of the chat-show medium's one-way mirror to reveal themselves in their most truly human form.

Part Two

13
David Baddiel Syndrome

or The tyranny of obligatory irreverence

'Is the English sense of humour little more than the temperamental reflection of such national characteristics as kindliness, tolerance, sentimentality, optimism, laziness, playfulness, childishness, dislike of extremes and a desire for physical and emotional ease?'
Harold Nicolson (from *The English Sense of Humour*)

'Not at all was I impressed with that programme'
Prince Naseem Hamed, talking about
Fantasy Football League

It's the winter of 1996–7 – the last of eighteen Tory cold seasons. Everywhere you go in Britain, there are giant new pubs full of people singing along to Oasis's 'Wonderwall'.

In the Pizzaland over the road from the St Albans Arena, a shy-looking father and his football-shirted son share a difficult meal. There is something very touching about their awkwardness. If they could read their futures in the mozzarella, the long-term forecast might say anything, but the short-term one would contain an element of reassurance. It would say: 'You are going to see David Baddiel, a man who doesn't think twice about expressing his inner-most feelings, even though sometimes it might be better if he did.'

There is no way of knowing how this particular father and son might react to the moment – later in the evening – when Baddiel confesses that sometimes his only goal in having sex with his girlfriend is to supply himself with mental images for later masturbational exploits. (There is no way of knowing how David Baddiel's girlfriend reacts to it either, come to that.) A nervous attempt at a collusive glance, maybe, or perhaps a half-stifled flush of embarrassment? Either way, the arteries of their masculinity will have been fattened beyond the wildest dreams of any wily pepperoni merchant.

When you're actually in the midst of it, however, the whole David Baddiel testosterone bonding experience is not quite as cut and dried as might have been imagined. Early on, when the chants of the crowd oblige him to down his pint in one, this is done not so much in a spirit of beery triumphalism but with genuine (and justifiable) concern that his fragile grip on the proceedings might be fatally weakened by any form of alcoholic overindulgence

Appearing on *This Morning* just before his 'Too Much Information' tour began, Baddiel confessed that he had only gone on the road in the first place because Frank Skinner said 'you had to perform live to be a proper comedian'. To lapse momentarily into a football-related figure of speech, this is a bit like Alan Shearer convincing Gareth Southgate that you have to take penalties to be worth your place in the international side.

If you take as an official index of stand-up prowess the list of comic attributes Bob Monkhouse draws up in *Crying with Laughter* – 'the perfect pause, the subtlest shading of a word, the sidelong glance, the sudden switch of expressions, mock-shock, simulated sanctimony, shared secrecy, faked frankness, genuine on-the-spot emotion' – then David Baddiel scores perhaps three. A master of the comedic arts such as, say, Skinner or the at-this-point-in-the-nineties-pacing-about-lithely-in-the-wings-waiting-for-his-cue Johnny Vegas would expect to tick all nine boxes and a few more besides in the space of a couple of minutes.

In technical terms, then, tonight's show is something of a débâcle. It's fine to be reading cues off the back of your monitors at this early stage in a long tour, but those cues really need to say something other than 'Play dialogue excerpt from your favourite porn film' or 'Now is the time to use the line "like Fergie on speed"'. It is a further harsh fact of comedic reality that any aspiring humorist who finds himself using the formula 'and while we're on the subject of . . .' more than twice in one evening needs to do some serious career stock-taking.

And yet, by all measures other than content and presentation, this performance is a howling success. The warmth with which Baddiel is received is more than equivalent to the loathing he traditionally inspires in those who do not admire him. There *is* something specious about Baddiel's much-vaunted honesty – his endless presentation of himself as a purveyor of the difficult truths which are so often just easy prejudices in drag – but there is something genuine about it as well. And any man who can describe his angle of erection as 'less that of a high-powered industrial crane and more that of a gently opened cat-flap' must have *something* going for him.

Towards the end of the show, when David Baddiel invites the audience to ask him questions to use up the time he would otherwise have had to fill with theoretically comedic material, a voice from the back of the auditorium demands 'Who's funnier, you or Frank?' When the answer rings out from across the stalls – with better comic timing than any the star of the show has managed in the course of the evening – 'Frank!' – Baddiel has no trouble laughing. And why should he? While his demonic *Fantasy Football League* sofa-mate's crowd-control abilities sometimes verge on the sinister, Baddiel simply relies – not unrealistically on tonight's evidence – on the hope that his audience likes him.

Baddiel and Skinner and the post-Hornby mindset

Speaking to Skinner at around this time, he is considering Baddiel's suggestion that the two of them should expand the public's apparently bottomless fascination with their opinions and domestic arrangements into a full-length question-and-answer show. While still sceptical at this stage, Frank is plainly weakening.

'I like the idea of people being able to ask genuine questions,' he admits. 'I might try it – it gives you a chance to completely improvise, because you don't know what's coming.'

At the next summer's Edinburgh Festival, *Baddiel and Skinner Unplanned* makes a triumphant live début, before eventually taking up residence on ITV as a central plank (alongside the *Friends-*

without-the-jokes aspirational couples drama *Cold Feet*) in the network's attempted demographic upgrade. Although, as it appears on TV, *Baddiel and Skinner Unplanned* certainly has the *fin-de-siècle* air of the final step in a long evolutionary process, it's actually this show's predecessor, *Fantasy Football League* (which moves from BBC2 to ITV for the 1998 World Cup as part of the multi-million-pound Frank Skinner transfer package), that is the purest embodiment of a tendency endemic in British cultural life.

At a stage in the United Kingdom's economic development when very few people can earn a living out of actually making things any more, it is easy to see how the idea of two men building a career by sitting in a replica version of their own front room discussing that week's football results might be attractive. But there is more to the success of *Fantasy Football League* than that. Alongside Nick Hornby's *Fever Pitch*, it seems to define a shift in cultural emphasis from direct to indirect participation: where actually doing things ourselves is no longer deemed to be quite as interesting – or important – as responding to other people doing them.

Coinciding fortuitously (or not, depending on your point of view) with a huge technologically inspired expansion in the amount of space to be filled in digital TV and radio schedules – not to mention endlessly proliferating newspaper supplements – this apotheosis of passivity prompts an orgy of heedless self-gratification on a scale unseen since the last days of the Roman Empire. Wherever you look, there are people revealing their inner selves via their cultural preferences, and no individual yen – from a liking for the odd game of tiddlywinks, to a mild fondness for the music of T-Rex – is too insignificant to stop someone thinking they can squeeze a heartwarming first-person memoir out of it.

What might reasonably be termed the Post-Hornby Mindset generally presents itself as a bluff, common-sense riposte to outdated intellectual hierarchies (which, in one sense, is exactly what it is). And yet the positive discrimination – *for* the consuming masses, *against* the talented individual – which it also entails actually corresponds far more closely to the oft-bemoaned notion of 'political correctness' than anything the overcompensating erstwhile liberal élites of the late 1980s ever managed to come up with.

You don't have to be Lord Baden-Powell or V. I. Lenin at this point to feel that a culture which is more at ease celebrating the state of fandom than the talents and achievements which actually earn that tribute is going to have a hard time supplying itself with worthy objects of admiration in the future.

Perhaps the clearest evidence of this mindset's innate vulnerability is its neurotic unease about any form of artistic expression which can't be justified solely in terms of the way it reflects the circumstances or emotions of its notional audience. Where you might think that a subliminal awareness of just how much was being got away with would prompt a greater open-mindedness towards those willing to take genuine risks, it actually has the reverse effect. Like Victorian doctors – covering up the gaps in their own knowledge by energetically poo-pahing old wives' tales and oriental medicine – the cultural gatekeepers of the late Major and early Blairite epochs assert their authority by striving to exclude all who would offer them something other than a mirror image of themselves.[157]

It would be nice to be able to claim that the conjunction of this era of intellectual conservatism with the unprecedented forwardness of the comedian as a cultural figure is purely coincidental. But that would not really be true. At the same time as, say, Vic and Bob (with the roots of their humour planted deep in the fertile soils of prog-rock and avant-garde art) or *Father Ted* (with its uniquely beguiling brand of transatlantic Irish whimsy) offer an instant passport to new worlds of fun and enlightenment, a vast *Lord of the Rings*-style Orc army of comedic conformists seems hell-bent on imposing its own narrow vision of the world on everyone else.

[157.] Talking with Mark and Lard on Radio 1 in early 2003 to promote his terrible book *31 Songs*, Nick Hornby claims that he doesn't have time for the music of Led Zeppelin any more, as it 'no longer has any connection with where his life is now'. As if this is somehow Robert Plant and Jimmy Page's responsibility! This is the pop-cultural equivalent of the people in TV programmes about buying holiday homes abroad who walk into exquisitely decorated Tuscan monastery conversions and say 'Sorry, but it's not my taste'.

A froth with a saline base

This is pretty much the sort of thing philosophical Frenchman Henri Bergson was talking about a century before, when he described comedy as 'a froth with a saline base'. Bergson's book *Le Rire* sees comedy almost as a means of social control. 'It is the business of laughter to suppress our separatist tendency,' he claims, somewhat ominously. 'Society', Bergson continues, 'holds suspended over each individual member, if not the threat of correction, at all events the prospect of a snubbing, which although it is slight is none the less dreaded.'

Anyone who has ever watched Mark Lamarr or Sean Hughes picking holes in the appearances of the poor unfortunate ex-pop stars and their unknown stooges in the *Never Mind the Buzzcocks* line-up round will know what Bergson meant. The predominance of this type of informal social discipline in the mid to late nineties contributes to a kind of tyranny of obligatory irreverence, wherein any individual who takes what they do seriously – or has high ambitions – is somehow to be derided for fear they might upset the less committed majority.

When Harold Nicolson wrote in 1946 of 'the tendency of the English to regard as comic, insincere or pretentious anything which they do not happen personally to understand', he was referring to those sections of society which an inveterate snob such as himself would probably still have felt comfortable referring to as 'the lower orders'. Yet the criticisms he made of the predominantly working-class music-hall audience – that it 'will respond immediately to the recognisable and will laugh aloud at stock jokes, repetitions, mimicry ... references to food or drink and any allusion to the topical' – would be at least as appropriate to the largely middle-class crowds of the thriving nineties comedy-club scene.

To understand why this streak of philistinism is historically every bit as apparent at the self-consciously upmarket end of the British comedy spectrum as it is in the more downmarket regions, you have to go back to the satire boom of the late fifties and early sixties. There are two separate camps within this movement. On the side of the good guys (in this, although not every, instance) is Peter Cook.

240

Far from liberal by instinct (in fact, in later life he describes his younger self as 'a complete Nazi'), Cook none the less embraces the comedic possibilities of high and low culture with equal alacrity. When (in conversation with Chris Morris's haughty radio interviewer) Cook's Sir Arthur Streeb-Greebling – 'statesman, scholar, tycoon' – recounts his leading role in the LA riots ('I like to think I mowed down as many whites as I did blacks') or describes Betty Grable as being 'like Alma Cogan without the bounce', it's the awareness of popular culture which informs his character that is amusing, rather than his ignorance of it.

Humphrey Carpenter's history of the *Beyond The Fringe* era, *That Was Satire That Was*, wisely notes that Cook's was a satire 'not so much of a corrupt or enfeebled old order . . . as the old guard pathetically trying to modernize itself in the age of TV and rock and roll'. The undertow of affection he retained for this beleaguered establishment (which would, after all, have probably been his own ultimate destination, had the siren call of show business not lured him away from a career in the diplomatic service) was matched by the natural gratitude of a born hedonist for the glorious vista of guilt-free pleasure-seeking afforded by the 1960s' relaxation of time-honoured social and behavioural restrictions.

While Cook (and Dudley Moore, and Jonathan Miller, and – in his own heroically buttoned-up way – Alan Bennett) could embrace the new possibilities of their era with open arms, the picture did not look quite so rosy on the other side of the ideological barricades. For the more authoritarian faction (as represented by tweedy curmudgeon Richard Ingrams), humorous insubordination as practised by himself and his fellow scions of the officer class was one thing, but watching the virus spread to the ranks – as it did when, in George Melly's felicitous phrase, satire 'handed on a license for irreverence' to pop – well, it was just too much for him.

Carpenter's book contains a superbly ominous excerpt from a review in Ingrams's school magazine, *The Salopian*, of one of his early forays into the dramatic arts. In a Shrewsbury School Passion Play, Ingrams was, apparently, 'very effective as leader of the mob when, with high, harsh and strained voice he shouted for the death of Christ'. It was in this same magazine, at Christmas 1954, that the adolescent Ingrams invented the concept of 'The Pseud':

241

turning the full weight of his scorn upon those of his fellow public schoolboys who affected an enthusiasm (because obviously no such enthusiasm could be genuine) for 'Chagall, Blake and Freud' (why he didn't throw in Darwin, Picasso and Louis Armstrong while he was at it, still remains a mystery). In the process, he instituted a tradition of hysterical suspicion of almost any form of culture (especially the popular variety) which would endure from the earliest days of *Private Eye* to Ian Hislop's team captaincy on *Have I Got News For You*.

The very purpose of irreverence is to rub against the grain, and yet by the mid to late 1990s, the all-seeing sneer is almost the official language of UK culture. The list of things it is possible to build a career out of being irreverent about has expanded to include pop music and sport as well as politics. And if there's a living embodiment of the Bergsonian dictum that 'laughter, by the fear which it inspires ... restrains eccentricity', it's the smirking presence of David Baddiel in his *Fantasy Football League* judgement seat, poking fun at the pineapple-headed appearance of the unfortunate Nottingham Forest striker Jason Lee.

In a few years' time, footballers with even more ludicrous hairstyles will be fêted for their tonsorial daring on the front of every newspaper and magazine in the country, but Jason Lee has made the fatal mistake of being ahead of his time. And while *Fantasy Football League* can sometimes be quite fun, there are points at which the show's persecution of Lee – who also, lest we forget, has the temerity to be of mixed ethnic origin – suggests that all it's really doing is opening up the illicit thrill of terrace bullying to a new middle-class constituency. A constituency which wouldn't have dared to participate for real in the dangerous days of the seventies and eighties, for fear of getting its head kicked in.

It's interesting to note that in *Fantasy Football League*'s final stages, after the transfer to ITV for the 1998 World Cup, Frank Skinner seems to become increasingly unhappy with the oafish demeanour of the studio audience. His poignantly embittered air might reflect the immortal words of Courtney Love – 'When you get what you want, you never want it again' – but it also prompts him to an act which future generations will look back upon as the apex (or, more aptly, the nadir) of late-nineties laddite sexual hysteria.

Promotional duties for the show give Frank the opportunity to get his hands on that holy grail of under-achieving British masculinity, the Jules Rimet Trophy. The most appropriate means he can come up with of celebrating this mystical moment (and the emotional truth underpinning his live TV confession to this effect makes it just as shocking in the – on the evidence of Frank's previous observations about his high regard for veracity, unlikely – event of it having been fabricated for the purposes of comedy) is to rub his penis against the trophy's bulbous tip. Thirty years of hurt obviously never stopped him dreaming.

In a culture where nothing is sacred, nothing is worth anything. In the context of *Fantasy Football League*, confirmation of this important point comes from an unexpected source.

As befits a Muslim Jungle fan, Prince Naseem Hamed's saucy aura of casual invincibility in the mid to late nineties is underpinned by a sense of belonging not to one culture, but to two.

'I was born in Britain and I'm proud to be English,' he says in a break between training sessions at the Sheffield gym of his Irish trainer, Brendon Ingle, 'but at the same time my parents are from the Yemen – that's the culture I come from – and I'm so proud to be an Arab it's not true.'

This pride is fiercely reciprocated. The Arab world is not over-populated with sporting heroes, and Prince Naseem fits the bill triumphantly. Desert monarchs shower him with Mercedes convertibles and hundred-thousand-pound watches. In the Yemen, his face appears on postage stamps – 'It's a wicked likeness!' – and he can't get the president off the phone.

In Britain, of course, we do things differently. To be admitted to the inner sanctum of nationwide celebrity here, our sporting champions have to allow themselves to be insulted by comedians. While Prince Naseem's uncomfortably acrimonious appearance on *Fantasy Football League* – 'Not at all was I impressed with that programme,' he observes afterwards, with imposing formality – is superficially the least successful of the many mid-nineties ventures into sports–showbiz cross-over territory, in the years that follow, Hamed's refusal to be the butt of Skinner and Baddiel's schoolboy jibes comes to be looked upon as a triumph of the human spirit.

Traditionally in this country, we are more at ease with plucky losers than the defiantly victorious. From Henry Cooper to Frank Bruno, it's a whiff of Dunkirk that we expect from our pugilistic heroes, not of El Alamein. And in the last years of the twentieth century and the early ones of the twenty-first, this cult of condescension spreads from the boxing ring into almost every walk of showbiz life.

From Neil and Christine Hamilton at one end of the socio-political spectrum to Keith Chegwin and supposedly disgraced *Blue Peter* presenter Richard Bacon at the other, the semi-ironic rehabilitation of those who have fallen from public grace will become one of the dominant narrative strands in all forms of entertainment. Before this can happen, a series of momentous public events must come to pass. While the role of David Baddiel in these dramatic tableaux is not initially apparent to the naked eye, closer examination with posterity's high-powered microscope will reveal that he is, at the very least, in the picture.

Before even *that* suspicion can be confirmed, though, we must consider the impact of that aforementioned cult of condescension on Baddiel's standing as an author.

'A tongue jabbing gingerly at the ashen dent of my anus'

As the comedic career infrastructure described in chapter 5 establishes itself ever more securely, the comedian-turned-novelist becomes to the late 1990s what the rock-star-turned-actor was to the seventies: someone with more cultural capital than they properly know what to do with. Even among the numerous bare-arsed hybrids of warmed-over stand-up material and diaphanously-clad autobiography that constitute the comedian-turned-novelist canon, David Baddiel's *Time For Bed* stands out as an especially regrettable triumph of personal ambition over actual literary talent.

A review copy falls open on page 119 and the phrase 'a tongue jabbing gingerly at the ashen dent of my anus' leaps up out of the print (I'm not sure why, perhaps because it is rather more finely tuned than many of those around it). Which makes it all the more surprising to read on the cover the fine Irish writer Roddy Doyle's avuncular assertion that he 'thought the book was terrific'.

David Baddiel Syndrome

Even the warmest advocate of Baddiel's prose would be forced to admit that 'terrific' (*adj*. very great or intense) is stretching it a bit. There is a hint of self-abnegation in Doyle's willingness to be quoted to this effect, but there's something quite crafty about it, too (and not only in the same way as when Oasis's Noel Gallagher used to cannily praise blatant second-raters like Dodgy and Ocean Colour Scene, secure in the knowledge that they made his own band look even more special by comparison).

It's hard to understand why the lot of the professional writer – solitary, often impoverished, prey to innumerable insecurities and the savage depredations of the reviewing fraternity – should still be deemed an aspirational one by large sectors of society at this point, but for some reason, it is. Yet heaven help the novelist in the intellectually jumpy climate of the mid to late nineties who has the temerity to suggest that perhaps there is something they can do that other people can't: that perhaps not everyone (not even every comedian) has a novel in them.

As the furore over Martin Amis's advance for *The Information* in 1995 demonstrates, all the public (or, more accurately, the media) demands in return for according novelists the ever-rarer distinction of high-cultural clout, is that they should live out their lives in penury and die in rented accommodation.[158] For some reason, these strictures do not apply to those who already make a very good living by other means. And whereas you might think this anomaly would cause a general closing of ranks on the part of a snooty publishing fraternity hell-bent on keeping out celebrity interlopers, it actually has the reverse effect.

Desperate for some of David Baddiel's showbiz glamour to rub off on them, the literary establishment follows Roddy Doyle's lead by welcoming him with open arms. A few years later, when Baddiel is appointed a judge of the 2002 Booker Prize, hardly a voice is raised in protest. People made a fuss when Mariella Frostrup was asked to do the same job, but at least as a former press officer for Spandau Ballet, she had some kind of cultural track record behind her.

[158.] As Amis notes to Melvyn Bragg on *The South Bank Show* at around this time, 'half a million pounds for crap would be fine'.

245

Those who are concerned that letting David Baddiel judge a literary prize is like letting an egg-eating snake judge an egg-and-spoon race find their worst fears are soon confirmed. Baddiel complains that of the books he has been asked to read, 'there are far too many with an obvious *gravitas*'. And, as anyone who has seen David Baddiel's sitcom for Sky[159] knows, obvious *gravitas* is not David's strong suit; his disdain for the self-consciously heavyweight being symptomatic of that 'desire for physical and emotional ease' identified by Harold Nicolson as central to the nation's sense of humour.

Goodbye England's rose, hello *OK!* magazine

In the late nineties, Britain is – perhaps more than at any other stage in its history – a country sitting back and waiting to be entertained. From the bungling of hapless criminals captured on CCTV footage to the face of an ambitious young Tory grandee losing his seat at the 1997 election, the range of things that people are willing to find funny seems almost infinitely extendable. (Henri Bergson's writings of a century earlier about 'the absence of feeling which usually accompanies laughter' speak to the nation's mental state at this point with rare directness: as the prescient Frenchman pointed out, there is hardly any activity which does not have a comedic aspect if viewed from sufficient distance.) And it is this condition of morally disconnected spectatorhood which *Fantasy Football League* posits as humanity's default state.

It may seem strange that the ascendancy of the particular spirit of comedic mean-mindedness here designated (perhaps a little mean-mindedly in turn, given that the man whose name we're taking in vain is merely its purest – not its only – embodiment) as David Baddiel Syndrome should coincide with one of the most astounding displays of public emotion ever seen in this country. But isn't it possible that the huge outpouring of formalized grief which followed the death of Princess Diana was at least at some level a response

---

[159.] Voted worst sitcom in the English language three years running by a poll of ex-readers of *The Listener* magazine.

to the idea of ourselves as a nation unable to take anything seriously?

Peter Cook once said that Britain was 'in danger of sinking giggling into the sea' and it is in this context that the veritable tsunami of humourlessness which sweeps across the nation in the immediate aftermath of Diana's death can most easily be understood. The portentous accoutrements of public mourning – the books of remembrance in supermarkets, the non-stop ballads on Radio 1 – might feel like the paraphernalia of a strange kind of invisible drug, but they actually represent a semi-conscious attempt to shake off that instinct for mocking laughter which Bergson defined as 'something like a momentary anaesthesia of the heart'.

As if in the belief that the tide has somehow turned against him, David Baddiel makes the hero of his second novel someone who uses the upset generated by Princess Diana's death as means of getting women into bed. While this ruse somehow fails to make those who have experienced heartfelt emotions realize their mistake, Baddiel needn't have worried about the British public losing its capacity for vindictiveness and cynicism.

For all the outbreak of soul-searching set in train by the British media's nagging suspicion that its own hands might have Diana's blood on them, the bold new resolutions which ensue last about as long as a New Year's diet. The vilification of David Beckham following his sending off in the second-round World Cup game against Argentina in France in 1998 is a *Fantasy Football League* victimization campaign operating at the level of an actual Salem witch-hunt.

You'd think that kicking an Argentinian would earn Beckham the undying gratitude of the nation's less forward-thinking football fans, but for some reason the spectacle of impotent petulance presented by his momentary (and in the circumstances, understandable) display of temperament accesses a deep well-spring of national rage and shame. In a further unexpected twist, the lustre of persecution nobly borne which the Beckhams acquire in the course of the subsequent hate-filled late summer and early autumn makes them ideal candidates to fill the gaping chasm left by Diana's untimely demise.

David and Victoria's increasingly regal aura does not end with the purple thrones at their wedding or the monarchical affectations of Beckingham Palace. It resides equally in their peculiarly Diana-like blend of tenderness, narcissism and conspicuous consumption, so precisely captured by both Alistair McGowan and Ronnie Ancona's long-running impressions and the Beckhams' memorable Comic Relief encounter with Ali G – a light-hearted echo of the princess's epoch-making *Panorama* interview.

The dynamic of confession and redemption established with such exquisite melodramatic grandeur by Martin Bashir's 'Queen Of Hearts' *coup* echoes on throughout the culture of celebrity, even as the latter expands like a kind of psychic airbag to cushion the impact of the princess's death. As the more sympathetic hearings (not to mention the copy approval, large sums of money and Caroline Aherne-style free holidays) which can be elicited from *OK!* and *Hello* magazines shift the balance of celebrity pulling-power decisively in their favour, a new post-Di age of sympathetic non-tabloid advocacy seems to be dawning.

Needless to say, things don't quite pan out that way in the end. But for a few weeks back there, it was a beautiful dream.

'Hankering after evil in the public mind'

In William Hazlitt's 'On The Pleasure of Hating', the great nineteenth-century essayist saves a straying spider from a premature end while speculating (with a clarity of thought matched only by taxonomical inexactitude) that 'a child, a woman, a clown, or a moralist a century ago would have crushed the little reptile to death'. On observing a general improvement in public manners since the dark days of universal spidercide, Hazlitt also observes the way in which 'the spirit of malevolence survives the practical exertion of it'. This 'hankering after evil in the public mind', he argues, finds expression in the general fascination with gossip.

At the turn of the twenty-first century, when *Heat* magazine (whose name, eagle-eyed readers will have noticed, is actually an anagram of 'Hate') endeavours to rebrand itself after an ignominious launch period, the advertising agency responsible briefly considers using quotes from Hazlitt's essay as the basis of its campaign. Having experimented with giant billboards bearing the legends

'Public nuisances are in the nature of public benefits', 'The heart rouses itself in its native lair and utters a wild cry of joy at being restored once more to freedom and lawless unrestrained impulse' and – perhaps most pertinently of all – 'We grow tired of everything but turning others to ridicule and congratulating ourselves on their defects',[160] the agency ditches the whole idea and opts for a more accessible slogan. One which proclaims intelligence to be directly proportional to the desire to speculate idly about the personal lives and fashion mistakes of others.

As *Heat* borrows a new template from cheap-and-cheerless *Now* magazine that sends its sales figures spiralling upwards into six figures and beyond (eventually overhauling *OK!* and *Hello* around the half-million mark), the magazine starts to supplement its frothy and essentially harmless blend of TV-led non-news and vacuous celebrity lifestyle ephemera with an authentic nasty streak. At once engorged with their own power and in thrall to what they imagine to be the small-mindedness of their readership, *Heat*'s editorial team works to enforce a level of social and cultural conformity that might have made even sharing-a-flat-with-Frank-Skinner-era David Baddiel a little nervous.

Thankfully, this erstwhile confirmed bachelor is married with a child by this time, so he fits in well enough with the prevailing mood of frenzied domesticity. But as competition between *Heat* and its rapidly proliferating (and blatantly imitative) rivals hots up, no one is safe from the judgemental lenses of its camera-toting drones. What began as a reaction against tabloid invasiveness ironically culminates – with high-powered telephotos scanning even the most low-rent of celebrities for any form of physical or sartorial imperfection – in a new pornography of intrusion.

Who's got an unsightly rash? Whose neck is showing their age? Which celebrity has 'freakishly long hands'? By the early 2000s the sort of questions it was good manners *not* to ask in the pre-*Fantasy Football League* era have become the meat and drink of everyday public discourse.

In fact, if comedy's only function was the one Vic Reeves came

---

[160.] To anyone who doubts that this actually happened, I can only say 'prove to me that it didn't'.

up with while pondering Nietszche – to provide a socially acceptable means of laughing at someone with 'a particularly goofy tooth' – there would no longer be any need for it. Happily, that is *not* comedy's only function. As the ensuing '*OK*-style celebrity home and garden exposé' will aim to confirm.

14
Vic Reeves Welcomes Us into His Beautiful Home

And shows us paintings differing markedly from those of Ronnie Wood

'A picture is finished when all means used to bring about the end have disappeared'

James Abbott McNeill Whistler

'Michael Jackson's just a teacup on the horizon at this point. He's being manufactured in a porcelain factory'

Vic Reeves

Hopelessly lost amid the genteel greenery of rural Kent in the autumn of 1997, a confused city-dweller wanders into the village post office, forlornly brandishing a photocopied map. 'It'll be Lady A's you're looking for,' says the nice woman behind the counter.

But it's not Lady A we're after, it's the new lord of the manor, the man who realized long ago where the real future was: not in computers or currency speculation, but in cannibalizing yourself a stage name from Jim Reeves and Vic Damone and then persuading Gordon Burns from *The Krypton Factor* to knock household cleaning products off piles of dogfood with a trombone.

At the entrance to the (then) Reeves residence, there's a big wooden gate that opens automatically when you've identified yourself over the intercom. If you proceed up the drive – past the two huge stone Buddhas on the left – and glance down the rolling green sward to your right, there's a fantastic view of the Kent coast and Dungeness power station in the distance.

251

At the bottom of the hill is the old black Austin that Vic and Bob Mortimer buried in September's *Omnibus* TV programme. 'I was going to bury it anyway,' Vic explains. 'I've had it about four years and it's never worked.'[161]

If he feels the urge to stand by the fence with a shotgun cocked over his arm shouting 'Get off my land', Vic manages not to give in to it. His handsome property is also home to a number of four-legged residents, including two fine pigs – a Berkshire and a Tamworth. They truffle about in their enclosure in the contented manner of farm animals which have good reason to suspect that their owner intends to let them live out their natural lifespan undaunted by the threat of the slaughterman. (As a teenager, Vic had a grim-sounding Saturday job performing porcine castrations, and is repaying a karmic debt.)

Also grazing contentedly in the garden is the newest addition to the Reeves menagerie: an Angora goat, which Vic recently bartered for a cow. Vic runs a luxurious hand through its silky hair.

'I might trim it at Christmas,' he speculates. 'See what I can make out of it.'

On the other side of the house is Vic and Bob's work-shed. As well as a couple of stuffed grebes and a cuckoo, the walls of this miniature cricket pavilion boast a well-realized self-portrait, dated 1985, of Vic in papal robes. He holds a scroll bearing the inscription 'res ipsa loquitur', which he translates for visitors with a significant look as 'the meaning lies on the surface'.

Like many of Vic's more grandiose proclamations, this one is best taken with a pinch of salt, but it would certainly be true to say that everything he and Bob do – from the fine tailoring of their suits to the Picasso-inspired serenity of the Dove From Above – is informed by an acute visual sense. In acknowledgement of this fact, and as a tentative first step towards exposing his painterly canon to a wider public gaze, Reeves has kindly fenced off a small paddock of time for a face-to-face discussion of his art.

[161.] This property seems to spell doom for cars. In 2003, some years after Vic has sold the house to Paul O'Grady, eagle-eyed viewers of Comic Relief's *Celebrity Driving School* watch in wonder as Lily Savage's representative on earth somehow manages to crash his vehicle in the driveway.

That's not 'his art' in the *look-at-the-horrible-watercolour-or-substandard-piece-of-graffiti-I-knocked-out-on-my-day-off-and-am-now-planning-to-sell-for-a-fortune-at-a-charity-auction-to-show-what-a-well-rounded-creative-individual-I-am* sort of way, but the art which has gone hand in hand with his comedy from the very beginning, and which shines a welcome Maglite of inspiration on to the obscure workings of his unique and deviant mind.

When Vic and Bob are creating, say, a mythical beast with Ron Atkinson's face and an apple and polythene halo, they still do drawings for the BBC's costume and set designers.

'If we just tell them what we want,' he admits, 'it never ends up looking like it does in our minds.'

His love of plans goes back a long way.

'At school I used to do really dull technical drawings of airplanes,' he remembers. 'I used to make kits as well – hundreds of them – and I'd paint all the men's faces and give them paisley shirts.' Vic's favourites were German aircraft of the Second World War, many bits of which are lying just beneath the surface of the countryside around his new home, as the Battle of Britain was fought overhead.

Even the four-year engineering apprenticeship he served at SAB brake regulators in Newton Aycliffe during his late teens does not seem to have extinguished his love of draughtsmanship. When Vic moved to London, he wanted to go to art school, but they wouldn't let him into Goldsmith's (conveniently located near his home in New Cross), so he used to sneak in and use their equipment anyway.

'I basically designed my own art course while signing on,' he remembers. 'It was somewhat arse about face, but the government was still paying for me.' He ended up going across the river to Sir John Cass in Whitechapel for a year – drawing pictures of Terry Thomas with his eyes far apart (for reasons which will be explained later on) and making light bulbs out of wax.

The German artist Joseph Beuys began to make chairs out of fat and pictures out of felt after the plane he was flying as a World War II pilot was brought down in the Arctic wastes and Eskimos rescued him from the crash-site and wrapped him up in those (under the circumstances) life-preserving substances. While Vic insists that 'exactly the same thing happened to me', there is no documentary evidence to support this claim, and it is hard to shake the suspicion that he made light bulbs out of wax for the same reason that he used to make models of planes like the one Joseph Beuys was shot down in: i.e. for fun.

Would it be fair to say that his (Vic, not Joseph's) art and his comedy are different ways of expressing the same thing?

Vic grins his assent. 'The art is just what I started with. I think it's getting too serious though . . . Art should be [assumes cheesy light-entertainment voice] *just for laughs.*'

It would not be unreasonable to speculate that before [official Goldsmith's graduate] Damien Hirst and his conceptualist fellow travellers in the Saatchi Collection's 1997 *Sensation* exhibition turned art into comedy, Vic and Bob were turning comedy into art. Shared obsessions with textures and meats – whether cooked or in carcass form – suggest the parallel might go even further.

'Damien has confessed to me', Vic admits proudly, 'that we were his first influence.'

Is it strange to find yourself becoming someone who has shaped the minds of a lot of other famous people?

'It's great, isn't it?' Vic nods vigorously. 'It means you can predict what they are going to become.'

In what way exactly?

'I wouldn't like to go into that.' As his sardonic laughter fades, five small birds land on the wire in front of him. 'Look at those goldfinches,' Vic says knowledgeably, 'they're like the Rolling Stones.' A goldfinch flies away. 'That's Bill Wyman!' Vic shouts excitedly. 'He's leaving the rest of the group.'

Who's going to be the next to jump off the fence?

'Charlie Watts.'

Another finch leaves.

'That was the one I thought was Charlie Watts as well!' Vic is suitably exultant: 'I've even influenced goldfinches in their natural behaviour.'

Going back into the kitchen to leaf through the artworks laid out on the table there, it's a different Rolling Stone who is on Vic's mind.

'Because I'm known for being on TV,' he insists with proper modesty, 'I don't think I should present myself as a serious artist. That'd feel like a bit of a cheat . . . like Ronnie Wood drawing on to the canvas from his astral projections.'

The shadow of Vic's day job certainly falls quite heavily across paintings and drawings such as 'Electrical Work Carried Out by Real "Live" Puppy', 'Queen Elizabeth I Urinating in the Style of a Man' or 'The Krankies Airlifting Mickey Mouse Out of a Dust Storm Full of Skeleton [*sic*]' (the subject-matter of this last, the artist insists, is 'quite self-explanatory'). There's the occasional straightforward pastiche too, notably of Italian surrealist Giorgio de Chirico, whom Vic describes as 'one of my favourites'.

The first thing you notice about the pictures in which Vic seems to be developing a style of his own is the prevalence of images of people with their eyes set widely apart.

'When I was at art school, I was just doing copies of Davids and things like you're supposed to,' he explains, 'and I got very bored. Then I found a picture in an Elvis Presley annual which had the eyes very far apart, so I set myself the task of trying to draw people with their eyes very far apart while still making them look like who they were meant to be . . .'

It's just the kind of challenge the contemporary art establishment is failing to rise to . . .

'Indeed,' Vic nods sagely. 'That's what they should be doing at the Royal Academy – a wide eye competition.'

There's certainly a wide range of pictures of Elvis: 'Elvis Eating Thrushes' Eggs' ('Just the sort of wholesome food he should have been eating'), Black Elvis ('He's more like a Welsh miner in this one, really') and last and, frankly, least, Elvis with a carrot strapped to his forehead. Why does the caption to the last of these read 'You shouldn't have'? 'It's like . . . [Vic's voice cracks with suppressed merriment] *it's your birthday!*'

Mr Presley seems to occupy the same central role in Reevesian iconography that Jesus or the Virgin Mary did for the great artists of the Renaissance . . .

'It's partly that, yes, but it's mainly because the first picture that got me doing the eyes wide apart was of him, so I did a lot of them. It works just as well with other people like Terry Thomas or Morrissey or Ronnie Corbett, though.'

None of those three would have had quite the iconic heft to carry 'Elvis, Priscilla & Lisa Marie As The Holy Family'. 'She [Priscilla] looks very sinister, doesn't she?' Vic enthuses. 'Look at that eye!

He's gripping her quite tightly: [Assumes scary Elvis voice.] *Smile, you bitch . . . look like you're enjoying it . . .* [Vic's eye turns tenderly now to the infant Lisa-Marie.] Michael Jackson's just a teacup on the horizon at this point. He's being manufactured in a porcelain factory.'

The warm response elicited by magazine exposure of Vic's pictures soon soothes his fears of Ronnie Wood overlap. And as his *œuvre* proceeds with apt rapidity through public exhibition to hardback publication, he becomes increasingly confident about it. While doing the publicity for *sunboiledonions* – a beautiful, funny and occasionally disturbing volume in the great tradition of Edward Lear – Reeves shows the world a newly straightforward public face.

Conscious of time-honoured British distrust of anything that might be deemed pretentious, Vic and Bob have traditionally done their best to conceal the possibility that they might actually think about what they do. Discussing his wide-eyed Elvises on *Clive Anderson*, however, Vic brazenly uses the word 'iconography', causing his unctuous interlocutor's eyes to bulge in the manner of one who eschews any form of genuine intellectual exchange.

While it's refreshing to see Reeves present such a forthright aspect, his new-found openness does bring problems of its own. Groucho Marx prudently never drew attention to his friendship with T. S. Eliot,[162] for fear of making explicit things about his comedy's affinity with literary modernism that would have been better off remaining implicit. And when the set of Vic and Bob's 1998 BBC2 series *Bang Bang . . . It's Reeves and Mortimer* is built around a cabinet which looks like it's been borrowed from Damien Hirst's guest bathroom, and giant Gilbert-and-George-style portraits of the show's stars peer down from the back wall, it feels rather like the tail is wagging the dog.

'I had one of those pieces of bevelled glass to put our images behind, so it would look strange when the cameras moved,' Vic

---

[162.] In *The Groucho Letters*, T. S. Eliot and Groucho Marx discuss the satisfactory conclusion of a much-postponed dinner engagement with a warmth which belies this discretion.

explains apologetically. 'But once it went up, I do remember saying "Shit! It's going to look like Gilbert and George".'

It's not that he has any more reason to be coy about high-cultural antecedents than he does about low-cultural ones. But at its most inspirational, Vic Reeves's comedy has made a glorious mockery of the very existence of that high–low division. So the prospect of it raising its ugly head within the dynamic of his own career comes as something of a shock.

Rather than squander his mojo in the manner of a dissolute eighteenth-century monarch, Reeves has always preferred to channel it into an extraordinarily broad range of creative activity. In the same way that when David Lynch is not making films, he paints pictures with glue or sculpts human heads out of cheese and turkey, then encourages ants to eat them, Vic's public acts are only a small subset of the total sum of his artistic endeavours.

Whether essaying a portrait of a goldfinch in the style of one of Rembrandt's assistants or recording horrifyingly scatological rap parodies in the dubious guise of MC Manmud, comedy is simply not a big enough storage tank to contain the torrential effusions of his subconscious, just as art and music haven't been. Only a judicious combination of all three will do the job.

The tricky question as Reeves's career enters what, in a less perennially playful performer, might be termed its 'mature' phase, is how to reconcile this broad creative urge with the more focused requirements of a continuing profile in top-flight show business. At some point, an element of giving the people what they want simply has to enter the equation.

Giving the people what they want

It's not often one gets the chance to say this, but the stage of the Cambridge Corn Exchange is a feast for the eyes. The day will no doubt come when colour therapists will study the uplifting impact on the soul of the set of *Shooting Stars* at the earliest stage in their training. But for the moment it is enough to bask in the invigorating combination of blues and yellows and oranges.

By rights, the 1996–7 'live edition' of the book of the video of the CD-ROM of the TV celebrity quiz ought to be a step too far. A *Shooting Stars* segment shoehorned into Vic and Bob's last stage show went off horribly half-cocked. And the second series on BBC2 has had the odd creaky moment, too – even the show's most ardent admirer could be forgiven for feeling that thirteen episodes was stretching it a bit. When something starts at the peak of conceptual perfection which was the *Shooting Stars'* base-camp, there is only really one way to go. And that is not up.

Yet somehow this show does not have the second-hand feel you might expect. Perhaps because watching comedy on TV is so often a more fulfilling experience than watching it live, a no-expense-spared reconstruction of a small-screen pleasure seems to get people more excited than a 'proper' live show would. Perhaps also because touring the same routines up and down the country has given the performers the chance to savour the quality of Vic and Bob's writing instead of just belting it out and moving on to the next show.

The atmosphere is certainly jollier than at an actual studio recording, where all concerned tend to have the air of being at work as they carry their cans of lager out on to the set. And judging by the strangled shouts of approbation that greet her every move, for a substantial portion of the audience the chance to see Ulrika Jonsson in the flesh is worth the price of admission on its own.

Far more than Angela Rippon to Vic and Bob's Morecambe and Wise, Ulrika's involvement in *Shooting Stars* seems to have taken on a life of its own – her status somewhere between muse and Aunt Sally. A delicate and peculiarly British balance of deconstruction and celebration seems to have been established here, in that the idea of Ulrika's beauty only really seemed to take flight when Vic and Bob started undermining it; whether by giving her a public platform from which to demonstrate her facility for drinking pints of lager in four seconds,[163] or by making indelicate reference to the 'strange and edible crabs' that, legend has it, 'live on her face'.

Conversely, the guest 'celebrities' who join the regulars at each new town on the tour – a shy man from local radio, a charming Cambridge United footballer, an unknown female pop singer and (by way of contrast) St Etienne's Sarah Cracknell – need to be built

---

[163.] Or pretending to do it. If the dark rumours are to be believed.

up a little. If this is not quite the way things turn out ('Favourite meal: steak and chips, favourite group: Simply Red, favourite TV: *Only Fools and Horses.* That's right, you *are* a footballer!'), Reeves and Mortimer can hardly be blamed. Show business is, after all, a stern mistress.

Anyone who wasn't fully aware of this before tonight's opening 'Legends' segment – wherein three fully costumed lookalikes struggle poignantly to bring to life the back catalogues of Freddie Mercury, Rod Stewart and Elton John, with the help of a live band and Mark Lamarr on occasional harmonica – certainly knows it afterwards. There are few more poignant sights in the world than a lookalike playing it for laughs. And there is a hint of cruelty in Vic and Bob's decision to allow this to happen on such a grand and awful scale which they (and we) need to be wary of.

For 1999's midnight Radio 1 special *Cock of the Wood*, Vic Reeves records the show in the woods surrounding his aforementioned Kentish domicile. In the company of a band of rowdy acolytes, he plays records by Todd Rundgren and Method Man while indulging in lewd and manly banter.

This is a vivid pagan tableau, eerily suggestive of the classical symbolism explored at such imposing length in J. G. Frazer's *The Golden Bough.* On the northern shore of Lake Nemi (or 'Diana's Mirror', as it was called by the ancients) in the region of Aricia in Italy's Alban Hills, there lurked amid the mists of myth a sacred grove, patrolled by a grim figure with a drawn sword. The latest in a long and unhappy line of murderer priests established by Virbius (male companion of the Goddess Diana) and somewhat misleadingly dubbed Kings of the Woods, this beleaguered individual would retain office until inevitably perishing by the hand of his successor.

For a candidate could only attain this illustrious position (and its concomitant privilege of loving physical relationships with the oaks and elms of the wood) by slaying the man who would, on expiring, become his predecessor. While some have sought to equate the bloody succession of the Arician priesthood with the pressures and rivalries at the top of the late-nineties UK comedy tree, I for one find such comparisons not just irresponsible, but downright offensive.

15
A Grove of His Own

Steve Coogan fights to maintain his position in Virbius's gory lineage

'The life of a wit is a warfare upon earth'
Alexander Pope

'I do have a letter from Michael Winner . . . it's not framed'
Steve Coogan

Six inches away, on the other side of a cramped lunch table, Steve Coogan is holding his cigarette at a very strange angle. His arm is wrenched painfully back over his left shoulder, as if in the grip of an invisible assailant. A clumsy attempt to reassure him of the superfluity of this exaggerated act of consideration meets with a brusque response.

'It's not for you,' Coogan says crisply, 'it's for me.'

But no one is forcing him to smoke.

'I like smoking,' he insists, 'I just can't stand smoky rooms.'

While it would probably be a mistake to read too much into Steve Coogan's desire to divorce actions from their consequences in this instance, contradictions do tend to pile up around him like sand dunes on tussock grass.

It is the summer of 2001 (which is skipping on a few years ahead of where we ought to be right now, but this encounter demonstrates the fraught nature of life at the very top of the comedy food chain with such exquisite clarity that it would be a shame to save it for later) and the reason we find ourselves in an especially notorious nest of media vipers is that Steve Coogan is returning to the business of self-promotion after almost three years out of the limelight.

He's making his big-screen starring début in *The Parole Officer*: a 'family comedy', co-written by himself and Henry Normal. The budget of around five million pounds might not sound all that big by Hollywood standards, but with the British film industry in the terminal stages of post-Lottery bloat, failure would be costly in more ways than one. Small wonder that, as the film's co-writer, co-producer and star, Coogan – smartly turned out today in expensive-looking sunglasses and well-laundered Chevignon shirt – seems focused almost to the point of distraction.

He starts out by explaining that he 'decided to make a film his parents would want to go and see' as a reaction to the sorry selection of sub-Guy Ritchie gangster efforts clogging up the cinematic release schedules. At this stage – before a finished version has been screened – it has not yet become fully clear that what Coogan has actually done is to make a film that *only* his parents would want to go and see.[164]

The rough cut which is available shows a promising – even polemical – premise of Lancastrian public-sector heroism, all too swiftly obscured by a blizzard of lame innuendo and weary slapstick. And that too eager titular concession to American cultural imperialism (given that it's set in Manchester and not Texas, shouldn't the film really be called *The Probation Officer*, not *The Parole Officer*?) sets an ominous tone of pre-emptive artistic compromise.

Soho House is an interview location of Steve Coogan's own choosing, and yet the sense of being on show that goes with it plainly makes him uncomfortable. It's not hard to understand why, as this members-and-their-guests-only hangout is one of those places designed to disillusion anyone who liked to imagine that they were living in a meritocracy.

Walking through the warren of bars and screening rooms whose denizens exhibit every known form of new-establishment ostentation, Coogan becomes embarrassed by the number of people claiming his acquaintance. He likes to drop in every now and again, he

---

[164.] In fact it does reasonably well at the UK box office, but only in the first week – until word gets around.

insists, sardonically, 'to keep in touch with what the kids on the street are thinking'.

The dark energy of these places is certainly powerful.

'They always sound so convinced anything they do will be brilliant,' marvels Coogan, unable to avoid mentioning the group of people behind us, who are discussing an upcoming film project in the sort of braying voices which are impossible to escape in this kind of environment, 'just because it's their idea! If I, or any of the people I write with, have an idea, our first impulse is always to think of reasons why it *won't* work.'

In some ways, Alan Partridge's unrepentant gaucheness is a way of channelling the pain of such social unease into a comedic safe haven. Talking about how much he's enjoyed his recent relocation to Brighton, Coogan mentions that he's become 'like that Pink Floyd song says, "comfortably known"'. On being informed, perhaps somewhat pedantically, that the song is actually called 'Comfortably Numb', Coogan's face falls with a suddenness that is no less comical for being entirely self-aware: 'I don't want to be that.'

A few minutes later, in an exchange which might have been transcribed directly from an episode of *The Larry Sanders Show*, Coogan is approached by a slightly nervous-seeming Johnny Vegas. As Vegas (of whose comic talents Steve is plainly in no doubt) withdraws from the table – not quite bowing, but almost – Coogan draws his right index finger across his throat, making the time-honoured gesture of impending oblivion popularized by Arabian assassins in Sinbad films, and simultaneously expressing heartfelt concern about the direction in which the younger man's current management is taking him.

As it happens, over the next few months Vegas will inscribe the most inspired televisual arc since Jarvis Cocker broke into the pop mainstream in 1994–5. But then anyone – even Steve Coogan – can make a mistake.[165] And thus established, the Sandersesque mood of the afternoon proves very hard to shake off.

Shortly afterwards, Coogan catches sight of his cousin Aidan McCardle across the restaurant. McCardle is a successful RSC

[165.] It is only fair to point out here that a change of management does play a part in at least the later stages of Vegas's TV apotheosis.

actor, fresh from a successful stint in the lead role of Richard III. In less starry boyhood times, the two cousins shared summer holidays in Ireland together, but in this socially pressured context they seem unsure of how to greet each other. After a certain amount of anxious to-ing and fro-ing, they eventually end up kissing full on the lips, which the ensuing air of embarrassment suggests is not the course that either had intended.

'I took the actor's route,' Coogan proclaims, once his cousin has taken his leave, 'went to drama school, bought a pair of tights and did what I was supposed to do . . . [from this point, his initial jocular grandiosity fades subtly into genuine bitterness] . . . When we came down for our London showcase, I did this piece from an Alan Ayckbourn play that I was really pleased with, and didn't get a spit or a fart in response. The only people who were signed up were people who had floppy hair and looked like they might do OK in a Merchant Ivory.' He beckons me in with a conspiratorial leer. 'To be honest, the only people who got signed up were twenty-one-year-old lads that the gay agents wanted to shag.'

This disillusioning encounter wasn't the young Coogan's first brush with the discriminatory practices of the acting establishment. In the mid-eighties, he came down to London to audition for smart drama schools like Central and RADA, but found himself overawed by 'all these people walking in with long scarves and big flowing overcoats who seemed to be called Sebastian and have fathers who knew the tutors and worked for the BBC World Service'.

Coogan, by his own regretful admission 'just didn't have that kind of confidence'. Consequently, he ended up studying drama in the less gilded surroundings of Manchester Poly (an *alma mater* which – in producing not only himself but also Caroline Aherne, Doon MacKichan and Coogan's erstwhile comedy helpmeet John Thomson – would ironically end up having a greater impact on the showbiz establishment of the future than many a supposedly more élite institution).

It seems strange that Coogan should still be holding a grudge about this. After all, if plan A had succeeded, he might now be auditioning for character parts in the same sub-standard Brit gangster flicks *The Parole Officer* was intended to satirize, rather than running his own multi-million-pound production company and opening one of the biggest British films of the year. But admirers of his work have good reason to be grateful for Steve's tendency to take rejection personally.

The way Coogan tells it, every crucial step forward in his career has been a response to some implied slight. The record-breaking West End stage show with dancing girls (1998's *The Man Who Thinks He's It*) was a response to overhearing a contemporary (he won't say who, but it would be funny if it was Frank Skinner) describe him as a talented TV performer who couldn't put on a live show. And he only went to the Edinburgh Festival in the first place to prove to a sceptical alternative-comedy establishment that there was more to him than just advertising voice-overs.

Coogan's competitive edge was already pretty sharp before he'd even graduated from drama school. 'I remember thinking, I can't wait for college to finish,' he says. 'I was quite happy for us all to be thrown overboard to see if we would sink or swim, because there were a few holier-than-thou people who turned up on time for every lesson and were heavily into Brecht and Stanislavsky. And I wanted them to have to audition for baked-bean adverts.'

Such a combative attitude to his professional fellows recalls a quote generally attributed to Coogan's eighteenth-century predecessor, the poet, polemicist and master of the literary put-down, Alexander Pope. 'The life of a wit', he asserted, 'is a warfare upon earth.' While Coogan has not – as Pope was – been disqualified for public office on account of his Catholicism, he often cites the religious background he shares with the wasp of Twickenham (and also with Chris Morris, Armando Ianucci, Frank Skinner, Caroline Aherne and Mike Yarwood, come to that) as a well-spring of his anti-establishment feelings.[166]

After perusing the menu at some length in search of a meal which exactly fits his requirements, Coogan eventually settles on chicken with braised pak choi. The waitress has inadvertently misled him

---

[166.] Pope's Victorian biographer Courthorpe observed: 'He knew nothing of the manly conflict between equals which does so much to strengthen and correct the character of boys in an English public school.' How Steve Coogan's personality might have been shaped had he, too, not been denied such a privileged start in life, one can only speculate.

into believing that pak choi is a delicious noodle. When a plate overrun by an unappetizing-looking fibrous vegetable is eventually placed – rather insouciantly – in front of him, Steve fights an epic battle against the rage which burgeons within.

For a while, he seems to be winning, but then something snaps. He pulls himself up a few inches higher in his seat and disdainfully raises the business end of his chicken leg with a designer fork. 'Excuse me,' he exclaims, with a misplaced (but oddly infectious) air of triumph, 'but do *you* see any noodles?'

The moment when status anxiety tugs away the mask of propriety to reveal the contorted face of human need and rage beneath is one of Steve Coogan's most reliable comic staples. In this context, there seems to be an intriguing conflict between the ostentatious consumerism for which – in the early stages of his career at least – he was generally renowned and a 'staunchly Labour-supporting Catholic' upbringing, wherein, to use Coogan's own proud words, 'everything was always about helping people less fortunate than yourself'.

Then again, maybe after a childhood of cheerful socialist self-sacrifice (an already large family – Steve initially had four brothers and one sister – having been extended still further with the adoption of another sister and a series of fostered siblings), the appeal of a span of hedonistic self-indulgence would not be so very mysterious.

'I think I was quite an excessive person for a while,' he admits. 'I'd do my work and then go out and get wrecked . . . But on a personal level, I'm much happier now.'

The usually genial Coogan doesn't seem much happier on this occasion, but that is often the way with people who have recently renounced decadent lifestyles.

Throughout Steve Coogan's working life, people have compared him with the late Peter Sellers. Understandably confused as to what this might mean (that he will die young and have a very annoying daughter?), Coogan's response sometimes seems to have been to emulate Sellers's automotive and carnal indulgences, rather than the range and intensity of his best work. In fact, there have been times when it's been hard to resist the conclusion that not only his personal life but also his career were being driven by that part of his anatomy which a character in *Ally McBeal* might call 'his dumb-stick'.

It is hard to square the concupiscent Coogan of tabloid kiss-and-tell exposés (or of Tony Ferrino or *Dr Terrible's House of Horrible*, come to that) with the shrewd, self-aware individual who describes himself as 'too anal to self-destruct'. Coogan has always been happy to admit that the reason so much of his other work – not least *The Parole Officer*'s gormless hero Simon Garden – reminds people of Alan Partridge is that there is so much of himself in that character. In this respect, perhaps there is some mileage left in the Peter Sellers comparison, but as a contrast rather than a likeness.

One of the reasons Sellers was able to submerge himself so completely in such a variety of roles – from *Dr Strangelove* to *The Pink Panther* to Chauncey Gardener in *Being There* – was that no one, least of all Sellers himself, seems to have had much idea of what he was really like as a person. (This confusion of identity was neatly enshrined in the title of Peter Evans's absorbing 1969 biography, *The Mask Behind the Mask*.) Steve Coogan, on the other hand, embraces the reality of who he is with an almost technical precision.

'My background', he explains, 'was in that kind of limbo between lower middle-class and upper working-class where you don't quite know whether you belong to one camp or the other. When I passed the eleven-plus and went to grammar school, I wasn't one of the tough kids from the housing estate, I was one of the softer boys from the place where people owned their own houses, mowed their lawns and washed their cars on a Sunday morning . . . it was kind of a Little Englander environment.'

Does he think he felt an obligation to behave badly in the early days to demonstrate the fact that he was coming up in the world?

'I don't think I thought about it that much. I just sort of did it,' Coogan smiles ruefully. 'I lived a very obvious lifestyle – I remember I bought a sports car before I bought a washing machine – and I think part of me didn't really care about what I was like as a person, because I knew I had integrity in my work. Looking back on it, I suppose my attitude was: people can say I'm a bastard, but they can't say I've sold out.'

Coogan's distinctive brand of principled unrepentance backs him into some strange ideological corners.

'I drive a fast car, but I don't feel guilty about it,' he explains gravely, 'because – as far as I know – I haven't fucked anyone over to get it. Whereas . . .' Coogan smiles, realizing how outrageous this is going to sound, but saying it anyway, 'if I see someone else in a flash car, I think they probably have done.'

So Steve Coogan is the only decent person in Britain to drive an expensive car?

'My theory may be full of holes,' he acknowledges, mock-defiantly, 'but it's still one I like . . .'

When someone from Coogan's religious and political back-ground starts getting paid a large amount of money for making people laugh, isn't there usually supposed to be an element of guilt involved?

'Even though I'm not really . . .' Coogan assumes a pensive air, 'I don't know what I'd describe myself as, as far as Catholicism is concerned, but I loathe that fashionable left-wing reaction which writes it off as repressive. A lot of Calvinist interpretations of Christianity are far worse in that regard, and even though it would be very media-friendly of me to say that I went to Catholic school and really hated it and the only way I could express myself was through comedy, it wouldn't be true.'

Coogan speaks very highly of his Catholic education. The order of brothers who ran his grammar school – the celebrated French order, De La Salle – were far from the briar-wielding ogres of Jesuit stereotype.

'I wasn't force-fed the catechism or told that sex was wicked unless it was for procreation,' he remembers. 'My religious lessons when I was fifteen were spent discussing whether the church should endorse the armed struggle by aligning itself with Marxists in South America.'

Like his old friend, rival and Manchester Poly drama degree course-mate Caroline Aherne, Steve Coogan was weaned on the socially conscious TV drama of the seventies and eighties. One of the intriguing things about both of their comedy-writing is the way it has taken on the social authenticity and concern with character detail that characterized the best work of, say, Ken Loach or Jim Allen (the veteran left-wing screenwriter whose son Coogan is proud to claim as a childhood friend) while abandoning their explicit political agenda.

'I think that's true,' Coogan nods pensively, 'and I'm not quite sure why. Personally I do have quite strong political convictions, but I think that people who are deliberately and consciously polemical in their work eventually lose their impact, because they only ever talk to the converted, whereas I feel that I've got all these brownie points with my enemies, because people who I have real political differences with still like what I do.' He pauses. 'I don't know whether to be pleased or displeased when I get a letter from Michael Winner saying how much he likes my comedy.' Coogan looks up sharply, as if concerned that this might be taken as a merely hypothetical example – 'I do have a letter from Michael Winner' – then decides that perhaps he has gone too far: 'It's not framed.'

The pat explanation for all of this would be that for some of those who reached voting age in the 1980s, the disjunction between an imaginative world of top-flight left-wing TV drama and a political reality in which Margaret Thatcher was trying to prove there was no such thing as society was simply too much to comprehend. And the conclusion they reached? That show business was the only truth.

While there is undoubtedly some validity to this view, there are also other factors which need to be taken into account. As specious as John Major's rhetoric about a 'classless Britain' was, there's no denying that the immediate post-Thatcher period ushered in the greatest broadening in comedy's social base since The Goons and Tony Hancock in the immediate post-war years. If you take the strangely subservient attitude towards what the author terms 'The Oxbridge Mafia' which prevails in Roger Wilmut's *From Fringe to Flying Circus* (first published in 1979) as a starting-point,[167] it's plain that comedy is one area in which dramatic progress was made in terms of equality of opportunity in the last quarter of the twentieth century.

Where Ben Elton, French and Saunders, Rik Mayall and other big wheels of the alternative epoch were mostly – with Lenny Henry and Alexei Sayle among the few exceptions – middle-class scions

---

[167.] Had Wilmut's Oxbridge Mafia not been 'sidetracked' from their pre-ordained career courses, apparently, 'the world might have gained three doctors, two solicitors, an advertising executive, a literary critic and a number of other solid citizens'.

of Birmingham or Manchester Universities, the post-alternative epoch has been dominated by those with less luxurious social ante- cedents. In the 1990s, writers and performers such as Vic Reeves, Caroline Aherne and Ricky Gervais,[168] all from emphatically non- BBC backgrounds, ended up not only creating and starring in but also, in the latter cases, directing (previously the last redoubt of the old TV caste system) their own beautifully realized artistic statements.

Having been on several sets and observed that the director almost invariably seems to be a somewhat diffident upper-middle-class man with a certain rumpled lustre to his hair, glasses and clothing,[169] the directorial part of the equation seems particularly significant.

'You're broadly right,' Coogan laughs. 'The old social balance does tend to remain in that area . . . but there is a sort of natural justice at work, in that mavericks do find their way through. If you take Peter [*Phoenix Nights*] Kay, for example, he has a reputation for being difficult, but that's just because he's someone who knows exactly what he wants and has no time for lily-livered southern jessies giving him their opinion.

'It's the same with Caroline Aherne,' Coogan continues. 'When someone like her who has real talent and vision and also directs comes along, the people who've gone through the normal channels of privileged education are left wondering, What's the point of us? I think that's why people in the industry are reassured by her being cast as a bit of a wild card.'

It's interesting how often the last half-decade or so's more auth- entic comedies of working-class life have come under fire from critics at the snootier end of the spectrum, who label them as 'exploitative', almost, it sometimes feels, as if trying to protect the lower orders from themselves.

Coogan nods earnestly. 'I remember in the case of *The Royle*

[168.] Although the latter, like Alan Bennett before him, 'only found out he was working-class when he went to university'.

[169.] When this vile slander is put to him, *League of Gentlemen* and *Royle Family* (series two) director Steve Bendelack – a rugged frontier individual who paid his dues at art school and *Spitting Image* before becoming one of the most widely respected of comedic helmsmen – says, 'I think that's probably true.'

Family, a *Guardian* journalist called Charlotte Raven slagging it off for being "by middle-class people for middle-class people". I read that and thought, You're just wrong. There are no more working-class people in TV than Craig Cash and Caroline Aherne!' – he pauses, as if alarmed at the prospect of them using this as a testimonial – 'They think I'm posh because my family had two cars.'

'The key thing with *The Royle Family* is,' Coogan picks up his thread again, 'if you compare it with, say, the films of Mike Leigh – which at their best can be very good and at their worst can be a middle-class bloke pointing at working-class people and going "aren't they peculiar?" – is that the people it's about find it funny. That's why *The Royle Family* could go out on BBC1 and get very healthy viewing figures, because the people it was based on were enjoying it. And that's why it's such an inspiring example of something which is very pure and yet has reached a broader audience.'

The Parole Officer's half-hearted stab at a contemporary Ealing comedy ultimately proves to be a not-so-inspiring example of exactly the opposite tendency. But hearing Coogan talk so warmly about Aherne's work (as a general rule, there's no quicker route to an awkward silence in the company of a comedian than to mention the achievements of a contemporary), it's hard to believe this is the same person as the serial avenger of slights who can cite possession of an expensive car as evidence of not having sold out.[170]

[170.] Talking about Michael Winterbottom (who directed his fine performance in *24 Hour Party People*, 2002's cinematically bold if commercially unsuccessful biopic of Factory Records boss and Alan Partridge role model Tony Wilson), Coogan says something rather startling.

'Why I like Michael,' he insists, 'is that he's a northern intellectual, and that, I suppose . . . ultimately . . . all cards on the table, is what I am.'

This apparently heartfelt admission cannot be allowed to pass unchallenged. Not because it is necessarily untrue – Coogan enjoys a discussion of the co-operative socialist pioneer Robert Owen as much as (in fact probably more than) the next millionaire playboy comedian – but in the certainty that if he felt circumstances demanded – if, for example, he were here today to promote one of the lascivious schoolboy romps with which his *œuvre* has been regularly punctuated – he would cheerfully say the exact opposite.

When this objection is still at the raised-eyebrow stage, a sheriff of

This intriguing disparity will be explored for a final time in the concluding chapter, but for the moment, a statement Coogan makes on a later occasion just about covers it. 'Vengeance is a pretty good motivation,' he observes, philosophically, 'but love is a pretty good motivation too.'

---

unspoken scepticism which hasn't yet had time to get its posse of words together, Coogan is already racing to head it off at the pass.

'You're right,' he nods vigorously. 'Next time I do a broad comedy, I'll probably say I can't stand all that intellectual stuff and I just want to reach out to the people.'

16
The *Royle* We

Caroline Aherne and the comedy of popular sovereignty

'Put in the first paragraph "She tried to top herself . . . she's had eye cancer"'
Carmel Morgan, Caroline Aherne's press officer, 1999

'Things happen in sitcoms. Real life is just people sitting around and sometimes saying funny things'
Caroline Aherne

In a moth-eaten make-up caravan on the set of the third series of *The Fast Show* in the summer of 1997, Caroline Aherne is talking about her new series, *The Royle Family*. She hopes it will show 'what's funny about normal lives, without being "Ooh, let's laugh at them" like the Two Ronnies in their donkey jackets'.

She's just won a big argument with the BBC about doing the show without a laughter track. 'It's brave of them to let us do it this way,' Caroline admits graciously. 'And at least now if it fails, we won't have to wonder if it *would've* worked. We know the dad is dead funny . . . just in the way that dads are. You don't tend to see naturally funny people in sitcoms, because everyone's always coming out with really long sentences, but he's very dry. His catchphrase is "My arse!"'

Set in real time, with no canned laughter, in a council house in Wythenshawe not dissimilar to the one Caroline herself grew up in, *The Royle Family* – as it slips on to BBC2 screens with minimal fanfare in the autumn of 1998 – turns out to be one of the most original pieces of British TV in years. The entertainment potential of a programme in which a hard-drinking sofa-bound layabout (Caroline), her fiancé (writing partner Craig Cash) and parents (Ricky Tomlinson and Sue Johnston, formerly Bobby and Sheila Grant in *Brookside*) sit around the small screen shouting at *The Antiques Roadshow* might seem to be somewhat limited, but only a fool would accuse *The Royle Family* of being a show about nothing.

Marked out from conventional British TV comedies by its heroic lack of plot ('Things happen in sitcoms,' its co-author prescribes strictly, 'real life is just people sitting around and sometimes saying funny things') and disciplined adherence to its own set of aesthetic principles, *The Royle Family* combines the intellectual rigour of *Seinfeld* with the ornery warmth of *Roseanne* at its unsentimental best. It's not just very funny, but a great deal more besides.

If a television series in which a father's fascination with his own bodily functions is one of the major recurring themes can possibly be described as lyrical, then lyrical is what *The Royle Family* is. Talking to Aherne about it again shortly after the end of the first series, in early 1998, she seems surprised at the warmth of its reception, though she was delighted when she showed the touching matrimonial finale to some of her friends and it made them cry (it reminded her of the way she herself burst into tears[171] when Simply Red's 'Holding Back the Years' came on at the end of Rodney's wedding in *Only Fools and Horses*).

The question which must occur to anyone who has shuddered at the acerbic brutality of Mrs Merton is, where did all this human feeling suddenly come from?[172] Within its enclosed, domestic setting, *The Royle Family* seems to enshrine all the ideals of working-

---

[171.] Didn't everybody?

[172.] Caroline explains the link between the two shows thus: 'I wanted to do it from the beginning, but the BBC wouldn't let me till I signed up for the last two series of Mrs Merton. Then they said "Go on, here's some money" – it was like a treat ... And I must hold my hands up and say they were dead supportive,' she continues archly, 'once we got a good review in.'

class familial and communal solidarity which were supposed to have been demolished by the Thatcher years.[173]

'Everyone in *The Royle Family* is based on someone real,' Caroline confides. 'We just remember what people say and exaggerate. My mum's obsessed with what people have to eat in exactly the same way that Barbara [Sue Johnston's character] is, and Ricky Tomlinson is Craig Cash's dad. He's obsessed with the price of everything.'

The Royle Family's unique understanding of the rough and tumble of family life – the way that Ricky Tomlinson can treat Sue Johnston with such appalling thoughtlessness while somehow still loving her to distraction – is the biggest single factor in making it one of the best-loved of all British TV comedies.

Caroline Aherne is used to having the support of her community behind her; from close-knit relationships with supportive male co-writers Henry Normal and Craig Cash, right back to her early childhood, when she and her brother Patrick were both diagnosed as suffering from rare cancers of the retina. Since the Ahernes didn't have much money – Caroline's mum Maureen was a dinner lady, her dad Bert worked in an unspecified capacity on the railways – their local Irish Catholic club in Wythenshawe held a dance to raise the funds to send them to Lourdes.[174]

The balance between tenderness and mischief which would later characterize her comedy seems to have been established early on in Caroline's relationship with her brother (in whom the eye condition was more advanced). 'I'd send him the wrong way sometimes for a joke, as you would as a child,' she remembers, 'but in her own daft old way my mum was really clever. She used to say to Patrick "Look after Caroline, look after Caroline, she's only tiny so you've always got to hold her hand", but really she was doing that because

---

[173.] It had been in reconciling these ideas with the ancient traditions of ducking and diving institutionalized as Thatcherite entrepreneurship that *Only Fools and Horses* had struck such a profound chord.

[174.] A cure was effected – miraculous or otherwise – but the Ahernes had to keep on popping down to Bart's hospital every few months for several years to come, supplementing faith with science. Caroline would later pay off this debt to her papist heritage by making one of her first characters a nun called Sister Mary Immaculate.

it meant I could guide him about and he didn't feel anyone was doing it.'

Aherne's roots are in the same doughty Manchester Irish stock that gave the world Oasis, Steve Coogan and her fellow *Fast Show* regular John Thomson. Can she think of any reason why this particular demographic should have been so fruitful in the early nineties? 'It's just a great place, Manchester . . . Manchester and London,' she beams vaguely, 'that's all there is really.'

This remark – of particular interest to Aherne fans in Nottingham, Scotland and the home counties – elicits the first of a series of warning twitches from her press officer, who has stayed in the room throughout the interview, even though her charge seems well able to look after herself.

Does she think that the fact that her parents had Irish accents – and she didn't – might have encouraged her acute ear for dialogue? 'I've never thought of that before,' she says sceptically. 'My dad's dead anyway, but *no one* spoke the same as he did. [She looks at her press officer.] You never met him, did you?' At this point her voice drops an octave or so into an impenetrably thick, rapid-fire Irish brogue, occasional guttural swear words being the only concession to comprehensibility. 'People would say "What's your dad on about?" and we'd say "We don't know – just smile" . . . My mum's voice is lovely though,' Caroline qualifies, 'it's dead soft.'

'You just grow up like other kids in your area really, though, don't you?' she continues, looking around for confirmation. 'We were no different from our neighbours on the estate. Except I went to a convent school rather than the local comprehensive. If I'd have gone to the comprehensive, I could've walked, but I ended up getting buses on my own at eleven.' She is thinking aloud now, which often seems to mean trouble. 'My mother would rather have me get raped on the two buses but knowing about God than walking to the comprehensive.' Caroline looks at her press officer for support again. 'It's rough round there, though . . .' She shakes her head in disgust. 'They don't care, do they?'

Unwilling to join in a general debate on the unfitness of Catholic mothers – especially Caroline's – her press officer sounds a note of caution: 'She'll be ringing me tonight saying "You don't think he'll put 'My mother would rather I got raped . . .', do you?"'

I'm sure Mrs Aherne senior will appreciate that her daughter meant it in fun.

As if caught up in the excitement of saying the wrong thing, Ms Aherne junior decides to grasp all the nettles in the garden at once. 'Caroline, *who has no boyfriend at the moment*,' she says with prurient emphasis. Her press officer joins in:[175] 'Put in the first paragraph "She tried to top herself, she's had eye cancer".' 'Dead dad,' Caroline chimes up again cheerfully. '"Her dad's dead" ... Oh yes, "and any time now, she's bound to get found out".'

At the 1998 South Bank Show awards, Caroline Aherne finally got to meet Ken Loach, the veteran social-realist film-maker whose gruelling but inspirational dole queue drama *Raining Stones* is her favourite film of all time. This encounter sounds like it might have been a bit of a culture shock on both sides, as at Caroline's approach the notoriously limelight-shy Loach suddenly found himself in the unaccustomed position of being blinded by papparazzi flashbulbs.

'I was expecting him to be like a madman, with his hair all wild, as if he was too busy thinking of the things he was working on to ever get a comb in it, but he just looked like the man over the road – a geography teacher or something ... I still love him though,' she continues, forgivingly. 'You know how it is on set – the big vans with all the catering? Ken Loach wouldn't have any of that. The actors only have one sandwich because he thinks – which is true – that you go a bit sleepy in the afternoon if you've eaten a lot. Ricky [Tomlinson, veteran of several Loach productions and a man known to like a pie in his lunch-break] told us all about it.'

It's funny that Loach's attitude to trying to capture the authentic texture of working-class life on film is that you can't have more than one sandwich, whereas the authentic working-class attitude would be ...

'Free food!' Caroline chimes in, happily. 'They're all sadists, those people, aren't they? I bet Ken was sat there in his Winnebago with all the sandwiches that he hadn't let everyone else have.'

To leave the libel courts free for the Catholic mothers, it should

---

[175.] In more ways than one. Around this time, Carmel Morgan leaves her press officer's post – at Caroline's typically maveric request – to help Aherne and Cash co-write the next two series of *The Royle Family*.

probably be emphasized that Caroline Aherne is joking at this point. Yet – banter aside – it's an interesting fact that while Aherne's generation of writer–performers have taken on the meticulous social observation of the left-leaning TV and film dramas they grew up with, they have also – by and large – abandoned the political objectives that lay behind them. As if to confirm the point, Caroline chooses this moment to remember that she has lent her video copy of Mike Leigh's *Meantime* to Steve Coogan, and he's not given it back.

Obviously, her loving representation of her own social reality is *implicitly* political . . .

'Is it? Oh, I am delighted, I've never been told that before.'

And what about Mrs Merton's heroic struggle to give a voice to the forgotten older sections of a greying population?

'That sounds like something dreamed up by a sad journo desperate to put a new angle on the fact that it's someone dressed as an old lady.'

You certainly couldn't say Aherne had been corrupted by money, because it was important to her right from the off.

'When I started doing Mrs Merton,' Caroline remembers, 'I couldn't believe how much I could get for three minutes on regional telly. I'd be quite happy for someone else to play her – or Denise in *The Royle Family* come to that – but you get paid so much more for performing than writing, and if you weren't in things, you wouldn't have the clout to get them made in the first place.'

In a world where the currency of celebrity has become so devalued that we are expected to find a pregnant Victoria Beckham 'taking her bump for a walk' an enduring source of fascination, the complex and contradictory personality of Caroline Aherne comes as a welcome respite. Guarded and indiscreet, knowing and naïve, brittle and spontaneous, crafty and self-destructive, this is a woman with an IQ tested at 176 who finds Benny Hill funny; an accomplished media powerbroker who played her husband at darts for the right to keep her name, and lost.

Ricky Tomlinson says Aherne 'acts the dizzy blonde but is actually as sharp as a box of razors'. And there's certainly no shortage of acuity in her explanation of *The Royle Family*'s housebound format. 'I remember they took Alf Garnett out of his house and put him in a restaurant scene once and he just looked *massive*. It was funny to see him sitting there with lots of extras, but you just couldn't believe in him in the same way as when he was sitting at home shouting at the TV.'

It was this same concern with the perils of overstatement which caused her to hold out against the wishes of BBC top brass and insist on *The Royle Family* being filmed in real time without an audience.

'Even with *The Fast Show*,' she remembers, 'I liked all the more naturalistic performances that were done on location much better than the stuff they did in the studio. The whole thing gets diluted in front of an audience, because you have to do the same bits again and again and again, and when people have had a laugh with a line once, they'll start doing it a different way and the performances just get bigger and bigger until the characters lose all their subtlety. Whereas out on location, cos there's only the crew and they don't care about them, they'll do it the same way fifteen times, which is what you need, really.'

The truth is that something that feels (and indeed is) as natural and spontaneous as *The Royle Family* doesn't happen without a great deal of careful thought. It's Caroline's uncanny instinct for what works and what doesn't that finds her preparing to direct the third series herself in the spring of 2000 (following in the accomplished footsteps of Mark Mylod and Steve Bendelack, who navigated the good ship *Royle* through its first two voyages).

'Craig wants it put on the credits "Director Caroline Aherne",' she laughs, '"for everyone except Craig Cash, who is his own man".'

Aherne is a bountiful hostess – visitors to the Maida Vale basement flat she's just bought from the TV presenter Dani Behr are quickly furnished with wine and a Cadbury's Flake, as she pours herself a glass from a half-bottle of something sparkling.

'I have got to watch it,' she says of the drinking she has now resumed in greater moderation. 'It was a big problem for me, and even though it's under control at the moment, I'll always have a tendency to go that way, because that's how my personality is.'

She hasn't been back to an AA meeting since the first drop of forbidden liquor passed her lips.

'They don't like it, do they? When people start drinking again,' she grins. 'For some reason it's frowned upon.'

Calculatedly outrageous one minute and alarmingly conventional the next, Caroline Aherne's interview persona strikes an intriguing balance between extreme caginess – urgently requesting 'don't use that' after what are often the most uncontroversial statements – and heroic indiscretion. Pointing out 'stains' on the sofa she inherited from her flat's previous owner, she jovially proclaims her intention to 'rub herself up and down against them and have a footballer's baby'.

The sideboard groaning with BAFTAs and British Comedy Awards is one of few personal touches the property has acquired in several months of habitation (unless the gongs are Dani's too, which seems unlikely) but they're not going to be hanging around for long. Later on this evening, Caroline plans to drag Craig Cash and producer Kenton Allen across North London to inspect a new property she's putting in an offer for.

'*Ground Force* did the patio,' says Caroline excitedly.

'To anyone else,' Craig smiles indulgently, stretched out on the floor in front of Aherne's cosy gas fire like a lanky visiting tom-cat, 'that wouldn't necessarily be a recommendation.' His durable alloy of affection and exasperation has been forged in the course of a creative partnership with Caroline which has at this stage lasted eleven years. Though she habitually refers to Cash as 'the wind beneath my wings', as with all the best double acts, the balance of power between the two of them is never quite as clear-cut as it seems.

They bicker constantly, in the time-honoured manner of people who spend a lot of time shut up in a stuffy room working together. Cash – a burly, affable Mancunian, who on first meeting might be Mark E. Smith's less splenetic half-brother – is sent flying into a rage by Caroline telling their producer Kenton Allen[176] to stop chewing gum.

'Who do you think you are, telling him what to do like that, a schoolteacher?'

[176.] Who attains TV immortality in *Back Passage to India* by banging his head very badly on a low doorframe.

'I *am* a schoolteacher,' Caroline insists, haughtily (if without obvious foundation in fact). 'And I don't let them eat apples either,' she continues, broadening the argument out, 'because I hate the noise of chewing . . . or anyone playing with their change, which Craig does all the time.'

'I find that quite relaxing,' insists the object of her strictures, 'in the same way that Caroline enjoys giving nicotine to the atmosphere and doesn't care about us maybe getting secondary lung cancer.'

Aherne has a deadly knack for projecting this kind of caustic workplace banter on to a wider public screen. When she's being presented with an award by Steve Coogan at the 1999 British Comedy Awards, the latter – in the midst of a quiet spell in his career – tries to cover up the slight sense of awkwardness that results with a vainglorious 'I know what it's like to be up here'.

'Yes, Steve,' concurs Caroline sympathetically, 'but it was such a long time ago.'

'It was a great old gag,' she recalls merrily, a few months later, 'because it *has* been a few years since he was up there.'

But didn't she think this fact might've been preying on Coogan's mind already? As evidence of her compassionate instincts, Caroline cites the routine she had originally planned, but ultimately thought better of, 'to be kind'.

'I was going to go [oozing fake showbiz compassion] "He'll be back again, won't he? He's still funny, ladies and gentlemen . . . *c'mon* . . . it's Steve!"' She chuckles at the memory of exactly how merciless this would have been. 'He'd *so* hate that, and the worst thing would be that he could never say it wasn't funny, because he'd hate to not have that great a sense of humour.'[177]

[177.] The delight she takes in tormenting Coogan is of such an order that – were it not the height of ill-manners to speculate on such a personal matter – it would be hard to imagine they were not at some point in the earlier stages of their association 'more than friends'.

'Caroline and I had what I suppose you might call a "flirty" relationship,' demurs an unusually bashful Coogan. 'I had a list of male friends [in itself a magnificently Cooganian concept] I could go out for a drink with, and when I thought "Who will make me laugh?" I'd always end up ringing Caroline because she was the funniest person I knew, and she would spent the whole evening taking the rise out of me.'

The Royal *Oui*: Where the actual house of windsor comes into it

By the time *The Royle Family* has made a successful transfer to BBC1 and rolled on through that third series – not to mention a couple of memorable Christmas specials – without any apparent loss of momentum, the show attains a regal aura all of its own. In fact, the episode where the Royles come to grips with the possibilities of Saturday morning, and Ralf Little's nobly put-upon teenage son returns from the shops to find the house empty as everyone's gone to the pub, scales heights of domestic verisimilitude unconquered since the legendary 'Sunday Afternoon at Home' edition of *Hancock's Half Hour*.[178]

The recurring sketch in *Alistair McGowan's Big Impression* where the actual royal family sit around the TV exhibiting the personality traits of their televisual almost-namesakes (with McGowan's Prince Charles as Craig Cash, Ronnie Ancona's Camilla Parker-Bowles as Caroline Aherne, the Queen as Sue Johnston and Prince Philip as Ricky Tomlinson) is more than just a tribute to *The Royle Family*'s increasingly institutional status. It also reflects the House of Windsor's achievement in suburbanizing itself to the extent that such a conceit should seem not only plausible but utterly appropriate.

Mike Yarwood's autobiography recounts a proud moment at the 1981 Royal Variety Performance, when the Queen and Prince Philip discussed the improvement in his impression of Prince Charles ('He's doing him better than he used to'). Twenty years on, in the heyday of his successor, McGowan (when it's still surprising how much better the writing in his show is than it actually needs to be,

---

[178] It is a measure of how things have changed in the intervening fifty years or so that when first broadcast by the BBC, this classic episode – wherein the residents of the Railway Cuttings, East Cheam, struggle to come to terms with the (to the present day's pampered sensibilities) incomprehensibly limited entertainment options of a mid-century Sunday afternoon – provoked complaints about undermining observance of the Lord's Day. The BBC was able to reassure anxious correspondents that since it was 'Sunday *Afternoon* at Home', that didn't preclude Hancock and co. having gone to church in the morning (a great lost episode, if ever there was one).

and before the whole thing gets too full of itself), the *Royle Family* skit is a regular feature alongside speeches from royal correspondent Jennie Bond, or a visit to David and Victoria at home in Beckingham Palace. But the monarchical bent of *Alistair McGowan's Big Impression* is no throwback to former times; it reflects a shrewd understanding of the way the cult of celebrity has intensified and mutated in the aftermath of Princess Diana's death.

While the basic workings of this process have already been discussed, there is one important aspect of the feverish few weeks following the princess's fatal Parisian car crash which has yet to be touched upon. It was at this fraught moment, not four months after coming to power, that Tony Blair staked an audacious claim to popular sovereignty by – in Andrew Rawnsley's sardonic formulation – 'posthumously rebranding the daughter of an earl who was divorced from a prince as a princess of the people'.

Servants of the People, Rawnsley's insider account of New Labour's first term, contains a detailed and perversely thrilling account of the mental gymnastics Blair and his right-hand man Alastair Campbell went through in a bid to save the British monarchy from itself. Of all the countries in the world, it is probably only this one that could be whipped up into a republican frenzy by the perception that its Queen was responding inappropriately to the death of her former daughter-in-law. And at the strange and – for a while – almost revolutionary juncture when, as Rawnsley recalls it, 'The palace switchboard was jammed with members of the public shouting obscenities at whichever hapless official answered', only Tony Blair knew what to do.

In sharp contrast to the oft-quoted (but sadly anonymous) Tory shadow minister who 'walked through the crowds in St James's and realized that Britain was a country he no longer understood', Blair understood precisely what his country needed. It wasn't so much *actual* feeling that the British people demanded – they had enough of that going on already – as a convincing show of something which could generally be accepted to look like it.

His initial entreaties that some form of live broadcast might convince her once loyal subjects that Elizabeth II at least cared enough to *pretend* to share their sense of collective loss met with obdurate refusal from the Palace on the imperious grounds that 'The Queen does not do live'. But she ultimately capitulated to Blair's wise counsel. The broadcast as finally delivered (receiving an instantaneous on-air seal of approval from famously gone-native BBC royal correspondent Jennie Bond) contained, according to Rawnsley, 'several humanising phrases', coined by Alastair Campbell to warm up a distinctly chilly original draft. Among them was the immortal, and marvellously unqueenly, 'speaking as a grandmother'.

Campbell's brief as Blair's press secretary was to fulfil approximately the same role as John Milton had for Cromwell's Commonwealth[179] (i.e. defending his administration before the court of public opinion with all the eloquence and fervour at his disposal). And given that his own views tended very much towards the republican end of the spectrum – he would, according to Rawnsley, 'laugh out loud listening to Blair trying to reconcile his dynamic, meritocratic new Britain with a hereditary monarchy of Old Hanoverian extraction' – it seems especially ironic that it should have been his silver tongue which came to the House of Windsor's rescue in its hour of direst need.

This was not the last piquant irony to follow on from the dramatic events of the late summer of 1997. Tony Blair would discover – in the course of the 2000 petrol uprising and the anti-war demonstrations of 2003 – that in mobilizing notions of popular sovereignty by identifying himself as spokesman for the nation,[180] he had actually made a rod for his own back. Meanwhile, the Queen, having acquired some of New Labour's oft-demonized spin-doctoring skills, would succeed in shoring up her own position at the prime minister's expense, by putting into practice the lessons of her grim

---

[179.] A fly-on-the-wall documentary screened in the middle of one of Campbell's periodic career crises does reveal him – though by general consensus an inferior poet to Milton – to have a nice line in sardonic asides. And there is a delicious air of the biters bit in parliamentary lobby correspondents bemoaning their unfair treatment at the hands of the former *Daily Mirror* political reporter. 'Look at *X*,' Campbell is once said to have sneered at a journalistic foe in a packed lobby briefing, '*masturbating* in the corner.'

[180.] 'The role of uniter and healer that had traditionally belonged to the monarch had been seized,' Rawnsley concludes, 'part by design, part from necessity, by Tony Blair, sovereign of national sentiment.'

night out singing 'Auld Lang Syne' in the South Greenwich UK PLC factory outlet.

Where the 31 December 1999 Millennium Dome débâcle ill-advisedly tweaked the noses of the real powers in the land by obliging Britain's national newspaper editors to wait for the Tube at Stratford, the Queen's Golden Jubilee celebrations – fortuitously timed to coincide with the inevitable patriotic frenzy of the 2002 World Cup – offered the nation the irresistibly ludicrous spectacle of Brian May playing 'God Save The Queen' on top of Buckingham Palace.[181] While some complained (not unreasonably) that this made all concerned look ridiculous, a willingness to be made a fool of has been the British monarchy's secret weapon since the time of the court jester.

The jester's privilege of free speech – as long as he continued to make the king or queen laugh, he could say more or less what he pleased – sometimes enabled the absolute ruler of the late middle ages to hear important truths no one else would have dared to utter in their presence. And while the institution of the jester's motley fell with the monarchy and did not reappear with it after Cromwell and Milton's brief republic came to an end (the self-denying ordinance of 1645 having applied the final *coup de grâce* when it proscribed the professional fool's cap and bells as, in R. H. Hill's words 'one of the influences that made men effeminate, stay at home and unfit for war'), the tradition of licensed insubordination has proved far more enduring.

Hill's *Tales of the Jesters* quotes from Samuel Pepys's diaries the memorable occasion on which the Master of the Revels (a seventeenth-century bridge between the office of court jester and a later age's directorship of the National Theatre), Tom Killigrew, came in front of Charles II dressed as a pilgrim. 'Whither goest?' asked the monarch. 'I am going to hell to ask the Devil to send back Oliver Cromwell to take charge of the affairs of England,' replied his fearless employee – fearing no loss of royal favour for

---

[181.] May's flatulent act of homage bears roughly the same relation to Jimi Hendrix's incendiary version of 'The Star-Spangled Banner' as a picture of some cats does to Picasso's *Guernica*.

his outspokenness – 'for as to his successor, he is always engaged on other business.'

In 1994, while receiving a lifetime achievement acknowledgement at the British Comedy Awards, Spike Milligan responded to a congratulatory message from lifelong fan Prince Charles by calling the heir to the throne 'a little grovelling bastard'. While this seemed somewhat graceless (if very funny) at the time, the white roses the prince sent to Milligan's graveside eight years later signalled that there were no hard feelings. And in truth – like Flanagan and Allen at the first televised Royal Variety Performance forty years before, suggesting that Her Majesty 'just fling the keys down' so they could move her car – Milligan was merely fulfilling the court jester's old function.

There is a rather poignant snapshot in Spike Milligan's biography[182] of a star-struck sixteen-year-old prince meeting The Goons at Sellers's palatial Hertfordshire manor house. It's poignant because in view of the truncated role destiny would have in store for him, submitting to the jibes of his teenage idols with regal good grace would ultimately be one of the few ways left open for Charles to live up to an old-fashioned ideal of kingship.

[182.] Taken by Peter Sellers's then wife, Britt Ekland.

17
'A Little Bit of Politics'

or Who do you think you are kidding, Mr Elton?

'A fool who is of a sad countenance and striveth after doing heroic deeds thereby faileth to make men merry, to which end he was hired'

R. H. Hill

'I think it was Supreme Court Justice Brandeis who said "Sunlight is the greatest disinfectant"'

Jerry Springer

Will Somers, court jester to the notoriously quick-tempered Henry VIII, is said to have set himself a worthy challenge; 'To be a kings fool, and yet be respected in himself and do things becoming to a man' was Somers's intention. The evidence of his subsequent career, as recounted in R. H. Hill's *Tales of the Jesters*, was that this was possible in some ways, but not in others.

The altruistic and principled funnyman became embroiled in a huge feud with the not so altruistic and principled Cardinal Wolsey, in the course of which the jester managed by way of a series of cunning pranks (a kind of Tudor dry run for Comic Relief's Red Nose Day) to trick the sour-faced prelate into giving a lot of money to the poor against his will. 'They that are most galled by my folly,' Somers congratulated himself aphoristically, 'they most must laugh.'

He also managed to lead a successful protest against the enclosure of common land in his home county of Shropshire. However, there were limits to what even Somers's sharp Shrewsbury wit could achieve, as was made all too plain when a courtier pointedly reminded him that 'A fool who is of a sad countenance and striveth after doing heroic deeds thereby faileth to make men merry, to which end he was hired'.

This shrewd summary of the difficulties facing any would-be political comedian echoes down almost four centuries of history to the notional audience in the Alexei Sayle short story discussed in the introduction, who had 'grown tired of being shouted at by fat men about things that weren't their fault'. To approach the age-old vista of ideological disillusionment from a less familiar aspect, it is worth bearing in mind that comedians aren't the only people who sometimes grow weary of trying to combine career advancement with the struggle for meaningful political change. It can happen to politicians, too.

Kilroy woz 'ere

In 1985, when the proto-Blairite Labour MP for Birmingham South (and alleged political heart-throb) Robert Kilroy-Silk resigned his parliamentary seat to present an American-style daytime talk show on BBC1, it seemed to confirm that the Labour Party was no longer a place for personal ambition. (While this made the successors of Keir Hardie and Ernest Bevin a rare beacon of idealism in the dark days of the 1980s, it didn't say much for its chances of ever getting into power, a fact of which Tony Blair and Gordon Brown – soon to be swearing blood oaths over their polenta in an Islington restaurant – were all too well aware.)

At this stage, it has to be remembered, the idea of an American-style talk show on domestic TV was a novelty in itself. Gilbert Harding might have shed the odd tear on *Face to Face*, back in the day, but the idea that our most reserved of nations would wish to discuss its most intimate affairs in front of an audience of strangers

287

still seemed highly improbable.[183] In this, as in many other respects, this country was about to surprise itself.

It wasn't just that the British stiff upper lip would come to tremble with practised ease under the heat of the studio lights. Robert Kilroy-Silk's demagogic persona – neatly preserved for posterity's vague distaste in the amber of one of Alasdair McGowan's better impressions – seemed (and seems, come to that) to embody all the qualities we used to find noteworthy in American TV preachers. His sturdy hybrid of crocodile-teared pseudo-sensitivity and madly overloading testosterone would later be dissected with clinical precision by Chris Morris's *Brass Eye*.

More detailed study of this important and troubling televisual landmark looms in the next chapter, but for the moment, consider *Brass Eye*'s characteristically shocking *Kilroy*-style debate about the difference between 'good AIDS and bad AIDS'. As Morris's rabble-rousing host berates an unfortunate HIV-sufferer for even coming into the studio – on the grounds that if a madman were to go on the rampage with a machine-gun, 'anyone here yawning would get your blood in their mouth' – the shock effect hammers home a picture-hook of truth.

The most pernicious thing about the *Kilroy*/GMTV school of televisual hand-wringing is the blend of sanctimony and prurience – of pretending to appeal to all that is morally best in an audience, while actually targeting all their basest and most primitive responses. Say what you like about Jerry Springer (who provides the sumptuous main course to *Kilroy*'s sickly appetizer in British TV's banquet of moral laxity), you can't accuse him of sugaring that particular pill.

[183.] When you consider the disastrous impact an emotional televised encounter with John Freeman had on Tony Hancock, another of his most celebrated interviewees, perhaps old-fashioned reserve had something to recommend it.

The Rite of Springer

When *The Jerry Springer Show* used to get respectful name-checks on *Roseanne*, British audiences wondered excitedly what sort of programme the Conner family might consider the last word in low-rent small-screen entertainment. Then UK Living brought us Jerry twice a day, and we were not disappointed. It wasn't so much the subject matter (though shows like 'The World's Oldest Living Siamese Twins' and 'My Pimp Won't Let Me Go' would have been hard to resist even in less capable hands), it was the host.

Never mind the egomania of Oprah Winfrey, the simpering of Tempestt, the smugness of Ricki Lake and the sheer spellbinding tedium of Sally Jesse Raphael. Whether fearlessly taking the piss out of the Ku Klux Klan or shamelessly encouraging grown adults to throw their shoes at each other, Jerry Springer quickly established himself as the people's talk-show host – a lion amongst minnows. Who else could have kept their composure throughout the immortal 'I Cut Off My Manhood', whose subject had become so bewildered by the attentions of a charismatic bisexual dwarf that he castrated himself with a pair of blunt scissors?

Born in London in 1944 (after his Jewish parents had escaped there from Hitler's Holocaust), in the late nineties Springer returned to the city that was his home until the age of five as a fully fledged folk hero.

So, does the object of all this adoration still believe in the essential goodness of humanity?

'Yes, absolutely,' Springer insists, chomping on a hefty Cuban stogie in his Piccadilly Circus hotel suite in the autumn of 1999.

More, or less so, since doing the show about the man who took his son-in-law out 'looking for hookers' while his daughter was in hospital having a miscarriage?

'Oh, more so, definitely more so . . . I think it was Supreme Court Justice Brandeis who said' – Jerry pauses to accentuate the effect of this impressive quotation – '"Sunlight is the greatest disinfectant".'

Jerry Springer used to work in TV news, but then decided it was 'too exploitative' and got involved with talk shows instead.

'The news involves talking about people against their wishes,' he insists. 'The only way you get on our show is if you call us.'

Like Robert Kilroy-Silk, Jerry Springer came to talk shows via politics.

Despite an early setback when he had to resign as a city council-lor after paying a prostitute by cheque, he was elected Mayor of Cleveland and later narrowly defeated as Democratic candidate in the race for Ohio state governor. How close did he get to the governorship?

'Pretty close. I could have made it if I'd given it another shot.'

Did he ever think he might have gone further?

'Well,' Springer looks genuinely regretful, 'I was born in England, so I could never have been president.'

The notion of President Springer is in some ways an enticing one. Not least because the bond of trust and admiration between the man and his studio audience ('We love you Jerry!') seems a stronger one than any mere politician could command. And a med-ley of Springer's Final Thoughts would certainly make a first-class inaugural address. On actually meeting him, though, the atmos-phere in his circle is rather how one imagines the heyday of Frank Sinatra's ratpack to have been. And this – as John F. Kennedy found to his cost – is not the ideal template for the application of political power.

Surrounded by sycophantic acolytes (including the legendary Steve, the large, dome-headed individual who always steps in onstage just after the fights have got nasty), Springer discusses the deal he's just signed for a feature film.

'We don't want it to be autobiographical, like the Howard Stern movie,'[184] he insists. 'It'll be more of a day-in-the-life type of thing, in the mould of The Beatles' *A Hard Day's Night*, except that at the end I'll reveal that I am really a woman.'[185]

[184.] The morally reprehensible but appallingly funny moment in Stern's *Private Parts* where the notorious US radio DJ (playing his own younger self) accidentally throws a frisbee into the face of someone who is educationally sub-normal marks one staging post in the development of film comedy that some might wish had never been passed.

[185.] Sadly, this feature film never materializes in this form, as a dreadful ITV chat show and the embarrassing Comedy Awards incident described in

Michael Moore, Michael Moore, riding through the glen

Jerry Springer's is not the only influential American political voice to make itself heard on British TV in the course of the 1990s. Anyone who saw *Roger and Me* – Michael Moore's defiantly mischievous film about the decline of the motor industry in his home town of Flint, Michigan – will have already suspected that this man had what it took to do great work on the small screen. 1994's first series of Moore's *TV Nation* confirms this, living up to and beyond the show's slightly off-putting billing as an 'international documentary magazine with attitude' [historical note: in 1994 it was still just about possible to use the suffix 'with attitude' without being instantly banished from respectable society].

This innovative BBC/NBC co-production begins outside Television Centre, as Moore indulges in idle banter with non-BBC2-watching passers-by – 'Oh great,' he exclaims archly, 'I'm stuck on the boring channel' (no, that would be BBC1) – but soon cuts to the chase. A genial, ursine figure with an incongruous penchant for jaunty baseball caps, Moore is not afraid to grapple with the big issues. He starts out with one that, in the mid-nineties, is among the very biggest: Bosnia.

Shuttling the few hundred yards between the Croatian and Serb embassies in Washington in a rented Fiat Yugo, Moore is soon making telling observations. For instance, that both warring protagonists represent themselves in blue on their ethnic maps. 'You've got the nicest colour,' he tells the rival ambassadors. 'Blue is the one everyone likes.' Serb and Croat alike are happy to indulge Moore's absurd whims – helping him fix his car, singing 'The

chapter 5 dull some of Springer's lustre. (He does get to play a talk-show host in 2003's *Citizen Verdict*, though.) Jerry also supplies the raw material for more bad stand-up routines in the late nineties than anyone else except the original cast of *Star Trek*, and – on a more elevated note – attains unasked-for high-cultural validation via the hugely successful 2003 National Theatre production of *Jerry Springer, the Opera*, co-written by Stewart Lee and Club Zarathustra's musical help meet Richard Thomas, which later transfers – following in the illustrious footsteps of Patrick Marber's *Closer* – to the West End and then Broadway.

Barney Song', even explaining the Bosnian conflict with reference to a large takeaway pizza ('The Muslims are the pepperoni . . . I would like a piece of Slovenia too, my mother was born there') – but when he suggests that perhaps they might simply talk to each other on the phone, refusal is swift and categorical. Some situations are so tragic that flippancy seems to be the only appropriate response.

Other items in the first episode of *TV Nation* definitely back this theory up. There's a poignantly one-sided battle for the attention of the New York cab-driving fraternity between a respected black film actor clutching a baby and a bunch of flowers, and a hardened criminal who happens to be white; and a truly shocking investigation into the brokerage of life-insurance policies belonging to people with AIDS, a business in which, one of the profiteers insists, 'there is no downside'.

Only with an over-jokey hunt for specific missiles in the former Soviet Union does the show lapse into self-regard, but even this segment has its compensations, as we get to see Moore turning his merciless interviewing technique on to his own parents. 'We had a lot of good times,' Mr and Mrs Moore senior insist valiantly. Their son's reply is instantaneous: 'Name three.'

At his best – taking a Wall Street collection to help pay Exxon's environmental fines while leading a large crowd in the mantra 'Give to those who take' – Moore is a genuinely provocative force, using the awesome power of TV in the manner of a latter-day Robin Hood. At his worst, hectoring innocent receptionists with a pomposity their bosses would struggle to match, he's the Sheriff of Nottingham in a baseball cap. The image of the rumpled iconoclast – fighting corporate evil with just a soundman for company – is so appealing that it can sometimes be hard for the person projecting that image not to fall in love with it.[186]

The increasing portability of camera and sound-recording technology encourages a growing number of televisual adventurers – P. J. O'Rourke and Jon Ronson among them – to scour the world's trouble spots in search of cheap laughs. And as the genre of bucca-

---

[186.] The huge commercial success of his 2002 book *Stupid White Men* suggests the public can't get enough of it either.

neer ironist documentary-making originally defined by the supremely supercilious Nick Broomfield develops, it becomes clear that whatever else you do, you should try not to leave home without a sense of moral perspective (or for those who don't seem to have one, subject matter so compelling that it can fill the space left by that absence).[187]

The insinuating quasi-modesty so ably practised by Moore, Ronson and Broomfield (the psychotically self-satisfied O'Rourke can't even manage *quasi*-modesty) becomes the dominant voice of TV and film documentary-making in the mid to late nineties. This dominance causes problems of its own, however, as a technique which relies upon a perception of the person with the camera as the underdog is necessarily compromised by overdog status.[188]

For example, the grim spectacle of Nick Broomfield harassing a plainly on-her-uppers ex-prime minister in his 1998 film *Tracking Down Maggie* achieves the seemingly impossible feat of making the viewer feel sorry for Margaret Thatcher. This is probably just the sort of thing Jonathan Swift had in mind when he observed that 'Satire is a sort of glass wherein beholders do generally discover everybody's face but their own'. But the particular cultural conditions of the 1990s – conducive as they are to narcissism in all its forms – suggest an alternative version of Swift's persuasive dictum.

There are a number of comedic contexts in this period wherein it might just as aptly be remarked that 'Satire is a sort of glass wherein the glazier exults in his own reflection above all others'. For instance, there's that awkward moment in a documentary about

---

[187.] Jon Ronson goes through the unusual and compelling rite of passage of discovering his moral centre on air, in the course of a Radio 4 programme he makes about a guest house near Auschwitz. This starts out in the (then) characteristically sly Ronsonian style and ends up as something altogether more emotionally engaged, establishing the increasingly humane template on which he bases later investigations of David Icke and other giant lizard conspiracy theorists.

[188.] *TV Nation* is also notable for launching the career of Louis Theroux, who takes Moore's using-the-camera-to-get-under-people's-skins methodology into new and unprecedentedly intimate areas, exploiting the desperation of politics' and showbiz's walking wounded for a return to active celebrity service to achieve levels of access that go beyond intrusive into the realms of outright home invasion.

The Simpsons when Matt Groening – the show's (as a rule) ferociously astute creator – boasts about seeing a giant billboard of Bart outside Fox Television's US HQ, as if this somehow represents the ascendancy of his personal ideology over that of the corporation he works for; not vice versa, as a disinterested observer might surmise.

'What exactly are you?' Tony Wright MP, chairman of the select committee on public administration, asks stand-up investigative journalist Mark Thomas in 2002, in another incidence of reflected satirical glory. 'Are you current affairs, entertainment, comedy?'[189] When this exchange is played back at the studio recording of Thomas's oh-so-wryly-titled Channel 4 show *The Mark Thomas Comedy Product*, there is much audience laughter at that unlikely abstract phenomenon defined by Terence Blacker in the *Independent* as 'the absurdity of someone needing to ask what Mark Thomas does'.

At a time when one of our most intensely felt needs seems to be to see ourselves reflected in anyone who has any kind of power over us, the inability to recognize one of the British public's non-elected celebrity representatives is a grave offence indeed. Stung into action by this profound slight, Thomas tells the committee that most of his friends do not have the remotest interest in politics, and goes on to advise all those sharing his own enlightened cynicism about the democratic process to make their own revolutionary protest at the forthcoming local elections and 'stay at home and sit in your fucking armchairs'.

And they said Wolfie Smith was a dangerous radical! [Historical note: Wolfie a.k.a. Citizen Smith was a Tooting-based seventies sitcom revolutionary, played by Robert Lindsay, the grouchy dad in *My Family*].

[189.] This apparently mystifying enquiry actually has a firm historical basis (it was because *That Was The Week That Was* went out under the current-affairs rather than light-entertainment umbrella that it was able to get away with as much as it did).

It's Tony Blair's party, and we'll cry if we want to

There's a brief period, just prior to New Labour's 1997 election victory, when it almost feels as if the ghosts of the alternative era have finally been exorcized. In the (up-to-that-point) rigorously non-partisan Harry Hill's 1996 *Comeback Special*, the grim fact of seventeen years of Conservative rule is seen in an entirely new light: through the eyes of the animal kingdom. 'It's a long time to you,' Hill begins, 'but it's a lifetime to a dog . . .', before fearlessly running the furry gamut to 'Fourteen generations of hamsters crying out for change!'

Unfortunately, when that long-awaited regime change actually does come about, the happy surge of rodent idealism swiftly dissipates. The infamous night of 10 December 1997 – when Tony Blair holds a party at Number 10 for Zoe Ball and Chris Evans, at the same time as Labour whips are using all the considerable muscle at their disposal to force a cut of £6 a week in single parent's benefit through the House of Commons – is just one of several notable staging posts on the road to disillusion.

If the unhappy sight of (as Andrew Rawnsley puts it) 'the prime minister pouring champagne down the throats of wealthy media stars while he takes money from the pockets of the poor' doesn't call for a hard-hitting satirical reprisal, it is hard to know what would. And yet by this time the very idea of such a response seems to have been discredited.

As *Have I Got News for You* producer Harry Thompson points out in Humphrey Carpenter's *That Was Satire That Was*, 'TV satirists are now paid more than captains of industry, which begs the question of whether they still have the moral authority to attack the rich and powerful merely for their rich and powerful-ness.' Thompson recalls reading a Sunday newspaper op-ed piece by an unspecified work associate. The article outlined what a scandal it was that some high-ranking employee of a former public utility should be paid a sum of money which Thompson knew the moralistic whistle-blower concerned was earning for three hours' work a week.

The day of the comedic conscience is not entirely done, though.

At a time when, as Establishment Club veteran John Bird has observed, 'Everything is a branch of comedy', it's an especially fitting irony that the only people who seem to be allowed to present political arguments without some form of showbiz trimming should be comedians themselves.

Veterans of the alternative epoch Mark Steel and Jeremy Hardy become *causes célèbres* – at the *Independent* and the *Guardian*, respectively – as just about the only unapologetically left-wing[190] voices remaining in the street that was once called Fleet. And when rumours emerge from the occupied West Bank in 2002 that Hardy is among a group of film-making European protesters caught up in the Yasser Arafat hostage situation while bravely standing up to the iron fist of the Israeli military–industrial complex, the spirit of Will Somers looks on with a smile.

Oh, Ben Elton, so much to answer for, *or* 'Bo Rhap could not be ignored'

No such bold gestures are forthcoming from the most prominent of Steel and Hardy's alternative peer group, Ben Elton having long ago let his radical credentials lapse in favour of a socio-cultural agenda some way to the right of *Kilroy*'s. It's a tribute to how successfully this erstwhile anti-Thatcherite firebrand acclimatizes to the John Major years when, in 1996, on being acclaimed by notorious tweedy curmudgeon A. N. Wilson as 'the funniest man in Britain', he does not do the decent thing and leave the country.

In fact, far from being chastened by this potentially fatal public-relations reversal, Elton flaunts his shame, live onstage at the London Palladium. There he is, bold as Brasso, demonstrating his contempt for our 'style-obsessed' contemporary society right from the off by wearing brown shoes after six o'clock. The strange thing is that for all Elton's jibes at 'fashionable, ironic' comedians, it is he, not they, whose message seems reactionary and depressing.

His obsessive equation of normality with pubs, curry and basic bodily functions seems unbearably condescending: as if that is the

---

[190.] Albeit in an annoyingly self-congratulatory and simple-minded way.

only culture 'normal' people have a right to. And at a point when even the not knowingly highbrow *Loaded* magazine is willing to put David Letterman and *The Simpsons* on its front cover, such narrow-mindedness is outdated as well as insulting.

If *Shooting Stars* feels – as it does at the time – like the high-water mark of an apolitical, post-alternative, post-Thatcherite comedy consensus, you'd expect the tide (in accordance with the Iron Law of Coastal Metaphors) to turn the other way shortly afterwards. And the apolitical nature of politics themselves in the age of sleaze and spin certainly seems to demand a politically committed comedic reaction. But wherever else such a response might be coming from, it's not coming from Ben Elton.

There are fifteen minutes of excellent material held hostage in the middle of Elton's rapturously received two-hour show, and most of it pertains to people who read books about the SAS. Otherwise, the level of comedic insight is so low as to be, well, not laughable. And Elton at his best (remember, this is the man who gave us *The Young Ones* as well as *Blackadder*) is too gifted a comic writer to be allowed to get away with such superannuated piffle as 'Car adverts bear no relation to our driving experience' and 'They're making designer lagers now'. (Hang on a minute, my mind's gone blank: what is it that bears do in the woods again?)

As the Blairite epoch gets into its sensibly shod stride, Elton's embrace of mediocrity seems to become ever more passionate. His gruesome big-screen directorial début, *Maybe Baby*, is a case in point. Not only is its determination to xerox the allure of his old *Blackadder* writing partner Richard Curtis's *Notting Hill* (theme song by Westlife, check, big reconciliation scene in West London park, check) sufficiently craven as to be a source of actual physical discomfort, it also contains a performance by Joely Richardson which is so bad it makes the cinema wallpaper curl. And these flaws are as nothing next to a central story-line – BBC executive cures writer's block by dramatizing his own infertility treatment – which is a sinister metaphorical justification for the death of fiction and a new world populated entirely by robots.

Within a few short months of the end of the second series of *Big Brother*, Ben Elton puts this evil gospel into practice by publishing a 'novel' about a reality TV series whose contestants get murdered (yes, murdered!) in which the bulk of the characters seem to be bloodless, two-dimensional replicants of those gloriously fully rounded human beings we've all been watching on TV.

It's at this point – just as there seems to be no further artistic depth for him to plumb – that Elton proclaims his masterstroke: a West End musical, based on the songs of Queen, produced by (it seems so obvious when you see it in black and white) Robert De Niro.

'Bo Rhap could not be ignored,' Elton writes in the Saturday *Telegraph*. [Historical note: 'Bo Rhap' was an abbreviation used by Ben Elton to indicate his special relationship with the most popular cod-operatic heavy-metal single of all time. It is not a coinage that catches on.] Accordingly, his lead character will be called Galileo Figaro.

Setting himself to write 'a story that reflected the feel of the words and music rather than their literal intent', Elton decides to draw further inspiration (as if the music of Queen were not inspiration enough) from 'heroic myths in which brave individuals take on the vast monolithic force of evil systems'. So enthused are they by this idea that even the surviving members of Queen chip in to the ensuing orgy of topical creativity (Elton reporting with justifiable pride that drummer Roger Taylor has 'slipped a reference to the internet into "Radio Gaga"').

Set in a terrifying future where 'Globalization is complete . . . Everyone watches the same movies, wears the same clothes and thinks the same thoughts', *We Will Rock You* employs the music of Queen as an unlikely rallying cry for freedom of thought and expression (unlikely because – as originally conceived – the music of Queen was right up there with the operas of Wagner and the films of Leni Riefenstahl as a statement of artistic individualism).

Magnificently undaunted by this minor intellectual obstacle, Elton rises fearlessly to the challenge of working the titles of as many Queen songs as possible into his narrative. Apparently, if the Ga Ga cops find Galileo, they will 'drag him before the Killer Queen and consign him into oblivion across the Seven Seas of Rye'.

The thing about cultural artefacts which are utterly devoid of any redeeming social value is that they can often – think of the TV series *Temptation Island*, for instance, or the music of Bon Jovi, *circa*

Slippery When Wet – be quite fun. Unfortunately, the same cannot be said of *We Will Rock You*. None the less, before the production has even opened, 'detailed discussions are already taking place for the show to be staged in North America, Australia, Scandinavia, Italy and Japan'.

Elton calls his Bacofoil dystopia Planet Mall. Planet Mall is a grim place where 'the company computers generate the music and the kids download it' and 'all musical instruments are banned', a place with a soul-sapping, homogenized culture which greedily uses up the world's resources, having no higher goal than the endless replication of itself. Planet Mall, you say? Well, to paraphrase the immortal words of Newman and Baddiel, 'That's Ben Elton, that is.'

All roads lead to Sir Rhodes

Given the pain of the Eltonian legacy, it makes sense that so many of the next generation's most telling satirical shafts – from the afore-mentioned Armando Ianucci sketch in which the poor people of Africa get together to raise money for the struggling British theatre establishment to Ricky Gervais's memorable 2003 appearance on *Comic Relief*[191] – should be directed not at the idea of trying to make the world a better place, but at the vanity and hypocrisy which are often engendered when those in the egotistical world of showbiz take it upon themselves to show concern for the lives of others.

In 2002, Steve Coogan's engaging Welsh protégé Rob Brydon is a guest on *Johnny Vaughan Tonight*, alongside old-school, hard-left rail-union leader Bob Crow. Vaughan is trying to do one of his serious political bits and Brydon has said beforehand that there is something he wishes to contribute to the discussion. He begins an anecdote about travelling into central London from the west and

---

[191.] To a soundtrack of Phil Collins's 'Another Day In Paradise', Gervais is filmed riding in the back of a limousine to the BBC studios. Glancing periodically out of the window to catch sight of obviously staged tableaux of urban deprivation, he repeatedly composes his features into a mask of anguish before growing bored and returning to his reading – a copy of the *Radio Times* proclaiming him the most influential person in comedy.

meeting a famous actor on the train (I can't remember exactly who, but someone in the Nigel Havers bracket).

Having created the expectation that he is going to go on with a story which will demonstrate his innate sympathy with trade-unionist goals in particular and the working man in general, Brydon tails off, unrepentantly, into nothing. The fact that he met a famous actor on the train was all he wanted to communicate. It's a cruel joke, but a brilliant one, simultaneously laying bare not only the egocentricity of the thespian mindset, but also the shaky foundations of the chat show's universal assumption of common ground between guests.

This is just the sort of thing you can imagine Chris Morris doing in the unlikely event of him ever appearing as a guest on a chat show (and the even more unlikely event of anyone else agreeing to appear with him). It's not a million miles from the kind of stunt Ali G pulls either, once he's become big enough to command a royal audience with David and Victoria Beckham.

As the character is initially developed by Sacha Baron Cohen on Channel 4's *Eleven O'Clock Show* in the very late nineties, Ali G offers a canny extrapolation of the Chris Morris Method. Morris employs the spurious authority of the current-affairs broadcasting establishment to back his victims into ever more ludicrous linguistic corners, thereby highlighting both their own foolishness and that of anyone who would pay unthinking heed to the words of confident, well-spoken young men in soberly cut suits.

Ali G, meanwhile, invests his comic capital in the old political order's fear of being seen to be unsympathetic to the increasingly dominant language of supposedly streetwise youth culture, thereby highlighting both the out-of-touchness of that old order and the foolishness of anyone who would pay unthinking heed to the words of brazen ignoramuses in co-ordinated Tommy Hilfiger rainwear.

Both rely for their success on that increasingly rare and precious resource: someone who can be relied upon not to get the joke. Cometh the hour, cometh the man, in the imposingly mutton-chopped shape of Sir Rhodes Boyson, no-nonsense former Tory education secretary. Boyson proves himself the ur-stooge by popping up twice, first nodding sagely at Morris's insanely draconian law and order proposals on the 'Crime' edition of *Brass Eye*, then rolling Ali G's Rizla of comedy two years later by agreeing with his suggestion that 'kids should get caned in school'.

The law of diminishing returns definitely comes into play here. Given that Sir Rhodes Boyson isn't revealing anything about what he thinks that we didn't know already, all we're really laughing at in these situations is his inability to identify Ali G or Chris Morris, which makes this comedy of non-recognition just one more expression of the politicized egotism mentioned earlier in the context of Mark Thomas and Michael Moore.

It would be easy (and not entirely wrong) to watch Chris Morris persuading MPs to ask a parliamentary question about the fictional drug 'Cake', or pressing Paul Boateng for his opinion on the cultural scourge that is 'Herman the Tosser', and conclude that he was dancing on the grave of the democratic process. The same would also seem to apply to Ali G's 2002 big-screen blockbuster *Ali G Indahouse*.

This film's basic storyline (Charles Dance's corrupt deputy prime minister tries to use Ali's stupidity as a stepping stone to the premiership, but is foiled by how in tune the new MP for Staines's simple-minded hedonistic agenda turns out to be with the actual desires of the electorate) can be encompassed within the following appropriately Ali-esque formulation: 'The Mother of Parliaments is a Slapper'. But its overall message is a little more complicated than that.

Ali G struggles to preserve the infrastructure of suburban community

The cause of Ali G's unlikely by-election victory in the film – a random insult to his rival candidate in the course of a televised debate on *Thames Valley Tonight*, which elicits the question-begging denial 'I did not suck off a horse' – seems to bespeak disillusionment with the existing political system. And the outrageous policies whose unexpected popularity secures his rapid parliamentary advancement ('free marijuana on the NHS for the treatment of chronic diseases such as itchy scrot' and – somewhat less forgivably – 'let in the fit refugees and turn away the rank ones') say equally little for the sophistication of the electorate.

It is important, however, to remember the reason Ali finds himself catapulted into public life in the first place. It's his heroic one-man campaign to save the John Nike Leisure Centre – 'spiritual home of the West Staines Massive' – which first brings him to the attention of Charles Dance's smooth Westminster operator. And while the 'Keep It Real' classes in US gangsta lore he teaches to impressionable pre-teens ('Most of you ain't never gonna see eleven') might be of doubtful educational value, they also embody just the kind of community-minded voluntary activity which would seem to have no place in Ali G's imaginary world of designer labels and drive-bys.

Ali G Indahouse's cinematic antecedents appear to be predominantly American – from *Wayne's World*, Quentin Tarantino and innumerable bad breakdance and rap movies, all the way back to Steve Martin's *The Jerk* and *Cheech and Chong* – but the film actually fits squarely into the very British tradition of the 1970s sitcom spin-off.

Alongside the last gasps of the *Carry On*s and the properly infamous *Confessions of . . .* series, the sitcom spin-off was one of the busiest divisions of the British film industry in the 1970s.[192] From *Porridge* to *Bless This House*, most UK TV comedy series worth their salt (and many that weren't) faced ritual elongation. The challenge was how to stretch characters and settings which often felt the strain over half an hour to three times their original length. Given that limitation is the lifeblood of sitcom, whereas film breathes through expanded possibilities, the interweaving of these two very different DNA strands was necessarily a perilous business, and the most reliable means of reconciling film's demand for closure with sitcom's need for continuity seemed to be to fabricate an extraordinary threat to the TV show's social framework.

Hence the unscrupulous property developers who threaten the destruction of Richard O'Sullivan and Paula Wilcox's NW8 idyll in 1974's feature-length *Man About the House* (scripted by *Rumpole of the Bailey* eminence John Mortimer). Hence also the slum clearance of the Newcastle street – and most notably the pub, The

---

[192.] The Richard Curtis/Hugh Grant milksop triptych excepted, it continues to predominate in major UK comedy film releases of this period, too, when you think about it (from *Mr Bean* to *Kevin and Perry Go Large*).

Fat Ox – where James Bolam and Rodney Bewes grew up, which kick-starts Dick Clement and Ian La Frenais's *The Likely Lads*.

Bewes's hen-pecked Bob has already moved up the accommodation ladder to the flesh-pots of the Elm Lodge housing estate, leaving James Bolam's socially immobile Terry looking forward to 'a modern kitchen, a lovely view and an inside toilet' in his new high-rise apartment. Unfortunately, when he finally moves in, these long-hoped-for amenities can only be experienced in the context of total societal breakdown, as lifts fail and unsupervised children – spiritual parents of Ali G's 'Keep It Real' students, a quarter of a century later – run riot in the concrete hallways.

The breakdown of family and community ties accelerated by the town planning dreamscapes of the 1960s and 1970s would create social conditions in many parts of the UK worthy of the grisliest of Ali G's American ghetto fantasies. And it's at the intersection between his imported hip-hop mythology and the actual psychogeography of West London's outer suburbia that just about everything funny which happens in *Ali G Indahouse* takes place (as opposed to the not-so-funny stuff, of which there's also quite a lot).

When Ali draws a verbal field sketch of the front line between East and West Staines – 'past Bumblebees Day Nursery, just before you get to the mini-roundabout' – it's the affection colouring the specificity that makes the picture so memorable, and which also makes the John Nike Leisure Centre worth saving. The film's ending throws up an unexpected environmental subtext, when the reason for the happily thwarted demolition turns out to have been a projected extra runway at Heathrow . . .[193]

There was even a dark rumour that Ben Elton planned to build a mall there.

[193.] The general approbation with which the alternative proposal of 'demolishing Slough' is received at the end of this film reflects not so much the environmentalist hostility enshrined in verse by John Betjeman as a subliminal attack on rival comedy sensation *The Office*, located just a few miles away from Staines, down the M4 corridor of comedy power.

18
Morals

Cartoons, *Brass Eye*, a brief history of swearing
and the real-life Mary Whitehouse Experience

*'Unless something is done and done quickly, we'll have four-letter
words littering our programmes in future, just as "bloody" does now'*
Mary Whitehouse

*'Fuck is the worst word that you can say. We shouldn't say fuck,
no, we shouldn't say fuck. Fuck, no!'*
Eric Cartman, Stan Marsh, Kenny McCormick and Kyle Broflovski in
South Park: Bigger, Longer & Uncut

The winter of 2002–3 is a happy time for people who are sick
enough to enjoy watching TV programmes about *That Was The
Week That Was*. In one of numerous additions to the *TW3* documentary canon wheeled out to commemorate the show's fortieth
anniversary, *Newsnight*'s Jeremy Vine – on the point of hauling his
Jeremy Paxman Lite anchor and setting sail into the prevailing
light-entertainment/current-affairs wind by taking over Radio 2's
The Jimmy Young Show – is talking about the importance of Bernard
Levin being rude to people.

'The reason the Levin section was so exciting at the time,' Vine
explains, 'was that it stripped away the automatic respect that people
are granted because they're part of the establishment – because
they're politicians, because they run a business, because they've
got a title. It put them in the studio and took all that away, and

you could see on their faces that they weren't ready for that to happen.'

On the one hand, everything Jeremy is saying is true. And contemporary evidence, such as the Church of England vicar who wrote a letter to the BBC abusing Levin in the most shockingly anti-Semitic terms,[194] certainly confirms that he touched a nerve.

The funny thing is, however, that for anyone seeking out a prophetic vision of what life in Britain would be like four decades later, it's not *That Was The Week That Was* itself which does the job (the black-and-white clips inevitably feel somewhat stiff and dated) so much as the attacks made on the programme by Mary Whitehouse's Clean Up TV campaign. Posterity has not so far been kind to the viewers' vigilante movement which the Saturday-night satirical shafts of David Frost and co. helped spur into action, but perhaps the time has come for a small-scale reassessment – at least in terms of the critical perspicacity of the organization's famously blue-rinsed founder.

'Anti-authority, anti-religion, anti-patriotism, pro-dirt and poorly produced, yet having the support of the corporation, and apparently impervious to discipline from within or discipline from without.' This was Whitehouse's verdict on *That Was The Week That Was*, as delivered at her campaign's inaugural meeting at Birmingham Town Hall in 1964.[195] Few people – with the possible exception of producer Ned Sherrin, who had to go through a libel trial after rashly insinuating that Mrs Whitehouse was a prostitute in an interview published in the *Daily Mail* at around the same time – would find much to disagree with there. In fact, the instinctive response of the twenty-first-century reader would be: 'Hmmm . . . sounds like my kind of show'.

It was always easy to laugh at Mary Whitehouse, and in some ways that was no reason not to. Among her experiences as senior mistress at Madeley Secondary School in the West Midlands (upon which she based her concerns about the moral impact of popular culture) Whitehouse remembered teenage boys coming to her and

---

[194] See Carpenter's *That Was Satire That Was*.
[195] Quoted in *Whitehouse*.

pleading: 'Will you please stop the girls teasing and tantalizing us into sexual relationships?'

Anyone who has ever known a teenage boy (or been one) will find it hard to take this recollection at face value, but some of Whitehouse's other observations about changing behaviour patterns among children in Birmingham in the early sixties – 'little boys don't scrap any more, they rabbit punch . . . the whole pattern of their play has changed' – ring a good deal truer (even to those who weren't born at the time). And you don't have to join Mary in blaming David Frost or Alf Garnett for such a serious decline in playground etiquette to admire her determination to do something about it.[196]

While views might differ on what that something ought to be, one of Mrs Whitehouse's more general observations still strikes a fairly deafening chord forty years on. When she complained that the youth of her day – and by extension society at large – was 'encouraged to believe that within adolescence and immaturity are ultimate values to be found', she might just as easily have been writing about the 1990s as the 1960s.[197]

'"Let's all be kids together" cry the adults,' she thunders, 'as if only child's play helps them to come to terms with what they have made of the world.' Michael Bracewell's *The Nineties: When Surface Was Depth* describes a similar process at work three decades later. 'A generational response to the problems of growing up in a society that is presumed to be increasingly complex and dangerous', he explains, 'has been to treat the perks of childhood – fizzy pop, cartoons, taste-treats, sweets, funny socks and toys – as a source of inspiration.'

'Serviced by adult cartoons, alcoholic pop, grown-up toys and pod-shaped cars,' Bracewell argues, 'the traditional nostalgia for childhood can now be replaced by something infinitely more appealing – the chance to have another one on your own terms.' There's more to it even than that, though. The fetishization of early child-

---

[196.] Among other achievements, in pioneering the application of moral pressure to a public corporation she was an unheralded forebear green and anti-capitalist strategies of four decades later.

[197.] cf. Gavin Hills in *The Idler* magazine: 'may we live forever on a Friday in the year I left school'.

hood which is such an integral part of the celebrity cult of the early twenty-first century recklessly posits *the business of child-rearing itself* as a means of achieving infantile satisfaction.

Whether uniting the generations in a festival of narcissistic consumption is a last-ditch evolutionary response to declining birth rates, or the final throw of a culture in the terminal stages of decadent collapse (or a bit of both), only time will tell. Either way, the spectacle of Brooklyn Beckham sitting alone in the back of his parents' car, listening to his portable CD player 'as a treat' on his way to receiving a Shetland pony and a miniature Mercedes for his third birthday, can do little else but chill the soul.

It's one of the neater ironies of the period that as well as being one of Bracewell's extensions of the 'perks of childhood', the nineties boom in 'adult' cartoons should have also supplied some of the decade's most morally sophisticated social commentary. As previously discussed, this was partly because animation proved less susceptible than live-action comedy to creative and political restriction by the US TV networks, but also because ideas of childhood were so overlain with collective neuroses as to be prime territory for comedic exploitation.

While the domestic animation industry could produce nothing to match them (let's not even mention that awful thing set in Brixton with Jane Horrocks doing most of the voices), the American lineage which stretches from *The Simpsons* to Matt Parker and Trey Stone's *South Park*, via *Beavis and Butthead*, *King of the Hill* and evolutionary missing-link *Ren & Stimpy* (see below),[198] would have a powerful influence on British comedy.

It is probably correct to surmise that Mrs Whitehouse would not have been a big fan of *South Park* (though even she would have struggled to resist the charms of Mr Hankey the Christmas Poo), but if she could just have seen beyond the show's gleeful and tireless profanity, she might have come to appreciate its underlying desire to celebrate the last vestiges of childhood innocence.

[198.] Given the concern with the verifiability of fatherhood intensified by all those paternity-test episodes of *Jerry Springer* and enshrined in the central story-lines of *Cartman's Mum's A Dirty Slut* and *Beavis and Butthead Do America*, it's interesting that this family line should be so firmly established.

Consider Michael McDonald's ballad 'Eyes of a Child' in *South Park: Bigger, Longer and Uncut* (the *South Park* movie's worthy riposte to the *Beavis and Butthead Do America* soundtrack casting *coup* which gave us Englebert Humperdink's immortal 'Lesbian Seagull'). 'There's a sparkle in their eyes,' sings the former Steely Dan vocalist, '[they've] yet to realize the bastards they really are.'

Ren & Stimpy: the bastards they really were

When Kyle and Kenny and Stan and Eric and the other third-graders of *South Park* were little more than a twinkle in their creators' bloodshot eyes, another frontier US animation was not so much pushing the outer edge of the envelope as posting the whole package to another destination. More than just a throwback to the golden days of Tex Avery, Chuck Jones and Bob 'Bugs Bunny' Clampett, the first two series of *Ren & Stimpy* (broadcast in the US – where at that point it was one of the most popular cable shows ever – in 1991–2, and on BBC2 a couple of years later) were new, dark and sometimes even frightening.

There is nothing intrinsically subversive about the relationship between Ren Hoek, an irascible chihuahua, and the heartbreakingly stupid Stimpson J. Cat; even though (like Morecambe and Wise before them) they share the same bed. As their maverick creator John Kricfalusi himself says: 'They're a classic double-act in the Laurel and Hardy mould; one's an asshole and the other's retarded.' But the animation lights up the screen with glowing colours, rakish angles and hallucinatory shape-changes, and the duo's adventures trash the barriers of time and space.

One week – in the unforgettable and terrifying 'Space Madness' episode – Ren and Stimpy journey to the outer reaches of the Crab Nebula; the next, they present their own nature programme. One minute they are erasing history, the next they are saving a horse from a burning skyscraper.

The emotional pyrotechnics are just as dazzling as the animatory ones. Stimpy, his idiotic tongue poking out from beneath his bulbous blue nose, endlessly torments his partner with misguided attempts to improve the quality of his life. Ren responds with a dazzling array of mood swings, veering without warning from cringing fearfulness – eyes filling with tears, heart pumping through paper-thin skin – to psychotic menace. Kricfalusi himself supplies the voice: three parts Peter Lorre to one part Jack Nicholson (he didn't want to do it, but none of the thirty actors auditioned could manage the requisite intensity).

Though he's never owned a chihuahua (he claims to be 'allergic to them') Kricfalusi does seem to have an intuitive grasp of that excellent breed's infinite capacity for rage. 'I was going into a restaurant once and someone had left two in their car, chained to the steering-wheel. They were screaming at me and their eyes were bulging,' he remembers admiringly, 'these two tiny little creatures who couldn't do a thing for themselves were aching to tear my throat out!'

In the glory days of the show's first two series, Kricfalusi's in-character tantrums used to bring letters back from Nickelodeon's head office saying 'lose the scenes where Ren is acting like an abusive father'. There's no denying the large element of psychosis in *Ren & Stimpy*. Kricfalusi regards this as 'a release of a lot of human genetic material that we'd probably be better off without; stuff that we don't need, but it's still in there and it's better that it should be released in a safe way, like in cartoons'.

Some of that unwanted genetic material takes on physical as well as emotional shape. *Ren & Stimpy* is consistently, at times almost unnervingly, scatological (and sometimes snotological too). Stimpy's abiding love is Gritty Kitty cat litter. His hairballs are large and luxuriant. In one episode, Ren climbs a single, Rapunzel-length hair up a castle tower, only to find that this one-strand rope ladder is actually of nasal origin.

'Mainly we put the fart and booger jokes in for kids, but we found out that grown-ups liked them as well,' admits Kricfalusi, who 'likes people watching to feel as if they got away with something'.

Nickelodeon certainly felt Kricfalusi was getting away with something (and watching the occasional appearances of homoerotic superhero Powdered Toast Man, you could kind of see what they meant). Having had to sign over the rights to the characters to get *Ren & Stimpy* made in the first place, he was ousted from his own show at the end of the second series. Several – sadly inferior – further series were made by a rather infamous alliance of Nickelodeon and Kricfalusi's former business partner, but nothing could tarnish the allure of the originals.

Brass Eye: 'Top this, you Quisling fucks!'

There is one show on British TV in the nineties which comes close to the vertiginous momentum and unrepentant extremity of early *Ren & Stimpy*. And that almost never gets broadcast at all.

The advance publicity for *Brass Eye* – the long-awaited follow-up show from *The Day Today*'s Chris Morris, which is hastily removed from Channel 4's schedules in the autumn of 1996 – has a suitably overstated feel about it. According to the programme's Channel 4 press release, Morris will not only 'take media terrorism to a level never seen on British TV before', he will also 'smack the issues till they bleed'.

A selection of fake headlines from the show ('Police have confirmed that all of Britain's women priests died yesterday – they are not treating the deaths as suspicious') seems to offer nothing new.

But a series of incendiary statements further down the page raise the stakes. Morris's scathing reference to 'feeble, under-realized prankster-drivel' (presumably a jibe at Channel 4's lesser lord of misrule, Mark Thomas, or even at Morris's mainstream ITV nemesis, Jeremy Beadle) is accompanied by splenetic exhortations to his imitators to 'top this, you Quisling fucks' and stern advice to viewers to 'watch this programme now because it will never be allowed a repeat'.

Curiosity as to the exact nature of *Brass Eye* has run high ever since a pilot version was turned down by the BBC. But Morris has imbued all those working on the show with a healthy respect for secrecy. 'It's a sitcom,' maintain two of the writers, Graham Linehan and Arthur Mathews, with just the faintest of twinkles in their collective eye. 'A very bad sitcom.' Others suggested that Morris had pulled off a series of situationist pranks so devastating that even to think about discussing them would bury the show in an avalanche of writs.

So, back to the press release. A finished copy of the first show, it says, won't be ready until the day of transmission. But there is a compilation tape of clips from the series, one of the highlights of which features Morris being clandestinely filmed approaching a series of street-corner drug-dealers. Nothing particularly out of the ordinary about that, you might think, except that Morris is wearing only a nappy, a combat blouse and a large orange sphere attached to the top of his head. He proceeds to bamboozle the bewildered and increasingly hostile dealers by barking at them, in absurdist drug slang, 'Jessup! Jessup! Jessup!'

The sampler tape also comes with an intriguing cover note. 'Please be aware that the last scene, where the person being interviewed has been blacked out, is not part of the show. In the transmitted version, the identity of the person will be revealed.' Fast-forwarding to the end of the tape, there is Morris – looking uncannily like Michael Hutchence in designer glasses and comedy goatee – introducing his unidentifiable pop-star victim with the words 'He's the puff-pastry hangman', before asking him such penetrating questions as: 'You sing all the notes. That's A to G, right? So you've never sung, like . . . an H?'

Early on in what is meant to be the week of transmission, a harassed-sounding Channel 4 press officer communicates the exciting news that the reclusive Morris will come out of hiding to discuss *Brass Eye* on the understanding that nothing he says will be printed as a direct quotation. The appointed day (Thursday) dawns with a Channel 4 'statement against enquiry' (media legalese for 'we're pretending to be doing you a favour by telling you this, but actually, it's just a load of rubbish') to the following effect: '*Brass Eye* is a bold, innovative, satirical format, and the channel needs more time to review the series before transmission so that we can screen the strongest possible programme.' In other words – for the moment at least – bye-bye *Brass Eye*.

At the height of his own censorship furore, a year or so later, someone asks David Cronenberg, the director of *Crash*, about the true nature of paranoia. He quotes the William Burroughs definition, which is 'seeing things as they really are'.

However, when *Brass Eye* is finally broadcast a few months later, the elaborate conspiracy theories which flourished in the intervening months die on the vine. No broadcasting regulatory system which allows Morris to get away with some of the things he gets away with in the course of these six episodes could really be said to be allowing its programme makers insufficient freedom.

The pop star whose face we couldn't see turns out to be Jas Mann, mainstay of Wolverhampton-based Levi's advert cross-over legends Babylon Zoo, and someone more than capable of saying ridiculous things without any prompting from maliciously inclined fake interviewers. If the activities at the more frivolous end of Morris's prankster spectrum sometimes leave viewers wondering what the point of them might be, there are plenty of other moments which give you a genuine jolt. For instance, when Nelson Koka makes his contribution to the crime debate, this august gentleman of African descent is captioned – in a brilliantly pithy summary of the habitual tendency of the UK media to play up the importance of its small number of non-Caucasian voices at the expense of the silent majority – as 'representing every single black person in Britain'.

The hallucinogenic graphics pioneered in *The Day Today* are taken to their logical extreme and beyond. For example, in the 'Animals' episode's snappily realized 'man vs evil continuum paradox': 'If you plot the number of animals abused against what makes people cruel, versus intelligence of either party,' Morris argues persuasively, 'the pattern is so unreadable you might as well draw in a chain of fox-heads on sticks, and if you do that, an interesting thing happens: the word "cruel" starts flashing.'

The most controversial of Morris's techniques is to lure unsuspecting celebrities into his web of issues-based madness and wrap them up in a deadly gossamer of fake production company information and media doublethink. He then gives them the opportunity to read out pre-prepared statements which make them look utterly ridiculous, thereby reducing themselves, in classic Bergsonian fashion, to the status of automata.

The sight of Margaret Thatcher's former press secretary and arch media manipulator Sir Bernard Ingham warning of the dangers of the 'made-up psycho-active drug' Cake is not one which anybody lucky enough to have seen it is going to forget in a hurry. (Especially once the allure of that deadly chemical has been amplified by the equally scientific estimation of Bernard Manning, who reveals that it 'stimulates the part of the brain called Shatner's Bassoon'.)

'A lot of people get this part of what Chris does confused,' says Morris's former *On The Hour* colleague Stewart Lee. 'The humiliation or not of Claire Rayner [another in the long line of hapless *Brass Eye* victims] is irrelevant – that's not anything he takes pleasure in.' The obvious relish with which Morris beguiles his victims into stripping themselves of whatever remains of their dignity might suggest otherwise – as do his own words[199] – but it certainly makes a nice change to encounter a comedian ready to go to another's defence.

'What's important about *Brass Eye*,' Lee continues, 'is that it exposes the duplicity of the media under a government which knows how to use it.' This is undeniably true, but if we're going to give Morris the credit for 'making us mistrust the way the message is being delivered', we should also pay him the compliment of extending this scepticism to his own methodology. After all, to paraphrase the immortal words of Gordon Ramsay, what's sauce for the goose is also sauce for the gander.

You can (as people often do) say that Morris is exposing the way the media confers authority on the undeserving. But the use of the word 'expose' implies a desire for change consistent with old-fashioned definitions of satire (e.g. Michael Frayn: 'satire's intentions are reformatory – it wants people to behave well') rather than Morris's more nihilistic, fun-seeking approach. 'Exploit' would probably be a better choice. This doesn't make what he does any less funny, it just stops people who enjoy Morris's work mistakenly trying to tether the unruly mule that is his sense of mischief to the rusty gatepost of a particular moral agenda.

Geoffrey Grigson observed that 'satire postulates an ideal condition of man, then despairs of it and enjoys the despair masochistically', but Chris Morris misses out steps one and two and skips straight to the 'enjoying the despair masochistically' segment. Consider veteran heavy-metal DJ Tommy Vance's 'message to a murderer' in *Brass Eye*'s 'Crime and Punishment' edition. 'I'm the

---

[199.] When asked about his primary comedic motivation in the *Independent on Sunday* in 1994, Morris confessed 'amusement really, and excitement'.

shopkeeper you shot in a mindless hold-up,' Vance intones dramatically, 'I'm Marvin Gaye, shot by my own father . . . Oh yes, you know me . . . All right, look in my eyes . . . What the hell did you do that for?'

If you had to guess Morris's reaction on the distressingly frequent occasions when real life horrors seem to use his imagination as a template (cf. the aforementioned influence of the 'War' edition of *The Day Today* on Bush/Blair policy towards Iraq in 2002–3, or the first Blair government's use of the 'Animals' episode of *Brass Eye* as a training video for handling the foot and mouth crisis), and it was an either/or question with the alternatives being (a) wry feeling of satisfaction, or (b) stomach cramps, only a fool would tick (b).

There's a coldness in Chris Morris's work sometimes which suggests that if you offered him the opportunity to end all the suffering in the world simply by flicking his fingers, he somehow wouldn't get around to it. Not because he'd be afraid of the consequent lack of material, but just because he'd be too busy doing something more important, like making a short film about a talking dog.

Only a proper understanding of this moral disconnectedness allows a full appreciation of the almost Jesuitical rigour he brings to his one-man revenge mission on bourgeois notions of taste and decency. Director of photography Andy Hollis remembers a four-hour wait while Morris ensured the colour of the blood an eight-year-old girl was meant to be clearing up was 'absolutely right'. 'It didn't help that he was writer, producer and director, as well as acting in it,' Hollis notes phlegmatically, 'as it meant there wasn't anyone telling him to stop because he'd gone too far.'

The job of trying to tell Chris Morris he was going too far would not, one suspects, be an easy one.

'He drives me absolutely crazy,' admits Morris's manager Caroline Chignell, affectionately. 'He has the most incredibly acute mind of anyone I know. We have these endless arguments where I'll be saying "But for God's sake . . . it isn't funny" and he'll just keep on "But why isn't it funny?" . . . I don't understand what he does for money either – even when he's about to get paid, I have to pretend I haven't done the deal, or can't remember how much it was for, otherwise he'd halve his cut.'

It's initially hard to discern any strain of altruism or self-sacrifice in the saga of Karla, the East German zoo elephant 'so upset by captivity she stuck her trunk in her anus'. And yet, as the 'Animals' episode of *Brass Eye* unfolds, and more and more celebrities express their sympathy for Karla's plight, there's a sense that for all their foolishness, there is something genuine about their compassion which the most gimlet-eyed of satirists would do well to emulate. Jilly Cooper's spontaneous line-drawing entitled 'Please free poor Karla from this fiendish hellhole' is especially endearing. And by the time Wolf from *Gladiators* pops up with a bulletin of his own – 'Urgent news: Karla has started to ingest her own head' – the fact that Karla is blatantly fictitious almost makes the whole thing more touching, not less.

As the dialogue fades out at the end of the programme, Morris is relaying new developments in Karla's plight over a transatlantic phone line to *Baywatch* star Alexandra Paul. 'I think you should get a press release and put it out over AP [the Associated Press newswire, which by a warped coincidence shares her initials],' suggests the horrified actress. She is genuinely trying to help, and Morris perhaps shows his inner schoolboy a little too clearly by repeatedly feigning bemusement and quizzically demanding 'Put it out over a pea?'

Morris's comedy godson Ali G does the same thing sometimes, too – when his desperation for the person whose eyes he is trying to pull the wool over to say something on which he can place a sexual or narcotic connotation overcomes him to the extent that he looks more foolish than his putative victim ever could. While it would be exciting to be able to say that Chris Morris and Sacha Baron Cohen were deliberately making themselves ridiculous in a cunning satirical double-bluff – reflecting the audience's misplaced confidence in the satirical mindset back at itself – it would probably not be true.

None the less, the strange and rather disturbing moment when Morris lies down on the studio floor amid *Brass Eye*'s jump-cut carnage and adopts the Christ on the cross pose (from the title sequence of *World in Action*) sets up at least one more strange note of resonance than was originally intended. In some ways, *Brass Eye*-era Morris – horizontal rather than perpendicular – is like Jesus in reverse: by being so evil, he brings out the best in sinners.

Of all the numerous opportunities British TV has given us to find Bernard Manning likeable in the past decade or so, the only one that's actually worked for him is the moment where – at Morris's prompting – he expresses his horror at the Hell of Cake. 'It's made from chemicals by sick bastards,' blusters Britain's leading exponent of the comedy of hate. 'It's a fucking disgrace!'

A few years later, after retreating from the public eye (and ear) for a few years into the phantasmagoric miasma of *Jam*, Morris returns with an almighty bang, as 2001's *Brass Eye* 'Paedophile Special' briefly threatens to clothe his messianic fantasies in the bloodstained shroud of fact. While it is hard to see what any reasonable person would find offensive in the spectacle of Phil Collins wearing a T-shirt which proclaims 'I'm talking Nonce-sense',[200] or Capital Radio DJ Dr Fox reading from a prepared script that proclaims the genetic make-up of the child-abuser to be the same as that of the crab, Morris's determination to press the buttons of Mary Whitehouse's spiritual children in the *Daily Mail* editorial department takes him into some territory that might have been better left unexplored.

On an emotional scale of one to eleven, with one being 'very upset at the unfair treatment of his work, which most of those concerned hadn't actually seen', and eleven being 'absolutely delighted, as it meant he must have got something right', it seems unlikely that Morris's response to the ensuing media furore would register in single figures. 'I don't think it upset him at all,' confirms Andy Hollis. 'I think he absolutely revelled in the coverage, because the effect it had rammed home the point he was aiming to make.'

That point is, presumably, that the prurient relish of the media in dealing with this most emotive of all issues taps into the same properly forbidden sources of sensual gratification as the offence

---

[200.] Phil Collins's status as pop's answer to Rhodes Boyson is thereby confirmed (robbing *South Park* creators Matt Parker and Trey Stone of the Oscar they deserved for *South Park: Bigger, Longer and Uncut*) had earlier made him the butt of a number of well-aimed satirical barbs.

itself. This is a valid and worthwhile criticism, successfully made in the programme by Morris's *Kilroy*-like interrogator proclaiming, 'I'm afraid we will have to see that little girl being upset in a rather more sustained way later on in tonight's deeply disturbing programme.'

And the fact that Labour culture minister Estelle Morris is willing to condemn the programme without actually seeing it does testify to the Blair administration's determination to pander to the prejudices of Middle England, as expressed in its house journal, the *Daily Mail*. But on the other hand, to employ the sort of extreme example which should connect with readers of that newspaper (which was, after all, the paper which backed Hitler and Mussolini in the thirties), you didn't have to actually *join* the Nazi party to know that being a Nazi was wrong.

The idea that you have to actually experience a work of art in order to have an opinion on it is, after all, an entirely bogus ploy designed by wilful seekers of controversy in the hope of getting bums on seats. The funny thing about satire is, it's very happy to use moral arguments to defend its own right to do whatever it wants, but less eager to apply the same kind of strictures to itself.

The point at which *Brass Eye* loses all sense of moral perspective is when it uses the names of actual, convicted paedophiles for comic effect. It's at this moment that you can't help questioning the nature of the thrill Morris is deriving from his satirical endeavours. After all, if what makes this programme funny is simply the fact that such terrible things do happen, doesn't that make its author just as guilty of profiting from the suffering of the innocent as any of the people he so waggishly points a finger at?

Perhaps in this regard – to resort momentarily to the kind of biblical language which a man with his religious education ought to be able to relate to – Morris should have removed the plank from his own eye before drawing attention to the splinters in everybody else's. Either way, it's at the moment when called upon to rub shoulders with reality that any form of satirical endeavour faces its sternest examination.

'Without realness we iz nuffink'

When Ali G teaches his 'Keep It Real' classes to the attentive eleven-year olds of the John Nike Leisure Centre, he is in some respects quoting himself. In an early appearance on Channel 4's *Eleven O'Clock Show*, Ali is observed teaching 'workshops in gang culture' to the elderly residents of the Aubrey House residential home in Guildford.

This is all very amusing as far as it goes, until Ali brandishes an AK-47 at an elderly woman called Ethel and she mutters fearfully under her breath 'I don't know anything, don't ask me today – I'm too worried'. There are two possible explanations for this strangely distressing scene. The first, and less likely, is that Ethel is acting. In this case, given how obvious the subtext about the average OAP's fear of crime already is, you'd have to wonder why anyone thought this needed to be further emphasized. In what seems (having watched the sequence a number of times) the far more likely of the two explanations – that the old woman is actually genuinely upset and confused, and the sequence was left in in the belief that no one would notice (or care) – the question which needs to be asked is more serious.

And that question is: how could such callousness come about? Bergson wrote that in order for the true voice of the comic to prevail, we had to 'put our affection out of court and impose silence on our pity'. There are some moments – for instance, when Ali harries an innocent Ulster Unionist ('Are you Irish?' 'No, I'm British' 'So, you're only here on holiday?') – where his calculated stupidity seems the ideal means of getting to the heart of the matter. But there are others, just as (in fact, probably more) numerous, where it seems to be there to be savoured for its own sake.

When Ali visits a coal-mining heritage attraction in Sacha Baron Cohen's Welsh motherland, he proclaims – to the evident (and understandable) disgust of his guide, Gordon Gratton – that 'miners lived in here before they became human beings'. At this point, it becomes difficult for anyone who lived through the dark days of the early eighties to suppress a shudder.

Ali G's lack of a redemptive voice was inherited from *Beavis and Butthead*. Yet, where Mike Judge's animation was a satire (and one motivated, in the admission of its author, by 'hatred and contempt') on the limited mental horizons of a specific phase of adolescence, as mediated through wilfully exploitative rock and rap videos, Ali G is a grown adult. What this implies about the evolutionary progress of British masculinity is not absolutely clear, but it seems probable that Mary Whitehouse wouldn't like it. And in this instance, she might even be right.

Max Wall, Margaret Thatcher, Les Dawson and the end of shame

'What is it like to live entirely without shame?' Peggy Hill asks her sexually liberated niece Luanne in a 1997 edition of Mike Judge's *King of the Hill*. 'Is it a good thing?'

'Yes,' observes this unnervingly well-adjusted fifteen-year old, after a momentary pause for reflection, 'it is.'

Ten years earlier, Ian Jack wrote that 'Mrs Thatcher wanted to liberate Britain from shame, and to a great extent, and in unpredictable ways, she did . . .' Whether or not this was a good thing was a much more complicated question. The Thatcherite project[201] was based on the hope – in Jack's formulation – that 'unfettered (and unsubsidized) by the state, the people of Britain would rediscover their ingenious aptitudes and entrepreneurial skills'. But this 'unfettering' would reach far beyond the industrial sphere, as the tentacles of the *laissez-faire* ideology she had customized from Victorian economic liberalism stretched into every corner of British public (and private) life.

Given that Mrs Whitehouse offered (along with Labour's redoubtable Barbara Castle) one of the few templates for a woman wielding political power in Britain, and Margaret Thatcher – in principle at least[202] – shared her conservative Christian convictions,

---

[201.] So that's where Tony Blair picked up that term from.

[202.] In practice, she seemed to regard religious conscience more as an inconvenience to be subordinated to the higher goods of the free market and a conception of British national interest rooted in Winston Churchill's more vainglorious moments.

it was ironic that the latter should preside over the final destruction of the former's dream of remaking Britain in her own image. As dividing lines between past and future go, they don't come much more clear-cut than the week in November 1984 when a strike started on the assembly line at British Leyland's Cowley plant over a supervisor's alleged use of profanity and Channel 4 – soon to be dubbed 'Channel Swore' by the nation's tabloid moral guardians – made its first broadcast.

Ian Jack's anguished contemporary commentary on 'The Rise of the 4-Letter Word' (reprinted in the 1987 essay collection *When the Oil Ran Out*) marks the significance of this occasion with a due sense of solemnity. In commemoration of this last hurrah of seventies-style union militancy, Jack calls, appropriately enough, upon Alan Bleasdale – author of that timeless landmark of anti-Thatcherite humanism, *Boys from the Blackstuff* – to mark the exact progress of the nation's decline into Anglo-Saxon vulgarity.

Bleasdale claims he 'first heard a woman [a fellow teacher at his school in Liverpool] swear' in 1967, two years after Kenneth Tynan used the word 'fuck' on a live TV discussion programme.[203] In 1971 he left the UK to work abroad (perhaps still in shock) and returned three years later to find a drastic change in the nation's linguistic landscape.

'When I left, I'd never heard a girl swear,' Bleasdale remembers, more in sorrow than in anger, 'and when I came back I found beautiful little eleven-year-olds shouting "you fucking twat" down the corridor.'

There was a little way to go before the third-grade innocents of *South Park* could join in their gleeful chorus of 'Fuck is the worst word that you can say', but not all that far. In short, it was still

---

[203.] Asked in the course of a discussion of stage censorship on 13 November 1965 (on a live talk show satirically entitled *BBC3*, because there could never be a channel called that, could there?) whether he could imagine the National Theatre putting on a play in which sexual intercourse was represented onstage, Kenneth Tynan responded: 'Well, I think so, certainly. I doubt if there are any rational people to whom the word "fuck" would be particularly diabolical, revolting or totally forbidden.' In this opinion at least, the man who would later bring us *Oh Calcutta!* might fairly be said to have been ahead of his time.

only 1974 and already – in the immortal words of Chris Morris's hardheaded TV news reporting *alter ego* Ted Maul – 'The language is Swear-hili'.

It would hardly be fair to blame Margaret Thatcher for a break-down in social niceties that was already well under way by the time she came to power (and after all, the British public did vote for her at three general elections, so we can hardly hold our hands up and claim it was nothing to do with us).[204] But there was a particular quality to the shamelessness of her epoch, which had something to do with a narrowing gap between public and private morality.[205]

Les Dawson's second volume of autobiography, 1992's *No Tears for the Clown*, recounts this much-loved comedian's touching last romance with a Fylde hotelier, some years younger than he was. Embarking on this love affair less than a year after the death of his

---

[204] The (two years pre-Thatcher) 1977 film version of *Are You Being Served?*, for example, offers a disturbing relief map of Britain's psychological land-scape in a key year in our country's cultural history. Both the shocking vulgarity of the jubilee and the warped patriotism of the Sex Pistols are here in plenty. Within the first minute or so of this department-store farce, Mrs Slocombe has revealed her Union Jack underwear and professed concern as to the state of her pussy, Mr Peacock has raised his eyebrows a lot and the evil caretaker Mr Harman has sucked off Shirley's drawers with a Hoover. From then on, it's downhill all the way.

At the point in the early nineties when *Are You Being Served?* is released on Warner Home Video, the end-of-the-pier tradition of homely vaudeville sauce to which Grace Brothers belongs (alongside such other comedic landmarks as Benny Hill and the *Carry On*s) is in the process of being elevated to an unprecedentedly exalted cultural position – an elevation which, in this case at least, is more patronizing than the neglect it super-sedes. 'This is the kind of thing that made Britain great. Stupid, but great,' opines Mr Grainger as the Grace Brothers staff – holidaying on the 'Costa Plonka' – take refuge from an unlikely Spanish *coup d'état*. The spiritual impoverishment on show in *Are You Being Served?* makes you worry for a decade that could have found pleasure in it in the first place, but even more for one that would want to watch it again.

Happily, a quarter of a century on from the film's original release, things have moved on a little. Silver jubilee has given way to golden, and *Ali G Indahouse* begins with its hero being fellated by his dog, Tupac.

[205] It's not so much that hypocrisy goes out of fashion – as John Major's 'back-to-basics' morality crusade of John Major's would demonstrate – just that it becomes less necessary.

beloved wife, Dawson looks back fearfully (if not all that pertinently, given the differences between their respective situations) to the example of Max Wall.

Wall – at that point one of the biggest comedy stars of his day – was appearing in the West End in a play called *The Pyjama Game* (in which a young Les had a minor role) when the break-up of his marriage became public news. Having had the temerity to embark on a liaison with a beauty queen who was, in Dawson's conservative estimation, 'a hundred years his junior', the great Wallofski found himself the target of all 1950s Britain's considerable capacity for censoriousness and hypocrisy.

'When Max and I came out of the stage door,' Dawson recalls, 'people turned their backs on him. I remember there was a light drizzle falling and it was misty – Max had had a lot to drink and I caught him as he stumbled against a wall. "What have I done that is so terrible?" he whispered to me. "All I did was to fall in love."' (Wall's own autobiography, *The Fool on the Hill*, expresses his pain in an even more dramatic fashion: 'I became the dog to be given bad news,' he laments, 'the one to be censored, judged, sent into mental exile.')[206]

Dawson agonizes over the possibility that his own May-to-December love affair might destroy his career in the same way, but a supportive tabloid press soon confirms that he needn't have worried. There is a price to be paid, however, for this newly easy-going attitude.

'The newspaper had brought in a medium who was supposed to have got in touch with Meg's spirit,' Dawson recalls, through gritted teeth, 'and my dead wife was supposed to have told her "carry on bonking, Les".' As a finishing touch, the article was 'tastefully illustrated with a photo of Meg's grave'.

[206.] A masterpiece of what you might term the 'non-confessional' style (containing, as it does, the immortal line 'Such little items as losing my driving licence after being breathalysed over the limit are hardly worth a mention'), this book traces Wall's career from humble music-hall beginnings as 'the boy with the obedient feet' to the ultimate validation of touring with Mott the Hoople.

19
Equal Opportunities, the Ones that Never Knock

Race and Ali G, sex and *Smack the Pony*, and *Spaced* – the final frontier

'Is it because I is black?'
Ali G

'Anyone who thinks women aren't funny is an idiot: two of my favourite comedians of the last twenty-five years are Lily Savage and Dame Edna Everage'
Ricky Gervais

It's a sunny summer morning in 2001, at the Fulham Road offices of Johnny Vaughan's production company, World's End. His producer, Paul Ross, snuffles around on the office floor, breathing heavily, while Vaughan's bulldog, Harvey, makes calls in the office next door. Vaughan has an interesting theory about the true significance of the bulldog's standing as an emblem of untainted Britishness, given that its actual status is as a 'pedigree mongrel' whose genetic make-up is based on nine breeds intermingled over hundreds of years.

He is not expounding that theory today, though. Instead he is fulminating at length about Jeffrey Archer, whose perjury trial has just come to a dramatic conclusion. Vaughan seems to be missing his *Big Breakfast* soapbox. His personal investment in the public disgrace and incarceration of a fellow icon of social mobility[207] goes far beyond the bet it won him with a next-door neighbour (coincidentally a barrister). Archer received the same prison sentence as Vaughan did for the pre-celebrity motorway-service-station cocaine bust which looms so large in his own personal mythology.

'I got four years as well, funnily enough . . .' says Vaughan, not sounding as if he necessarily thinks it's all that funny. 'One of the first books I read when I was sent away was *Bonfire of the Vanities*, and that's roughly how Jeffrey Archer must have felt – like a master of the universe, with his Krug parties in his penthouse. And the law, almost like *Columbo*, has doggedly tracked him down and put them all on trial: all those people who knew exactly what he was up to – that band of high-Tory thieves who thought it was one rule for us and another for them, the people who sold the family silver and lined their own pockets . . .' Vaughan is working up a fine head of rhetorical steam now. 'To see this happen to the person who personified it all,' he nods his head with evident satisfaction, 'it was like the dying scream of the eighties.'

A name which doesn't crop up in Vaughan's genial diatribe – or anything anyone else says about the Archer case, come to that – is that of Aziz Kurtha. Kurtha is a Pakistani-born businessman and occasional TV presenter who might – had the cards of fate fallen a little differently – have ended up being considered Karachi's answer to Darcus Howe. It was Kurtha who supplied the original story of Jeffrey Archer's brothel-based indiscretions to the *Daily Star*, and whose evidence at the original 1987 libel trial placed the slippery Tory grandee firmly where he said he wasn't.

Exhibiting a faith in British justice as touching as it was naïve, Kurtha had his character totally assassinated by Archer's lawyers (a refrain picked up by Archer himself, who branded him 'a very evil man'). After the death of Monica Coughlan (the unfortunate

---

[207.] Vaughan proved that, like the value of investments, icons of social mobility can go down instead of up. On the 2003 Comic Relief 'Town & Gown' edition of *University Challenge*, he is plainly delighted to find himself on the opposite side to Stephen Fry – a man with whom he shares two formative institutional experiences: Uppingham public school and subsequently (rather to the detriment of the former exclusive establishment's disciplinary reputation) jail.

brothel employee at the centre of the case) in a car crash, Kurtha
– who had been effectively ruined by the original trial – was the
main person who might seem to have had something to gain when
the truth about Archer's perjury finally came to light. And yet, in the
excitement of the great man's downfall, the vindication of Kurtha
remained very much a public secret.

Why none of the other brave seekers after truth who had pursued
Archer down the years chose to take up cudgels on his innocent
victim's behalf, we can only conjecture. But you would not have to
be the most cynical observer of British attitudes to people from the
Indian subcontinent to suspect that the fact that he (to quote the
immortal words of Ben Stiller's faked 911 call in *The Cable Guy*)
'looked Asian' might have had something to do with it.

Consider one of the things Aziz Kurtha said at the time[208] about
the way people's responses to him are informed by his ethnicity.
'Sometimes English people tell me I sound quite "English" in the
way I speak, or "not at all like Indians talk". I regularly joke that
my accent is put on, and then go into a long "Goodness gracious
me" Peter Sellers routine.'

The gap between Kurtha's idealization of the English establishment and the way he is actually treated by it renders his eagerness to
please in this context extremely poignant. And the place of Sellers's
simpering Indian character[209] in British comedy's pantheon of racist
infamy is finally sealed when his catch-phrase supplies the title for
BBC2's somewhat belated mid-nineties anti-colonial fightback (see
below).

Sellers was not short of company there: from Alf Garnett to
Mind Your Language, from *It Ain't Half Hot Mum* to fellow ex-Goon
Spike Milligan's rightly infamous *Curry and Chips*, the back pages of
UK comedy positively bulge with ethnic slurs. That last unlamented
televisual vehicle (in which a blacked-up Milligan's takeaway proprietor maintains a painful *Never The Twain*-style rivalry with Eric
Sykes's neighbouring chip-shop owner) makes a particularly
uncomfortable remembrance, even – or rather especially – for Milligan's most devoted admirers.

[208.] In Jack's *Before the Oil Ran Out*.
[209.] This character first appeared as the doctor in 1960's *The Millionairess*.

Pauline Scudamore's admirable biography faces the issue of Milligan's racism (and if the word is to have any meaning, it's the only one a proper respect for Spike's genius will allow us to use) head on. Unsurprisingly, she locates its origins in his colonial upbringing in India and Burma. In that youthful setting, the fact that white people were 'supposed to be superior' was, Milligan remembers, 'emphasized by every facet of our lives'. On the one hand painfully aware of the inequities of imperial circumstance, on the other unable to shake off the reflex condescension fostered by 'constant attentions of deferential native servants', Milligan was 'pressed into a sort of acceptance that everything non-British was just a load of shit'.[210] Milligan's childhood experiences would seem to confirm the commonsensical contention of Anne Dummett's authoritative 1973 study *A Portrait of English Racism* that 'Racism is essentially a mystique created by Europeans as a definition of their *own* identity as being greater and stronger than anyone else's'. While enforced relocation as an adolescent to not-so-sunny Catford proved that life in Britain could be a load of shit too, neither this disillusioning experience nor the mind-expanding impact of the war years seem to have been quite strong enough to overcome the pernicious effects of Milligan's early indoctrination.

There's a truly unhappy passage in *Where Have All the Bullets Gone?* – the fifth volume of Milligan's military memoirs – where Spike, on the move in wartime Italy, hitches a ride from a black American GI amid a shower of ash from an erupting volcano. His inability to see past the colour of the American's skin to the calibre of his kindness is almost as painful to the reader as it must have been to the lift-giver.

'He offers me a cigarette, then gum, then chocolates,' Milligan begins. 'I wait for money but nothing comes. The fall of ash has turned his hair grey. He looked every bit like Uncle Tom,' he con-

---

[210.] An Anglo-supremacist strand persists in what you might call the neo-colonial school of British comedy – i.e. those who are influenced by Milligan above all others – from Reeves and Mortimer being unable to understand why anyone should be offended by them blacking up as Marvin Gaye and Smokey Robinson to Harry Hill's mystifying insistence that there is something intrinsically funny about the name of Channel 4 newsreader Zeinab Badawi.

tinues – instinctively denying the camaraderie so effortlessly extended to fellow combatants elsewhere in his wartime recollections – 'Goodbye, said his teeth.' The fact that Milligan's capacity for empathy – with people, animals and even plants – is at other times so well-developed as to be actively self-destructive makes his total disregard for the humanity of his benefactor doubly shocking.

Anne Dummett probably had this sort of thing in mind when she wrote that racism's crude stereotypes 'tell us no truths about black people at all; but they tell us much that is true and important about white people's picture of themselves'. In the same connection, consider for a moment the two non-white characters who flit momentarily across the screen in that movie spin-off of *Man About the House* (released a year after the publication of Dummett's book) which came up a couple of chapters back.

One of them is a harassed single mother who is there only to wring a (very) cheap laugh from the fact her child is called Enoch. The other is a now mercifully forgotten Thames television celebrity called Sambo the Nig-nog. How or why such an infamous creation could have remained a figure of national prominence in the era of Roxy Music and *The Morecambe and Wise Christmas Show* is a question that is just too distressing to enter into. In any event, the heartfelt lament of Paula Wilcox's Chrissy – 'You can do anything in London except live!' – might have been designed for such marginalized figures.

Jim Davidson's panto, *or* the wages of *Sinderella* is death

It would be nice to think that this kind of systematic social exclusion had been left behind in the 1970s, but the ongoing career of Jim Davidson suggests otherwise. Thus in the spring of 1995, the fact that Davidson is putting on an 'adult' panto in London's West End and the theatre is not full suggests there might be hope for this country after all.

Whatever anyone's individual feelings about Davidson – lovable Charlton roughneck, or one of the ten most evil men in Europe – his popularity has never previously been in dispute. Maybe terrestrial TV's admirable system of low-key censorship (whereby really

right-wing comedians are only allowed on television when presenting game shows) is starting to take effect.[211] Then again, perhaps
March is just a mad month to open a panto.

Sinderella starts badly. 'Are there any fairies in London?' asks
Mia Carla's drunken Fairy Godmother. 'Yes . . . John Major!' shouts
the man next to me. Yet, for all this show's renegade proletarian
ambience, there aren't all that many jokes in it that might not have
been made just as easily by a mainstream (i.e. alternative) comedian.

Everyone now seems to be fishing in the same pool of showbiz
self-referentiality. Jim's remorselessly priapic Buttons makes frequent references to failed marriages and drink-driving convictions.
Among the supporting cast are Jess Conrad's 'ageing Sixties heart-
throb', the same role he played in *The Great Rock'n'Roll Swindle*
(this man has deconstructed himself so many times that he might
as well be made of Lego) and Diane Lee in the title role. If the
name is not familiar, just add the prefix 'Peters and'.

Lee's Sinders lacks spark, but ''Ello my darlings' legend Charlie
Drake (last seen as an impeccable Smallweed in the BBC's *Hard
Times* – no one can deny this man has range) cuts a compellingly
obscene figure as Baron Hard-on. He sets the tone for a production
that plumbs Shakespearian heights of bawdiness. The stage is awash
with giant vibrators and the pantomime horse has a huge penis, but
one of the most striking things about *Sinderella* is the pleasure it
seems to take in overturning the conventional sexual hierarchy. The
naked flesh on display is almost all male and the show's closing
line, from its rapacious Fairy Godmother, is a forthright statement
of carnal intent towards Buttons.

If only Jim Davidson's attitude to race was similarly enlightened.
He insists that his racial jibes are 'just a bit of fun', but that's what
Adolf Hitler said about *Kristallnacht*. He ties up an ugly string of
them by looking round the crowd for a non-white face, affirming
his delight when he finds none by saying, with a roguish wink, 'The
shops are still open, I think we're safe.' There's no arguing with
the fact that a Jim Davidson audience provides a nightmare vision

---

[211.] Unfortunately, this policy seems to lapse as the decade proceeds, until Jim
Davidson 'specials', live from the Falkland Islands, become almost a weekly
feature on BBC1.

of what an all-white Britain might be like. There's a black man in the cast, though: a dancer called Paul Bailey. Most of his co-hoofers learned their trade at the Performers Dance College in Essex. Bailey trained with the Ballet Rambert.

The Thea Vidale and Lenny Henry calling-your-mother-a-bitch or not contrast

By an actual coincidence, it is at around this time that Oprah Winfrey makes her celebrated declaration that 'excellence is a deterrent to racism'. It would be fair to say that Texan comedian Thea Vidale – who makes a big splash on *Clive Anderson Talks Back* by leaving her Tina Turner fright-wig on the host's head ('Clive was very gracious to me') – is not impressed by Winfrey's contribution to the equal-opportunities debate. In fact, she is hopping mad about it.

'Oprah is one of the few out of millions of black women who have made it big,' insists Vidale, 'and she has a responsibility to all the others to think about what she says. Excellence is not a deterrent to racism. Racism is a deterrent to excellence. That's what racism is about – blocking and deflecting other races from greatness. I hate this "I pulled myself up by my bootstraps and so can you" mentality: some people ain't got no boots, let alone bootstraps.'

Having taken first the Hackney Empire (with the sort of much-extended run only Oliver Samuels – the Jamaican Max Miller – can usually manage) and then the West End by storm, Vidale is at this point vigorously resisting attempts to dub her 'the black Roseanne' on account of her combative demeanour and unlikely comedic bedrock of ten years in a violent and unhappy marriage. 'I'd like to be as popular as Roseanne,' she concedes, 'but I'm not "the black . . ."' *anything.*[212]

Does she think there is any intrinsic difference between black and white comedy?

'Well, you have to think about what comedy is – it's a form of

---

[212.] ABC thoughtfully stops such media simplifications becoming a long-term worry by cancelling Thea's sitcom.

reality brought out in a humorous way. And white people have a very different reality to black people.'

As the point of intersection between these two realities, the black comedian is in a position which is at once strategically powerful and yet highly vulnerable to attack from both sides. Vidale pushes her luck further than most: 'Black men love for you to go down on them . . . but you can't get a nigger to lick a stamp' being a representative sample of her determination to milk the established tradition of black female sassiness for all its worth.

'There's something about a big black woman telling the truth that white people love,' Vidale observes, with an engaging hint of cynicism. There are some truths that people just aren't ready to hear, though. When Thea calls her mother a bitch on daytime TV – 'She's a wonderful woman . . . and as long as she lives in Texas and I live in Los Angeles, that's how it's going to stay' – the *Pebble Mill* studio audience plainly wants her dead. This should not be taken as evidence of Black Country small-mindedness. Even the *Jerry Springer* crowd boos people who disrespect their mums.

You wouldn't catch Lenny Henry calling *his* mother a bitch. Watching the burly West Midlander go through his paces in the mid-nineties – recording his *Loud* video in the suburban spotlight of the Wimbledon Theatre – most of his jokes, even the good ones ('The Birmingham Six, The Guildford Four . . . The Dave Clark Five must be shitting themselves') have that floating-rootlessly-in-time-and-space feel peculiar to the traditional club performer. There is a tension in Henry's act, however; between the celebration of sameness which is mainstream comedy's cosy heart, and the overwhelming sense of his difference as a black British man which is central to the way he presents himself and the way his audience sees him.

With his endlessly accommodating blues, funk and rap pastiches and his gallery of affable characters, Henry seems to be trying to soften images of black masculinity; to make them less threatening to his largely white (and not especially liberal) audience – 'That's why Linford Christie runs so fast,' he asserts in the midst of a discourse on discipline in Jamaican parenting. 'His mum's after him.' Priapic soulman Theophilus P. Wildebeest's 'love rocket' (a huge phallic contraption on which Henry seats an understandably reluctant member of the audience) even detumesces at the crucial moment.

It's Henry's very determination not to intimidate or offend which sharpens his occasional edgy moment.

'That's my solution to racism,' he observes pointedly – with regard to the special treatment his familiar face earns him – 'all black people should become famous.'

Q: When is a dichotomy not a dichotomy?
A: When it's the historically crucial Cosby–Pryor interface

If the founder of the 'all black people should become famous' school of comedy might reasonably be said to be Bill Cosby, the principal of the rival 'there are some wounds that fame cannot heal' academy is certainly Richard Pryor. Sexually abused as a six-year-old child by a boy ten years his senior, Pryor was never able to tell anyone what had happened to him. Years later, his abuser turned up at his film trailer with a young son of his own in tow, and calmly asked for an autograph.

There is an idea – popular with the sort of people who love Bill Hicks but would never be caught dead enjoying Denis Leary – that the Cosby–Pryor divide represents some kind of primal bifurcation in black comedy between bourgeois assimilation and heroic outsider status. As appealing as this theory might be, it just does not stand up to closer examination. Thea Vidale claims them both as equal influences, and perhaps – as with the two apparently contradictory quotes at the end of Spike Lee's *Do The Right Thing* (one from Malcolm X and the other from Martin Luther King) – it's not so much an either/or situation as a case of complementary opposites.

By his own admission – in his Todd Gold-ghosted autobiography, *Pryor Convictions*, among other places – when Richard Pryor started out in the early 1960s, it was as a craven Bill Cosby copyist. Among those who encouraged him to wake up and smell the coffee were Groucho Marx and Miles Davis (with that kind of encouragement, Bradley Walsh might have grown into a cockney Sadowitz).

Having been raised in a whorehouse in Peoria, Illinois, it was hardly surprising that when he did begin to develop a style of his own, Pryor's concerns should tend towards the earthier end of the comedic spectrum. The world that he saw in his early years shaped not only Pryor's rough-and-ready attitude to sex, but also his scathing take on respectable hypocrisy. 'White dude used to come down and ask "Do you have any girls who'll cover you with ice cream, and little boys that'll lick it off?"' he remembers, not all that fondly. '. ... And he was the mayor.'

Even as he was boldly laughing in the face of sexual and racial taboos, Pryor's private life became the acme of domestic repression, as he subjected his various wives to a series of grievous degradations while willingly enslaving himself to alcohol and freebase cocaine. It would be wrong, however, to see too much of a contradiction between the joy of Richard Pryor's best comedy (a kind of one-man call and response routine or, as he himself describes it in somewhat more formal terms, 'a dialogue between his inner and outer selves') and his unhappy personal circumstances. The abusive behaviour for which he became notorious – emptying a magazine of bullets into one wife's car being the best-publicized among a veritable catalogue of misdeeds – was bound up in the same self-hatred with which his comedy heroically attempted to wrestle.

A check-list on the inside cover of his autobiography marks the staging posts in a chaotic life: 'The money, the women, the cocaine addiction, the attempt at self-immolation [in 1980, in the midst of a cocaine funk, Pryor doused himself with cognac, set himself on fire and ran through the streets of LA as a human torch], the six marriages, the quadruple-bypass surgery, the diagnosis of multiple sclerosis'. And among the tributes on the back is one from Bill Cosby, who says that Pryor 'finds laughter where none has a right to exist', which – as celebrity encomiums go – seems to be pretty much on the money.

In sharp but welcome contrast to Pryor's unending turbulence, Cosby reigns serene in slickness and in health. Despite more than thirty years as one of the top people in his field, the man who was Dr Huxtable never got around to performing on this side of the Atlantic before the spring of 1995. When the time finally comes for Cosby to make his London début, he jets in without so much as a single sycophantic retainer in tow, has dinner with some friends, brings a dressed-up-to-the-elevens Royal Albert Hall to its feet with two hours of elegantly crafted domestic discontentment, then meanders off home again without so much as a word to Richard and Judy.

Happily married and in the throes of a sumptuously well-provided-for early retirement, you might think Cosby would not have much to complain about, but that would be to miss an important point. It's complaining that has got him where he is today. So it's strange that so many people should express concern about his plans for an American version of *One Foot in the Grave:*[213] it's the children in *The Cosby Show* who are nauseatingly cute – the old man can out-grump the best of them.

And therein, strangely enough, lies Bill Cosby's political importance. In establishing that black Americans can have little problems as well as big ones, he has been a soft-shoe subversive rather than the social-climbing sell-out of critical imagining. Watching Cosby onstage in this country for the first time, it is easy to see what made Richard Pryor admire him so much. The subject matter might be as familiar as an old slipper, but the easy elegance of its delivery and desiccated cool of Cosby's endless rhetorical flourishes are unique.

It's not all good, wholesome family fun either. Cosby's celebration of intramarital flatulence strays into realms where even Billy Connolly might fear to tread. And his *pièce de résistance* is the longest and most graphic description of a prostate check-up ever attempted in a British theatre: the midst of a stool examination, apparently, is 'the only time when black is not beautiful'.

The man behind the *Real McCoy/Goodness Gracious Me* Divergence explains exactly where Tony Blair comes into it

In the summer of 1995, Anil Gupta approaches BBC Head of Comedy Jon Plowman with the suggestion that the time might be right for an all-Asian sketch show. In Gupta's estimation, a couple of the writers and performers he's worked with as a script editor

---

[213.] They needn't have worried: like the American *Absolutely Fabulous* and *Royle Family* and Boothby Graffoe's prime-time Hollywood talk show, it somehow never materializes.

on the somewhat rickety black talent vehicle *The Real McCoy*[214] (notably Meera Syal), together with a duo called The Secret Asians (a.k.a. Sanjeev Bhaskar and musician Nitin Sawnhey) who have been performing with some success on the London circuit, have the makings of a successful TV team.

Plowman gives him ten thousand pounds of development money to put on a one-off performance which he can come and see. After just four days of writing and rehearsal, the show – now rejoicing in the polemical title *Peter Sellers Is Dead* ('It wasn't that we had anything against Peter Sellers,' Gupta insists. 'We just wanted to move on from the old "comedy Indian" stereotype of Sellers or Spike Milligan browned-up and doing a funny voice') – goes ahead on a Friday night at Hammersmith's Riverside Studios, in front of an audience judiciously packed with friends and family of the cast and crew.

The experiment is pronounced a success. However, with no money available to commission a full series until the next year's budget comes through, Gupta and his willing ensemble finalize their collective aesthetic via a couple of well-received Radio 4 series before the TV show – now called *Goodness Gracious Me* in ironic tribute to Peter Sellers's aforementioned simpering Indian character – makes its TV début in early 1997.

'The "going for an English" sketch was just about the first one we wrote in that four-day rehearsal period,' Gupta remembers, of the routine which becomes the show's signature. The idea of a confident group of young Indians crowning a drunken night out with a contemptuous experience of English cuisine speaks to the very heart of the British Asian experience – not only cocking a snook at years of racially motivated curry-house abuse but also ridiculing the Anglo-Saxon penchant for treating ethnic-minority fellow countrymen as a kind of exotic resource.

In one sense, this justly celebrated *Goodness Gracious Me* sketch is a victim of its own success, as the classic simplicity of its reversal

---

[214.] Growing out of the London black comedy circuit based around Hackney Empire's famously boisterous 291 Club, this series would ultimately look like a transatlantic trial run for Russell Simmons's hugely successful Def Comedy Jam.

of convention quickly becomes a formula which is – in itself – creatively limiting. In another way, though, it's the very focused nature of the show's comedic outreach programme which enables it to achieve, and even surpass, so many of its original goals.

Goodness Gracious Me's self-consciously traditional approach – notably its live-in-the-studio format – is designed to appeal to a slightly more conservative audience than might be expected to relish the prospect of an all-Asian cast. And what Gupta himself calls a 'don't scare the horses' mentality ('It's enough for people to deal with that they've got brown faces,' he remembers himself thinking, 'so let's not do anything else that's going to alarm them') turns out to be a very effective tactic.

Gupta and his team are triumphantly vindicated in their determination that *Goodness Gracious Me* should be broadcast before – rather than after – *Newsnight* (as BBC high-ups had initially intended). And ultimately, in winning more than five million viewers, the show paves the way for a period when – from *East Is East* to *Bend It Like Beckham* – the British film industry's Asian wing is just about the only one turning a profit. So how did this triumph of integrational advancement come about?

'With *The Real McCoy*,' Gupta remembers, 'the crowds in the studio were 90 per cent black. They loved the show, and every time someone would say something bad about the police, it would bring the house down. In that environment, you have to be quite disciplined not to just go in there and say "white people are stupid" and have everyone think you're a genius.' This was one of several pitfalls that *Goodness Gracious Me* managed not to fall into.

'Our approach', says Gupta, 'was more that we wanted to make some serious points, but not necessarily have them noticed, because the fundamental issue we were trying to address was "Can Asians be funny to a broad UK TV audience?" And this was a question which, at that stage, even we didn't know the answer to. It was all quite New Labour,' Gupta continues, 'in that you had to be "on message". There would be sketches that we wouldn't do, even though we knew they were good, because they didn't quite fit in with the overall things we were trying to say. We knew this could be our big breakthrough show and that, in turn, carried a certain responsibility, so we were willing to do whatever it took.'

Just as with New Labour, the *Goodness Gracious Me* ensemble's sense of 'all being in it together' within an authoritarian leadership structure was based on formative experiences of rudderless chaos.

'When I worked on *The Real McCoy*,' Gupta remembers, 'there was such a lot of politics involved – even among the cast – with everyone saying "you can't do this" or "you're not allowed to say that". But people were arguing about things that were irrelevant to a wider audience! That was how I knew *Goodness Gracious Me* had to speak with one voice. Someone [i.e. Gupta] needed to be in charge, saying "this is what we're going to say and how we're going to say it".'

While the finely honed nature of the show which results proves highly effective in reaching out to a new audience, it still doesn't cut much ice with the comedy *cognoscenti*.

'You're either fashionable, or you're not,' Gupta concedes phlegmatically, 'and *Goodness Gracious Me* was vastly more popular with the under-fifteens and the over-thirties. Ironically, and slightly gallingly – given that, in social terms at least, it was a very significant show – our generation thought it was all a bit tame.'

Caroline Aherne – acerbic as ever – describes the show as being 'like Bernard Manning, but without the timing'. This seems a little harsh, but there are certainly times when the *Goodness Gracious Me* team fall back a little too readily on old-fashioned notions of ethnic difference (the bossy-old-women routine Meera Syal and Nina Wadia do at the Ben Elton-hosted Golden Jubilee concert, for example, might have been lifted word for word from *It Ain't Half Hot Mum*).

When you consider what happened to some other graduates of *The Real McCoy*, however, the reality behind Gupta's strategy is shown in stark relief. The fine character actor Felix Dexter, for example, made an excellent BBC pilot show – 'executive-produced' by *The Fast Show*'s Paul Whitehouse and Charlie Higson – which somehow didn't get a series ('There wasn't really a champion for it,' Gupta remembers, 'and Felix was not quite powerful enough – or in the loop enough – to get it made') and Dexter had no option but to move on to the RSC.

It is only in this context of restrictions on black comedic career advancement limitation that the true significance of Ali G can fully be appreciated. When some black comedians (*Real McCoy* veteran Curtis Walker among them) complain about Sacha Baron Cohen's character 'appropriating black culture', a lot of people find such criticism outrageous.[215]

Don't these people realize – the counter-argument runs – that the whole point of Ali G is that he is not actually a black man, but a white man pretending to be black? Surely, then, every aspect of his success – right down to his timeless catch-phrase 'Is it because I is black?' – must be a comment on white culture's appropriation of black culture, rather than merely a reflection of it?

Well, yes and no. Consider how the tabloids might react if a comedian who actually *was* black recorded a sketch (as Baron Cohen does in *Ali G Indahouse*) in which he lasciviously kissed the Queen's finger, pronounced 'You is much fitter than you look on the coins', then – after accidentally removing Her Majesty's undergarments – commented approvingly on her 'shaven haven'. Yet because Baron Cohen is a non-black, public-school-educated Cambridge graduate, that somehow makes it OK.

It's not Sacha Baron Cohen's *fault* that he has more freedom to do what he wants than a black comedian would have. But it is his responsibility to remember this fact when he's making use of that ethnicity-based licence extension. Accordingly, he's at his best – in 1999's *Alternative Christmas Message*, in *Ali G Indahouse*'s tart satire of the futility of *Colors*-style gang conflict ('In the ghetto, washing non-colourfast synthetics at 60 degrees can cost you your life') – when he uses that power to say things no one else would dare to.

In the opening episode of 2003's *Ali G In Da USAiii*, for example, Baron Cohen outrages respectable US opinion by talking about 'the terrible events of 7/11'. On first hearing, this joke seems crassly obvious, but it also enables him to make a devastating satirical point in the space of five words. By mistaking the date of the attack on the World Trade Centre for the name of the grocery chain which pioneered late-night opening, he not only alludes to capitalism's capacity for making a fast buck out of unthinkable

---

[215.] Just as the BBC used to condescendingly reassure black people complaining about Alf Garnett's racism that it was 'meant to be' for their benefit.

horror, but also to the ever-tightening global grip of the US military –capitalist complex which was instrumental in provoking that murderous attack in the first place.

But when he takes the easy option – which, as the (at least in its own mind) sophisticated late-night audience of *The 11 O'Clock Show* gives way to a more explicitly hormonal teenage following, he all too often does – it's not just himself Baron Cohen lets down. Celebrating what he affects to satirize and satirizing what he affects to celebrate, he offers up a compendium of stereotypical images to a culture which is already overloaded with them, and in the process strips black culture of the one thing about it that really scares people: its actual blackness.[216]

A Savage Culture

A Savage Culture is the title of a book by Remi Kapo, first published in 1981. Kapo came to Britain – aged seven – from Lagos, Nigeria, in the year of the Queen's coronation, and as he reflects on his personal experiences at the hands of his colonial hosts, the grim prevailing mood is illuminated by occasional moments of optimism. 'Each generation', Kapo notes hopefully, 'is one more moment removed from the traditions that can hold a nation back.'

Beyond the numerous thought-provoking revelations which the book itself contains (not least the fact that the Smethwick Labour Club – later to be one of Frank Skinner's youthful haunts – was one of two West Midlands drinking dens to institute an explicit colour bar in the wake of the 1962 Commonwealth Immigrants Act), Kapo's title might have been designed for a society which extends all its available capacity for indulging the outrageousness of black culture to a comedian who is not actually black. Or, for

---

[216.] The court scene in *Ali G Indahouse* reveals that his real name is Alasdair Leslie Graham, so he's not even Asian, like everyone tends to think. (Hence David Brent's repeated imprecations to brown-skinned employees of Wernham Hogg to 'Do your Ali G' – a comic conceit which might be said to contain as much of the truth about race relations in Britain as any viewer can be expected to take in.)

that matter, looks for its most gleeful celebration of the essence of womanhood to a female comedy character who urinates standing up.

As Lily Savage – the partially reformed Birkenhead scrubber with a pompadour worthy of Marie Antoinette – teeters grandiosely across the stage of the Southend Cliffs Pavilion, her mascara does not just run, it flees.

The haul has not been short for Birkenhead-raised ex-social-worker Paul O'Grady. The stately progress of his imperious, cheese-wire-tongued creation from south-east London's least salubrious gay pubs to presenting *Top of the Pops*, sharing a regular coffee with Richard and Judy ('She's wearing nipple clamps under that C&A blouse') and opening Barry Grant's restaurant in *Brookside* has taken nigh on a decade. Yet Lily has not lost her edge in the process.

In the course of an extended stand-up set, she attains a level of scabrous piquancy unattainable in the bite-sized portions in which television usually serves her up. The voice is a nicotine rasp, the face – to borrow its owner's memorable phrase – looks 'like a ferret licking snot off a nettle'. Savage's world (like that of her closest peer, Jenny Eclair) is one in which piles constantly get stuck in gussets and children's faces might at any moment be disfigured by scalding Pop Tarts. But the filth and tragedy of everyday life find comic release through her heightened descriptive powers and baroque imagination. A verruca might be a verruca, or it might be 'a bit of chewing gum with a rosary bead stuck in it' – you can never quite be sure.

Savage does light and dark with equal facility. Her impression of *Coronation Street*'s Tracy Barlow is second to none, but her vision of the ageing process would depress Ingmar Bergman. Only the musical routines lack focus, and even they have their moments: 'It had to be you ... It had to be you ... Followed me round like some mangy hound/Like shit on a shoe.'

At the same time as sending up drag's – somewhat played out – notion of glamour by being more ruin than façade, Savage upholds its subversive tradition of making homosexual jokes acceptable to a non-gay audience. I'm not sure what a Southend crowd would make of Lily's very funny oral-sex routine ('. . . balls swinging against your chin like two used tea-bags') if it was delivered by a man who wasn't wearing a dress.

Perhaps O'Grady's most impressive *coup*, though, is to strip drag of its paradoxical anti-female bias. His act comes across not as a mockery of womanhood but rather as a genuine tribute to it. It is a measure of the extent of this achievement that his supporting act – Brenda Gilhooley's one-dimensional Page Three parody Gayle Tuesday – has the crowd laughing at her, and with her attitudes, not vice versa as she presumably intends.

It does say something about this country (though I'm not exactly sure what) that from Dame Edna Everage, to Les Dawson and Roy Barraclough's Dottie and Ada, to Lily Savage, it should still be easier for a man to build a career as a female comedy character than it is for a woman.

Female comedy performers who are actually female

There's nothing quite like the feeling you get in a room that contains more than one male comedian. The crackle of competing egos lights up the air like the aurora borealis. Rock stars, supermodels and Siamese Fighting Fish – all species celebrated for their inability to interact without natural rivalry escalating into outright violence – look on in appalled bewilderment.

The atmosphere which prevails in a draughty Groucho Club ante-room in the spring of 1999 is very different. Doon MacKichan and Sally Phillips, two thirds of the starring troika in *Smack the Pony* (the stylish and imaginative Channel 4 sketch show which returns for a second series with a slew of well-deserved awards, including an International Emmy, to its name), are waiting to have their photos taken. And the closest MacKichan and Phillips come to self-aggrandizement is to nervously ask the waitress for another croissant.

'The thing with us,' insists Phillips – previously best known as the mischievous motel receptionist in *I'm Alan Partridge* – 'is that we do an awful lot of guff, and then they save it in the edit.'

All three of the *Smack the Pony* principals are accomplished comedy writer–performers whose turn in the spotlight is long overdue, but after years of playing dignified second fiddle in unsuccessful TV pilots and male-dominated Edinburgh revue shows, being the centre of attention is plainly taking a bit of getting used to. 'Arriving at the Emmys,' Phillips says, savouring how grand this sounds, 'we were – well, I was going to say mobbed, but that would be an exaggeration of the foulest nature – *approached and greeted* by an enthusiastic group of Scandinavian documentary-makers.'

The Scandinavians were much taken with 'The Butterfly Song', one of the breezily lightweight (and often rather embarrassing) pop pastiches with which each programme ends, but it is the *Smack the Pony* team's deft timing and brilliantly economical characterizations that mark their work out from the sketch-show crowd.

'What's great', Phillips insists wryly, 'is we've all played the straight parts for years, so those are always done very well.'

It's almost as if the store of *gravitas* accumulated in years of poker-faced support play has given them a layer of extra comedic authority now that they're finally out on their own.

'We've probably learned more acting skills,' agrees *The Day Today* and *Beast* veteran MacKichan, 'because normally you're the only woman on a show with four or five blokes, so you sort of get used to doing whatever comes up. Also, a lot of the things we've had to do have been very thin, and we've had to make them better. It's great to be let loose on something bigger after years of people saying "I really liked that nurse you did" and thinking "Cheers, it was *two lines*".'

At this point, acerbic Lancastrian Fiona Allen – the third member of the triumvirate,[217] then best known outside *Smack the Pony* for an eventful stint on *Coronation Street* – makes her belated entrance. A spikier, more confident presence than her two colleagues (as anyone who saw her demurely put Frank Skinner to the sword on the Brummie motormouth's BBC1 chat show will have noticed), Allen wonders whether to bother with an excuse for her tardiness and settles on 'I overslept'.

The conversation turns to the proper means of dealing with the

---

[217.] And last to join, having stepped in as an eleventh-hour replacement when Amanda Holden decided more effective means of career advancement lay elsewhere.

men who take the sort of faintly demeaning minor roles in *Smack the Pony* that the show's stars always used to get.

'We cram them all into a tiny Winnebago afterwards,' MacKichan confesses, 'and say "Thanks *so* much, we're *really pleased* you could do it", in a very patronizing tone . . . well, *I* do.'

Allen chuckles admiringly: 'You do it really well, too.'

This may sound a little stringent, but with the balance of power between men and women as it is in the world of comedy – and after years of striving to do their best with 'the excuses for female characters some male comedy writers come up with' – revenge is a dish best served whenever you can get it.

'Do you like the guys in the show?' MacKichan asks guilelessly.

I can't remember much about them.

'Great!' Allen smacks a fist into her palm in celebration.

'They've got their own show now,' MacKichan continues. I assume she is joking. 'No, really,' she insists, 'they've been offered a commission.'[218]

Don't they find that a little bit outrageous?

'It is sort of hilarious,' says MacKichan. 'You spend fucking years being a comedy whore and then . . . No . . . *we love them.*'

It takes about eleven minutes of conversation to realize that all that stuff at the start of this section about female comedians not being as rivalrous as their male counterparts is in fact patronizing rubbish. MacKichan is actually the most competitive person I have ever met. This suspicion is confirmed on an amusingly grand stage a few years later when – drafted in as a last-minute replacement on 2003's celebrity *Fame Academy* – MacKichan at one point physically shoves Ulrika Jonsson (no pushover herself when it comes to claiming centre stage) out of the way in a bid to claim the spotlight for herself.

It's not that the comedian's traditional competitive edge isn't there in the *Smack the Pony* context, just that it's wrapped up in a layer of supportive muslin. A case in point is MacKichan and Allen's collective look of anguished solidarity – barely masking a mutual *frisson* of inner delight – when it comes up in conversation that Sally

---

[218.] She needn't have worried. A short period of time after its eventual broadcast, no one can remember what this show was called.

Phillips got her start in showbiz taking tickets for former boyfriend Richard Herring's early-nineties Edinburgh shows.

'Once Richard and I split up, my career really took off,' Phillips insists gamely. 'Up until then, people didn't want to employ me because I was just his girlfriend.' Her self-penned mid-nineties anti-Herring revenge monologue as Ophelia in Arthur Smith's *Hamlet* certainly leaves no one in any doubt as to the somewhat unreconstructed attitudes of her former beau (not that anyone who had sat through any of his plays would have been in all that much doubt about them anyway).

'They always referred to me as "an actress",' says MacKichan of her former *On The Hour* and *The Day Today* colleagues, 'and they still do. There's nothing I could do that would convince them I was a comic – well, I don't think I *am*, but "a comedienne" or "a writer–performer" would be nice. Even if I exclusively write and perform comedy for the rest of my life, I will always be an actress to them.'

Traditionally in male-dominated sketch shows (at least from *Not the Nine O'Clock News* onwards) female performers seem to have been there as much for the possibility that they might be persuaded to take their clothes off as for any other reason. Not that male comedians have been reluctant to show their bodies themselves. Indeed, some of them – Steve Coogan, Charlie Higson and Armstrong and Miller being names that spring to mind – insist on appearing naked on our TV screens as often as possible, as if daring the women of the world not to find them attractive.

Without lapsing into the realms of outright personal abuse, it would probably be fair to say that none of the above individuals were gifted by nature with the looks of the born romantic lead. That's probably half the reason why they became comedians in the first place. (In this connection, it is worth remembering the boast of the great eighteenth-century wit and radical gadabout John Wilkes, who once proclaimed that – insofar as his extensive relations with the opposite sex were concerned – 'it took him about half an hour to talk away his face'.)

The women from *Smack the Pony*, on the other hand – having had to be able to scratch a living in the actress mines when the comedy-revue support roles dried up – necessarily conform to a higher standard of conventional attractiveness. It's in this context that the show's somewhat mystifying emphasis on broad physical comedy – especially the kind which will coincidentally allow its stars to confirm their position in the upper echelons of feminine comeliness – can best be understood. This is one competition with their male peers which Phillips, MacKichan and Allen (and oddly under-credited fourth Pony, Sarah Alexander) cannot help but win.

Epilogue: *Spaced* – the final frontier

In early 2000, a woman in her early thirties employed in the luxurious world of the London media (the audience demographic at which *Smack the Pony* targets itself with an almost clinical single-mindedness) observes over dinner that while she's never previously understood what it was that made men want to go into work quoting lines from the previous night's TV comedy shows before, for the first time in her life, *Smack the Pony* has opened that particular door to her. She announces this as if it's an entirely good thing. But is it?

There's no denying that one feature of gender equalization – as it is experienced in the 1990s – is increasing numbers of women behaving in those particular sorts of irritating, self-indulgent ways that only men used to get away with. There is an upside, however. The next phase in the ongoing process of female liberation described in chapter 7 (from the suffragette and the king's horse to Jo Brand disparaging Malcolm Hardee's sexual prowess on the cover of the latter's autobiography) is the colonization of cultural enjoyments that were once almost exclusively male preserves.

It begins – as do so many positive social trends – in the world of pop, where the late eighties see an increasingly high proportion of women in the concert audiences for sweet-natured Glaswegian underground rock band Teenage Fanclub. It culminates in the beguiling gender-neutral geekery of Simon Pegg and Jessica Stevenson's *Spaced*, a show whose distinctive and sometimes almost overwhelming visual style perfectly captures the disorientation of a world in which all doors seem to be open.

(Sadly, the inspirational gender-neutrality of the whole *Spaced*

phenomenon is about to be horribly undermined by the fact that –
at the time of writing – only Pegg was available for interview.)

'LWT [who co-produced the show with the Paramount Comedy
Channel for Channel 4] were desperate for something a bit young,'
Pegg explains, 'so they left us alone with absolutely no interference.
I look back and I'm amazed the whole thing got through in as pure
a form as it did. I remember a rehearsed reading in front of some
executives . . .' He pauses, as if the memory is almost too painful.
'But it was at that time just before *The League of Gentlemen* took
off, when everyone was so desperate to find the next wave that if
anything came along which seemed remotely fresh, they were all
going "Yes, let's do that".'

Were Pegg and Stevenson (who were going out together when
they started writing *Spaced*, but aren't at the time of writing) aware
as they embarked upon it what an inspiring vision of sexual equality
their working relationship would offer?

'That's exactly what we wanted,' says Pegg, whose comedy
beginnings were in the 'fascistically PC' surroundings of Bristol
University in the very late eighties.[219] 'It was very collaborative,' he
says of their co-writing methodology, 'more like a conversation than
working, really.

'We wanted to come up with something that was very much our
own,' he remembers, 'to replicate that feeling of identification, of
watching a show and thinking, This is not for people who are older
than I am, it's for *me* . . . I remember going to see *ET* when I was
twelve,' he continues nostalgically, 'and there's a scene when they're
trick or treating, and ET sees a kid dressed as Yoda, and John
Williams drops a bit of *The Empire Strikes Back* into the soundtrack,
and I remember just feeling such a connection with the film at that
moment.'

If the adolescent Pegg seems at this point to have confused artistic
success with the calculated (and self-congratulatory) fostering of
brand loyalty, he would not be the last of his generation to do so.

[219.] A later, less ideologically rigorous comedy training ground – replacing
Charlie Creed-Miles as genial layabout boyfriend to Lynda Bellingham's
daughter Julia Sawalha in the defiantly above-average mid-nineties ITV
sitcom *Faith in the Future* – was probably just as significant.

'That's why *Spaced* is so heavily and quietly referential,' he maintains, still in *Dawson's Creek* mode, 'because there *is* something really gratifying about being spoken to personally by a film or TV programme ... When, say, *The Young Ones* came out, there was this furious railing against Margaret Thatcher and all that she stood for, whereas the most dramatic feature of our times seemed to be the *lack* of any kind of incendiary political situation, the death of opposition, and the question of how to make the best of this kind of extension to your childhood afforded by the fact that no one has been encouraged to get married and have children and perpetuate the capitalist hierarchy.' [Historical note: this was before the advent of *Heat* magazine, when getting married, having children and perpetuating the capitalist hierarchy returned to the top of the agenda, smartish.] Presumably it's in such carefree times that cultural manifestations like sci-fi and comics, which connect directly – and in the most childlike way – to the imagination, seem especially appropriate. Hence the *modus operandi* of *Spaced* as North London's very own 'cross between *Northern Exposure* and *The X-Files*'.

Director of photography Andy Hollis confirms that 'It was almost like a running competition between Simon and Jessica and Edgar Wright, the director, to see how many TV or film spoof scenes they could get into each episode'. If *Spaced* had been nothing more than a movie buff's love-in, there wouldn't have been much point to it. But beyond its celebration of the cultural ephemera so beloved of easy-living twenty-, thirty-, forty- and fiftysomethings, the two series of *Spaced* also add up to a funny and strangely moving study of what it means to be – in Pegg's words – 'living in a strange place and never quite feeling at home there'.

That's not strange just in terms of physical or geographical reality (though the house they're living in *is* quite strange). Or even in terms of the cultural alienation so often experienced by ex-students moving to London after going to college.[220] But rather, 'strange' in the very modern sense, wherein 'no matter how close to

---

[220.] After all, as Pegg explains, the show's central characters are not exactly newcomers to the delights or otherwise of the capital: 'Tim was born just down the road from where the house is in Highgate, and Daisy comes from South London.'

home you are, you can still feel disenfranchised and disconnected'.

This sense of disconnection is hammered home by the tirelessly zappy direction of Edgar Wright (with whom Pegg and Stevenson had worked together previously, some years before, on a 'very dark' Paramount Comedy Channel series called *Asylum* which, the former insists, 'was the natural precursor to *Spaced*'). Beyond the show's seemingly overriding concern with surface, with visual surprises and skate-ramp jumpcuts, there lies a deeper feeling of cultural shock.

It would not be reading between the lines too much (well, I don't *think* it would) to see that this underlying sense of shock stems from the break-up of those old family and social structures so affectingly and unsentimentally eulogized in *The Royle Family*. In that show (also, lest we forget, the product of a harmonious writerly blend of yin and yang) Jessica Stevenson has a poignant recurring role as a socially unsuccessful next-door neighbour – who, while officially struggling with her weight, never misses an opportunity to truffle around in search of leftovers.

Popping next door for a cup of sugar (or, more likely in this case, a stray fondant fancy) is one thing, but an entirely new social infrastructure is rather harder to come by. The replacement of old bonds of class and family with the less permanent ties of friendship, fun and shared cultural affinities for, well, shows like *Spaced* was always going to be an ambitious project. It's rather like removing a load-bearing wall and replacing it with a pile of attractively decorated beer crates.

As the century turns, *Spaced*'s eternal teen dreamworld, free of sexual or racial prejudice (OK, there aren't any actual black people in the show, but if there were, their characters would probably be just as fully rounded as everyone else's, and – unlike the haunted cyphers of *Man About the House* – no one would think they had no right to be there), looks less and less like becoming a reality. Amid such grim real-life events as the murders of Stephen Lawrence and Damilola Taylor, the refuge of fantasy becomes ever more alluring.[221]

[221.] Perhaps this also explains the otherwise mystifying late 1990s/early 2000s vogue for full-grown adults – apparently in command of their mental faculties – reading children's books about posh kids learning to become wizards.

'What amazes me', marvels Andy Hollis, 'is that people go to the house. Every time the people who live there look out of the window, they've got all these *Spaced* fans standing in the garden, having their photo taken.'

20
Families at War

The Reeves and Mortimer despot/democrat
trajectory reaches its terrifying conclusion

*'We were struggling with the skills the contestants had. Two hours
before a show, we'd be saying "Fuck it, he's going to have to sniff
kettles"'*

Bob Mortimer

'Now our work is done, we shall return to the tundra'
Vic Reeves

A BBC TV studio resounds with the unmistakable sound of a
human being in terrible pain. This anguished cry does not come
from the audience, who have sat patiently for three week-night
hours through a series of lengthy weekend game-show set-ups with
only the services of an above-average warm-up man[222] for distraction. Neither does it come from the floor manager, mumbling officiously into his earpiece. Nor from the contestants: two competing
families who, among a series of other privations, have just been
obliged to introduce themselves in song, wallpaper at speed and
dance energetically on rollerskates before eating a large plate of fish
and chips (and all this to impress a 'jury' comprising six pairs of
twins).

.The human being who is suffering so horribly is the star of the
show. Vic Reeves is suspended approximately thirty feet above

---

[222.] Ross Noble.

the stage in an uncomfortable-looking harness. He is dressed in a marvellously sinister black spider costume, incorporating a cannibalized flying helmet and legs that hang as limp as the lettuce in one of Franz Kafka's recurring salad-based nightmares. Beneath him, inside a huge structure – futuristically dubbed 'The Cubiscus' – minions busy themselves setting up a selection of unappealing-looking prizes on plinths. Unfortunately, they have not busied themselves quite enough to stop Vic's harness from cutting into him in all sorts of places a man would rather not be cut into.

'If we can't go now,' he pleads, 'can you please let me down for a minute?' But the camera is an unforgiving dominatrix and Vic is left dangling for several minutes more until the night's climax finally creaks into motion. Manœuvred by the winning family – false legs spinning absurdly beneath him as he emits strangled but triumphant cries of 'I am the spider' – Vic is winched perilously up and down, struggling heroically to procure prizes and propel them down a shute. His accomplice, Bob Mortimer, supplies musical accompaniment at the keyboard, wearing a strange and terrifying hat.

As a general rule, nothing robs top TV entertainment of its magic like being there when it's recorded, but in this case, a sense of small-screen history in the making is hard to shake off. The programme being filmed is called *Families at War* and, for Reeves and Mortimer, it marks a long overdue emergence from the shelter of Friday-night cultdom into the harsh glare of the Saturday-evening prime-time spotlight. For the British people at large, it offers a precious opportunity to heal the psychic wounds inflicted on the national psyche by the advent of the televised Lottery draw.

Watching strangers win huge sums of money they have done nothing to earn has not been good for us. Consider such dubious Lottery-inspired TV formats as Cilla Black's *Moment Of Truth*[223] – wherein one member of a family trains for a week to perform a complex and pointless task in the hope of winning an improbably lavish series of prizes for their avaricious kin. (If one of the parents loses, mum and dad divorce; if a child loses, they're slammed into care.) Even less edifying is Carol Vorderman's *Better Homes*,

---

[223.] Updated by the BBC in the summer of 2003 as Ian Wright's aptly titled *I'd Do Anything*.

wherein two rival sets of neighbours get décor improvements done by a team of experts (they don't even have to help with the work themselves) and whichever is deemed to have added more to the value of their house wins an extra fifty grand (the losing family is torn to pieces by a pack of wild dogs).

Not only do these disturbing small-screen spectacles sow envy and dissension within the homes and communities of Britain, they also testify to a televisual culture of greed run riot. The time is out of joint and – not for the first time – Vic and Bob are here to put it right. Thus the plan for *Families at War* is that it should hark back to a healthier era of paltry BBC prizes and honest family fun: a time before the TV schedules became an unfenced adventure-playground for corporate sponsors. A time when the lure for prospective game-show contestants was not the prospect of winning life-altering sums of money, but the chance to make fools of themselves in front of millions of people.

'We've had a bloke who plays snooker in the pitch dark,' Bob enthuses, during a quick break in rehearsals, 'and a nineteen-year-old who has to dance with a pig that's got the face of Chris Tarrant.'

'Last week's winners walked away with a Hoover and a footspa,' Vic adds proudly, 'and I think the Hoover might have been broken.'

The additional nasal foundation underpinning Vic's familiar north-eastern twang suggests that he is battling the flu (Bob helpfully points towards a confirmatory ruff of white tissue fragments forming across the shoulders of Vic's characteristically tasteful jumper), but he is soon to catch a cold of a very different kind.

The thinking behind *Families at War* is presumably that by isolating and emphasizing the light-entertainment dynamic which has always been integral to Vic and Bob's career, the show will blast them through the eight-figure audience pain barrier and into Morecambe and Wise hyper-space. More excitingly even than that, *Families at War* promises to be the glorious final stage in the revolutionary process of democratization which can be traced back to the very beginnings of Reeves and Mortimer's TV career.

Where *Vic Reeves Big Night Out* reduced celebrity to a physical substance, *Shooting Stars* enabled them to conduct their experiments on human guinea pigs. Now, by plucking regular folk off the street and inducting them into the same surreal fraternity, they could seize the means of production and overturn the established social order once and for all.

Vic and Bob even go so far as to imagine themselves disappearing in a puff of smoke at the end of the series, with a grandiose declaration of 'Now our work is done, we shall return to the tundra'. Unfortunately for them (but fortunately for us, as we would have missed them if they *had* returned to the tundra), this is not quite how things turn out.

The *Families at War* pilot, broadcast on August Bank Holiday in 1998, contains a deliciously mischievous outside-broadcast segment, in which the contestants are introduced by means of Vic and Bob breaking into their houses and deriding their interior décor. [Historical note: at this point – before *Ground Force, Changing Rooms* and Trinny and Susannah have had time to complete the final demolition of the old-fashioned notion of personal space – the concept of a celebrity home invasion still generates a genuine *frisson*.][224]

The sight of Vic inspecting a hapless teenage girl's collection of Leonardo DiCaprio posters will live long in the memory. 'A picture of a boy!' Reeves expostulates, moving on to the next image with the bemusedly malevolent expression of one of the extra-terrestrial invaders in *Mars Attacks!* '. . . But it's the *same* boy.' And the prospect of these two very strange men picking through the sock-drawers and private possessions of the nation's adolescents is way beyond delightful.

Unfortunately, by the time the actual series gets on to the screen (six months or so later), the purity of the original vision has been somewhat compromised. Whether the Reeves and Mortimer housebreaking segment was deemed too disturbing for tea-time viewing, or the men in question simply couldn't be bothered doing the extra filming (Bob's sheepish admission that 'It was just a bit too much trouble to be honest' eventually confirms the latter theory), the replacement introductory device – a song wherein contestants introduce themselves by making a fearful hash of lines Vic and Bob have written for them – turns out to be a poor substitute.

A rather limited public talent pool adds to the impression that

---

[224.] Just as it did in Barry Humphries's last great subversive TV *coup, Dame Edna's Neighbourhood Watch.*

this time perhaps the democratizing impulse has run ahead of itself.

'We were struggling with the skills the contestants had,' Bob admits later. 'Two hours before a show, we'd be saying "Fuck it, he's going to have to sniff kettles".'

There are still some great moments, like the housewife who gives an unerringly well-modulated performance of Celine Dion's theme-song to *Titanic*, breaking off every few bars to emit a piercing bark. As if this display is not proof enough of her desire to entertain, Bob subjects the poor woman's barking ability to further stringent investigation by making her yelp behind a screen with a series of actual dogs, with an international show judge and breeder of champion beagles there to make the call as to which noise is of human origin.

If this sort of thing had been explicitly designed as a despotic antidote to the phoney democratization of the docusoap (and such an openly satirical intention is the last thing Vic or Bob would own up to), it could hardly have done a better job. Far from adding to the endless stream of professional 'characters' turned up by programmes like *Driving School* and *Airport*, the intention behind *Families at War* seems to be to reassert the primacy of the gifted amateur. But there is a contradiction here that is too big to ignore.

One of the many strange things about Reeves and Mortimer's comedy is that – like many of anarchism's most successful and enduring applications – it relies on a rigidly hierarchical command structure. Not so much within the duo's own dynamic – where power relations are constantly and cleverly shifted around, with Vic the comic supremo one minute and Bob the real funnyman the next – as in their relations with the outside world.

It's significant that, just as with *Shooting Stars* – the celebrity game show whose success first brought them to an audience wider than the one Bob affectionately refers to as 'the two million diehards who like to watch us arsing about' – the most uncomfortable moments at the recording of *Families at War* are caused by those people who don't know when to shut up and let the experts get on with it. In this case, it's a painfully unamusing Glaswegian Elvis impersonator; on *Shooting Stars*, it was anyone who tried to be funny.

The increasingly self-congratulatory atmosphere of the latter

show is one reason Vic and Bob decide – for the moment at least
– to make the third series the last. 'When everyone gets the joke,'
Vic explains, 'you have to knock it on the head.'[225] Hence, presumably, the bold step out into the real world beyond the closeted
enclave of TV celebrity. And yet, one of the main reasons *Families
at War* doesn't ultimately work is that it's a celebration of the Corin-
thian spirit whose underlying message is all about the value of
professionalism.

There's nothing quite like watching people off the street do Vic
and Bob's lines really badly to make you yearn to see someone with
at least a City and Guilds qualification in showbiz have a go. Even
Ulrika Jonsson (by this time presenting the resonantly titled *National
Lottery Dreamworld*) would have brought a bit of additional polish
to the proceedings. In fact, as badly received as it was at the time, the
controversial Swede's bizarre and intermittently gruesome one-off
Reeves-and-Mortimer-scripted starring vehicle *It's Ulrika* has begun
to take on an increasingly mythic air as the years have passed since
its initial broadcast.

Sitting in their management offices on Soho Square towards the
end of 1999, Vic and Bob are plainly sensible of the fact that their
great leap forward didn't take them quite as far as they'd imagined
it would.

'We'd start off with a million viewers at half five, and end up
with six and a half million, but get a viewing figure of three,' Bob
reflects ruefully.

'People still stop us in the street and say "I'm a big fan of *Shooting
Stars*",' adds Vic with a rather poignant expression, 'but I don't
think anyone's ever stopped us to say they're a big fan of *Families
at War* – maybe a little kid asking questions about the spider.'

'It's amazing how many people can't scan, let alone sing,' a
disillusioned Mortimer observes of the disastrous opening song segment, 'because very few of them could, could they?'

---

225. While *Shooting Stars*'s eventual return in 2001 is largely a pragmatic
response to the less than overwhelming success of *Families at War* and,
later, *Randall and Hopkirk (Deceased)*, the fourth and fifth series seem much
fresher than might have been anticipated, if only because it's fun to watch
Vic and Bob's somewhat bemused response to the cultural climate they
have done so much to shape.

Perhaps the other problem was (I gently interject) that there *was* an actual war going on . . .

'You mean', comes the puzzled response, 'that we really *did* pit them against each other too much?'

No, an actual war in Bosnia.

While it would be fair to say that Vic and Bob's comedy has not traditionally been shaped by the course of international events, the conflict in the former Yugoslavia – especially the bombing of Sarajevo, which coincided rather unhappily with the series's opening episodes – did make *Families at War*'s jokey martial trappings (searchlights, Blitz paraphernalia, Alice Beer acting the wartime adjutant) look a bit shabby. If only the show's title had been 'Families in Vague Competition' or 'Families Struggling for the Ascendancy, Although It Doesn't Really Matter Who Wins', there wouldn't have been such a problem.[226]

'It's difficult with the public, too,' admits Vic, 'because it's harder to be cheeky with them in a friendly way.' For all Bob's assurances that his comedy partner has 'always had that Bruce Forsyth thing going', the evidence he cites of Vic's instinctive rapport with contestants (telling one bewildered woman she has 'Titian hair', for example) seems more likely to confirm his fears than assuage them.

Offscreen, happily, things pan out a good deal more smoothly. 'We went back to the hotels with the families after the shows,' Vic remembers. 'They presumably think we're "stars" [he pronounces the word with the sort of at-arm's-length disdain with which someone doing community service might pick up a used nappy off the motorway hard-shoulder], but when you go out drinking till the early hours, everyone realizes they're all the same.[227] It just reminds you of being back working in foundries and stuff, and it's strange, because we've been out of that world for so long.' He turns to Bob: 'When we were out drinking with that Geordie family, I remember you saying "the punchline to every joke is 'cock'".'

Bob joins in, fondly, '. . . And he had his *fucking cock out*!'

[226.] The title takes on a further unfortunate new resonance in the light of the public break-up of Vic's marriage, and his ensuing trial by tabloid.

[227.] Obviously you'd have to track down the contestants to be sure they felt the same way.

Presumably what gave Vic and Bob's reacquaintance with their erstwhile socio-geographic peer group its wistful, nostalgic quality was the fact that this is not their peer group any more. When they're talking about these encounters, it's almost as if they're pleased that despite being cut off from their origins by virtue of aesthetic and commercial success, they can still be in a room with people who come from the same place they used to, and not be hated.[228] A howl of protest might be expected at this outrageous suggestion, but Vic just says 'Yes'.

Writing about 1872's celebrated Whistler libel trial (in which the flamboyant artist and wit sued the critic John Ruskin for being rude about a painting he'd done of his mother), D. B. Wyndham Lewis describes what he calls 'the Whistler apparition'. The flamboyant Victorian would arrive at court each day to the delighted consternation of the assembled crowds – 'foppishly-costumed, higher hatted than the average, flaunting a tall cane, an eyeglass and the famous white lock[229] [of hair – Whistler wore his forelock in the style later modelled by infamous seventies TV family *The Mallens*], emitting at intervals the strident, famous and feared "Ha Ha"'. In the early years of his fame, Vic Reeves used to cultivate just the same kind of strikingly individual demeanour.

Even as far back as the late 1970s, when Vic was out earning an honest crust with the people he now entertains for a living, he used to wear a leather jacket which – rather than the customary 'Motorhead' or 'AC/DC' – bore the legend 'Debussy', spelt out in silver studs. This desire to set himself apart from the crowd was the hallmark of the late-nineteenth-century dandy. But by the time Vic's fame was at its height, exactly a century later, the narcissism of the few was becoming the indulgence of the many.

---

228. There's a grim scene in the ITV Frank Skinner documentary that accompanies the release of his (unusually well-written) autobiography in 2002 where Frank goes back to his old haunts – the Smethwick British Legion among them – and the ghosts he used to haunt them with bemoan the fact that he is no longer an alcoholic before wondering why he doesn't drop in more often.

229. Whether it was Oscar Wilde or Quentin Crisp who said that 'for the truly exotic, normality is the one foreign land to which your passport has no visa', the point still holds good.

In this context, the Reeves and Mortimer despot/democrat trajectory has another twist to it. In combining the Roundhead's levelling urge with the Cavalier's hierarchical reflex, Vic Reeves's comedic universe has both prefigured and actively influenced the strange and paradoxical atmosphere of celebrity-fixated egalitarianism which currently prevails throughout huge swathes of our national culture. And in the same way that *Vic Reeves Big Night Out* begat *Noel's House Party*, whose 'Gotcha Oscar' (where a celebrity – or Gary Bushell if no celebrity was available – would be surprised in their own home by a camera behind their own TV screen) would in its turn become the template for the bulk of British light-entertainment scheduling in the early twenty-first century, *Families at War*'s influence also proves to be out of all proportion to its ratings.

Not only does it trigger a whole new wave of Saturday-night shows in which people less likely than Vic and Bob to scare a wider audience (Ant and Dec, say, or Ian Wright) supervise groups of friends competing with each other in ways which are not entirely based on material gain. It also – in demonstrating the general public's chronic lack of singing and dancing ability – fuels the craving for old-fashioned performance skills upon which the triumphant rebirth of the TV talent show (in the merciless guise of *Popstars* and *Pop Idol*)[230] will be predicated.

Perhaps most importantly of all, in moving out of their natural habitat and into the mainstream netherworld of BBC1, Vic and Bob leave a vacuum behind them. The best of those who rush to fill it (The League of Gentlemen, Johnny Vegas, Ricky Gervais) will deftly twist the Reeves and Mortimer legacy into strange and compelling new shapes.

[230.] The secret of the success of the first series of *Popstars* is the judges' brutal assessments of those who don't measure up (even if it is to standards set by Simon Cowell and Pete Waterman . . .). The novelty at this stage in the UK's cultural history of someone being told they aren't good enough at something to succeed at it is strangely exhilarating. In a last-ditch defence of the mediocrity which is so dear to it, *Heat* magazine tries to make stars of the worst contestants, and one of them subsequently gets to do a pizza advert.

21
The League of Gentlemen
Three character actors no longer in search of
an author

'What we do is comedy, but we're not stand-ups . . . Stand-ups are
all about personality, and I don't think any of us have that'

Reece Shearsmith

'I prefer to sleep with the light on: it's in the darkness that I see the
boy's face'

Mark Gatiss as a Peak District cavern tour guide,
haunted by awful memories

The Pleasance Theatre courtyard is the hub of the Edinburgh Festival's endlessly rotating wheel of fortune. For one month each year,
its cobbles seethe with up-and-coming comedians, striving to
impress each other with their disdain for the blatant career moves
of their peers. In August 1996, an unlikely looking quartet are
sighted on the fringes of this showbiz bear-pit, exuding – not physically, just in their urgent and slightly paranoid demeanour – the
stench of desperation which is so often the precursor to true artistic
excellence.

The League of Gentlemen live up to their name (taken from the
superior 1960 British heist comedy, starring Jack Hawkins as the
leader of a ring of ex-army bank robbers) by maintaining a clannish
and slightly defensive presence. Comedy pariah dogs, clutching
their own scruffy self-penned fanzine for moral support, their
onstage garb of dinner suits and Brylcreemed 1940s hair gives them

the heroically unfashionable air of a pre-*Beyond The Fringe* Oxbridge revue. And yet something undeniably modern leaks out from their cuffs and their collars.

Having announced each other with verbose, *Shooting Stars*-style introductions, the three of the four League members who actually make it on to the stage waste no time in creating their own compellingly grotesque world of sinister village shopkeepers and haunted tour guides. Their dark brand of homespun Gothic represents a triumph of imaginative morbidity over budgetary restriction – one effective, if painful, ruse being to stretch Sellotape across the bases of their noses to create a series of alarmingly porcine facial expressions. The League appear to be at least as happy playing women as men, and their show as a whole bears eloquent testimony to the positive impact of sexual frustration on creativity.

Just a couple of months after shutting up shop at the end of the Edinburgh Festival, they already have a polished and perverse new show in residence at Maida Vale's cosy Canal Café. By this stage, The League of Gentlemen already look ready for a much wider audience: the only possible reason for them not yet having their own series on Radio 4 is that the corporation fears they might show everyone else – except Harry Hill and John Shuttleworth – up.

The big problem with sketch comedy is that it can often be a means for resting thespians to prove that scriptwriting will never really be an option for them (and for exhibitionist scriptwriters to find out why they'll never see their names in lights). But The League's writing is crisp, clever and full of detail, and the ensemble's performance faction of Mark Gatiss, Steve Pemberton and Reece Shearsmith (fourth member Jeremy Dyson maintains a shadowy presence in the wings) are all excellent actors, capable of twisting vaguely recognizable situations into ever more bizarre shapes, until the original familiarity itself seems outlandish.

Most of their sketches begin with an extreme premise and then spiral with horrifying rapidity towards a baroque and often violent climax. Walk out of one of their shows quoting the best lines and you're liable to get yourself in trouble. 'Semen is such a persistent stain.' That's a good one. Or how about 'I prefer to sleep with the light on: it's in the darkness that I see the boy's face'?

The League of Gentlemen are not the first comic performers to derive inspiration from raw material that seems more the stuff of nightmares than conventional light entertainment. (In fact, doing this makes them part of a great British tradition, stretching back from Reeves and Mortimer to Monty Python and Spike Milligan before them.) They just take the idea further than anyone else has.

Imagine an hour-long *Fast Show* special, co-written by Alfred Hitchcock and the Marquis de Sade, and you have a visitor's passport to their strange kingdom. It's a place where Mike Leigh rubs shoulders with Christopher Lee and the resulting spark ignites the fuel vapour of a passing charabanc, bringing the earthly existences of a party of holidaying pensioners to an unexpectedly spectacular conclusion.

For men preoccupied with loneliness, guilt, sexual obsession and violent death, Gatiss, Shearsmith, Pemberton and Jeremy 'Ringo' Dyson have a very mild-mannered look about them (far from being raised in caves by sadistic newsagents, all four come from what Pemberton calls 'similar ordinary northern backgrounds': a quick survey of parental occupations throws up a secretary, an accountant, a car salesman and a relationship counsellor), although – as any occasional reader of serial-killer biographies will know – it's the quiet ones you've got to watch.

Classic League characters like Mr Denton (the crazed masturbation-obsessed toad-fancier, hell-bent on forcing his hapless houseguests to drink their own urine), or the dour cavern tour guide who points out amusingly shaped rock formations while struggling with visions of a dying child, attest to a sensibility that goes way beyond twisted. If The League of Gentlemen were only interested in shocking people, their work would not be nearly so entertaining. But even their most grotesque creations – Pemberton's ghoulishly predatory German exchange teacher Herr Lipp springs to mind – have a hard core of humanity that makes their desperation all the more affecting.

It comes as no surprise to discover that the quartet possess a hefty video archive of *Cutting Edge*-type TV documentaries from which to cull inspirational instances of human fallibility. Other influences range from Hammer Horror to the work of Alan Bennett – 'Which is horrific in its own way,' Pemberton explains, as the quartet gather slightly nervously round a tape recorder at the PBJ office in the autumn of 1997, 'but it's the horror of embarrassment and awkardness rather than the gothic variety.'

Would it be fair to say that The League of Gentlemen's aim is to unite the horror of social embarrassment with actual physical horror?

'I suppose so,' Shearsmith nods doubtfully.

'*Rising Damp* is the sitcom version of *10 Rillington Place*,' adds Gatiss, showing an alarming familiarity with the venue of one of the most notorious British murders. It's appropriate that he should mention *Rising Damp*, though, as The League's ability to wring laughs from the mangle of human desperation is unparalleled since the hilariously grim seventies sitcom heyday of Rigsby, *Steptoe & Son* and Basil Fawlty.

Any group of performers who can excite public shows of admiration from both Chris Morris and Ronnie Corbett (a man who, as his earlier advocacy of the Harry Hill live experience confirms, has his finger placed determinedly on the pulse of British comedy) must be doing something right. Perhaps because they are cursed with the social stigma of having met at drama school (with the exception of Dyson, who was sucked into the nightmare world of their Dickensian-sounding actors' training institute, Bretton Hall, from nearby Leeds University, where he was innocently studying philosophy), the respect of their comedic peers clearly matters to The League of Gentlemen.

While they're obviously delighted to have walked off with the Perrier Award on returning to Edinburgh in the summer of 1997, another less glitzy accolade seems to mean more to them.

'At last year's festival,' Gatiss remembers, 'I went up to Graham Fellows [a.k.a. John Shuttleworth] and told him that I loved him.[231] Twelve months later, I told him again, and this time he replied!'

So do The League now feel like part of the British comedy establishment?

An earnest shaking of heads ensues.

'What we do *is* comedy,' Shearsmith explains, 'but we're not stand-ups. We never appear as ourselves. Stand-ups are all about

---

[231.] Shuttleworth's uncanny ear for macabre local detail – such as day trips to 'the plague village of Eyam' – is clearly a major influence on The League.

personality,' he allows himself a strangely bitter smile, 'and I don't think any of us have that.'

The League have dined on more than their fair share of humble pie over the years, and for the next eighteen months or so there still won't be much else on the menu. Nurtured with exemplary patience by their far-sighted management company, they opt – albeit somewhat reluctantly – not to cash in on their Perrier Award. (When she first signed them up, after the 1996 Edinburgh Festival, Caroline Chignell warned them they 'wouldn't earn any money for two years', and she proves as good as her word.) Instead, they continue to develop their ideas for radio and in small venues like the Canal Café.

'We were all aware that there was a kind of vision at the heart of the whole thing,' Chiggy remembers, 'but no real idea of how it was going to be realized, and it seemed to me that so long as that was the case, it would be a grave mistake to go in and do an approximate TV version too quickly, because it might have been *terrible*. What primarily interested me about what The League were doing,' she continues, 'was the incredible strength of the perform-ances – they were scary and weird and done with incredible convic-tion and no apology. And it was a question of finding a way to contain them; to make sure they didn't become hammy.'

When The League of Gentlemen made their broadcast début on Radio 4 in November 1997, the numerous different narrative strands are loosely bound together within a single setting – the fictional northern town of Spent – which at this stage feels more like a plot device than an actual place. However, by the time the TV series finally hits the screen in early 1999, The League's scary fictional burgh (now renamed Royston Vasey in honour of dirty-mouthed muse Roy 'Chubby' Brown, who eventually makes a mem-orable cameo appearance as the mayor) is no longer just a means of linking together disparate sketches: it has come, unnervingly, to life.

To understand the extent of this achievement, it's worth con-sidering two of The League's televisual precursors, only one of which actually reached the screen. Steve Coogan's 1995 *Coogan's Run* located its variable sextet of characterizations – a pub singer, a salesman, a handyman, a quiz fanatic and an obsessive museum curator, as well as the sacred Calfs – in the fictional northern town of Ottle. While the idea was a good one and there were some great moments (many of them involving evil salesman Gareth Cheeseman, who with the benefit of hindsight looks like a distant ancestor of Ricky Gervais's David Brent),[232] the whole thing didn't hang together quite as well as it might have.

The use of different writers for separate episodes prevented the series from establishing a consistent overall tone, and the sight of Coogan occasionally drifting across the background in another guise wasn't enough to generate the requisite sense of community. In retrospect, the series looks like a kind of dry run for *The League of Gentlemen* as it finally appears on BBC2, in all its completed magnificence. The same might also be said, with a small stretch of the imagination, for the best show Reeves and Mortimer never made.

Asked about their future plans in 1996, Vic and Bob insist: 'We desperately want to do a Cox and Evans sitcom [Cox and Evans are two local councillors with severe hairpiece difficulties who first appear in the second series of *The Smell of . . .*], that's our dream.' When questioned as to what it is about these two worthy citizens that appeals as a subject for further comic investigation, Vic explains: 'They're probably slightly more joined to the real world than our other characters, and that means that there are more exploits they can get up to. Also, because they're councillors, you could have a lot of other people round them – all it'd need would be a mayor and a secretary and we'd be up and running. One of our wives would be a lesbian, and I quite fancy the idea of Bob having seven very wide-eyed identical daughters.'

If this scenario now sounds (which it does) like a Royston Vasey out-take, perhaps that explains Vic's rather ambivalent response when *The League of Gentlemen* first hits the screen. In idle conversation in the spring of 1999, Bob's determination to give due credit to its all-round excellence gets on Vic's wick to the extent that he at one point grouchily likens the show to superannuated kids' TV landmark *Rentaghost*. (He eventually overcomes this initial hostility sufficiently to allow individual League members to make suitably

---

232. As for that matter, does Gordon Brittas, Chris Barrie's heroically annoying leisure centre manager in *The Brittas Empire*.

obsequious sub-Reevesian cameo appearances[233] in *Randall and Hopkirk (Deceased)* – a series which ironically bears closer comparison with *Rentaghost* than *The League* ever did.)

As Bob Mortimer rightly and generously surmises, an exquisitely detailed and well-performed production has in fact elevated *The League of Gentlemen* about as close as TV comedy gets to art (which is very close indeed). The episode in the second series where the sinister circus of Papa Lazarou comes to town – Shearsmith's despotic ringmaster abducting innocent housewives by forcing his way into their homes and pretending to find a blockage in their domestic plumbing – is as disturbing (and as horrifyingly funny) as anything in Todd Browning's infamous silent horror *Freaks*, or the immortal cinematic canon of Luis Buñuel.

What's fascinating is, first, the success with which writing and characterization substantially unaltered since The League's humble mid-nineties origins (for instance, the local shop where the arrival of a customer prompts the husband-and-wife proprietors – the infamous Edward and Tubbs, whose catch-phrase 'This is a local shop, for local people' echoes round offices and school playgrounds well into the twenty-first century – into a murderous psycho-sexual frenzy) are overlain with Oscar-worthy production values (miraculously realized on a BAFTA budget). And then the warmth with which the resulting – still magnificently strange – entertainment is embraced by public and TV establishment alike.

Beyond the fanatical cult following which might have been anticipated, The League's unrepentantly dysfunctional characters win them national and international renown – from numerous BAFTAs and Comedy Awards to a prestigious Golden Rose of Montreux – to the point where even such diehard non Roy 'Chubby' Brown fans as Richard and Judy can be heard describing things that are weird or perverse as 'very Royston Vasey'. As gratifying as this must be for The League, it inevitably raises the problem – experienced by all celebrants of outsiderdom who find their work achieving widespread critical or popular acclaim – of how to respond to their new-found social acceptability.

[233.] Shearsmith's appearance seems to be a heartfelt tribute to former Vic and Bob staples Donald and Davey Stott.

At first they seem to want to test how far they can push it. But by the end of 2000's second series – particularly in a climax so outrageously sanguinary it makes Herod's slaughter of the firstborn seem like a minor shaving cut – The League of Gentlemen's obsession with Grand Guignol is threatening to get the better of them. All of which makes their decision to strike out in a new direction a wise move, and it's hard not to be thrilled by the prospect of a third series in which The League's army of baroque creations will leave behind the blasted heathland locations of Royston Vasey and march – like some grotesque post-millennial peasants' revolt – on the bright lights of the nation's capital.

The bright lights on this particular autumn morning in 2002 mean the Canal Café – the same beleaguered-seeming fringe venue on the edge of London's Little Venice where six years before they used to come up with new material every week in the hope of persuading their friends to return at seven-day intervals. 'We got a bit nostalgic going back there this morning,' Gatiss will admit later, '. . . for about five minutes.'

Dog-eared posters on the hallway wall advertise a selection of unappealing sketch-comedy attractions. (It would be nice to think that the ever resourceful BBC2 art department had come up with these, but sadly they are probably real.) Upstairs, The League are filming 'Legz Akimbo', the nightmarish theatre-in-education troupe which has been responsible for some of their most gruesomely unforgettable moments. Shearsmith plays the benighted Ollie Plimsouls: a man condemned by a malevolent destiny to funnel all the disappointments and failures of his life into superficially well-meaning but actually deeply offensive plays about 'issues', to be performed to restless audiences of uninterested schoolchildren by a tortured and despairing company. Like some fearful car breaker's yard of the soul, these vignettes compress the horror of a whole life of thespian underachievement into unnervingly compact cubes of suffering.

Following in the footsteps of such earlier Legz Akimbo landmarks as 'Everybody Out' ('A play about homosexuality', with the unforgettable mock-triumphant conclusion 'Me? I'm happy with who I am . . . and if you're not happy with that, why don't you go and kill yourself, like mum did?' which was lent an added bite by the fact that leading man Gatiss is himself gay), today's production is 'Vegetable Soup'. It addresses questions of mental and physical disability with a level of tactlessness that would make Robert Kilroy-Silk blush.

Plimsouls, like many of The League's most outlandish characters, is based on a real person (not a famous TV presenter, but someone Shearsmith was once lucky enough to go on a theatre-in-education tour with). Does Jeremy Dyson agree that some of the acuity his colleagues bring to Legz Akimbo comes from an apprehension of the misery which might have awaited them had a glorious career in the world of small-screen comedy not beckoned?

'Yes – that's definitely the case. There was a lot of frustration and bitterness in the early days of The League, and that sort of thing is very good fuel for comedy.'

In the course of 2001's triumphant live tour, The League of Gentlemen found themselves realizing their dark and tormented vision on a grand theatrical scale. It must have been strange for the three actors to perform these fraught mini-dramas of creative frustration to a succession of ecstatic packed houses at the Theatre Royal, Drury Lane.

'All I can say', Dyson smiles, 'is that from when we started the tour to when we finished it, the three of them all became happier people.' Having steadfastly resisted the temptation to compromise the uniformly high quality of The League's acting by having a go himself ('It would have undermined the whole operation,' he insists, 'and we were always determined to avoid giving anyone that feeling you get as a fan when something that's not quite right makes you wince'), Dyson finally slaked his thirst for public acclaim by taking a bow on the show's press night. 'It was nice, because *they* invited *me*,' he affirms. 'I didn't have to ask.'

As all four League members have lunch together in their trailer – scenically located in the car park of London Zoo – the bond between the quartet is clear. Potentially their interrelations are quite complex, writing as they do in two groups of two (Pemberton and Shearsmith in one, Dyson and Gatiss in the other) and yet the atmosphere seems entirely free of the vicious rivalries which usually prevail in such set-ups. Though the fact that Shearsmith almost shrieks 'Don't mention *The Office*!' when someone inadvertently refers to Ricky Gervais's much-praised new kid on the TV comedy block, suggests they do at least have a *collective* ego.

Without the accusation even having to be made, The League of Gentlemen are very keen to refute the suggestion that a combination of professional success and an end to twentysomething romantic uncertainty (all are now settled in marriages or long-term relationships) might have made them go soft. The new series, they promise, will contain 'quite a lot of unpleasantness', including two debt collectors savagely beating a simpleton ('It was just us and a camera in a Portacabin on a rubbish tip,' Gatiss remembers with a shudder. 'Watching through the monitor was like looking into *Kes*') and 'a lot of people gathered together inside the skin of an elephant'.

Any lingering fears that a new-found emotional maturity might have undermined the strangeness which makes The League of Gentlemen special are swiftly banished. Having been spotted at the summer première of the abysmal Ben Elton and Queen musical *We Will Rock You*, Pemberton insists that he was there with a single goal. To make actual physical contact with the show's co-producer, Robert De Niro. 'I brushed right up against him,' he proclaims proudly, before adding – with a meaningful look that, while stopping just short of being a leer, none the less contains more than a hint of menace – 'He's only little'.

The League's commendable determination to make the most of the advantageous situation in which they find themselves is reflected in their eagerness to embrace new challenges – like removing their characters from the protective embrace of Royston Vasey ('I remember [*Only Fools and Horses* creator] John Sullivan saying he instantly knew what Del-Boy would do in any particular situation,' Gatiss says admiringly. 'He knows the character so well, he can plonk him anywhere') or forsaking their usual portmanteau format in favour of extended linear narratives.

Rather than the previous sets of artfully linked sketches, each episode of the third series will focus on a single pre-established character or group of characters (i.e. the strangely symbiotic relationship between Pauline – the sadistic Re-Start interviewer who seems hell-bent on ensuring her clients never work again – and Micky, her educationally subnormal surrogate son), with some new faces (the aforementioned debt collectors, for example) as a subplot.

All the stories will then connect up at the end in a grand finale, which is rumoured to depart from League tradition by containing elements of joy as well as pain. 'In amongst all the bile,' Pemberton insists, 'there's compassion too.'

The chance to develop actual human relationships between their characters was not a luxury The League expected to enjoy when they first came up with them.

'If you're going to tell a story within a sketch,' Gatiss explains, 'you've got to get to it very quickly, and I think that's something we became quite good at . . .'

The League's knack for compressing an entire emotional world into a single phrase or gesture is up there with such masters of the art as Alan Bennett or (one of their most significant but least oft-cited sources of inspiration) Victoria Wood.[234] The problem is, once you've learned this trick of reaching a great intensity of emotion very quickly, it's hard to unlearn it so as to achieve the same effect within the structure of a longer, more traditional story-line. And while The League embark on their third series on the basis that their feature-length 2001 Christmas Special – containing three longer sections of continuous narrative – offers the best way forward, there are some grounds for arguing that this show was actually a creative blind alley.

Not because The League's characters and situations don't have enough juice in them to sustain longer stories – quite the reverse – but because some of the tenderness which was formerly bound up in their lovingly prepared parcels of psychic anguish seems to be seeping away when the story-lines are extended. The actual horror

---

[234.] *Acorn Antiques* was a big influence on *The Office*, too. But watching Wood hold a packed Royal Albert Hall in thrall in the mid-nineties, it's hard to pinpoint exactly what it is about this experience that is slightly depressing. Perhaps it's that – as with the lyrics of Damon Albarn – there is an uncomfortable suspicion that Wood's much-vaunted flair for the everyday might actually be rooted in contempt rather than sympathy. The objects of her scorn – women who don't enjoy sex, alternative therapists, Anthea Turner, people who eat free-range eggs – are rather easier targets than she pretends. And while Wood is anything but prim (she will happily bandy tampons and orgasms with the Brands and Eclairs of this world), it would be refreshing if, just occasionally, her comic standpoint could be other than one of aggressive common sense.

seems to be edging out the social anxiety, and there's a callousness about the Christmas Special which rather belies its authors' talk of a new-found warmth towards their characters, as if they've forgotten the affection – the love, even – which used to be implicit.

Accordingly, when the third series is finally broadcast, it's actually a somewhat chillier affair than its predecessors. Although the assault on the nation's capital does not materialize in quite the apocalyptic form that had been anticipated, The League's characters prove themselves more than capable of standing on their own two feet outside the safe haven of Royston Vasey. And the interweaving of different narrative strands at the end of each episode is thoroughly ingenious, in a Peak District Tarantino kind of way. But there's a disappointing conformist undertow to the way some of the stories are resolved.

For example, when Pauline has sex with Mickey, the potentially huge subversive impact of this unexpected turn of events is greatly undermined by her subsequently being sexually exploited by some-one else. It's almost as if where The League were identifying *with* their characters *against* the outside world in the first two series, there's now a tendency to indulge the audience's prejudices at the expense of their own creations: as if they're actually frightened of bringing out the tenderness they always felt towards their characters, and trying to cover that up with recourse to easy shock tactics.

It's not even the extremity in itself that's the problem – the sex party episode in series three, for example, is probably the single most extreme thing ever seen on British TV, and none the worse for that – but the moments when the characters' integrity seems to be wilfully sacrificed on the altar of heartlessness. Returning for a moment to the instructive model of Mr Quentin Tarantino's film career, just as it's the less violent, less wham-bam-thank-you-mam *Jackie Brown* that now feels by far his boldest movie, so it's always been in their quieter, kinder moments – like Tubbs giving suck to a piglet – that The League of Gentlemen have been at their most enduringly outrageous.

The League's decision to write their own stuff in the first place arose from the impossibility of ever getting roles that were worthy of them written by anyone else. The realization (presumably ham-mered home by those faintly unsatisfactory guest appearances in

Randall and Hopkirk (Deceased),[235] collective cameos in mid-ranking Brit-flicks like *Birthday Girl*, and joining Jamie Theakston and Jack Dee on the West End honour roll by co-starring in *Art*) that their subsequent self-propelled ascent up the thespian food chain hasn't really changed this must have been somewhat dispiriting.

Rather than turning their understandable anger back on to what is – after all – the perfect vehicle for their talents (which they themselves have so carefully buffed and polished), perhaps they should climb back on board and drive off somewhere new.

There's a fantastic moment in the final episode of the third series where Laurence Llewelyn-Bowen descends upon Royston Vasey like some foppish *deus ex machina*, and his familiar presence in this most unfamiliar of contexts seems to open up a new world of possibilities. If The League of Gentlemen can renew their pledge of allegiance to the wretched of this earth – the fops and the freaks, the demonized and the excluded – then they might have it in them to revive that great maverick tradition of British comedy film-making which seemed to expire with Monty Python.

[235.] Gatiss and Dyson even end up writing an episode.

22
Ceramics Revue

The Johnny Vegas story

'Why not put your energy into making a teapot of your own?'
Michael Pennington

'I'd like to thank Channel 4 for putting my career back five years'
Johnny Vegas at the British Comedy Awards, 2002

Of all the captivating comedic spectacles which present themselves within the timespan of this book, there is none more imposing than the sight of Johnny Vegas in full spate. To see this self-styled 'twenty-eight-year-old failed potter from St Helens' appear live onstage in 1997–8 is to marvel at a performer who can mould an audience in his hands with all the suppleness and application of a master craftsman.

Vegas is an emotional volcano, a veritable Mount St Helens – his fleshy slopes tattooed with rivulets of beer, sweat and clay – who somehow persuades women to let him kiss them and men to give him their designer shirts to 'clothe his nakedness' by the forcible eruption of his gargantuan personality. Johnny Vegas reflects people's anxieties back at them through the distorting mirror of his own desperation, and then they watch, spellbound, as he overcomes the class divide with an uplifting chorus of the 'Hokey Cokey'.

The ease with which he subjugates a live crowd does not preclude potential problems in making the all-important transfer to TV. After all, in that context, the key element of the Vegas live experience –

the fact that the audience are shut in a room with him and can't escape because they've already paid – will no longer be a factor. Furthermore, in small-screen terms, several aspects of the Vegas persona have a naggingly familiar look about them.

Since that red letter day when Vic Reeves proclaimed himself Britain's top light entertainer, there's been no shortage of able cultivators in that field, farming the hinterland of bottom-flight showbiz for a quick laugh (the names of John Shuttleworth and Alan Partridge are just two of the several hundred that spring to mind, and that scouse club comic Alexei Sayle used to do – the one who slept in his Jag and was on pills for his nerves – might fairly be said to have pioneered the genre).

The line between acting drunk and actually being drunk is hardly one that's never been walked before, either. But the rich ore Vegas extracts is all the more valuable for coming from such well-mined seams.[236] And the one-off *Johnny Vegas Television Show*, broadcast by Channel 4 on 27 December 1998 (with a series widely expected to follow some time in the New Year) is the most instantly legendary British TV comedy début since the first episode of *Father Ted*.

Think Les Dawson at his best, think John Kennedy Toole's literary masterpiece *Confederacy of Dunces* translated to a small northern boating lake. *The Johnny Vegas Television Show* suggests both of these things and more. Its hero's proud but desperate catch-phrase 'I'm not a comedian, I'm an entertainer' echoes on in the memory long after the stale taste of the rest of the season's supposedly festive viewing has faded from the palate.

Resplendently out of place in a bustling Soho champagne bar, Johnny Vegas's representative on earth – twenty-eight-year-old failed potter Michael Pennington – reflects on all the different ways it could have gone wrong. More sober in dress and demeanour than his flamboyantly flared-trousered and car-coated creation (at this stage in the evening anyway), it's no surprise to hear him talk about

---

[236.] 'It does seem to me that I rather honoured your party,' the eighteenth-century English wit Charles Lamb once wrote (in an endearingly Vegas-like manner) by way of apology for an alcohol-induced misdemeanour, 'for everyone that was not drunk . . . must have been set off greatly in the contrast to me.'

his *alter ego* in the third person. There's no doubt, however, about where Vegas gets his gift for a rhetorical flourish from.

'The question was,' Pennington muses, 'how did we get Johnny on the screen without making him a TV person? We didn't want to make a mock documentary: "*This is how he lives*". We didn't want to do a stand-up show, because Johnny Vegas is not a presenter: he's a very sad bloke who lives on his own, who's an alcoholic . . . Every now and then, he ventures out into the world and he's *very, very* bitter.'

There's one reason why *The Johnny Vegas Television Show* succeeds where so many other attempts to translate hit Edinburgh Festival shows (Vegas was Perrier-nominated in 1997 and successfully built his next year's show around the emotional disturbance he suffered on being beaten to that prize by The League of Gentlemen) to TV have failed. That's because it manages to establish its own integrity, rather than striving vainly to shoehorn a well-honed club act into an inappropriate new format.

'These are Johnny's dark years,' Pennington explains, 'the bit that never gets explained. It's like if you don't see [heroically grumpy ventriloquist] Bernie Clifton for ages and you wonder what he's been up to, and then you come across him somewhere, rummaging in Stationery Box for a cheap 200-sheet A4 pad so he can start writing his new show, and you can imagine he goes home and says "I'm ditching the bird", and his wife's saying "You'd be a fool: I'm your wife and I love you, but without that bird you're nothing".'[237]

The cameras follow Vegas around his home town of St Helens in Lancashire, with occasional flashbacks to his glory days at Butlins in Skegness. 'I never wanted personally to laugh at St Helens,' Pennington insists, 'because I live there, but this is the only place on earth where Johnny can exist. When we were filming, nobody said "What are you doing, stood there looking like that?" All we'd

---

[237.] Four years later, when Clifton turns up on the Louis Theroux spin-off series, *The Entertainers*, this vision proves uncannily accurate. *The Office* also taps into the rich vein of Cliftonian poignancy, when David Brent, having just been sacked on Red Nose Day ('How could you do this? . . . today of all days'), stands up to reveal a replica of 'that bird' clinging lifelessly to his midriff.

get was "I haven't got time" or "Sorry son, I think you're drunk".'

Thus we see Johnny hassling a hapless entertainments secretary at his local Labour Club, Johnny hassling an ice-cream man, ('They'll carve my face into lollies!'), Johnny getting chased by a kite.

'There's something of a "care in the community" element to it,' Pennington explains. 'You look at Johnny and think, Why is somebody not looking after him during the day? The feeling we wanted to get was "You shouldn't be laughing at this, but . . ." Some people think it's too dark, but it *couldn't* be too dark.'

Almost as compelling as Vegas's whirlpool of misplaced moral energy ('I deserve to be loved!') is the unforced naturalism of the people he comes up against. The secret of *The Johnny Vegas Television Show*'s imposingly realistic collection of ice-cream men and park-keepers is that they *are* ice-cream men and park-keepers. 'People have said "What's he been in before? I know I've seen him in something", and we're like "You haven't, he's an ice-cream man from St Helens".

'If you went to them with something scripted – "do this and be natural" – it would never work,' Pennington explains. 'We just said "You are an ice-cream man and this, here, is a pain in the arse, just react as you would". With the live show, the people in the audience are thinking to themselves, I just came out for a drink . . . and in the TV it's I'm just doing my job. What I'm basically saying is "I know your job is basically to look after the park, and you're a nice bloke, and the last thing you want to do is lose your temper with someone, so what I'm going to do is annoy you to the point where you have to".'

How do his untrained collaborators tend to react to this?

'They're patient at first, but after five minutes I have to remind them they're only acting before they strangle me.'

If Pennington's primary motivating force was not so obviously compassion, there might be a hint of Jeremy Beadle in all of this. As it is, *The Johnny Vegas Television Show* offers us not just a welcome riposte to those endless docusoap series about airports and cruise ships whose intermingling of show business and reality at this time so demeaning to both, but also a seismic shift in TV's approach to the ordinary.

'There's somebody like Johnny in everybody's community,' Pennington insists. 'This person talking to you who you think is a nutter quite possibly was Butlins boy number one at some point – all he wanted to do was make people happy and he's been denied that opportunity.'

Would it be fair to suggest that there might be a political element to all of this?

'I'd like to think it's a commentary, without being a lecture.'

Ideals of personal and collective responsibility do loom surprisingly large in the Johnny Vegas persona: whether he's justifying his lack of conventional comic material on ideological grounds – 'Jokes don't unite people, they divide them: they pick someone out and say "Laugh at him, laugh at her, she's a nun, he's an Irishman . . ."' – or, best of all, confronting paperboys with their moral stake in the evils of the media. 'It isn't just the reporters, it starts with kids like you – you're the ones *delivering* the papers.'

Perhaps this is why, where other comedians talk in terms of being true to comedic traditions – Peter Sellers or Monty Python or whoever – Pennington talks about his work in terms of being true to the spirit of people in pubs. He stopped watching other people's comedy when he started to do his own.

'I'm always wary of aspiring to be like someone else. It's like you're in a shop and you can't afford the stuff they're selling, so you look at a teapot and think, I'll go home and make one of those, and you do it and it looks fuck all like the one you wanted, so why waste your time? Why not put your energy into making a teapot of your own?'

Now that teapot is finally on display, we can all see what a lovely piece of work it is. Perhaps too lovely for its own good. Just as everyone's looking forward to admiring the saucers and sugar-bowl that will complete Vegas's beautifully crafted comedy tea service, there's a change of regime at Channel 4. Out goes *Father Ted* commissioning editor Seamus Cassidy and in comes Kevin Lygo, whose idea of the sort of Friday-night entertainment Channel 4's adventurous remit demands runs more along the lines of former Ned Sherrin underling Graham Norton, or Davina McCall's (admittedly excellent) *Streetmate*.

'I think the series is definite,' insists Pennington, shortly before the pilot airs to fully warranted critical acclaim in December 1998. 'I bloody hope it is, because I'll be really miffed if it's not.'

Unfortunately, his one-way ticket to the people's republic of really miffed is already booked and paid for. Lygo turns out to be among those who deem *The Johnny Vegas Television Show* 'too dark',[238] and what would have been one of the finest TV comedy series of the late nineties is cruelly consigned to the dustbin of history.

Michael Pennington goes back to the drawing board, doing live shows at the Victoria and Albert Museum – one aspect of which is a short film (shot by *Spitting Image*'s Roger Fluck) in the course of which Johnny breaks a roomful of pots in an orgy of unhappiness and recrimination. The idea of Johnny Vegas turning his back on his craft is a deeply distressing one, but presumably at this point Pennington feels *his* craft has turned its back on him. It's easy to see how such a lapse into self-hatred might have come about. If you've done something sub-standard and people don't like it, that's one thing, but to do something which embodies all the highest possibilities of your art and have it rejected so callously must be very hard to bear.

To add insult to injury, shortly afterwards Channel 4 screens *That Peter Kay Thing*, which is basically a more sanitized, less threatening version of *The Johnny Vegas Television Show* – sort of Vanilla Ice to Vegas's Eminem – stretched out to a six-part series. Among the characters 'introduced' in this show by the burly Boltonian Kay are an ice-cream man and a hard-pressed working men's club promoter.

Ever since Kay pipped Vegas at the post to win North-West Comedian of the Year in 1996 – coming on last and cunningly over-running – the two Lancastrians' careers have developed very much in parallel. Though there were never formal plans for them to work as a double act, before going up to Edinburgh in 1997 they did try out new material together at Manchester venues such as The Buzz Club and the Frog and Bucket.

Steve Coogan, who saw them perform at this time, is delighted

---

[238.] Though anything darker than, say, Norton's later hypocritical treatment of *Big Brother 3* superstar Jade Goody would be hard to imagine.

by the old-fashioned, pre-alternative aesthetic both men seem to share.

'People like Peter Kay and Johnny Vegas are just like my uncles,' he marvels in the summer of 2001, 'and I love the way the veneration of those traditions has become a social reality.'

The descriptions of the northern clubland environment on which Les Dawson cut his teeth in Mick Middles's biography could be stage directions for Kay's *Phoenix Nights* (the British Comedy Award-winning series later developed from the club-promoter episode of *That Peter Kay Thing*). As Middles writes about 'vast brick chasms thick with cigarette smoke and run on a draconian schedule' or 'dour foreboding interiors enlivened by occasional strips of tinsel, with a tiny stage patrolled by a viciously sarcastic compère', you can almost see Kay's genial goateed doorman looming up out of the Mancunian night.[239]

Dawsonian historical precedent also holds the key to the essential difference between Kay and Vegas. It was what Middles identifies as a 'hunger for the expected' on the part of those clubland audiences – and the resulting *get on, fit in, get off before the bingo* management mentality – that originally provoked Dawson's trademark epiphanies of dourness. The important thing to remember is that in surroundings where 'the clientele were the gods and artists bowed to their every reactionary whim', Dawson himself – who had, after all, once played piano in a Parisian brothel, and saw himself as a writer at least as much as a comic – was considered a dangerous comedic radical.

In the post-alternative epoch, the appearance of pre-alternative

---

[239.] A minor character loosely based on Middles is played by Simon Pegg in Michael Winterbottom's *24 Hour Party People*, wherein – in a neat twist of Mancunian aptness – Steve Coogan's Tony Wilson starts off the Factory night-club at a dive run by a venal promoter played by – of course – Peter Kay. Pub-quiz *aficionados* should note that of all the many comedians in the cast of this film (with the honourable exception of *Smack the Pony*'s Fiona Allen, who earned her momentary cameo with hard graft as a Hacienda cloakroom attendant), the only one with some actual connection to the Manchester music scene – the former Mrs Caroline Hook – is not in it. Perhaps it was anger at this injustice which prompted her former husband to describe *24 Hour Party People* as 'a film about the biggest cunt in Manchester, starring the second biggest'.

authenticity – as conveyed by Kay's drily Dawsonesque demeanour – is just what people want.[240] 'It's like watching Freddie Starr or someone like that,' Addison Cresswell notes happily (and without swearing) of Kay's *Phoenix Nights*. 'There just isn't really a division any more – half the people working on the show are old northern club comics.'[241]

While there's no denying Kay's shrewdness in exploiting this gap in the market – 'He is interesting,' Steve Coogan insists admiringly, 'in terms of knowing where he comes from and exploiting that fact, but celebrating that culture rather than laughing at it . . .' – it's hard not to feel that if the prevailing comedic wind were moving in a different direction, this man might be moving with it. There's nothing wrong with such a pragmatic approach, indeed some (Harry Secombe among them) might argue that it's a prerequisite for sustaining any kind of long-term showbiz career.

But the difference between a high-class craftsman (which Kay undoubtedly is, as the elegant and often very witty *Phoenix Nights* confirms) and a true comic artist like Johnny Vegas, is a willingness – even a determination – to do or say something just because it's really funny, irrespective of whether the audience are likely to agree with them or not.[242] It was Les Dawson's readiness to die a thousand deaths onstage at the Hull British Legion in the early sixties that gave his later hosting of *Blankety Blank* its awesome moral authority,

---

[240.] There is no shortage of anecdotal evidence of Kay's crowd-pleasing instincts. In 2003, he tells the *Big Issue* about a tape he's been compiling since 1988 filled with nothing but thirty-second fragments of TV show opening credits. 'There must be 160 on there,' he boasts. 'People think it's sad, but put it on late at a party and everyone goes mad.'

[241.] Though when Dave Spikey, a.k.a *Phoenix Nights'* Jerry St Clair, turns up on 2003's *The Live Floor Show* doing material about 'mongs', it's hard to be sure if this is such a good thing. And when one of the producers of *Phoenix Nights* brandishes his 2002 British Comedy Award in triumph, proclaiming 'This is for all the comedy in the north', you don't have to have been born within the sound of Bow Bells to think 'Oh, fuck off'.

[242.] This dangerous line was most famously walked by the frequently bewildering Andy Kaufman, whose cinematic inhabitant, the great Jim Carrey, can be seen responding to Vegas's shameless grandstanding with impeccable generosity and verve on a memorable 2003 edition of *Friday Night with Jonathan Ross*.

and if Peter Kay were really the visionary that a lot of people seem to want to claim him to be, he'd be doing this stuff at a time when the world *wasn't* crying out for it.

Mick Middles makes an intriguing connection between Les Dawson's bold leap into the abyss of audience disapproval and a similar show of daring by deadpan West Midlander Ted Chippington, who 'specialized in inciting the same reaction' from confused indie-rock audiences in the mid-eighties.[243] Having been lucky enough to see the mighty Chippington perform on numerous occasions around that time, I'd always thought it probable that this man would one day be viewed as a significant figure in the history of comedy, if only on the basis of such classic material as 'I just got back from 'Nam . . . Chelte-*nham*'.

But only in the Zippo glare of Middles's observation does the true grandeur of Chippington's standing in the comedy pantheon at last become clear. After all these years, the truth can finally be told. Ted Chippington – with his mercilessly downbeat one-liners and provocative cover-versions of Ottawan's 'D-I-S-C-O' – was actually the John the Baptist of the Old School Comedy Resurrection.

However, as the headless figure of John the Baptist can often be heard to observe at New Testament reunions, the life of a prophet is not always the easiest. Hence for Kay's wheelchair-bound *Phoenix Nights* club manager Brian Potter (even that name testifies to Vegas's subliminal influence) the now familiar trappings of post-Reevesian top light entertainer-dom are the logical accoutrements of a well-realized comic character. For Johnny Vegas, on the other hand, the Butlins boy number one stuff is not so much there to mark his audience's cultural card, as to establish a bridgehead into an inner world of barely controllable emotion, and to prompt rival comics into pondering 'Why is this bloke so unhappy, when he's got his own tour?'

Sometimes this characterization falls victim to its own success, as the poignant blend of self-awareness and self-delusion he projects so successfully as Vegas ('What I can do, you can't put it on paper!')

[243.] They were unsure of how to react to a set in which every joke began 'I was walking down this road the other day'.

sometimes feeds into the industry's perception of Pennington himself. Kay, on the other hand, is universally acknowledged as a formidable operator whose knowledge of his own mind is second to
no one's.

At Christmas 2001, Kay – styling himself enticingly as 'The
Young Alf Roberts' – lights up the Channel 5 schedules with a
dynamic and engaging stand-up show (later released on video).
'We're at the top . . .' Kay announces exultantly, *vis-à-vis* his career
as well as his specific geographical location (the glamorous Black-
pool Tower ballroom), 'and we're going higher.'

There have been times in that same year when Johnny Vegas has
appeared to be locked on a very different trajectory, as Steve
Coogan's regretful throat-slitting gesture eloquently attests. But
over the six-month period which follows that unpropitious July
encounter, Johnny Vegas effects one of the most miraculous career
turnarounds in British comedy history. A couple of suitably maverick showings on *Never Mind the Buzzcocks* having confirmed how
well his uniquely unfettered brand of spontaneity can work within
the confines of tightly formatted TV, Vegas embarks on a once-in-a-
lifetime small-screen odyssey.

His triumphant showing on 25 August's special comedians' edition of *The Weakest Link* (which he not only wins, but reduces the
legendarily unapproachable Anne Robinson to a giggling schoolgirl
with a crush in the process) inaugurates a magical mini-epoch
wherein you can hardly turn on the television without seeing Johnny
Vegas being just about as amusing as anyone has ever been in that
medium.

From *Friday Night with Jonathan Ross* to Paul Merton's *Room
101* (where a routine about the happy times he's spent in an internet
chat room called 'Beauty's Castle' scales heights of pathos analogous
to actual physical pain); from a bravura showing at the British
Comedy Awards (where he finds himself unable to thank others as
he'd like because his success is all down to his own hard work) to
The Frank Skinner Show, the televisual arc Vegas inscribes is too
perfect to last for ever.

The wary look on the face of Skinner[244] – who generally eyes

---

[244.] And Ross, and Merton, for that matter.

other comedians with the same implacable air a rattlesnake might adopt towards a badly wounded gerbil – is evidence of the admiration Pennington's talents inspire among his peers. There's something else in there, too – perhaps born of Frank's own pre-fame battles with the bottle. It's not so much a desire for the younger man to fail as a realization that he is probably flying too close to the sun. And Skinner is not the only one of Vegas's comedic elders who seems to feel this way.

'I tell him "You love all this",' says Paul Whitehouse – whose strangely (some might even say malevolently) underwritten part for him in *Happiness* inexplicably wins Vegas his Best TV Newcomer statuette at those fateful 2001 British Comedy Awards – '"but it's the end for you. Because it's all shit, and one day you'll turn round and it'll be like it never happened, and you'll be back in the poxy clubs".'

Does Whitehouse not think this sounds a little harsh?

He shrugs: 'I just see it as my responsibility to nurture him along those lines.'

The truth is that Vegas's TV *schtick* in the autumn/winter of 2001 – i.e. the moment we the viewers have tuned in to see him is, by a happy coincidence, just the one at which he has decided to make a full and frank confession of his innermost personal thoughts – *is* inevitably subject to the law of diminishing returns. What he's doing is catering to our hunger for the *un*expected, which is a much more demanding and voracious appetite than the more conventional, conservative one Peter Kay is feeding.

When Vegas starts to put himself about a bit too much – appearing naked on *The Big Breakfast*, shouting drunken rubbish into Sara Cox's microphone in a celebrity box at the 2002 FA Cup Final and having it replayed endlessly on the Radio 1 breakfast show as if it's the funniest thing he's ever said – you can almost feel his fellow comics rubbing their hands with glee. And this notional peer group *Schadenfreude* does not diminish when he gets married (in Las Vegas) and starts talking about how his pregnant wife is going to have to make allowances for the father of her child being an alcoholic. It's one thing to flirt with disaster for the purposes of comedy and quite another to wilfully shack up with it in a celebrity Barratt show home.

You can hardly blame Michael Pennington for getting his priorities a bit mixed up, though. The fact that someone who's done work of his quality should be most celebrated for the unfunny drunk he plays in *Happiness* and a series of adverts for a collapsing digital franchise in which he co-starred with a knitted monkey suggests that both the public and his own industry find a watered-down version of Johnny easier to take than the technical mastery of the 80 per cent proof grain spirit version.

Watching him as Ulrika Jonsson's left-hand man on the fourth and fifth series of *Shooting Stars* in 2002–3, he seems rather unsympathetically cast as a kind of philistine counterpart to Will Self (especially given that the whole original point of the Vegas character was that his life should be a celebration of unfulfilled artistic potential). The awful possibility that he might end up as a caricature of this unrealized self grows more real with every empty Guinness glass that piles up in front of him. And Johnny's apparently keen appreciation of what is going on doesn't make it any less painful.

At the 2002 British Comedy Awards, he gives what is – on the face of it – a vintage performance of shambolic grandiloquence, passing on his best-newcomer baton to one of the posh kids from *My Family* with a suitably gritted-teeth thank you to Channel 4 'for putting my career back five years'. When the blamelessly undeserving award recipient rashly tries to stand up for himself ('I'd like to thank Johnny for showing me how I'll be in twelve months time . . .'), the angry old-stager crushes him like a bug. There's still tenderness, as well as cruelty, in Vegas's lethal riposte – 'You'll never be me' – but the balance is shifting.

What Johnny Vegas really needs at this juncture is a way out, and a *Happiness*-facilitated move into movie acting seems to offer him one. But while none of the three films Michael Pennington completes back to back in the late autumn of 2002 have seen the dark of day at the time of writing (and it would be nice to be proved wrong), on the evidence of the British film industry's comedic output in the previous decade, it seems unlikely that all – or even any – of these will stretch him to anything like his full awesome comedic potential.

The most likely potential escape route from Johnny Vegas's creative impasse seems to come from the unlikely quarter of Radio 4.

While the largely self-penned 2002 series *The Night Class* (in which he plays a maverick ceramics tutor) sounds, on the face of it, like a step in the wrong direction – an attempt to reinvent the (potter's) wheel even – sometimes you have to go back to go forwards. And to hear Johnny imposing any kind of structural discipline on himself at this stage in his career is strangely exhilarating.

It might not be as innovative as *The Johnny Vegas Television Show*, but in the prevailing televisual climate ('The hardest thing with TV people,' Pennington observed ominously in 1998, 'is they ask you for summat new, then you do something new for them, and they want it to be the same') *The Night Class* seems to offer Johnny the most likely blueprint for a small-screen home of his own.

'You can practise pottery every day for the rest of your life,' he counsels one of his students, resonantly, 'but it won't make you a potter. You've got to take what makes you tick, and you've got to put that bit of yourself into the pot.'

23
Script for a Jester's Tear
Reality TV and the comedification of the self

'What the fuck am I talking to a reflection of me for?'
Alex Sibley, peering drunkenly into a bathroom mirror
in *Big Brother 3*, summer 2002

'We've gone into reality . . . We've gone the other way!'
Les Dennis on *Celebrity Big Brother 2*, autumn 2002

Of all the exotic things about Johnny Vegas – and there are many – one of the *most* exotic is his possession of an honest trade. In a 2001 survey of British schoolchildren under the age of twelve, when asked what they wanted to be when they grew up, 97 per cent said they wanted to be famous and the other three referred the question to their agents.

With the prospect of serious skill shortages in the second and third decades of the twenty-first century already looking likely, the advent of the top-rated Channel 4 show *Faking It* is a most unwelcome development. This – often genuinely entertaining – programme is built around the premise of three unglamorous people (who have actually trained to acquire a particular skill) being humiliated by a slightly more glamorous individual (who has been taught over the course of a month to *act* as if they know how to do something).

It's a kind of mirror image of that peculiarly late-nineties televisual process whereby people going about their normal business of

384

singing on cruise ships or failing driving tests became 'stars' by virtue of their leading roles in TV shows about the salt-of-the-earth normality of their lives.

At 11.35 p.m. on day four of *Celebrity Big Brother 2* in the autumn of 2002, the anxiety this kind of thing causes comes to a head. And – as so often – the spokesman for the confusion of a generation is Les Dennis.

'If I was going on *Room 101* at this point [the splendid irony inherent in a former game-show host taking part in one TV programme inspired by George Orwell's supposedly superannuated dystopia *1984* speculating about what he would like to do on another will be addressed later on in the chapter] there's someone I'd put in – well, not him, but the type . . . it's the Jeremy Spake Syndrome . . . [historical note: Jeremy Spake is a camply heterosexual clerk in a show programme about an airport who gets some daytime and holiday presenting work as a consequence][245] . . . reality TV people who've gone on to do what *we* do . . .'

Sue Perkins (of 'Mel and Sue' semi-renown) eyes Les nervously from across the divide between post-alternative comedy and old showbiz.

'There's an element of hypocrisy there . . .' she asserts, concerned that she is going to be inveigled by the silver-tongued Dennis into appearing to agree with something that might alienate her employers at Kingsmill.

'There is, isn't there?' agrees drum and bass don turned *East-Enders* actor Goldie.

'But why?' demands Les, with the anguished air of a man who is totally wrong in one sense but has at least a smidgen of rightness about him in another. 'We've gone *into* reality . . . We've gone the *other* way . . . Because we can do something we have always had a skill at doing – we have not come from the public into the business, we are *in* the business . . .'

For all its apparent logical flaws – his characterization of appear-

---

[245.] As further testimony to the size of the shadow he casts over the celebrity subconscious, Spake also appears in an obscene drawing by Mackenzie Crook which Ricky Gervais makes great capital out of at his Soho Theatre live season in the summer of 2002.

ing on a charity-motivated TV game show as 'going into reality', for instance, would seem to suggest that life away from the cameras was somehow a fantasy version of the truth that only the small screen could show – Dennis's concern about the erosion of the line between 'the public' and 'the business' is actually right on the money. There is no more entertaining demonstration of the increasingly promiscuous interplay across the previously closed border between the famous and the not-so-famous than what historians will come to know as the *Mr Right* farrago.

Mr Right is a belated (not to say benighted) 2002 entry into the reality TV stakes wherein a large group of single women, ranging from the merely predatory to the utterly desperate, are moved into a London house to compete for the favours of one man – thirty-five-year-old former royal functionary Major Lance Gerrard-Wright – dubbed 'Britain's most eligible bachelor'. From the outset, there appears to be something compellingly wrong with this show, even beyond the fact that its early stages are mired in bad publicity surrounding the date-rape allegations contained within host Ulrika Jonsson's recently published autobiography.

As the series proceeds (broadcast a little later in the evening each week, almost as if ITV, the network which brings us *Club Reps*, might be embarrassed by it), early suspicions that something is deeply amiss here gradually intensify. When one of the marginally more characterful participants expresses attention-seeking doubts about her continued participation, expecting Ulrika to beg her to stay (as is customary in that staple situation of reality TV pseudo-drama), she finds herself out on her ear before you can say 'bus fare home'.

Only after the last show has fizzled out in one of the limpest finales in TV history, and the resentful ex-contestants get around to selling their stories to the tabloids, does the shocking truth become clear. Mr Right has found his Ms, in the familiar form of Ulrika Jonsson, thereby giving new meaning to the phrase 'the hostess with the mostest'.

To imagine a breach of propriety on this level in an earlier tele-visual epoch, it is necessary to visualize Bruce Forsyth man-handling the winning *Generation Game* contestant from their seat behind the prize-laden conveyor belt and running off with the cuddly toy.[246] In the age of *I'm A Celebrity Get Me Out Of Here!*, however, Ulrika's casting-couch *coup* barely excites comment.

This is where the Reeves and Mortimer despot/democrat trajectory has ultimately led us. Two comedians possessed of an autocratic instinct and a mutual fondness for the unreconstructed phallocentric swagger of seventies pomp-rock have set in train an entertainment revolution culminating in the total decentralization of celebrity.

It is an oft-remarked historical irony – from Cromwell's English republic to the Russian revolution – that a democratic upsurge will often culminate in despotism. But in certain very particular circumstances (for example, when Napoleon's attempts to subjugate Europe spread the headily divisive doctrines of nationalism and liberalism across the continent, or strong government enthusiast Tony Blair endeavoured to establish a puppet London mayoralty only to see it taken over by his Old Labour nemesis Ken Livingstone) the reverse can also be the case.

This is roughly what's happened with Vic and Bob. Their triumphant success in hitching the wayward mule of late-twentieth-century celebrity culture to their own comedic wagon has culminated in a situation wherein Les Dennis's (admittedly – on the evidence of his performance in the *Big Brother* panto – somewhat questionable) assertion that he possesses a skill which non-celebrity *Big Brother* contestants don't is actually breaching the ultimate taboo. A situation wherein (from *Celebrity Fame Academy* to *Celebrity Driving School* to *Celebrity Fit Club* to *Reborn In The USA*) a willingness to endure the same humiliations that members of the public have been willing to put themselves through in the dogged pursuit of fame becomes pretty much a mandatory condition for continued celebrity status.

Presumably this explains why when Reeves and Mortimer themselves bow to peer pressure and start appearing on celebrities-instead-of-real-people substitution shows – Bob organizing 2002's disturbingly atavistic boxing bout between Ricky Gervais and Grant Bovey, Vic performing rather poorly on a celebrity edition of *Mastermind* – there is always a slight air of bewilderment about

---

[246.] As opposed to Anthea Redfern.

them. It's as if they're thinking, along the lines established by a certain Dr Frankenstein, *What have we wrought?*

They shouldn't be too hard on themselves, however, as the erosion of the professional demarcation between comedic and non-comedic fields is a phenomenon with well-established historical precedents. R. H. Hill's *Tales of the Jesters* records the dying days of the cap and bells, when 'growing freedom of thought and speech caused the fool's ancient prerogative to be of less account' and the late-sixteenth- and early-seventeenth-century craze for 'jest bookes' mutated in a direction eerily prophetic of the development of reality TV, more than three hundred years in the future. Hence the advent of such an ahead-of-its-time publishing phenomenon as 1679's *The Wittie Companion* – 'whose heroes', Hill notes, 'were not jesters but ambassadors, courtiers, squires, barbers and the man who is now spoken of as being in the street'.

Watching some of the things which *Big Brother* contestants get up to – Brian and Narinder's hilarious dry-humping, for example, or Alex Sibley's diverting game of 'Follow the van' – you would be hard-pressed not to see the programme as evidence of 'growing freedom of thought and speech' (well, if not of growing freedom of thought and speech, then certainly of actions, which generally speak louder than words anyway). Yet at the same time, everything about the show – from its Orwellian premise to its visual language, to the actual physical means of putting it together – is bound up with the seemingly unstoppable advance of surveillance technology.

This paradox – encapsulated within Michael Bracewell's judicious observation that 'Reality TV taught people how to empathise with one another as [both] a continuance and a riposte to depersonalising information technology systems' – takes a fair bit of getting to the bottom of. By what quirk of evolutionary development has humanity reached a point – *pace* Les Dennis – where situations in which a camera isn't present can seem 'less real' than those in which one is? How did the watchful eye of closed-circuit TV escape the realm of dystopian literature to become something people not only take for granted but even actively yearn for?

Fifty years after Orwell's death, the media has developed with such subtlety that it actually incorporates Orwell's grim prophecies into its reassuring consensual vision as a form of entertainment.

Accordingly, *Room 101* is not a place where you are forced to confront your darkest fears, but a repository into which they can be comfortingly banished. Similarly, rather than a screen you're not *allowed* to turn off, *Big Brother* initiates an – utterly pleasurable – addictive cycle you *don't want* to break out of (and don't have to, if you're lucky enough to have E4). It's not so much a case of Big Brother watching you against your will, as you willingly watching *Big Brother* watching other people who have filmed themselves running naked into the sea with video cameras in the hope of earning that privilege.

By a further piquant irony, the advance of surveillance technology within Western capitalist society follows on directly from the end of the Cold War and the demise of the totalitarian Soviet superpower – whose apparent invulnerability Orwell's *1984* was originally written to bemoan. As military suppliers remarketed their products to civilian populations, it was fitting – as well as inevitable – that Britain, one of the leading players in the international arms trade, should become the world's most observed nation, with more cameras per capita than any other country on the planet.

Channel 4's *The History of Surveillance* – first broadcast in the summer of 2001 – claims that the average busy British city-dweller can now expect to be filmed between three and four hundred times a day (though by my reckoning, you'd have to spend a fair amount of time gawping into the CCTV in Dixons window to fill this quota). It's partly the law and order lobby's battle-cry that those who have nothing to hide have nothing to fear which has changed us from a population that is nervous about being watched to one that is nervous about *not* being watched. But plain old-fashioned fear has probably played a role, too.

As is appropriate for a technological innovation designed to make people feel safer (and which has brought such nightmare visions as the abduction of Jamie Bulger into everybody's living-room), the reassuringly familiar and the downright sinister are never far apart in this small-screen history of the even smaller screen. For example, only a mile and a half in distance separates the already nostalgia-inducing footage of *Big Brother 2* sweethearts Paul and Helen frolicking in their East London garden of Eden and the anonymous-looking 'control centre' where – in an extremely scary police pilot scheme – computers 'harvest' faces off the streets from banks of surveillance TV monitors.

By the process of biometric mapping, a 'golden triangle' – stretching from the base of the nose to the corners of the eyes – allows the main identificatory features of each different human face to be encoded in just 84 bytes of information (which is barely a mouthful). Once recorded on the central computer, these details can bring every detail of a person's life up on a screen within seconds of their passing in front of a camera. In the face of such real and daunting threats to the freedom and privacy of the individual, perhaps the widespread fixation on such meaningless markers of pseudo-individuality as the personalized mobile ringtone becomes a little more understandable.

Half-way between the site of the original *Big Brother* house and that Orwellian Newham control centre lies the monument to 1970s retail brutalism that is Stratford's shopping centre. It is in – or near – this mausoleum of capitalism's broken dreams that Jack Dee reaches the end of his break for freedom in the first *Celebrity Big Brother* in the autumn of 2001.

Before the awe-inspiring symbolic significance of this dramatic tableau can be properly appreciated, three different strands of backstory must be patiently unravelled. The most efficient way of doing this would seem to be by pausing the action for a moment and resorting to the triple parallel flashback device employed so effectively in the aforementioned *Jackie Brown*.

1. Reality TV

Any potted history of this life-enhancing phenomenon must inevitably begin with *The Family*, Paul Watson's pioneering fly-on-the-wall depiction of working-class life in 1970s Reading (no-one remembers *An American Family*, the US prototype).

'The shock of seeing people as they really were on television at that point was very intense,' remembers local-boy-made-good Ricky Gervais, who was growing up in the town at the time. 'It was funny because they did change,' he recalls of the human guinea pigs in that epoch-making behavioural experiment. 'For the first couple of episodes they were very cagey, and by episodes three and four they were walking around in their pants.' The extent to which this transformation would impact on *The Office* – Gervais's later observational *Meisterwerk* – will become clear in the next chapter. But the reality TV/comedy interface did not begin or end there.

When *The Family* was reshown in full on BBC2 in the late eighties, it found a receptive audience, some of whom remembered how brilliant it was from the first time around, and some of whom didn't. Its influence could clearly be seen, for example, in *The Smell of Reeves and Mortimer*'s 'Slade in Residence' – based on a similar premise, except with skinhead/glam cross-over legends Slade as the family – which would in turn provide the template for *The Osbournes*.

If the 2001 MTV apotheosis of Noddy Holder's fellow hard-rocking West Midlander Ozzy Osbourne marked – in pure enter-tainment terms – reality TV's most advanced evolutionary phase, the same channel's disingenuously titled *The Real World* (first screened in the US in 1990 and in Britain a year or so later) marked the moment it crawled out of the primordial ooze. Ensuring from the beginning that the cross-over between what you might (if granted a special licence from the oxymoron police) call *real* reality and the more narratively malleable phoney version should be seductively blurred, this pioneering show took an artificially constructed family group of showbiz wannabes, moved them into a house together in an American city and filmed the ensuing quarrels, crushes and brazen emotional grandstanding twenty-four hours a day.

It is interesting to note that when BBC2 tried out this format in the early nineties, there was a general outcry about how un-British it was. The show eventually had to be abandoned after its subjects – mostly students at Manchester University – began to get beaten up in the street by mobs incensed at their emotional exhibitionism and all-round lack of class.

The nation's stiff upper lip had certainly loosened up a bit by the time the first series of *Big Brother* hit the screen in the early summer of 2000, but the omens were still not propitious. All those shows about vets and hotels had started to get very boring by this stage. And footage of crowds gathered outside the pioneering Dutch *Big Brother* house to whistle and hoot their acclaim for the lunkishlooking individual who was the inaugural winner seemed like TV interference from an alien world of low-country hysteria.

But then our own show started: slowly at first, then rapidly picking up momentum, until the deranged exploits of 'Nasty' Nick Bateman (if not a brother, then at the very least a cousin to Bret Easton-Ellis's *American Psycho* anti-hero Patrick, who shared the same second name) held the attention in a grip as secure as any TV show had ever managed.

Subsequent events would prove that – far from the genetic aberration he seemed to be – Nasty Nick was actually a faulty prototype for a new kind of human being. As this fresh genus developed over the second and third series to the awe-inspiring levels of sophistication exhibited by Irish air-steward Brian Dowling and half-German Essex-based model Alex Sibley, the nature of its evolutionary journey became ever more apparent.

The challenge facing the *Big Brother* contestant is to incorporate an awareness of how everything they do will look onscreen into their behaviour without being *seen* to do so. (After all, if you go too far in this direction, you might be labelled 'fake and false': an accusation which, in the *Lord of the Flies*-like atmosphere of the third series,[247] would attain the same terrifying power as an earlier generation's cry of 'witch'.)

It's hard to be certain exactly why their success in this regard should give us such joy – perhaps because their situation strikes a chord with our ever more surveillance-prone day-to-day lives, or perhaps because there's something perversely liberating about the extent of their self-obsession. Either way, the sight of Brian Dowling, left behind in the house at the moment of his 2001 *Big Brother* triumph, at once utterly alone and yet cradled in the loving arms of the nation; or latter-day Narcissus Alex Sibley, drunkenly hectoring himself in a bathroom mirror before demanding 'What the fuck am I talking to a reflection of me for?' are among the most entrancing visions of modernity with which the early twenty-first century has yet provided us.

[247.] Carefully nurtured by a wilfully irresponsible production team.

2. Capitalism

2002's BBC2 series *The Century of the Self* adds an intriguing new dimension to our understanding of the previous hundred-and-two-year period. To put it in a simplistic peanut-husk, the programme's argument goes roughly like this: that Sigmund Freud's nephew cunningly applied his uncle's teachings through the medium of advertising and thereby convinced first America and then its political and economic satellites that the only realistic way to achieve fulfilment was by buying stuff.

The idea of 'branding' (imbuing particular products with a – generally fallacious – set of moral, emotional and aesthetic values, so as to foster the illusion that these deeper requirements are met by the item or service's purchase, alongside whichever material need they are actually designed to cater for) is identified in this and other contexts as the acme of modernity. Yet one strand of its development can actually be traced back to the same primitive joke books whose evolution prefigured the growth of reality TV. Anyone who has ever, for example, bought John Smith's bitter because it was recommended by the teetotaller Jack Dee will appreciate the significance of the landmark 1630 volume *The Banquet of Jests*.

Though it purports to detail the exploits of King Charles I's jester Archie Armstrong, only one story in the book actually contains any reference to him. And as R. H. Hill's *Tales of the Jesters* reports, in suitably shocked tones, 'The same collection printed anonymously had already gone through four editions in the same shape' before Armstrong's name first became associated with it. Even in the version which purported to be the work of the great funnyman, 'the printer had left the word "anonymos" standing on the title page' – whether 'because he did not know what it meant, or in sheer cynical indifference, will never be known'.

The extension of such entrepreneurial liberty-taking from the independent acts of business-minded individuals to a fully integrated global economic system is a long and somewhat complex process which it would not be appropriate to go into too deeply at this juncture (curious readers are advised to seek out Rob Newman and ask him to explain it). But one important feature of this procedure's later stages is the development of the shopping mall (to whose fully realized present form the aforementioned Stratford Centre bears the same malfunctioningly prototypical relation that *Big Brother 1*'s Nick Bateman does to *Big Brother 2*'s Brian Dowling).

A physical environment devoted to inculcating the kind of child-like state which will maximize expenditure has no room for non-consumerist dissenters. In the consequent spread of areas from which you can be excluded simply for not shopping, the idea of public space is being gradually replaced by what are chillingly termed 'privately owned and administered places of public aggregation' – wherein there is no one to uphold the inalienable right of the UK citizen to sit on the bench drinking Strongbow.

It's intriguing that as society becomes more and more about who we keep out – from kids annoying people with their skateboards outside Budgens to (on a wider social canvas) asylum seekers and economic migrants – the inclusiveness of our culture becomes more and more frenzied. The broadcast and print media's endless imprecations to viewers, listeners and readers to 'take part' and 'get involved' by expressing a preference on every issue under the sun (from votes on the nation's favourite poem/food/book/film/Radiohead album to whether one of the stylists in *The Salon* should be obliged to have her hair cut, to which of a series of live session tracks should be played on bank holiday editions of Radio 1's *The Jo Whiley Show*) are partly inspired by practical considerations – making money where there's a premium phone line, or establishing a cross-media foothold – and partly by the need to demonstrate accountability to a fickle and potentially fractious public.

There's a broader element of consolation here too, though. It's almost as if constant reminders of our ability to 'make a difference' in such trivial matters might act as simultaneous compensation and smokescreen for progressive alienation from the actual process of political decision-making. 'Use your vote,' proclaims Davina McCall at the height of *Big Brother 2* hysteria. 'We live in a democracy!'

Characteristic of the many important issues on which the British public is invited to speak out in the early twenty-first century is Channel 4's 2002 commemoration of our *100 Worst TV Moments*.

The curious thing about this particular poll is that the winning worst moment – Richard Madeley's impression of Ali G – is not, objectively, all that bad. In fact, it's not that much worse than Ali G's impression of Ali G. And given that the whole point of the character is to be a satirical reflection of people trying to appear more 'down with the kids' than they actually are, Madeley has in fact shown a more intuitive understanding of what Ali G's all about – and has less cause for embarrassment – than all the people rushing to avenge this appalling slight on his coolness and integrity.

It's not so much Richard's Ali G impression in itself that's the problem here, as the impulse to commemorate it: a lodestone of this – otherwise very unecological – age's determination to recycle every cultural event almost before it has even happened (cf. the *Big Brother* tradition of reviewing people's 'best moments' just a few minutes after they've been evicted from the house). This tendency found physical expression in the appropriately hollow form of the Millennium Dome. The existence of a structure whose physical shape could be (and has been) 'entirely occluded by the received idea of its presence . . .' prompted Michael Bracewell to speculate 'how to reclaim one's subjectivity in the face of the near simultaneous translation of culture into received ideas of itself?'

If a survey was conducted to find the nation's favourite way of expressing this question in slightly less intimidating terms, without straying too far from the Dome and its brackish girdle yet somehow touching on the deliciously bogus formality of Carrie Bradshaw's laptop voice-over in *Sex and the City*, the winner might go something like this: if culture is like drinking water from the Thames – digested and processed so many times before it reaches us that its primal freshness is just a haunting memory – how can it leave anything but a nasty taste in your mouth?

3. Jack Dee and the comedy of consumerist despair

While the saucy Manhattan antics of Carrie and her enchanted circle – the Jimmy Choo shoe fetishism, the shameless sexual indulgence – cater for the more aspirational end of the comedic materialism market, Jack Dee has its B&Q sector covered. When Dee first strolled on to the stand-up circuit in the late eighties, his concern with the everyday helped him stand out from the mass of news-led comedians. As the pendulum swung the other way, and it became increasingly hard to move for comics saying: 'You know what it's like when . . .' with imploring looks on their faces, Dee was forced to place increasing reliance on the style and economy of his presentation to keep ahead of the pack.

Having started out as one of the first explicitly 'post-alternative' comedians, Dee remained true to his apolitical roots ('If you asked me what was going on in Parliament,' he admitted unapologetically in the early nineties, 'I probably wouldn't know'). But as the political landscape changed, this constancy in itself presented problems, as the Britain of bad service and underwhelming ambition at which Dee liked to look askance was based on a predominantly Thatcherite model.

In the happier, more dynamic atmosphere of the mid to late nineties, his preoccupation with domestic minutiae – how teachers behave when they go out with their friends, the way men hold power drills when there's no one else around – began to look like a kind of consumerist despair. A tacit acknowledgement that our only purpose on this earth is to be vaguely dissatisfied with the level of service we receive at out-of-town DIY emporia.

Occasionally, as in his merciless dissection of the fast-food eating experience, Jack Dee would go beyond mere observational comedy to the very essence of the human condition. At other – less transcendent – moments, he'd come across as the sort of tedious person who is always demanding to see the manager (which is odd, really, because in his pre-comedy catering career, he used to *be* the manager).

By the start of the next decade, after a couple of misfiring TV vehicles – including a supremely misguided attempt to make this famously dour individual the host of a zappy prime-time Saturday-night ITV variety show – Dee's career seemed to be going nowhere. This was one attribute he seemed to share with his fellow participants in the historic first celebrity series of *Big Brother* – notoriously brittle daytime TV casualty Vanessa Feltz, minor *Brookside* actress Claire Sweeney, erstwhile Boyzone makeweight Keith Duffy, tabloid whipping girl Anthea Turner and one-time boxing champion turned professional eccentric Chris Eubank – but that was where the common ground ended.

It is at this point – with Dee rolling his eyes at the benign verbosity of Eubank and the pugilistic aggression of a newly welterweight Feltz in front of the watching eyes of the nation – that the three strands of our narrative come back together again.

On the face of it, there is nothing all that surprising or significant about what happens next. A general certainty that Dee is going to win this competition (in which one celebrity is voted off each night for a week with the money from the phone votes going to charity) sets in very early. It's not just that his mix of dry wit, wry cynicism and occasional grouchiness is perfectly calculated to appeal to an image the British love to have of themselves. When you think about it, that thing which successful *Big Brother* contestants have to do – which is to project themselves in a way which is calculated to make everyone like them, while at the same time not seeming to care too much about what other people think – is the stock-in-trade of any successful comic. (It's in this sense that the commodification of the self which reality TV entails is also a comedification.)

When Dee escapes, breaking out of the house in the dead of night and wandering unfettered and unprotected through the wilds of East London, it seems like just the sort of class-joker-type move you'd expect of him. The fact he turns around and comes back seems to confirm a lot of people's suspicions about the consensual nature of the comedian's role in society.

Yet when you consider the precise circumstances of Dee's break-out – following hard on the heels, as it does, of a traumatic shock to his entire worldview – a less calculating and more dramatic story emerges. At the very affecting moment when Dee's pose of studied disdain is overcome by human sympathy for the plight of Vanessa Feltz (the pressure of being up for an inevitable early eviction telling, she starts swearing at Big Brother and writing obscenities on the furniture), he turns his back on the fundamental Bergsonian dictum that the pursuit of laughter obliges us to 'put sympathy out of court and impose silence on our pity'.

In the embarrassed aftermath following Feltz's lapse into total public meltdown, Jack looks around, in desperation, for someone else to take on the mantle of carer, but all his fellow survivors are either too self-obsessed or too scared of vilification by association to offer Vanessa the sympathetic ear she so obviously needs. This unlikely duo's ensuing exchange is inevitably an awkward one, which seems to cause him even more pain than it does her, but Dee is a better man for allowing it to happen.

In the light of all this, it would not be unreasonable to characterize his subsequent flight from the *Big Brother* house as an attempt to escape the onerous new responsibility of fellow human feeling. In which case, Jack Dee's ultimate decision to return – startled by the looming spectre of Stratford's concrete consumer mausoleum into a renewed appreciation of the connectedness of things and the dignity of his own standing as an individual entertainer within the capitalist entertainment framework (at least, I like to think this is how it happened) – is a fit cause for general celebration.

It's interesting that one of the few people who make no real effort to exploit the huge public interest surrounding *Celebrity Big Brother* is Dee himself. Duffy gets a part in *Coronation Street*, Sweeney's blatant self-mythologizing (ingratiatingly caterwauling 'me and my show-tunes' at every possible opportunity) somehow lands her a career in West End musicals, even Vanessa Feltz dines out regularly (metaphorically speaking) on her own humiliation.

It's probably their awareness of our awareness of their – perfectly legitimate – careerist motivation that makes Sue Perkins and Goldie so nervous about Les Dennis's anti-Spake crusade next time around. But for the moment, Dee's almost-silence strikes a rare note of dignity amid the familiar frenzy of celebrity self-advancement. And if his *Big Brother* experience makes him question the kind of callousness that once allowed him to make comic capital out of the commercial difficulties of a much-loved UK retail insti-tution ('Shame about Marks & Spencer's . . . If they go out of business, I'll have to switch to Waitrose'), then perhaps he is ulti-mately the biggest winner.

Seinfeld Coda

There's a strange echo of Dee's East End epiphany in the final episodes of that most unrepentantly consumer-minded of US sit-coms, *Seinfeld*. Filmed in 1998 but hoarded by BBC2 in a special cupboard until three years later, the concluding two-part special (broadcast within a month or so of *Celebrity Big Brother*) finds Jerry and George's 'sitcom about nothing' idea reactivated by new management at NBC. Offered the use of a private jet, the fractious foursome (Elaine and Kramer having come along for the ride) find themselves marooned in a small town in Massachusetts, after Kramer's violent attempts to rid himself of an aqueous blockage in his ear almost give rise to an airborne tragedy.

On the streets of this apparently civilized north-eastern enclave, they find themselves looking on as a fat man is robbed of his wallet and his car. The New Yorkers comment on his plight with charac-teristic sensitivity (George: 'He's doing him a favour – it's less money for him to buy food') while Kramer captures the entire incident on video. Unbeknownst to them, a 'Good Samaritan' law has recently been passed in this community – inspired (a touch would-be *Seinfeld* duplicator David Baddiel might presumably have appreciated) by the callous photographers who stood by while Prin-cess Di met her untimely end – which makes it an offence not to help someone in danger.

The ensuing judicial hearing turns into a show trial, wherein the selfishness so lovingly celebrated throughout the show's preceding seven-year history is exposed mercilessly to the public gaze, culmin-ating – via a series of entertaining court-room reappearances by such much-loved minor characters as Babu and The Soup Nazi – in our heroes receiving a (richly deserved) one-year prison sentence for 'criminal indifference'.

The spectacle of a jailed Jerry, describing being obliged to reduce the amount of milk he has on his cereal as 'one of the hardest things I've ever had to do', seems designed to bring as much joy to the show's detractors as to the people who love it. On the face of it, *Seinfeld*'s last-minute change of heart amounts almost to a deathbed confession – a final renunciation of unashamed capitalist decadence in favour of the ersatz humanist values the show has hitherto striven so hard to reject[248] (contrasting sharply therein with *Seinfeld*'s West Coast counterpart *The Larry Sanders Show*, which maintains its habitual flinty cynicism right to the very last moment).

In fact, it's a brave step forward into the unknown; an unknown where comedy defines the limits of our lack of feeling, rather than the extent of it. Where Jack Dee selflessly offers the spare change of his humanity to the emotionally destitute. And four endlessly flippant New Yorkers embrace the possibility that perhaps the thing we need to be most cold-heartedly sceptical about is our capacity for cold-hearted scepticism.

[248.] Larry David's next venture – the gleefully merciless *Curb Your Enthusiasm* – confirms that, for him at least, such a change of heart could never be more than a temporary blip.

24
The Office

Yea, though I walk through the Thames Valley of the shadow of death . . .

'I had grown to my desk as it were, and the wood had entered into my soul'

Charles Lamb

'It [The Office] *isn't a snide look at people who do regular jobs: we can't all be pop stars or astronauts'*

Ricky Gervais

'A lot of it is watching the clock, or watching someone else' – Ricky Gervais rolls his eyes distractedly, pushes out his lower lip and blows upwards in a time-honoured sign of boredom – 'doing this . . . I think those are the things people recognize first, beyond particular characters or lines.'

Sitting in an anonymous West End edit-suite in the summer of 2002 (the noticeboard on the wall is covered in Post-it notes, but the stapler is not – yet – set in jelly) with his co-writer and directorial accomplice Stephen Merchant, Ricky Gervais is trying to work out what it is about their subtle, complex and emotionally gruelling sitcom *The Office* that strikes such a powerful chord with so many people.

'I suppose it could be anywhere,' Gervais continues, of *The Office*'s unglamorous home counties location. 'There's something quite generic about that type of open-plan office, about a paper merchants, middle-managers, about the age group, about Slough.'

401

So they're not trying to avoid intimidating people by making everything recognizable, but rather using the trappings of a familiar world as a springboard for a breath-taking creative swallow dive?

'The reason we set it in an office and not an oil-rig,' Gervais demurs, 'is because we wanted to get the minutiae right. We wanted everyone to know the setting – the boredom of it, the sense of the clock ticking on the wall – so we could go deeper. It isn't a snide look at people who do regular jobs: we can't all be pop stars or astronauts ... In the end, the backdrop doesn't really matter as much as the characters and what they're saying. The important thing with *Dad's Army* was that they were ten middle-aged men – there didn't have to be a war going on. Just as with *Porridge* it wasn't so much about them being in prison as the fact that Fletch was a bit of a loser and he had to look after Godber.'

'We're not just a couple of media types laughing at people stuck in Slough working in an office,' reiterates Stephen Merchant, who seems worried about being thought of as snobbish. 'It doesn't matter if you're an international playboy,' he continues, somewhat more inscrutably, 'if you're not enjoying your life.'

'I imagine surgeons and people who work with NASA,' Gervais muses, 'going "Why has he got a bigger chair than me? He's only been here six months." You can't help it, you pick up symptoms. You compare yourself to your neighbour, not someone who lives 10,000 miles away ... If a country sinks, it's not as bad as your boss who's a twat.'

The great English wit Charles Lamb was obliged to work as a clerk at East India House to support his sister, who suffered from periodic bouts of violent mental disturbance. 'You arrive late, Mr Lamb,' his colleagues would greet him censoriously. 'Yes,' would come the great man's retort, 'but see how early I leave.' The poetic expression Lamb gave to the dissatisfactions of his working life – 'I had grown to my desk as it were, and the wood had entered into my soul' – will ring a bell with anyone who has ever done a job they don't like, but it might also have made a good workplace motto for *The Office* (if 'You don't have to be crazy to work here, but it helps' hadn't got there first).

Do Gervais and Merchant subscribe to the view that a crucial ingredient in most great sitcoms is people being stuck in a situation?

'It's not just *being* stuck,' Gervais insists, 'it's *knowing* you're stuck.' Gervais (who did a philosophy degree at University College London before a lengthy stint as entertainments officer at the University of London Union, managing an early incarnation of Suede, doing the music for *This Life* and earning sundry other distinctions at the university of life) waxes metaphysical. 'To be the dissatisfied Socrates or the satisfied fool ... that's the dilemma: do you trade happiness for wisdom?'

And what would *their* answers be to that tricky question?

Gervais points at Merchant: 'He's a dissatisfied fool.'

When the first series of *The Office* emerged, with minimal fanfare, in the summer of 2001, portents of the hoopla to come were thin on the ground. This was a low-budget BBC2 début, written and directed by a pair of virtual unknowns, in which nothing very much seemed to happen in the first couple of weeks. And yet those little somethings that did happen – such as a pornographic e-mail being doctored to feature the boss's face[249] – seemed to capture the atmosphere of contemporary working life with a precision that was as hilarious as it was excruciatingly painful.

As the growing numbers of people tuning in each week to the goings-on at Wernham Hogg paper merchants found out, that boss – regional manager David Brent, played by the series's co-creator Ricky Gervais – was a classic comic creation. Striving manfully to hide his predatory intentions behind politically correct platitudes, somehow balancing heartfelt concern for the welfare of his workforce with appalling self-interest, Brent miraculously retained just enough humanity to leave a question mark over his widespread designation as 'the boss from hell'.

If there is a comedic equivalent of the alchemist's magic formula, it's the capacity to make an audience empathize with someone even as they behave in an indefensible manner. And as *The Office* went through a frenziedly acclaimed repeat screening and started to rack up well-deserved British Comedy Awards and BAFTAs, the bulk of the attention was naturally focused on Gervais.

[249.] David Brent objects to this 'not because he's in it, but because it degrades women, which he hates'.

Yet it's not so much as the star of the show but as the hub of a perfect ensemble – alongside heroically gormless acolyte Gareth (Mackenzie Crook), tortured but acerbic Everyman Tim (Martin Freeman) and Dawn (Lucy Davis), the inscrutable receptionist for whom Tim's love should perhaps always have remained a secret (even to himself) – that he's earned his place alongside Captain Mainwaring and *Rising Damp*'s Rigsby as one of the true sitcom immortals.

While office manager David Brent's almost psychotic tactlessness plainly originates from a dark recess in Gervais's twisted mind, the extent to which his gullible right-hand man Gareth Keenan derives from the personality of Stephen Merchant has been somewhat less well documented. In fact, Brent's delusional sidekick sounds *so* like Merchant that Mackenzie Crook often finds himself getting half the credit for the Saturday-morning radio show Gervais and Merchant co-host on indie radio station XFM.[250]

When the spry Londoner went to audition for the part, they asked him to 'try it in a West Country accent'. Merchant grew up in Bristol, just down the M4 from the Gervais family home in Reading. 'We think there's nothing funnier than a man from Reading onwards towards Bristol trying to be taken seriously,' the latter explains compassionately.[251] It is this despotic duo's apparently random but actually very clearly thought out attention to such details – rigorously enforced throughout every aspect of the show, from script to casting to direction – that makes *The Office*'s unique brand of Thames Valley naturalism so uniquely engrossing.

'When we first started,' Merchant admits, 'we didn't know anything about casting. We just knew we had to get the best naturalistic actors ever. "I tell you what we should do,"' Merchant remembers himself and Gervais thinking. '"We should get people who aren't

---

250. It was in this relaxed environment that their comic partnership was first cemented, though they were sacked shortly before *The Office* took off, only to be taken back on (much to Gervais's delight) on much more favourable terms once it started to become successful.

251. Merchant's rarely seen stand-up act as a 'pedantic, Gareth-style character' is also based on this somewhat fragile premise – 'I hope we haven't used that card up though,' he says anxiously, 'because as a performer it's all I've got.'

actors – we'll get real people to do it!" But the thing is, real people *can't* do it.[252] In fact, most *actors* can't do it.

'The most flattering thing for us', he continues, 'is when people think it's improvised.' Getting actors to say lines as if they're doing it for the first time is a fairly precise science. 'We keep on top of them,' Gervais grins malevolently, 'almost to the point of embarrassment. It's not necessarily that they're doing it wrong, just that sometimes there might be ten ways to do something and we want number seven.'

'Because we've acted it all out together in the writing room first,' explains Merchant, 'it's kind of like we know how every word should sound.' That level of preparation must be quite a challenge to the humble performers. 'When you're asking someone who's twice as good an actor as you "Can you go up at the end of that sentence, because it's funnier?"' Gervais grimaces, 'that's where it gets tricky.'

'I don't know what the cast's opinion is of us as directors,' Merchant muses, 'I would imagine it's like we're pretending.'

Gervais affects a world-weary thespian grimace: '. . . So now the fat bloke who thinks he's an actor is telling me how to say my line.'

Lucy Davis – whose voice should be naggingly familiar to fans of *The Archers* as that of good-natured Brummie interloper, Hayley; and who also turns out, somewhat against the run of play, to be Jasper Carrott's daughter – is rather more complimentary about their direction. (And it is very much *their* direction: since Gervais is acting most of the time, it's generally Merchant who 'carries the red book').

'I imagine John Cleese must have been like Ricky and Stephen when he did *Fawlty Towers*,' she says, 'because he could see Basil so clearly inside his head.' Someone who worked with Gervais and Merchant for the first time on the second series sent them a thank-you note afterwards. It read: 'It's always interesting when an actor's being directed by being told "that's a bit mental".'

'But that's nicer than telling them they're overacting!' insists an affronted Gervais.

[252.] It's interesting that while this is the diametrically opposite view to Johnny Vegas's, both of them seem to be right.

Martin Freeman – whose pivotal role as the sensitive cynic awash in a sea of mediocrity gives *The Office*'s audience the vital luxury of someone to identify with – mentions a running joke he and Ricky share about the latter's lack of formal acting qualifications. Endeavouring to capture the spirit of this friendly on-set banter, Freeman describes 'waving my certificate from Central Drama School in his [Gervais's] big fat face'.

But when it comes to assessing the actual performance of *The Office*'s untrained leading man, Freeman will not hear a word against the burly thespian neophyte. 'You don't need to be taught to be an actor,' he insists. 'It's all about being an observant person: paying attention to other people, and paying attention to the shit that's in your mind.' He laughs. '. . . And there's enough shit in Ricky's mind for all of us!'

Ricky Gervais's offscreen persona is an entertaining blend of bluff common sense and fairly advanced neurosis. Asked in an *Evening Standard* questionnaire what he might say to tourists on the streets around his Bloomsbury home, Gervais responded: 'Either move faster or get out of my way.' In the course of a nervy appearance on *Room 101*, he revealed that he couldn't bear to enter a pub or restaurant before the person he was meeting had arrived, and would rather circle the venue shiftily several times than go in and wait on his own.

'The thing about Ricky,' says Lucy Davis fondly, 'is that there are so many tales you can tell where if you know him you'll roar along, but if you don't you might go "Oh".' As if to underline the truth of this observation, she then embarks on a fond reminiscence of the time Gervais tried to blind her on set with an aerosol deodorant.

'I don't smoke,' insists this self-styled 'grumpy old man from Reading'. 'I don't do extreme sports.' He leans forward conspiratorially in his seat, as if on the brink of a damaging personal confession. 'My only risk', he proclaims with a daredevil flourish, 'is cheese . . .' Gervais grins, somewhat goatishly. 'I'll have a healthy pasta meal with half a pound of Parmesan.'

In fact, this nutritional maverick seems to have embraced Gustave Flaubert's dictum that 'You must be regular and natural in your habits like a bourgeois, so that you may be violent and original in your work'. Eschewing the unfettered hedonism and egotistical promiscuity which is the general run of comedians' private lives, Gervais has lived with the same woman (*This Life* producer Jane Fallon) since he met her twenty years ago. So – lacking any of the customary priapic or narcotic-based pointers as to the roots of his comic genius – it's going to be necessary to delve a little deeper into the 'shit in Ricky's mind'.

'A clown running around in trifle is only so funny,' Gervais announces, back at the Fitzrovia editing suite where he and Merchant are putting the finishing touches to the second series. 'But a man whose wife has just left him *falling over* in some trifle, that is absolutely hilarious . . . because that's where the darkness comes in.'

His voice gets slightly louder, which is one of two signals Gervais tends to give when a comic extrapolation is under way. (The other is a mildly hysterical bared-teeth laugh, in the manner of much-loved *Carry On* star Sid James.)

'Oh, his wife's left him, and he's covered in custard, and there she comes with her new boyfriend,' Gervais laments.

'That's real bad luck, mind,' chips in Merchant, archly. 'And who left the custard there anyway – do you think it was the boyfriend? I never liked him.'

'Nerd!' barks Gervais damningly.

'Loser!' Merchant snaps back.

What initially seems like the rambling of an impenetrable music-hall double-act is actually a kind of character shorthand. Rather than obvious TV comedy precedents – like Alan Partridge or Victoria Wood – *The Office*'s inspirations are, Gervais claims, largely cinematic.

The flashes of almost unbearable emotional acuity with which *The Office* is illuminated have such unlikely starting-points as the final scenes in *The Bridges of Madison County* – 'When you think she's going to maybe go and pursue this other life and then realize she isn't' – or the fact that in Billy Wilder's *The Apartment* Shirley Maclaine says she noticed Jack Lemmon because he was 'the only man who ever took his hat off in the elevator'. ('There's no exposition!' Gervais enthuses. 'Don't expose things completely!')

Of every eight hours he and Merchant spend working on *The Office*'s scripts, 'Six will be spent talking about films, and what worked and what didn't.' Lots of people manage to while away their working days talking about films without coming up with ideas for award-winning sitcoms, though. So how did these two 'total chancers' (their own phrase: Merchant introduces himself in similarly unflattering terms as 'a lanky, bespectacled West Country oik', and Gervais's pre-*Office* employment record was bulked out by spells as a traffic warden and singer in a doomed new-romantic pop group)[253] come to hit upon such a paragon of televisual perfection?

The Office was originally developed from a twenty-minute film of the David Brent character (then known, more generically, as 'Seedy Boss') which Gervais and Merchant had recorded for the latter's BBC production training course in the summer of 1998. During the three years it took to get the show on to the screen with the painstaking attention to detail both felt was requisite, Gervais's career threatened to take off in another direction.

He graduated from Channel 4's *Eleven O'Clock Show* – the same little-lamented launch pad which also gave the world Ali G – to presenting his own late-night chat show, *Meet Ricky Gervais*, in which he managed to offend more or less everyone by bombarding his guests with bigoted opinions (e.g. on Comic Relief's annual contribution to global charity: 'What did they do with last year's?') without letting anyone know that these were intended satirically.

'My character in *Meet Ricky Gervais* was obviously a TV bigot in the classic *Till Death Us Do Part* sense,' Gervais explains, with a slightly pained expression. 'The problem people had with it was that I used my own name – I didn't wear a hat and I didn't wink to the camera. I was very proud of that at the time, but in retrospect I think it was probably a mistake.[254] I wasn't so much worried about the upper-middle-class people who didn't get it and were offended, I was more concerned by the ones who agreed with what the character was saying. You can't legislate against stupidity, but [and here the ghosts of Loadsamoney and Alf Garnett loom large] it's a Pyr-

---

253. A kind of poor man's Blancmange.
254. 'I hate it when comedians say "It went over people's heads",' says Gervais ruefully. ' "No – you got it wrong." '

rhic victory if you end up with a Fascist following and everyone else hates you.'

One of the keys to *The Office*'s success as opposed to *Meet Ricky Gervais*'s relative failure was the skilful way it employed the omni-present docusoap format. The idea of having its central character followed around by a camera crew came about not so much as a response to what Gervais calls 'the *Zeitgeist* of documentaries being made about everything', but because, he insists, 'doing it that way gives you more access to people's emotions and how they behave'.

There's a slight element of rewriting history here, in that in its pilot incarnation *The Office* was – as head of BBC comedy Jon Plowman confirms – 'very much a parody of a docusoap'. But like the show which was in some ways seen within the channel as a prototype for it, Chris Langham's *People Like Us* (whose journalist anti-hero Roy Mallard was a brilliantly conceived game-bird hybrid of Alan Partridge and real-life microphone-toter Ray Gosling, but whose televisual embodiment for some reason never worked quite as well as the original Radio 4 incarnation), the idea was to use the conventions of the genre to get to the reality of the workplace, not vice versa.

'At no point in the life of *The Office* has it *ever* been a spoof documentary,' Ricky Gervais reiterates forcefully. 'It's been a *fake* documentary – not so much faking a genre, but because we wanted you to watch it as if David Brent was real, and that seemed the best way to do it. We liked the fact that he is a normal person who, when given his platform, thinks, This is it: I'm a philosopher! I'm the next Jane McDonald! [genetically modified star of BBC TV's *The Cruise*] . . . but he opens his mouth and he blows it.' Gervais pauses. 'When someone says "You should meet Ted, he's the funni-est bloke you'll ever meet", I can guarantee you that he won't be – he'll come up with one of those buzzer things in his hand and go [Gervais makes irritating buzzer noise] and you'll go [he winces] "Isn't he great?"'

The feeling of embarrassment he describes has become ever more familiar over the last few years as traditions of British reserve have been washed away by reality TV's exhibitionist floodtide. In the early summer of 2002, *The Office* even spawned its own docusoap

409

spin-off series – *The Real Life of the Office* – about a Swansea car-hire firm whose boss made David Brent look like Albert Schweitzer.

Needless to say, Gervais is delighted by this development, and quotes verbatim from a newspaper review of the profoundly disturbing programme which resulted. 'If Ricky Gervais was watching, he'd probably have been flattered and saddened – flattered that he got everything right, and saddened that it changes nothing.'

Gervais pauses. 'But I *love* the fact that *The Office* changes nothing,' he insists. 'And all those people in offices who used to do impressions of Harry Enfield will now be doing impressions of David Brent.' It's often those who are most clearly the subject of satire who feel most compelled to embrace it. 'Of course the blind spot is dangerous,' Gervais nods sagely, 'and by definition, you don't notice it.'

As to the exact nature of Gervais's own blind spot, it might be a kamikaze instinct for saying the worst thing imaginable in any situation, just to see what will happen (an unexpected trait, this, in a man who claims his only adrenalin surge comes from risks involving the excess consumption of dairy products).

Thus it was that in the autumn of 2001, going up to receive a British Comedy Award live on prime-time ITV, Gervais decided it would be a good idea to 'run the risk of offending everyone in the country'. Accompanied to the podium by his producer Ash Attalla, who is in a wheelchair, Gervais says: 'Aah, look at his little face', before adding that Attalla 'wants to make it clear that he is not a competition winner'. Attalla makes a 'wanker' hand gesture. After a momentary but very awkward pause, while a roomful of comedy professionals decides whether it is appropriate to find this funny, everyone laughs.

Did they plan this beforehand?

Not specifically, admits Attalla, 'though Ricky warned me he might say something'.

Did his long-suffering producer think it was funny?

He seems to have done. 'I've worked with Ricky for four years,' Attalla notes indulgently, 'and he's still more obsessed by my wheelchair than anyone else I know.'

But what about Gervais himself – does he never worry about the moral impact getting away with this kind of thing might have on him?

'My mum', he remembers fondly (his mother died two years ago), 'always used to say "The worst thing that could happen to you when you go to the bookies is that you win".' Ricky flashes his incisors, 'But I never really agreed with her.'

The frenzied air of anticipation which intensifies throughout the run-up to the first screening of the second series of *The Office* seems to offer Gervais plenty of scope to indulge his gambler's instincts. Speaking to the other actors on their mobile phones throughout the last days of shooting, they seem as excited about it as anyone else.

So, does Mackenzie Crook have any sympathy for the demonic Gareth?

'A little bit, but not too much ... He can look after himself anyway: even though he's twenty-six or -seven, it's more like he's fifteen, and he always comes swaggering back like a kid.'

And how does Lucy Davis feel the contrast between Dawn's magnetically clandestine romance with Tim and her less complicated relationship with official boyfriend Lee might play out?

'She's not married to him, so she could move on, but it's really hard for her. Lee isn't a bastard, he isn't vile, he doesn't hit her, and sometimes reliability wins out over Hollywood.'

Last but not least, does the awful moment at the end of the first series when Tim abandons the get-out clause of a psychology degree in favour of Brent's offer of a promotion and a modest pay-rise set him up for a life of unhappiness?

'The thing about Tim is,' Martin Freeman explains, 'he can see stuff clear as day, but he pussies out. He thinks, I'm going on thirty, it *is* five hundred quid and I'll go next year. That's a man fooling himself, which is something we all do every day, but really he's just an ordinary bloke who's as scared of failure as anyone else, and he knows that as long as he stays in that job, he'll always be the smartest person there.'

'If you'll be happy retiring at fifty-five, there's nothing wrong with that,' Gervais amplifies later, *à propos* of Tim's pivotal dilemma. 'Family-making is fine, being in a job you don't like is fine – they're all fine if they're what you want. It's *kidding* yourself they're what you want when they're not that causes problems.'

Seeing all these characters again in the first episode of the new series is like meeting up with old friends who've been abroad for six months. They've all changed slightly in ways you can't quite put your finger on. Even though the second series follows on in real time from the first – with the camera crew staying on (and what self-respecting notional but non-spoof documentarist would think of missing such an opportunity?) to cover the drama that will inevitably accompany the merger between the Slough and Swindon branches – there is something fantastically convincing about these subtle changes in appearance and demeanour.

The amazing thing about the second series of *The Office* is that for all the factors conspiring to spoil it – not least everyone going on about how great it is all the time (one overwrought correspondent to internet comedy forum 'Not The BBC'[255] even complains that the show is undermining the quality of debate, because everyone keeps comparing everything else to it inappropriately) – *The Office* actually manages to *surpass* expectations. Like the music of The White Stripes, it proves that even in our grievously over-mediated culture it is possible to do something which is so great that all the hyperbole and overkill which inevitably ensue can do nothing to diminish the joy of it.

There are a couple of episodes in the course of the second series where Ricky Gervais seems to be getting too big for the show: leaving behind the naturalistic environs of Wernham Hogg for his own private world of loneliness and humiliation. But the whole thing is brought back together so seamlessly in the end – when it is made agonizingly clear just how desperately David Brent needs his job – that you can't help wondering if this internal detour was a kind of controlled explosion of the Gervaisian ego (which must surely have burgeoned to some extent amid all the 'genius of our time' hyperbole).

The fragile mental equilibrium of its star and co-author notwithstanding, it's actually a good thing that everyone has made so much fuss about *The Office*. First, because the BBC are right to be proud

---

[255.] Virtual beneficiary of the struggle to build a national forum for comedy appreciation which began in the mid-nineties with *Deadpan* magazine and the other one no one remembers whose first issue had Craig Charles on the cover in the week he was charged with a serious criminal offence.

of it, but more importantly, because the example of the way the show got made is an extremely positive one. And anything that rams home what a great decision it was to respect Gervais and Merchant's vision (creating, in Jon Plowman's phrase, 'a complete first-hand package that hasn't had to go through another brain') can only be for the best.

In letting *The Office* be everything that its creators knew it could be, rather than doing what – as Martin Freeman points out – they so easily could have done and 'handing the whole thing over to some forty-five-year-old generic Oxbridge blokes so they could make it look the same as everything else', the BBC set themselves a worthy managerial yardstick.

The Office's producer Ash Attalla first worked with Stephen Merchant on a short-lived BBC2 show called *Comedy Nation*. He then developed the disability-based sketch show *Yes Sir, I Can Boogie* (unsympathetically tagged 'Goodness Gracious Wheelchair' by BBC insiders) for Radio 4, before going on to produce the alarmingly titled *Come Together with Ricky Gervais* for rarely watched comedy cable channel UK Play.

With *Goodness Gracious Me* mainstay Anil Gupta having put himself forward as *The Office*'s man on the inside at the BBC on the basis of Merchant and Gervais's homespun 'Seedy Boss' pre-pilot, a delicate negotiation had to be entered into. Ricky and Stephen's determination to control everything had to be balanced with the requirements of a sometimes conservative financing organization.

To calm the fears of BBC high-ups about letting such relative unknowns direct as well as write, and – in Ricky's case – star in *The Office*, Gupta offered to direct the pilot (which, given Gervais and Merchant's fanatical attention to every detail and already well-established creative shorthand, must have been a bit like coming between The Silent Twins) on the basis that they'd be allowed to take over if the show got the go-ahead for a series. This, Gupta remembers happily, 'was pretty much exactly what happened'.

And it was in the leap from official pilot to actual broadcast series that *The Office*'s distinctive character was finalized. In the planning stages of the former full-length prototype, Attalla remembers, they'd 'toyed with' the idea of employing a voice-over from one of the kings of that lucrative art, such as John *Bergerac* Nettles or Andrew 'Manuel from *Fawlty Towers* but he doesn't sound like that now' Sachs. In the transition to the version of the show that was ultimately broadcast, the 'mockusoap element' was very much toned down.

First because, as Jon Plowman remembers, 'the channel felt that the *Driving School* moment had kind of passed', but really more in response to practical concerns that the more rigidly documentary-style pilot (thoughtfully included in the million-selling first series DVD package, for those who want to check this out for themselves) was not exploiting *The Office*'s comedic potential to its fullest extent.

'I think the thing that irritated us all most about the pilot,' Ash Attalla remembers, 'was that because the way we filmed it was very true to documentary conventions, we had to capture everything in one shot, so when we watched it back with our friends, there were bits we were laughing at because we knew there were jokes there, which no one who wasn't there at the time could actually see.' Accordingly, they decided to – as executive producer Gupta puts it – 'cut themselves a bit of slack' in terms of strict adherence to the documentary form.

What *The Office* ended up as was, in Jon Plowman's estimation, 'basically a sitcom that happens to be filmed quite like a documentary. In that you can imagine those scripts being performed in front of an audience in a three-and-a-half-walled set, but the something extra you get from the way they've actually been done is a feeling of naturalism, and the impression that the characters are owning up to more than they would under normal circumstances.'

A vital and often overlooked element in *The Office*'s overall impact is the way the show's visual language complements its underlying story-line of inadvertent emotional disclosure. It was experienced director of photography Andy Hollis (a veteran of both Chris Morris's endlessly mutating film stocks and *Spaced*'s seemingly insatiable yen for Hollywood parody) who helped directorial novices Gervais and Merchant to get the best out of their new situmentary hybrid.

'I think after the pilot, they realized it was never going to be possible to get everything from one take,' Hollis explains, 'but when we had a cutaway shot of people reacting, we tried to justify it as though it was from the same position. And we never had big set-ups where the camera turns right round and looks back at itself – we always tried to make it look as though a documentary-maker had cobbled together lots of different bits of pieces of film in the hope of telling one story.

'As a general rule,' Hollis continues, 'it's my job to stop the audience noticing where the cameras are, but in this case we made a *point* of letting them know, so the actors could play to them. And that helped us get everyone's reactions across a lot more clearly. The beauty of *The Office* is you get to see the whole of people's faces, rather than just watching them square on, like you do in a normal TV programme.'

There are two particular moments in the second series when content and delivery harmonize with eerie precision. The first is in the magnificently gruesome fire-drill episode, when David Brent insists on unnecessarily carrying a wheelchair-bound formerly Swindon-based employee down the fire escape in the hope of impressing everybody, then tires of the physical effort required and abandons her in the stairwell. In a scene whose subliminal echo of the heroism of September 11 office workers trying to get their colleagues out of the World Trade Centre is just as clear in Brent's mind as it is in ours, his betrayal seems all the more absolute. And the camera pulls back as if almost unable to look.

This idea – that there are some things which are so terrible or so private that they should not actually be broadcast for the idle diversion of strangers – is just about as close to heresy as it is possible to get on twenty-first-century TV. And it recurs in the final episode, when Tim makes a second doomed formal play for Dawn's affections. Heading into closed conference to face his romantic destiny, he unclips his microphone, and for nigh on a minute there's no sound. At first those watching at home feel cheated, and then they realize that by way of those few moments of silence, a little bit of lost humanity has been restored to them.

In the quarter century or so since the advent of Reading's last great contribution to the history of the small screen, *The Family*, we've grown increasingly used to watching people on TV behaving as people actually do. And in some ways, *The Office* is a comment on the extent to which that has raised our expectations of how much comedy can (and should) achieve.

By actually fulfilling those raised expectations, *The Office* raises the bar for the competition. But it also does something else. One of the most mysterious things about David Brent is the way he constantly presents himself as a showbiz figure – a 'chilled-out entertainer' – in the most non-showbiz context imaginable. This seems most straightforwardly explicable in terms of the 'comedification of the self' outlined in the previous chapter. (Gervais's creation being, above all things, a man who is conscious of the presence of the camera, it can presumably be deduced by extension that there is now a little bit of David Brent in all of us.)

But one of the most inspiring things about *The Office* is how stubbornly it resists being boiled down into something less than it is. There are times – especially in the second series – when David Brent's self-consciousness is so extreme that it pushes on through to the other side and becomes a crazy kind of freedom. One of these is the already legendary scene in the second series's Red Nose Day episode, where Brent endeavours to trump his suave and likeable new boss's exquisitely well-delivered John Travolta dance routine by improvising his own nightmarish assemblage of acid-house and break-dance moves.

As Brent flails around – haplessly but with absolute conviction – daring anyone to break the spell, he becomes a kind of human Catherine wheel, illuminating the Slough of despond. It takes two or three viewings to work out what that strange look in his new boss's eyes is, and then you realize . . . It's *jealousy*.

25
'I Told You I Was Ill'

Spike's last resting place and *Back Passage to India*

'"Pleasure in nonsense" . . . is concealed in serious life to a vanishing point'

Sigmund Freud

'It was like Stockport in the sixties . . . everybody helping each other – all the doors open'

Craig Cash

In a moment of mellifluous reflection during the first series of *The Office*, David Brent muses on who he might choose if asked to name three geniuses. While accepting that other people might plump for Einstein or Newton, his choices follow a different course: 'Milligan, Cleese, Everett, Sessions'.

The addition of a fourth genius – especially in the unexpected form of vocal gymnast John Sessions – is a great maverick touch, but no one is going to disagree with Brent's opening choice. At least, almost no one.

When Spike Milligan dies, in February 2002, his passing is mourned with a rare intensity and eloquence. The *Daily Mirror* even achieves the ultimate tabloid ambition of capturing the national mood – by devoting its entire front page to a mocked-up gravestone bearing the best of Milligan's well-stocked cellar of possible epitaphs, 'I told you I was ill'.

That well-chosen phrase also supplies the title for a strangely edgy televised tribute show at the Guidhall, a few months later. Anyone who still doubts the extent to which Milligan was feared as well as admired by the eager comedic legions who followed in his pioneering footsteps cannot help but notice the nervous looks on the faces of Eddie Izzard, Terry Jones et al. as they struggle to perform selections from his scripts and poems.

The only one of the performers who doesn't seem overwhelmed by the significance of the occasion is a characteristically ebullient Kathy Burke.

'They were all very much in awe of him, and I wasn't really,' Burke confirms afterwards. 'I just really liked his kids' poems.' In endeavouring to master the voice of *Goon Show* stalwart 'Min', she was sternly told to pinch her throat between her fingers and wobble it as she spoke by the show's director Sir George Martin – 'he didn't seem to think it would be possible to get it right without actually doing that'.

There's a distinctly poignant moment in the show when Terry Jones starts telling a story which is meant to demonstrate how not everything Monty Python did was directly inspired by Spike Milligan, but ends up implying the opposite. As he starts to feel this happening, Jones becomes visibly flustered – almost as if he thinks the great man is about to jump out from behind a pillar and shout 'boo'.

Sometimes in such reverential situations, it's not the rolling acres of well-intentioned encomiums but the rare, ugly dissenting voice that gets to the heart of the matter. In this instance, it's a voice so grating that it seems unfair to identify its source. But then again, as Nick Bateman used to say, 'live by the sword, die by the sword'. It's a columnist called Tom Utley, writing in the Saturday *Telegraph*.

The gist of Utley's position – outlined a week or so after Milligan's death – is as follows. Utley has never found Spike Milligan funny, because his comedic trademarks (sudden switches of subject, struggling to control his laughter on *Parkinson*, say) seemed to him to be merely the straightforward manifestations of mental illness.

The reason this seems so heartless and uncalled for (it's a free country after all, and anyone has the right not to find someone else funny) is because it is so obvious to anyone with the smallest capacity for human sympathy that Spike Milligan's sickness – in the form of the battle he fought with manic depression for the better part of his adult life – *was* a part of the story.

It was partly the intensity with which he felt the bad things in life that made the intensity with which he felt the good so moving and so readily communicable. To lapse momentarily into the language of Hollywood, it was the darkness that made the light so precious.

The impact of Milligan's psychic torments on his creativity is considered in great depth in *Depression and How to Survive It*, a grimly gripping case-study cum survival handbook on which he collaborated with Dr Anthony Clare. The descriptions of general depressive states – of living life 'as though you are sitting with an eider-down over you and you hear the doorbell ring' – and the horrors of actual breakdowns are vivid enough to dispel any romantic illusions about the causal links between madness and genius.

There is no doubt that – at least in Milligan's case – there was a strong connection between suffering and artistic sensitivity. The sense of 'skinlessness' he noted in the aftermath of nervous collapse – 'a breakdown is like being burnt alive: you come out of it with a higher degree of sensitivity' – was a creative resource as much as an emotional blight.

The mental frailty described by Clare as 'a hairline fracture waiting for fundamental stress' originated in the fateful events of 2 June 1944 – when Milligan 'folded up' delivering heavy batteries under fire in Italy (his subsequent ordeal at the hands of an unsympathetic sergeant-major is commemorated in *Puckoon*'s show trial of 'a hero with a coward's legs') – but intensified through the burst of creativity surrounding the writing of the *Goon Show* scripts. 'I wrote a lot of my best scripts when I was ill,' Milligan admitted of the escalating mania which culminated in his attack on Peter Sellers, and subsequent hospitalization, in 1953.

The relationship between Milligan's mental fluctuations and his work is probably best illustrated in tandem with another, more cheerful creative influence: childhood wordplay. One of the shared features of infancy and psychic disturbance[256] is an absence of what

---

[256.] And drunkenness or any other form of chemical intoxication, come to that.

Freud calls 'the constraints that prevent free association' of words and thoughts. Interacting with those whose minds were too young to have settled into the steady rhythms of custom was one of Milligan's surest sources of comfort.

One of the children's poems which Kathy Burke reads at the Guildhall celebrates Spike's daughter's attempt to come to terms with the idea of the world spinning on its axis – 'Well, it's making me dizzy'. This would probably be a good place to bring in Reeves and Mortimer. Partly because it was a version of Tommy Roe's 'Dizzy' that (with a little help from The Wonderstuff) gave Vic his only number-one hit single. And partly because Spike Milligan is not the only comedian to have savoured the pleasures of childish free association.

In 'The Mechanism of Pleasure and the Psychogenesis of Jokes', Freud states that 'During the period in which a child is learning how to handle the vocabulary of his [it's always 'his' with Freud, isn't it? But I'm sure he means girls as well] mother tongue, it gives him obvious pleasure to "experiment with it in play" . . . And he puts words together without regard to the condition that they should make sense, in order to obtain from them the pleasurable effect of rhythm or rhyme.'[257]

Asked if they agree with Freud about the highest purpose of jokes and laughter being to help us to recapture 'the mood of our childhood, when we had no need of humour to make us feel happy', Reeves and Mortimer's responses are about as unequivocal as they ever get.

'I think anyone could see that that probably is our motto,' Bob insists. 'It's just turning things on their head really, isn't it?'

Vic says, laughing, 'My mother always tells me that when I was tiny we used to go shopping at Littlewoods in Leeds and I used to call it Bigwoods, and I used to think that was absolutely hilarious.'

Beyond establishing a link to the primal bliss of infancy, Freud argues that the shared mechanisms of jokes and dreams – the rever-

---

[257.] This response was shared, Freud noted, with 'certain categories of mental patients' and Milligan and Clare's harrowing descriptions of the former's disturbed mental states – of 'mental imagery speeded up and verbalised uncensored' – seem to bear that out.

sals and substitutions, the compressions and expansions – suggest that both are a vital outlet for the things in our heads which can't get out in any other way. It was actually Henri Bergson, however, who came up with the linkages between comedy and the subconscious mind that are most germane to Vic and Bob.

Observing, with Freud, that comic absurdity often had 'the same nature as that of dreams', he remarked upon 'the strange fusion that a dream often effects between two persons, who henceforth form only one and yet remain distinct'. And if that's not the perfect description of a great double act, then I don't know what is.

Eric and Terence's big adventure

The account of Ronnie Kray's funeral in Iain Sinclair's *Lights Out for the Territory* describes an occasion thoroughly impregnated with meaning. Spike Milligan's funeral is not really like that, yet as a black Morris Oxford glides noiselessly through a stone arch, there's no denying the dreamlike quality of the occasion.

This is a private, family affair, presided over by that most Milliganesque of figures – a solitary piper in an ill-fitting kilt – with the bare minimum of media fuss. When the coffin arrives at Winchelsea churchyard in East Sussex,[258] wrapped in an Irish tricolour (Milligan's Irish citizenship was a legacy of his long-running feud with the UK passport authorities, who'd summarily revoked his Britishness in 1960), local residents – taking a genteel interest in this discreetly unpublicized occasion – half-expect to hear the volley of shots that would signal the involvement of the IRA.

In an eerie echo of the arbitrary religious divides which characterize his 1963 novel *Puckoon*, Milligan – the British army veteran – has had a Catholic funeral (at the church nearest his home, just outside Rye) before being buried in an Anglican cemetery. Watching a pre-release video of the long-awaited film version of this much-loved book seems as good a way as any of shedding light on the complexities of Milligan's passing.

Given that the book had been through countless paperback

[258.] A lovely, peaceful place, where Milligan used to do brass rubbings.

421

editions, it might seem surprising that no serious attempt was ever previously made to film it. To anyone familiar with the vertiginous switchbacks of Milligan's thought processes in general, and the genial chaos of *Puckoon* in particular, the delay is not so mysterious. The story is set in a fictional small town, heedlessly bisected by the boundary commission at the Partition of Ireland in 1924, and this motif of random division is extrapolated into a gleeful miasma of sub-Joycean Paddywhackery.

When the film's director Terence Ryan bravely suggested to Milligan that 'the story does jump around a bit', the latter confided that on holiday at his father's home in Australia while in possession of the galley proofs, he got drunk and – with emotions running high (it was Milligan senior's memories of growing up in Ireland, passed on to Spike in the course of the latter's own childhood in India, which gave the book its emotional foundation) – set fire to thirty pages which were never replaced.

Puckoon's tart satire of the futility of sectarianism – indeed of borders and boundaries of any kind – has proved thoroughly resistant to the ravages of time, but the film has a strangely dated look to it, and the thing which comes through most strongly in the faithfulness of Ryan's adaptation is the intensity of Spike's absence.[259] In a way, perhaps this is as apt a tribute as any.

Watching a late-night repeat of the eighty-year-old Milligan's appearance on *Room 101*, it's funny to imagine him – as a child in Burma – befriending the colonial policeman who would one day become the author of the book behind the TV concept. 'Hello, Millie,' the young George Orwell (then Eric Blair) would greet the pre-teen Spike (then Terence) on their occasional meetings in 1920s Rangoon. Milligan's chief childhood memory of the great man – as

---

[259.] Reservations about the ability of Sean Hughes to fill such giant shoes – and the comedian would certainly be more convincing as a leading man if he had spent less of the last few years taking easy money to be rude to people on TV quiz shows – are mitigated by the discovery that he stepped out of a minor part and into the breach at the last minute, the film-makers' previous choice (the seemingly even less suitable John Gordon Sinclair) having pulled out the weekend before shooting began. 'You cannot play Spike,' insists the film's producer sympathetically. 'He was – I don't know what Spike was . . . he was an *energy*.'

recounted in Pauline Scudamore's biography – was that he had 'very thin knees'.

When you start thinking about how different Britain would be now if Orwell had perished in some gruesome blunderbus incident, or Milligan had met his end in the WWII foxhole where he penned that poignant epitaph – 'I died for the England I dreamed of, not for the England I know' – it's hard not to get carried away with the significance of their meeting. To think of all the cultural DNA strands that ended up being Big Brother and Eddie Izzard, Monty Python and The Beatles,[260] randomly brushing up against each other years before, without anyone there being any the wiser . . . Well, the mystery and excitement of it all is almost too much to contemplate.

Caroline and Craig's big adventure

Seventy-five years or so after Eric Blair and Terence Milligan's historic imperial rendezvous, another strange and poignant encounter takes place on what was once patronizingly termed the Indian subcontinent. But this time – happily – TV cameras are present.

Back Passage to India is an off-puttingly titled BBC documentary (screened at Easter 2000) which turns out to be nigh on a work of art. The programme follows Caroline Aherne and Craig Cash to a remote eye hospital in the Indian state of Rajasthan, where they look on embarrassedly as a brave twelve-year-old boy called Hemuran undergoes an operation to save his sight. The exquisite scenery, dramatic central story-line and shamelessly manipulative sound-track are subtly offset by the hilarious bitchery of the moonlighting *Royle Family* stars.

[260.] The most oft-cited instance of Milligan's influence on The Beatles was the way his work with director Richard Lester on the groundbreaking 1950s TV vehicle *A Show Called Fred*, as well as the prize-winning 1960 short, *The Running, Jumping and Standing Still Film*, would shape the latter's film work with The Fab Four, but Milligan's impact did not end there. 'Look at John Lennon's book *In My Own Write*,' asserts *Puckoon* producer Ken Tuohy unarguably. 'If you'd put Spike's name on, no one would have known any different.'

One of the many striking things about this compelling piece of television is that the Aherne family's own personal experience of visual impairment is not even alluded to. 'I was never going to mention it,' Caroline insists. 'Andy Harries [the programme's executive producer] and a few other people asked me to, but I just thought it would be a bit, well,' she shrugs, 'pointless. When you become famous and you pick what charities to do,' she continues, matter-of-factly, 'everybody chooses something close to home, because it gives them more of an impetus – you always find people doing breast cancer because their mum's died of it.'

There is little in either of Caroline Aherne's most famous comic creations – acidic housewife and chat-show host Mrs Merton or couch-bound layabout Denise Best (née Royle) – to suggest a vocation for international charity work. And her own life seems to contain so many dramas that you wouldn't think there'd be time for anyone else's.[261] But it's Caroline and the heroically reluctant Cash's very unsuitability for the task of dramatizing the plight of those less fortunate than themselves which makes *Back Passage to India* so emotionally affecting.

'We can't help but say the wrong thing,' says Craig – a sarcastic Sancho Panza to Aherne's Wet-Wipe-toting Don Quixote – 'because we don't know what the right thing to say is.'

Some of Caroline's off-the-cuff proposals for combating Indian social problems – for example, that the Taj Mahal should be sold off to raise money to build a new sewage system ('Don't tell me the Americans wouldn't buy everything that's got a bit of sparkle') – will certainly have raised a few eyebrows.

'I still don't know why that can't happen,' Aherne maintains gamely, back in the comfort of her Maida Vale living-room.

'She's not got a clue, has she?' splutters Cash.

The sight of the ever-beauty-conscious Caroline Aherne tottering

---

[261.] When Caroline decamps for Australia shortly afterwards, it seems worryingly as if she might be following in Tony Hancock's footsteps once again (the latter's relocation to the Antipodes having coincided with his final decline and ultimate suicide) but she confounds the doom-mongers by returning with a new series in her luggage, *Dossa And Joe* – another minutely observed domestic microdrama in which Madge from *Neighbours* fills Sue Johnston's soap-legend fluffy slippers.

out of the Indian savannah on her platform sandals – having been obliged to relieve herself behind a bush – is just one of *Back Passage to India*'s many enduring images. There's another great scene where she is forced to make a speech at a formal welcoming ceremony. After stumbling through a few gracious phrases, she hands the microphone to her even more reticent associate, proclaiming, with deceptive guilelessness, 'I think Craig would like to say a few words.'

'She did that on purpose,' Cash snarls genially, 'because she knew I'd have nothing to say to them.'

In fact, as on several other occasions (notably when he tries to comfort the tearful hospital director by telling him 'You're a good man'), Craig's attempts to do the right thing under unfamiliar social pressure bear noble and affecting fruit. In this case, however, the impact of his touching speech – 'You have a beautiful country' – is somewhat diminished by his later assertion that he would rather die than go to India on holiday.

'I'm full of shit as far as the Third World's concerned, aren't I?' Craig admits. And yet by being similarly upfront about the hypocrisy that is inevitably involved in any encounter between Third World and First, *Back Passage to India* somehow manages to avoid the off-putting atmosphere of self-righteousness that so often prevails when celebrities do onscreen charity work.

It's not hard to imagine what *The Royle Family*'s curmudgeonly patriarch Jim Royle would have to say about TV stars swanning off to help the needy at the licence-payers' expense (his observations would almost certainly involve the words 'my' and 'arse'), but *Back Passage to India* disarms these objections to such good effect that it might even persuade that notorious old skinflint to put his hand in his pocket.

'Cataracts are something old people suffer from in this country,' Caroline explains, 'and maybe there would be people here whose nannas would be waiting for an operation on the NHS. But the very fact of a little boy like Hemuran being unable to see, which is a God-given right, just for the sake of fifteen pounds – well, it's fifteen pounds an eye, so it's thirty pounds the pair,' she smiles, aware of how like an antique dealer offering a concession on a pair of candlesticks this makes her sound. 'I knew that would make more people want to give money than maybe an old person would.'

'Nannas aren't saleable,' Craig shakes his head in mock resignation. 'There's no profit in a nanna.'

'Craig is very jealous of the fact', Caroline insists vaingloriously, 'that since we've come back from India, I've moved on in my life a little bit, spiritually.'

'In what way?' Cash howls with fury, his voice fluking up an octave with the outrageousness of it. 'You've not progressed one bit, spiritually or otherwise!'

'Anyone watching' – Aherne insists of the scenes in which she touches villagers' outstretched hands in the manner of visiting royalty – 'will say "What does she think she's doing? She's just an old piss-head", but it's lovely to think you can make someone happy just by holding their hands – they're all smiling away, and it's like two nations meeting.'

Craig harrumphs at this, but far from presenting herself as a regal benefactress, Caroline insists she got more out of the whole thing than anyone else did.

'Hemuran would have got his sight back anyway, even if we hadn't been there to film it. And it was so beautiful to see the kind of love his whole community had for each other. When he was setting out for the hospital, everyone came to see him off: all they wish for each other is the best,' she continues wistfully, 'and that's not the way we are any more.'

'It was like Stockport in the sixties,' says Craig, only half-joking this time. 'Everybody helping each other – all the doors open.'

'That's why old ladies are always saying "It sounds terrible, but the best time of my life was in the war",' Caroline continues, suddenly impassioned. 'Because we have lost that sense of community, and we'll never get it back.'

It seems strange that she should say this, because the survival of that sense of community is one of the main things *The Royle Family* is about.

Does she see any parallels between her family's trip to Lourdes and the one the Indian boy makes in the film?

'It's weird you should say that, for two reasons. First, because it was probably very similar, in that – in a very innocent way – we did feel that we were going to get my brother's sight back, albeit by different means – the power of prayer rather than faith in the doctor. Secondly, because we just went back to Lourdes for the first time recently, in fact yesterday.'

From a crumpled paper bag which looks as if it ought to contain old-fashioned sweets, Cash starts to produce material evidence of Caroline's weekend pilgrimage: 'A bottle of holy water, some prayer thing . . .'

She shoots him a warning look that would stun a charging bullock. 'Don't you dare take the piss, Craig.'

It's too late to stop. He has already removed the last item from the bag and now holds it – rather sheepishly – aloft. It's a very unreligious-looking green child's biro. 'And a pen!' he concludes, with an infectious air of triumph.

The sublimely affectionate quality of Aherne and Cash's bickering is lent an added piquancy – in retrospect – by the subsequent dissolution of their writing partnership. (In the autumn of 2002, arguments over a new pub-based sitcom, *Early Doors*,[262] precipitate a seemingly final breach in their creative association.)

Returning to the Winchelsea churchyard a year after Spike's funeral, there's still no headstone above the grave. Much to the distress of all concerned, an agreement on what form it should take awaits the resolution of a dispute over different versions of Milligan's will between his widow, Shelagh, and some of this doughty campaigner against overpopulation's six (count them) children.

A contradiction to – even beyond – the last: there could be no more apt tribute to this restless creative spirit. Looking around at Britain in the early twenty-first century, anyone seeking out one last

---

[262.] When *Early Doors* finally screens, it is initially – as with Spike Milligan and the film of *Puckoon* – Caroline's absence which comes through most strongly (she had originally been going to play the pub's landlady), but as the series develops, those who can set aside their objections to some of the most gratuitous communal singalongs since Terence Davies's *Distant Voices Still Lives* find plenty to reward them. Not least the two most engagingly pragmatic policemen since *The Fast Show*'s 'Fat Sweaty Coppers'.

Milligan epitaph could do a lot worse than the famous words inscribed on Sir Christopher Wren's memorial in St Paul's Cathedral: 'his monument is all around you'.

Conclusion

'What this vision may mean, ye men that make merry,
Discern ye! I dare not discern it myself'

Piers Plowman

'Hoorah for transparency . . . I have returned as a spectre'
Vic Reeves, on the last page of *sunboiledonions*

'The idea of Jim as a ghost', Bob Mortimer enthuses in the spring of 2000 – shortly before Reeves and Mortimer make what is formally their professional acting début, in Charlie Higson's big-budget BBC1 remake of minor cult TV landmark *Randall and Hopkirk (Deceased)* – 'it just seems right'.[263]

The well-established sense of Bob as Vic's representative on earth – recruited from the august ranks of the legal profession to notarize the otherworldly transmissions of his ethereal mindset –

[263.] Anyone doubting Reeves's ghostly propensities might like to take a trip back in a time machine to the Lyceum Ballroom in London on a grey autumn Sunday in 1982. (This might not seem the most obvious choice of destination, but then again, the opportunity to experience seven hours of music notionally originating from the city of Norwich does not come along every day.) The headliners are John Peel favourites The Higsons, who play white funk for students but are still somehow quite good. They take their name from singer Charlie Higson, whose performance of their single 'I Don't Want To Live With Monkeys' makes up in confidence for what it lacks in musical subtlety. The evening's standout showing, though, comes lower down the bill, from non-East Anglian infiltrators Design For Living, who, in their own oddball country-gentlemen-trying-to-play-free-jazz kind of way, project a truly demonic energy. Most of this energy comes from their then unknown bass-player, Jim Moir.

also dovetails nicely with the show's original late-sixties template. But there are some problems with the whole idea.

In co-starring amicably with the sort of people – Tom Baker, Peter Barkworth, Charles Dance even – Vic would once have jovially eaten marzipan effigies of, aren't the Joseph Beuys-influenced textural provocateurs becoming what they set out to destroy? Well yes, they probably are. But that eventuality comes to many an artistic iconoclast in the end, and sometimes there's nothing else for it but to accept the inevitable with good grace.[264]

Besides, Vic and Bob have got to do *something*. By the early twenty-first century, turning on their TV sets must be like the scene in *Being John Malkovich* where the actor takes a trip into his own head and sees everyone being him. The magical sight (in May 2003's *I'm A Celebrity Get Me Out Of Here!*) of Phil Tufnell tenderly washing the cockroaches off Daniella Westbrook in a jungle pool is transcribed so directly from a lost drawing for an early episode of *Vic Reeves Big Night Out* that it's actually scary.

There's an intriguing demographic undertow to all this, too. For the generation of TV viewers who have grown up on Reeves and Mortimer, *Randall and Hopkirk (Deceased)* is one of those old programmes repeated so late at night they were probably too drunk to remember what actually happens in it. But for Vic and Bob themselves, the memory of its original late-tea-time weekend broadcast is still as fresh as a newly baked Victoria sponge.

'It was my favourite programme at the age of nine or ten,' Vic enthuses. 'Seeing people disappear is always going to be a lure, isn't it?'

How would they like their version to relate to the original – to capture the spirit of the thing itself, or merely the innocence of their reaction to that thing?

'I'm not sure if that sort of reaction is still available,' says Bob pensively. 'We certainly can't compete with *The Matrix*.' (He pronounces it to rhyme with 'hat-tricks' rather than 'hay-ricks', as if to emphasize the alien nature of its modernity.)

[264.] In January 2003, Vic Reeves consummates a solemn act of union with the British showbiz establishment by marrying one of the models with whom he co-presented TV nostalgia show *I Love 1991* at a ceremony attended by Lenny Henry and Ben Elton.

'When *Randall and Hopkirk* was first on,' Vic remembers, also harking back to a lost age of technological innocence, 'it was about the same time colour TVs were really coming in, and I remember a friend of mine inviting everyone in the street back to his house to have a look at his new set. When we got there, it was just a normal black-and-white TV, but with red, yellow and blue gel Sellotaped on in strips to make it look like it was vaguely in colour.'

The memory of such shared experiences of cultural awakening looms large with a lot of the people who feature in this book. Caroline Aherne with *Parkinson*, Ricky Gervais with *The Family*, Steve Coogan and *Fawlty Towers* – all refer to formative instances of interaction with a reassuringly formal and integrated televisual culture.

'Television as I grew up with it – addicted to it,' Coogan insists, 'could be a wonderful experience. It sounds pretentious, I know, but it was a really *unifying* thing. Sitting down in front of a programme that you knew half the country was watching at the same time was a very different experience from watching something on video or digital[265] TV. I remember calling my dad who was working in the attic on something – "*Fawlty Towers* is starting! Come down *now!*" It was on then and you couldn't record it, so you watched it or you missed it.[266] Because there were far fewer entertainment outlets at that point,' Coogan continues, warming to his theme now, 'whole families – from eleven to forty or fifty – would sit down and watch the same thing and all get something from it . . . That's one

---

[265.] In the barren entertainment landscapes of the pre-Sky and acid house and PlayStation epochs, even the smallest cultural oasis would be drained of every last drop of moisture. Without lapsing entirely into an 'I remember when all this was nobbut sand' state of mind, when Johnny Vaughan refers nostalgically to 'the days when you'd have to watch *Paint Along with Nancy* all the way through because there wasn't any other choice, and you'd end up actually learning something, if only by osmosis', you can kind of see his point.

[266.] In *Mrs Slocombe's Pussy*, Stuart Jeffries talks of 'defrosting something from the freezer aisles' of cable channel or video, and this analogy with the difference between fresh and frozen food is very well chosen: you can't quite put your finger on why the former is better for you, it just is.

of my most nostalgic memories,' he concludes euphorically, 'turning the TV off afterwards and everyone saying what their favourite bit was, and just really appreciating it.'

If there's a common strand which binds together the greatest British TV comedy of the Reeves/*Office* epoch, it's people raised in that era of mass entertainment reaching back into their memory of its inclusiveness, and striving to recreate that feeling within a new, more fragmented televisual environment. An environment whose specific cultural circumstances allowed them greater creative freedom than their original inspirations would ever have been granted.

What Vic and Bob were doing in the mid to late eighties, then, was basically sending forth that Eric and Ernie Christmas Show vibration to a roomful of people in a scabby south-east London pub.

'Because there wasn't anything like that in mainstream culture at that point!' Steve Coogan exclaims. 'And it was the fact that the whole "shared" thing had gone which actually inspired people. I was in a taxi the other day,' Coogan continues, 'and they had one of these video screens playing old comedy clips. Every TV series you've ever heard of was on – apart from any of mine – and they were playing *The Two Ronnies* from 1980. It was that sketch where Ronnie Corbett is on *Mastermind* and he keeps answering the question before last. Ronnie Barker wrote it under a pseudonym. I was literally crying with laughter, thinking, This is glorious, because it's so funny and so accessible and so well crafted.'

In the early years of the twenty-first century – as the West End fills up with plays about Tommy Cooper or Morecambe and Wise, and an East London gallery hosts an exhibition of painstakingly worked replicas of the paintings in Tony Hancock's London art-world satire *The Rebel* – that lost world of inclusive comedy continues to exercise an ever-increasing fascination for people. On the face of it, this is a straightforward nostalgic impulse, but something rather more complex and interesting is going on, too, in the form of an underlying suspicion that these old warriors of the variety circuit might in some way have been the architects of what we now know to be modernity.

The idea of looking back to old comedians for the basis of contemporary reality is not a new one.[267] But it is an intriguing possibility that in updating the playful intertextuality of *Morecambe and Wise* and *The Two Ronnies* for a new televisual era, the Vic and Bob generation inadvertently created the template for a new form of entertainment which would not only supersede those unifying 1970s comedies as a new form of One Nation TV, but at times threaten to render comedy itself unnecessary.

Watching whatever validity Harry Enfield's 'imaginary' rock star in *Celeb* might once have had being fatally undermined by the existence of the infinitely more outlandish and entertaining *The Osbournes* in the autumn of 2002, it is certainly hard not to conclude that where satire once kept watch over reality, the reverse is now the case. And yet – just like satire's before it – reality TV's one-way mirror is not the sure protection from embarrassment it might initially appear. As Jonathan Swift would probably have noted, if invited to appear with Dermot O'Leary on *Big Brother's Little Brother*, 'Reality TV is a sort of glass, wherein beholders do generally discover everybody's face but their own.'

This observation applies to viewers and programme-makers with equal severity. Just as people who like to harp on about the mediocrity of Hear'Say are really passing judgement on themselves for ever having been interested, so the production team on 2003's second series of *I'm A Celebrity Get Me Out Of Here!* show themselves – in pandering to the racism inherent in the British public's desire to humiliate John Fashanu – to be as morally ignorant as the young Americans who subjected a terrified kidnap victim to the same ordeal as that depicted in *The Blair Witch Project*. When questioned, they claimed that they hadn't really done anything wrong because they were 'only doing it for the camera'.

Just because you're filming something doesn't mean it's not actually happening. This is just one of a number of lessons that need to be learned if the limitless entertainment potential of reality TV

[267.] A long time before Johnny Rotten realized Max Wall and Tommy Cooper were the roots of English culture, people had been asking themselves just what it was that was so revolutionary about Vladimir Nabokov's *Pale Fire*, when Buster Keaton's projectionist was climbing into the cinema screen as early as 1924's *Sherlock Jnr*.

is to be realized without toxic moral side-effects. In showing that everyone – even Vanessa Feltz, or traditional comedic whipping boy Bobby Davro (featured to poignant and sympathetic effect on Louis Theroux's *The Entertainers*) – has the right to a measure of understanding, reality TV has the capacity to engender a huge extension of human sympathy. The fact that it so often tends to have the reverse effect is just the sort of high-protein subject matter you can imagine Ricky Gervais getting his teeth into once *The Office* is over and done with.[268]

Whatever direction Gervais and Coogan and Aherne and Reeves (and Ross, for that matter) choose to move in next, the one thing that is certain is that they'll be doing it as elder statespeople. For the same reason that it has such a precise starting-point, the finishing line of their comedic golden age can also be clearly discerned. If only because the next generation coming through – raised in the aftermath of the Thatcher era, with its obsessive pursuit of individual choice above all other political or social considerations – will inevitably lack the emotional and psychic bedrock of not having had things all their own way (culturally, at least) to start off with.[269]

You can see this already in a number of those televisual entertainments which might – for the want of a better term – be called Post-*Office*. Like the self-consciously Wernham Hogg-style ads for Nokia mobile phones or *Heat* magazine which are so conspicuously lacking in the emotional delicacy of the TV show they're modelled on. Or Channel 4's *The Richard Taylor Interviews*, in which a well-spoken and frankly rather creepy man tricks people who have the temerity to want a job into humiliating themselves by means of the sort of sickening manifestations of terroristic management which *The Office* understood so well.

You can see it most of all, though, in the live show of 2002

---

[268] This would certainly be a more appealing prospect than the idea the indefatigable Jonathan Ross is discussing excitedly in 2002. This act – honed in the privacy of their own homes, but drawing worryingly closer to a public airing – involves himself and his friend Ricky 'just being as offensive as possible to everyone who comes into the room'.

[269] It's not that this new generation will necessarily fail to produce equally great work, just that its achievements will have to be built on different foundations.

Perrier Award-winner Daniel Kitson. An engaging and eloquent individual with a very well-developed vocabulary, Kitson just seems to lack a crucial element of moral focus. Like the deputy editor of *Dazed and Confused* magazine who made a TV programme about her generation needing everything parcelled up into bite-size chunks for easy consumption, and called it *The A to Z of Now*, Kitson knows there's a problem, he just doesn't realize it's him.[270]

Appearing at the Soho Theatre in a new stand-up guise in July 2002, Gervais skewers Kitson's 'here I am, now entertain me' attitude with characteristically deadly aim. The character he inhabits has spent so much time slack-jawed in front of History Channel programmes about Hitler that he has lost all sense of human perspective. 'Not a *great* war,' he observes competitively, of the less oft-televised horrors of the 1914–18 conflict, 'a *good* war.'

The possibility of a period of all-out conflict between the new old guard and an emerging generation of morally disconnected twenty- and thirtysomethings is a fascinating one. But watching BBC Scotland's *Live Floor Show* in the winter of 2002–3, it seems unlikely that such an apocalyptic scenario will ever materialize. As hosted by burly Irish wag Dara Braian, this unexpectedly enjoyable showcase for new comic talent is like *Friday* and *Saturday Night Live*, but without the pain.

A warm welcome is extended to returning veterans Jo Brand and Jenny Eclair, and Simon Munnery appears 'as himself' – a large beard intensifying his prophetic aura[271] as he utters the despairing

---

[270.] The one thing Kitson hates, he tells us – between a series of well-judged assaults on people whose personalized mobile ringtones are perhaps not the trusty markers of originality and independent-mindedness they like to imagine – is R'n'B. He describes this form of musical endeavour as 'bland and corporate', but the thing about it that really seems to make him angry is that it is a *discipline* – wherein a whole world of love and heartbreak is described within a pre-established framework – and because this idea of creativity doesn't fall within his own (shockingly narrow) parameters of individual self expression, he doesn't feel it should be allowed to exist.

[271.] The double act God and Jesus – in which Munnery first honed his Nietzschean ethos in the mid to late eighties (before his career took a lengthy detour with *Alan Parker – Urban Warrior*) – can with hindsight be seen to vie with Ted Chippington in the post-alternative John the Baptist stakes.

anti-stand-up mantra 'Does anybody come from anywhere? Does anybody remember anything?' The most exciting of the show's new faces is probably Matt Blaze, a handsome Hackney-based newcomer who – having obviously paid Chris Rock's famously confrontational HBO Special the attention it deserves – capitalizes on his rarity value as a black face north of the border by telling the studio audience a series of things it really doesn't want to hear.

Steve Coogan in 'Cashback'

When *I'm Alan Partridge* finally returns for its long-awaited – perhaps too long-awaited – third series in the autumn of 2002, time seems to have caught up with it slightly.

First, there's the competition.

'What *The Office* does so well', Coogan concedes gamely, shortly before the series airs, 'is a very subtle, almost *über*-naturalism' – he grimaces at how pretentious he thinks this sounds – 'if I can use the word *"über"*, whereas *Partridge*, while it has a semblance of naturalism, is actually *hyper*-real. Alan is not really a real character – although when you watch him you kind of buy into the idea that he might be.'

Perhaps even more threateningly to Alan Partridge's long-term viability, TV reality has caught up once and for all with the imagination of satirists. While not all the ludicrous ideas Alan floated despairingly to a BBC executive in the first series (anyone for *Monkey Tennis*?) have subsequently been commissioned, it feels like most of them have.

'Lots of presenters now deliver things ironically in a slightly naff way and are happy about it because it's "Partridge-esque",'[272] Coogan grimaces, 'and that's made our life very difficult.'

While there are some great moments in the series, there's also an overwhelming self-consciousness about detail which suggests Coogan's decision to knock Alan gently on the head is the right one. His beautifully judged and surprisingly tender performance in

---

[272.] 'That which does not kill us,' Richard Madeley has sometimes been heard to observe, 'makes us stronger.'

the BBC's Christmas 2002 drama highlight *Cruise of the Gods* suggests that whatever choppy waters the post-reality TV seascape has to offer, he at least should have what it takes to ride them out.

One long-time collaborator asserts: 'It's when Steve plays up that he's really a man of the people, not when he goes for the lowest common denominator.' And, from Julian Barratt and Noel Fielding's Arctic Circle-bound post-Reevesian zookeepers in the brilliant (Baby Cow-produced) BBC3 pilot episode of *The Mighty Boosh*, to the new form of naturalism Sean Lock seems to be pioneering in his desert-dry social-surrealist tower-block comedy *15 Storeys High*, a willingness to aim high is a common feature of all the most promising (and funniest) comedic manifestations of early 2003.

Something new certainly needs to happen. The distended latex faces and distorted northern accents of Leigh Francis's *Bo' Selecta* seem like a rather mirthless and inhumane end to the family line Vic Reeves and Bob Mortimer began thirteen years earlier by donning masks and doing a silly dance. And when otherwise lovable *Big Brother 4* loose cannon Federico Martone starts intimidating the woman in the diary room by doing an impression of Francis's celebrity stalker Avid Merrion (who had first come to prominence as a bloated tick on the arse of the *Big Brother* phenomenon a year earlier), it seems like comedy and reality TV might actually be eating each other.

This seems the appropriate moment to address the fundamental ambiguity encapsulated in the title *Sunshine on Putty*. The question which has to be asked is 'Did the comedy of this period warm our hearts, or did it harden us up?' The answer, of course, is that it did both. Not in the way that when writing history essays at school or college you have to say 'the causes were social, political *and* economic'. But in the manner identified in William Empson's *Seven Types of Ambiguity* as type number three, i.e. where 'alternative meanings combine to make clear a complex state of mind'.

Final thoughts

In his graduation speech at New York's Fredonia College on 20 May 1978, the American novelist Kurt Vonnegut asked the question 'How do jokes work?' (employing the timeless example 'Why is cream more expensive than milk? . . . because cows hate to squat on those little bottles' for the purposes of exposition).

'The beginning of each good one challenges you to think,' Vonnegut asserts. 'We are such earnest animals . . . When I asked you about cream, you could not help yourselves – you really tried to think of a sensible answer . . . The second part of the joke announces that nobody wants you to think, nobody wants to hear your wonderful answer. You are so relieved to at last meet somebody who doesn't demand that you be so intelligent, you laugh for joy.'

'Why could the jester say what he liked without giving offence?' demands R. H. Hill in *Tales of the Jesters*. 'Why was he free from the general obligation to defer to and flatter the ruler, unless it were because he had been a simpleton originally?'

Whatever the enduring significance of the early middle ages' gradual replacement of village idiots (those 'so simple as to make the baron's modest intellectual attainments seem more impressive by comparison') by 'intelligent fellows who had brains enough to act the fool', one thing is very clear.

In the immortal words of *Spinal Tap's* Nigel Tufnel (or it might have been David St Hubbins, but either way, the point stands), 'There's a thin line between clever and stupid.'

Bibliography

Caroline Aherne, Craig Cash and Dave Gorman *Mrs Merton's World of Television* (Hodder & Stoughton, 1997)

David Baddiel *Time For Bed* (Little, Brown, 1996)

David Baddiel *Whatever Love Means* (Little, Brown, 1999)

Henri Bergson *Laughter [Le Rire]* (Macmillan & Co., 1911)

Michael Bracewell *The Nineties: When Surface Was Depth* (Flamingo, 2002)

Humphrey Carpenter *That Was Satire That Was* (Victor Gollancz, 2000)

Karl von Clausewitz *On War* (Penguin Classics, 1982)

Nik Cohn *Yes We Have No* (Secker & Warburg, 1999)

William Cook *Ha Bloody Ha: Comedians Talking* (Fourth Estate, 1994)

Ian Davidson, ed. *The Two Ronnies: And It's Goodnight From Him* (Star, 1982)

Les Dawson *A Card for the Clubs* (Sphere, 1974)

Les Dawson *No Tears for the Clown* (Robson Books, 1992)

Daniel Defoe *The True-Born Englishman and Other Writings* (Penguin, 1997)

Bruce Dessau *Reeves & Mortimer* (Orion, 1998)

Emma Donoghue *We Are Michael Field* (Absolute Press, 1998)

Anne Dummett *A History of British Racism* (Penguin, 1973)

William Empson *Seven Types of Ambiguity* (Chatto & Windus, 1930)

Peter Evans *Peter Sellers: The Mask Behind the Mask* (Leslie Frewin, 1969)

Kenny Everett *The Custard Stops At Hatfield* (Willow, 1982)

Sigmund Freud *Jokes and Their Relation to the Unconscious* (Penguin, 1991)

Malcolm Hardee *I Stole Freddie Mercury's Birthday Cake* (Fourth Estate, 1996)

William Hazlitt *The Fight and Other Writings* (Penguin, 2000)

Peter Hennessy *Never Again: Britain 1945–51* (Jonathan Cape, 1992)

Christopher Hill *England's Turning Point: Essays on 17th Century English History* (Bookmarks, 1998)

R. H. Hill *Tales of the Jesters* (William Blackwood & Sons, 1934)

439

Gavin Hills *Bliss to Be Alive* (Penguin, 2000)

Ian Jack *Before the Oil Ran Out: Britain in the Brutal Years* (Vintage, 1997)

Stuart Jeffries *Mrs Slocombe's Pussy: Growing Up In Front of the Telly* (Flamingo, 2000)

Remi Kapo *A Savage Culture: Racism – A Black British View* (Quartet, 1981)

The League of Gentlemen *A Local Book For Local People* (Fourth Estate, 2001)

David Marquand and Anthony Seldon, eds *The Ideas That Shaped Post-War Britain* (Fontana, 1996)

Groucho Marx *The Groucho Letters* (Michael Joseph, 1967)

Graham McCann *Morecambe & Wise* (Fourth Estate, 1998)

Graham McCann *Dad's Army: The Story of a Classic Television Show* (Fourth Estate, 2001)

Mick Middles *When You're Laughing: The Illustrated Biography of Les Dawson* (André Deutsch, 1999)

Spike Milligan *Puckoon* (Anthony Blond, 1963)

Spike Milligan *Mussolini: His Part in My Downfall* (Michael Joseph, 1978)

Spike Milligan *Q Annual* (Michael Joseph, 1979)

Spike Milligan *Where Have All the Bullets Gone?* (Michael Joseph, 1985)

Spike Milligan *Peace Work* (Michael Joseph, 1991)

Spike Milligan and Anthony Clare *Depression and How to Survive It* (Ebury Press, 1993)

Bob Monkhouse *Crying with Laughter* (Arrow, 1994)

Eric Morecambe *Mr Lonely* (Eyre Methuen, 1981)

Eric Morecambe and Ernie Wise (with Dennis Holman) *Eric & Ernie: The Autobiography of Morecambe & Wise* (W. H. Allen Ltd, 1972)

Robert Newman *Dependence Day* (Century, 1994)

Robert Newman *Manners* (Hamish Hamilton, 1998)

Harold Nicolson *The English Sense Of Humour and Other Essays* (Dropmore Press, 1946)

George Orwell *Shooting an Elephant and Other Essays* (Secker & Warburg, 1950)

J. B. Priestley *Let The People Sing* (The Book Club, 1940)

Richard Pryor (with Todd Gold) *Pryor Convictions And Other Life Sentences* (William Heinemann, 1995)

Andrew Rawnsley *Servants of the People* (Hamish Hamilton, 2000)

Vic Reeves *sunboiledonions* (Michael Joseph, 1999)

Henry C. Roberts, ed. *The Complete Prophecies of Nostradamus* (Crown Publishers, NY, 1947)

Leonard Russell, ed. *English Wits* (Hutchinson, 1940)

Alexei Sayle *Barcelona Plates* (Hodder & Stoughton, 2000)

Bibliography

Pauline Scudamore *Spike Milligan: A Biography* (Grafton, 1987)

Iain Sinclair *Lights Out for the Territory* (Granta, 1997)

Michael Tracey and David Morrison *Whitehouse* (Macmillan, 1979)

Kurt Vonnegut *Palm Sunday* (Grafton, 1982)

Max Wall (with Peter Ford) *The Fool on the Hill* (Quartet, 1975)

Roger Wilmut *The Goon Show Companion* (Robson Books, 1976)

Roger Wilmut *Tony Hancock: Artiste* (Eyre Methuen, 1978)

Roger Wilmut *From Fringe to Flying Circus: Celebrating a Unique Generation of Comedy 1960–80* (Eyre Methuen, 1980)

Roger Wilmut and Peter Rosengard *Didn't You Kill My Mother-in-Law?: The Story of Alternative Comedy in Britain from the Comedy Store to Saturday Live* (Methuen, 1989)

Mike Yarwood *Impressions of My Life* (Willow, 1986)

Acknowledgements

Thanks are due to the following helpful and in some cases intimidatingly charismatic individuals:

Firstly to my editor, the irrepressible 'publishing insider' Andy Miller, for – to pick out at random just one of many significant contributions – not letting his hatred of *Seinfeld* get in the way of his professional judgement

To Nick Davies and all at Fourth Estate for their exemplary blend of patience and enthusiasm

To contributing commissioners through the ages including Lucy Tuck, Jessamy Calkin, Vicki Reid, Francesca Ryan, Kathryn Holiday, James Brown, Sheryll Garratt, Tim De Lisle, Philip Dodd, John Ferguson and Gavin Martin

To suppliers of pictures, videos, cassettes, books and information, including Chiggy, Janette Linden and Jo Beasy at PBJ, Vic Reeves, Louise Pickett at Hat Trick, Carlton B. Morgan, Paul Wright, Bill Menniss, Gary Beggerow, Jon Savage, Mark Sinker, Andrew Male (for the Graham Chapman anecdote), Bev Dickinson, Ian Preece, Philip Gwyn Jones, Richard Williams and Steve McEntee in the library at *The Independent*

To all those who arranged or granted interviews outside the immediate demands of the promotional merry-go-round, including Kathy Burke, Addison Cresswell, Amanda Emery, Caroline Chignell (to use her formal title), James Herring, Andy Hollis, Steve Bendelack, Brian Glanville, Anil Gupta, Stewart Lee, Patrick Marber, Dan Lloyd, Al Murray, Richard Allen-Turner, Jon Thoday, Jon Plowman, Simon Pegg, Joe Norris and Jonathan Ross

To everyone connected with *Rab C. Nesbitt*, an excellent TV programme, which has somehow eluded mention in this book until the final possible moment

Acknowledgements

And last, and most, to Nicola Barker – the wings above my wind – for comedy-related forbearance far beyond the dictates of romantic entanglement.

Picture credits

All pictures are courtesy of the BBC Photo Library, except Vic Reeves on his motorbike (Jim Moir/PBJ Management) and Father Ted and Bishop Brennan (Hat Trick Productions Ltd/Channel 4).

Index